AROUND PARLIAMENT
See pages 104–119.

*Around
Városliget*

Central Pest

AROUND VÁROSLIGET
See pages 140–151.

CENTRAL PEST
See pages 120–139.

EYEWITNESS TRAVEL
BUDAPEST

EYEWITNESS TRAVEL

BUDAPEST

MAIN CONTRIBUTORS:
BARBARA OLSZAŃSKA, TADEUSZ OLSZAŃSKI

LONDON, NEW YORK,
MELBOURNE, MUNICH AND DELHI
www.dk.com

PRODUCED BY Wydawnictwo Wiedza i Życie, Warsaw
SERIES EDITOR Ewa Szwagrzyk
CONSULTANTS András Hadik, Małgorzata Omilanowska,
Katalin Szokolay
EDITORS Joanna Egert, Anna Kożurno-Królikowska,
Bożena Leszkowicz
DESIGNER Paweł Pasternak

Dorling Kindersley Ltd
PROJECT EDITOR Jane Oliver
EDITORS Felicity Crowe, Nancy Jones

TRANSLATORS
Magda Hannay, Anna Johnson, Ian Wisniewski

PHOTOGRAPHERS
Gábor Barka, Dorota and Mariusz Jarymowiczowie

ILLUSTRATORS
Paweł Mistewicz, Piotr Zubrzycki

REPRODUCED BY Colourscan, Singapore
Printed and bound by South China Printing Co. Ltd., China

First American Edition, 1999
07 08 09 10 9 8 7 6 5 4 3 2 1
Reprinted with revisions 2000, 2001, 2004, 2007

Published in the United States by
DK Publishing, Inc., 375 Hudson Street,
New York, New York 10014

Copyright 1999, 2007 © Dorling Kindersley Limited, London

ISSN 1542-1554
ISBN 13: 978-0-75662-435-4
ISBN 10: 0-75662-435-5

FLOORS ARE REFERRED TO THROUGHOUT IN ACCORDANCE WITH EUROPEAN
USAGE; IE THE "FIRST FLOOR" IS THE FLOOR ABOVE GROUND LEVEL.

Front cover main image: Chain Bridge, Budapest

**The information in this
DK Eyewitness Travel Guide is checked regularly.**

Every effort has been made to ensure that this book is as up-to-date
as possible at the time of going to press. Some details, however,
such as telephone numbers, opening hours, prices, gallery hanging
arrangements and travel information are liable to change. The
publishers cannot accept responsibility for any consequences
arising from the use of this book, nor for any material on third party
websites, and cannot guarantee that any website address in this
book will be a suitable source of travel information. We value the
views and suggestions of our readers very highly. Please write to:
Publisher, DK Eyewitness Travel Guides,
Dorling Kindersley, 80 Strand, London WC2R 0RL, Great Britain.

CONTENTS

Pallas Athene on the Old Town Hall

INTRODUCING BUDAPEST

Hungarian crest adorning a wall
close to the Tunnel *(see p100)*

◁ The Parliament building *(see pp108–9)*, standing on the Danube

The Hungarian National Gallery *(see pp74–7)*, in the former Royal Palace

View across the Danube towards
St Stephen's Basilica *(see p116–17)*

Porcelain in the Museum of
Applied Arts *(see pp136–7)*

Barrel-organ player in the historic
Castle District *(see pp68–85)*

The landmark domes and towers of four of Budapest's most striking places of worship

HOW TO USE THIS GUIDE

This Eyewitness Travel Guide helps you get the most from your stay in Budapest with the minimum of difficulty. The opening section, *Introducing Budapest*, locates the city geographically, sets modern Budapest in its historical context and describes events through the entire year. *Budapest at a Glance* is an overview of the city's main attractions. *Budapest Area by Area* starts on page 66. This is the main sightseeing

Plotting the route

section, which covers all of the important sights, with photographs, maps and illustrations. It also includes day trips from Budapest and three walks around the city. Information about hotels, restaurants, shops and markets, entertainment and sports is found in *Travellers' Needs*. The *Survival Guide* has advice on everything from using the postal service and telephones to Budapest's public transport system and medical services.

FINDING YOUR WAY AROUND THE SIGHTSEEING SECTION

Each of six sightseeing areas in Budapest is colour-coded for easy reference. Every chapter opens with an introduction to the area of the city it covers, describing its history and character, and has one or two *Street-by-Street* maps illustrating typical parts of that area. Finding your way around the chapter is made simple by the numbering system used throughout. The most important sights are covered in detail in two or more full pages.

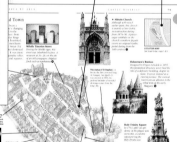

Each area has colour-coded thumb tabs.

Locator map

The area shaded pink is shown in greater detail on the Street-by-Street map.

A suggested route takes in some of the most interesting and attractive streets in the area.

The list of star sights recommends the places that no visitor should miss.

1 Introduction to the area
For easy reference, the sights in each area are numbered and plotted on an area map. To help the visitor, this map also shows underground stations, main bus and tram stops and parking areas. The area's key sights are listed by category: Museums and Galleries; Churches; Historic Streets and Squares; Palaces and Historic Buildings; Hotels and Baths; and Parks and Gardens.

A locator map shows where you are in relation to the other areas in the city centre.

2 Street-by-Street map
This gives a bird's-eye view of interesting and important parts of each sightseeing area. The numbering of the sights ties up with the area map and the fuller description on the pages that follow.

BUDAPEST AREA MAP

The coloured areas shown on this map *(see inside front cover)* are the six main sightseeing areas used in this guide. Each is covered in a full chapter in *Budapest Area by Area (pp66–167)*. They are highlighted on other maps throughout the book. In *Budapest at a Glance*, for example, they help you locate the top sights. They are also used to help you find the position of the three walks *(pp168–75)*.

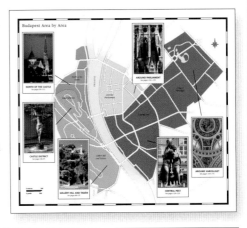

Numbers refer to each sight's position on the area map and its place in the chapter.

Practical information provides everything you need to know to visit each sight. Map references pinpoint the sight's location on the Street Finder map *(pp242–53)*.

Façades of important buildings are often shown to help you recognize them quickly.

The visitors' checklist provides all the practical information needed to plan your visit.

3 Detailed information on each sight
All the important sights in Budapest are described individually. They are listed in order following the numbering on the area map at the start of the section. Practical information includes a map reference, opening hours, telephone numbers and admission charges. The key to the symbols used is on the back flap.

Stars indicate the features no visitor should miss.

4 Budapest's major sights
Historic buildings are dissected to reveal their interiors; museums and galleries have colour-coded floorplans to help you find important exhibits.

A timeline charts the key events in the history of the building.

INTRODUCING
BUDAPEST

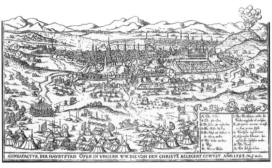

FOUR GREAT DAYS IN BUDAPEST

It can be difficult to plan a visit to this historic, sprawling city, particularly if time is short. These four days provide a taste of Budapest, with a variety of sights and experiences, and together include much of the best in architecture, museums, shopping and fun that the city

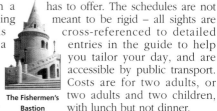

The Fishermen's Bastion

has to offer. The schedules are not meant to be rigid – all sights are cross-referenced to detailed entries in the guide to help you tailor your day, and are accessible by public transport. Costs are for two adults, or two adults and two children, with lunch but not dinner.

Passengers ride the antique Sikló funicular railway up Castle Hill

A DAY ON CASTLE HILL

- **Art at the ÒRoyal Palace**
- **Lunch in a Castle courtyard**
- **Concert at Mátyás Church**
- **A subterranean Labyrinth**

TWO ADULTS allow at least 10,000 HUF

Morning
Buda's **Castle District** *(see pp69–85)* towers over Pest. Winding paths lead up Castle Hill from Clark Adám tér, but the traditional way up is by the **Sikló** *(see p69)*, a 100-year-old funicular railway. Start the day with a tour of the grounds of the **Royal Palace** *(see pp70–1)*. Take time to admire the Romantic design of **Mátyás Fountain** *(see p72)*, and to visit the wonderful collection of 19th-century Hungarian paintings at the **National Gallery** *(see pp74–7)*. Leave the Palace area through the ornamental Habsburg Gate, then stop at **Rivalda** *(see p196)* for a splendid *al fresco* lunch.

Afternoon
A short walk along Tárnok utca into central Buda, past myriad souvenir shops, leads to **Fishermen's Bastion** *(see p80)*. From here there are glorious views of Pest, especially **Parliament** *(see pp108–9)* and **Chain Bridge** *(see p62)*, almost directly below. Do not fail to visit ancient **Mátyás Church** *(see pp82–3)* – where there are organ concerts some summer evenings – before walking along the wonderfully preserved streets of Buda's Old Town. Follow Fortuna utca round to Kapisztran tér and the lone, ruined tower of **St Mary Magdalena** *(see p84)*.

Peerless **Lords' Street** *(see p85)*, with its gothic details and peaceful courtyards, leads to the bizarre subterranean **Labyrinth** *(see p85)*. Nearby **Alabardos** *(see p196)* is the perfect place for an early dinner in a medieval setting.

THE FINER SIDE OF LIFE

- **A morning at the spa baths**
- **The Museum of Fine Arts**
- **A walk to the Opera House**
- **Dinner at Gresham Kávéház**

TWO ADULTS allow at least 17,500 HUF

Morning
Start with coffee in **Gerbeaud Cukrászda** *(see p206)*, the city's most famous café. Then ride the beautifully preserved **Millennium Line** *(see p238)* to **Széchenyi Baths** *(see p151)*, and spend at least three hours indulging in bathing, sauna and massage in glorious imperial surroundings. Stop for lunch at **Gundel Étterem** *(see p204)*.

Afternoon
Walk off the effects of lunch in the **Museum of Fine Arts** *(see pp146–9)*, which houses

One of three outdoor pools at Széchenyi Baths, the hottest in Budapest

Hungary's finest collection of foreign art in a monumental building facing **Heroes' Square** (see pp142–3).

On leaving the museum, walk past the **Millennium Monument** (see p145) and down Andrássy út – a superb avenue of embassies and consulates, giving way to restaurants and shops – and stop at one of the many cafés on **Liszt Ferenc tér** (see p206). The highlight of Andrássy út is No. 22, the **State Opera House** (see pp118–9), which offers guided tours in the late afternoon. From here, walk along lower Andrássy út, over Erzsébet tér, to the **Gresham Palace** hotel (see p114), facing Chain Bridge. Finally, spend the evening dining at the informal **Gresham Kávéház** (see p199), famous for its "Three Foie Gras", a Hungarian speciality.

FAMILY FUN AL FRESCO

- **A tour of the Buda Hills on the Children's Railway**
- **A walking safari round Budakeszi Wildlife Park**
- **Supper and folk music**

FAMILY of 4 allow at least 17,500 HUF

Morning

Head for the **Buda Hills** (see p161) by means of the Széchenyi Hill cog railway (5am–11pm, tel. 355 41 67), which begins at Szilagy Erzsebet fasor, just north of Moskva tér metro station. At the top, a short walk leads to the TV tower (closed) and the terminus of the **Children's Railway** (open May–Aug: 10am–5pm). The steam engine departs on the hour and meanders through the Buda hills to Hűvösvölgy, passing the **Erszébet Look-Out Tower**. Disembark at Szép Juhászné station for lunch at the outdoor café.

Afternoon

A well-marked path runs from the café to **Budakeszi Wildlife Park** (open Mar–Oct: 9am–6pm; Nov–Feb: 9am–3pm.

Children relax at Budakeszi Wildlife Park in the Buda Hills

Tel. 023 45 17, 83). The park is set across 3 sq km (1 sq mile) and contains a wide variety of animals, from wild boar (which also roam the surrounding country-side), to wolves. There is a separate reserve for plants and flora. A walking safari tours the best of both areas. The on-site restaurant is a great place for supper, and offers folk music after 6pm. At going-home time the Children's Railway will be closed, but bus No. 22 runs from the park to Moszkva tér.

HISTORY AND SHOPPING

- **The surviving monuments of the Jewish Quarter**
- **A Middle Eastern lunch**
- **Shopping on Váci utca and in Central Market**

TWO ADULTS allow at least 8,700 HUF

Morning

Start at the **Hungarian National Museum** (see pp130–3), where Sándor Petőfi read his National Song in 1848 (see p31). Spend an hour amongst the treasures of Hungary's turbulent past, then go to another historic location – the **Jewish Quarter** (see p134). The **Great Synagogue** on Dohány utca is a splendid Byzantine-style building, attached to which is the **Jewish Museum**. The **Holocaust Memorial** is found

in the synagogue's courtyard. The rest of the quarter is known for its gift shops and book stores, and the less ostentatious synagogues on Rumbach S. utca and Kazinczy utca. On the same street, stop for a non-Kosher but authen-tic Middle Eastern lunch at **Carmel Pince** (see p200).

Afternoon

Váci utca (see p127) offers great shopping at its northern end – for souvenirs, fashion and fine Hungarian porcelain at Goda (No. 9). Do visit the **Inner City Parish Church** (see pp124–5), then cross Kossuth Lajos út, and head south past the **Klotild Palaces** (see p127) and more shops, to Fóva tér. Rest here in a café. Across the road is the final retail challenge of the day – the huge, renovated **Central Market** (see p211).

One of the many busy terrace cafés that line Váci utca

ting Budapest on the Map

e capital of the Republic of Hungary, Budapest has over 1.8 million inhabitants, a fifth of the country's total population. The city is situated on the Danube and covers an area of 525 sq km (200 sq miles). One third of the city is taken up by hilly Buda and Óbuda, on the western bank of the Danube, and the remaining two thirds by flat Pest, on the eastern bank. Budapest has a pivotal location at the heart of central Europe. From here one can easily reach other major cities such as Vienna, Zagreb, Bratislava, Belgrade, Bucharest and Prague.

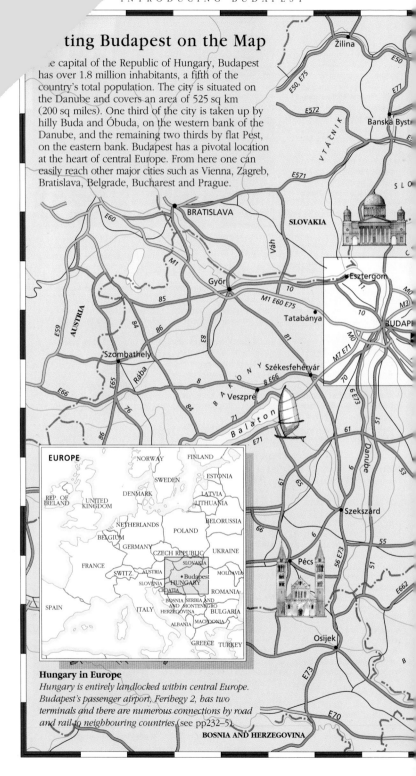

Hungary in Europe

Hungary is entirely landlocked within central Europe. Budapest's passenger airport, Ferihegy 2, has two terminals and there are numerous connections by road and rail to neighbouring countries (see pp232–5).

BOSNIA AND HERZEGOVINA

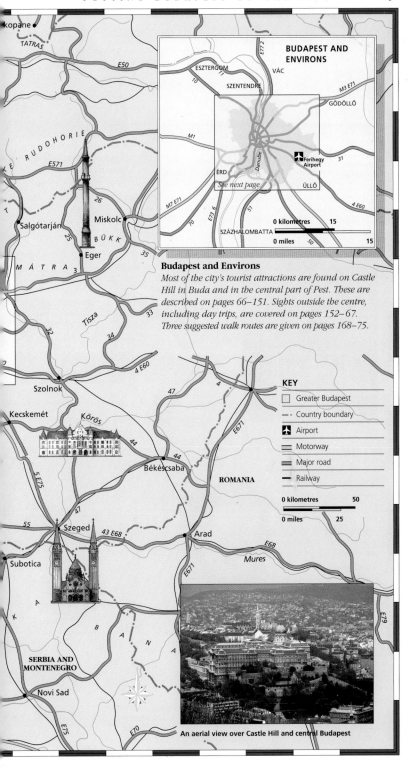

**BUDAPEST AND
ENVIRONS**

ESZTERGOM

VÁC

SZENTENDRE

GÖDÖLLŐ

Ferihegy
Airport

ÉRD

See next page

ÜLLŐ

SZÁZHALOMBATTA

0 kilometres   15

0 miles   15

Budapest and Environs

*Most of the city's tourist attractions are found on Castle
Hill in Buda and in the central part of Pest. These are
described on pages 66–151. Sights outside the centre,
including day trips, are covered on pages 152–67.
Three suggested walk routes are given on pages 168–75.*

kopane

TATRAS

RUDOHORIE

Salgótarján

Miskolc

BÜKK

Eger

MÁTRA

Tisza

Szolnok

Kecskemét

Körös

Békéscsaba

ROMANIA

Szeged

Arad

Mures

Subotica

**SERBIA AND
MONTENEGRO**

Novi Sad

KEY

☐	Greater Budapest
- - -	Country boundary
✈	Airport
▬	Motorway
▬	Major road
▬	Railway

0 kilometres   50

0 miles   25

An aerial view over Castle Hill and central Budapest

Central Budapest

Detail on the Stock Exchange

The centre of town includes Castle Hill (district I) on the western bank of the Danube and districts V, VI, VII, VIII and IX of Pest on the river's eastern bank, bounded by the city's original tram line. The Roman numerals denote the official administrative districts *(see p223)*. For the purposes of this guide, the centre is divided into six areas. Each area has its own chapter containing a selection of sights that convey its character and history. Sights on the outskirts of the city, and suggested day trips and walks, are covered in separate chapters.

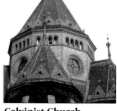

Calvinist Church
Situated close to the Danube, this church is distinguished by its eye-catching, poly-chromatic roof (see p100).

Royal Palace
The Royal Palace has been destroyed and pains-takingly rebuilt many times. It was last meticulously recon-structed after World War II, to the form that the Habsburgs had given it (see pp70–71).

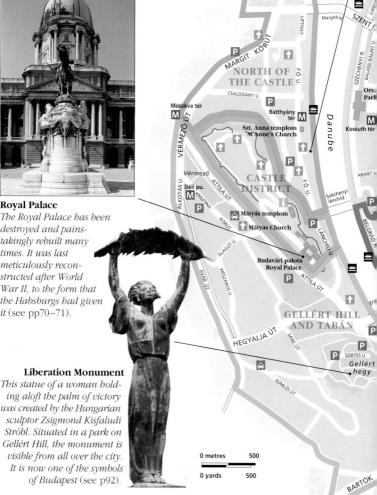

Liberation Monument
This statue of a woman hold-ing aloft the palm of victory was created by the Hungarian sculptor Zsigmond Kisfaludi Stróbl. Situated in a park on Gellért Hill, the monument is visible from all over the city. It is now one of the symbols of Budapest (see p92).

0 metres 500

0 yards 500

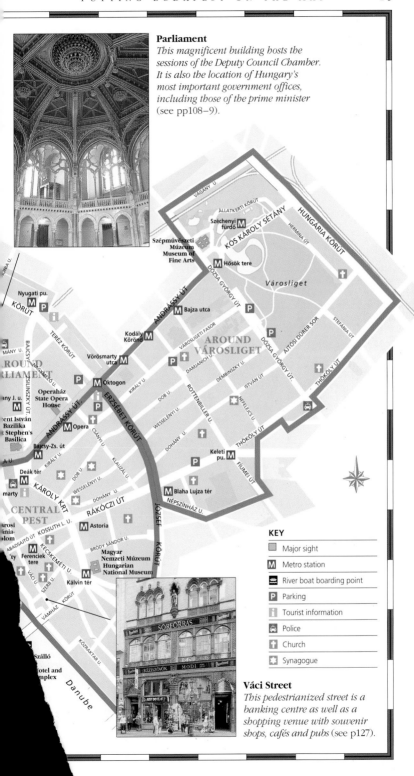

Parliament
This magnificent building hosts the sessions of the Deputy Council Chamber. It is also the location of Hungary's most important government offices, including those of the prime minister (see pp108–9).

VÁGÁNY U.

ÁLLATKERTI KÖRÚT

Széchenyi M fürdő

KÓS KÁROLY SÉTÁNY

HERMINA ÚT

HUNGÁRIA KÖRÚT

Szépművészeti Múzeum **Museum of Fine Arts**

M Hősök tere

Városliget

Nyugati pu.
M P

KÖRÚT

TERÉZ KÖRÚT

BAJCSY

VÁGÁNY U.

MANY U.

ANDRÁSSY ÚT

M Bajza utca

DÓZSA GYÖRGY ÚT

P

STEFÁNIA ÚT

AITÓSI DÜRER SOR

Kodály Körönd M

VÁROSLIGETI FASOR

AROUND VÁROSLIGET

DÓZSA GYÖRGY ÚT

THÖKÖLY ÚT

Vörösmarty utca M

P

DAMJANICH U.

ány J. u.

SILINSZKY U.

VÁGMEZŐ U.

KIRÁLY U.

DEMBINSZKY U.

ROUND RLIAMENT

P M Oktogon

DOB U.

ROTTENBILLER U.

ISTVÁN ÚT

NEFELICS U.

ent István Bazilika t Stephen's Basilica

Operaház State Opera House

ERZSÉBET KÖRÚT

CSÁNYI U.

WESSELÉNYI U.

M Opera

Bajcsy-Zs. út

DOHÁNY U.

THÖKÖLY ÚT

Keleti pu. M

FIUMEI ÚT

KIRÁLY U.

DOB U.

KLAUZÁL U.

Deák tér M

WESSELÉNYI U.

marty

KÁROLY KRT

DOHÁNY U.

M Blaha Lujza tér

NÉPSZÍNHÁZ U.

RÁKÓCZI ÚT

JÓZSEF KÖRÚT

CENTRAL PEST

arosi inia- olom

KOSSUTH L. U.

M Astoria

BRÓDY SÁNDOR U.

ABADSAJTÓ ÚT

KECSKEMÉTI U.

'ty Ferenciek tere

Magyar Nemzeti Múzeum Hungarian National Museum

VÁCI U.

SZERB U.

Kálvin tér

VÁMHÁZ KÖRÚT

KÖZRAKTÁR U.

szálló

otel and mplex

Danube

KEY

▢	Major sight
M	Metro station
⛴	River boat boarding point
P	Parking
ℹ	Tourist information
⌘	Police
✝	Church
✡	Synagogue

Váci Street
This pedestrianized street is a banking centre as well as a shopping venue with souvenir shops, cafés and pubs (see p127).

THE HISTORY OF BUDAPEST

As early as the Palaeolithic era, there were settlements in the area of Budapest: the narrowing of the Danube made the crossing of the river easy at this particular spot. In around AD 100, the Romans established the town of Aquincum here. Their rule lasted until the early 5th century AD, when the region fell to Attila the Hun. It was subsequently ruled by the Goths, the Longobards and, for nearly 300 years, by the Avars.

The ancestors of modern Hungarians, the Magyars, migrated from the Urals and arrived in the Budapest region in 896. They were led by Prince Árpád, whose dynasty ruled until the 13th century. At the turn of the first millennium, St István, whose heathen name was Vajk, accepted Christianity for the Hungarians. As their first crowned king, István I also laid the basis of the modern Hungarian state.

It was Béla IV who, in 1247, after the Mongol invasion, moved the capital to Buda. Much of the expansion of Buda took place under kings from the dynasty of the Angevins. Buda reached a zenith during the reign of Mátyás Corvinus in the 15th century, but further development was hindered by the advancing Turks, who took the region and ruled Buda for 150 years.

Crest of the Hunyadis

Liberation by the Christian armies resulted in the submission of the country as a whole to the Habsburgs. They suppressed all nationalist rebellions, but at the same time took care of economic development. Empress Maria Theresa and Archduke Joseph, the emperor's governor, made particular contributions to the modernization of both Buda and Pest. Yet, the slow pace of reforms led to an uprising in 1848, which was brutally crushed by Franz Joseph I. Compromise in 1867 and the creation of an Austro-Hungarian Empire stimulated economic and cultural life once more. Soon after, in 1873, Buda and Pest were united to create the city of Budapest.

Following World War I, the monarchy fell and Hungary lost two thirds of its territory. The desire to regain this contributed to its support of Germany in World War II. However, Budapest was taken by Russian troops in 1945 and large sections of it levelled. Under the subsequent Communist rule, the popular uprising of 1956 was ruthlessly suppressed by Soviet tanks but it initiated a crisis that shook the regime. Free elections took place in 1990, resulting in the victory of the democratic opposition, and the emergence of a new bourgeoisie.

Dating from 1686, when the Turks were expelled, this map shows the fortified towns of Pest and Buda

◁ Gyula Benczúr's *The Baptism of Vajk*, displayed in the Hungarian National Gallery *(see pp74–7)*

The City's Rulers

In the 13th century, Béla IV built a castle in Buda and designated the town as his new capital. Until that time, the Árpád dynasty, the first family of Hungarian kings, had ruled their domain from elsewhere. When, at the beginning of the 14th century, there were no male heirs to the Árpád throne, Hungary began a long period during which it was mainly ruled by foreign kings including the French Angevins and the Polish Jagiełłos. Under Mátyás Corvinus, a great Hungarian king, Buda became one of Europe's most impressive cities. The Habsburgs, while suppressing national insurrections, rebuilt Buda and Pest after the devastation left by the Turks, adding fine pieces of architecture.

LADISLAUS HUN BOHEM REX

1440–44
Władysław (Ulászló) I of Poland

1637–
Ferdinand

1301–5
Wenceslas II of Bohemia

1541–66
Sultan Süleyman, "the Magnificient"

1385–6
Charles II of Durazzo

1386–95
Maria (crowned)

1490–1516
Władysław (Ulászló) II

1608–19
Mátyás II

1272–90
Ladislas IV, "the Cuman"

1270–72
István V

1307–42
Charles I Robert of Anjou

1437–9
Albert of Austria

1526–64
Ferdinand I

1200	1300	1400	1500	1600
ÁRPÁDS	ANGEVINS		JAGIEŁŁOS	OTTOMANS
1200	1300	1400	1500	1600

1445–57
Ladislas V, "Posthumus"

1290–1301
András III

1382–5
Maria (un-crowned)

1235–70
Béla IV

1458–90
Mátyás I, "Corvinus"

1516–26
Louis II

1526–40
János I Zápolyai

1342–82
Louis I (Lajos), "the Great"

1564–76
Maximilian I

1576–1608
Rudolf I

1305–7
Otto Wittelsbach of Bavaria

1387–1437
Sigismund of Luxembourg (initially as Maria's consort)

1619–37
Ferdinand II

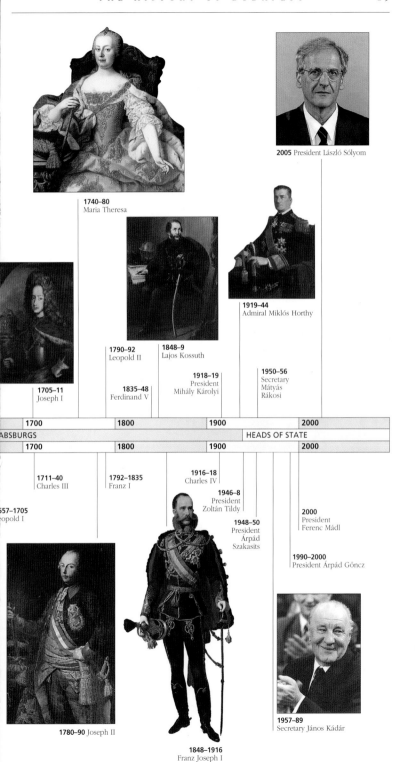

2005 President László Sólyom

1740–80
Maria Theresa

1919–44
Admiral Miklós Horthy

1790–92
Leopold II

1848–9
Lajos Kossuth

1918–19
President
Mihály Károlyi

1950–56
Secretary
Mátyás
Rákosi

1705–11
Joseph I

1835–48
Ferdinand V

| 1700 | 1800 | 1900 | 2000 |

ABSBURGS · HEADS OF STATE

| 1700 | 1800 | 1900 | 2000 |

1711–40
Charles III

1792–1835
Franz I

1916–18
Charles IV

1946–8
President
Zoltán Tildy

1948–50
President
Árpád
Szakasits

2000
President
Ferenc Mádl

1990–2000
President Árpád Göncz

657–1705
eopold I

1780–90 Joseph II

1848–1916
Franz Joseph I

1957–89
Secretary János Kádár

Early Settlers

Bronze Age vessel

Traces of settlements in the region by the Scythians and the Celtic Eravi date from around 400 BC onwards. In the 1st century AD, the Romans conquered the area as their province of Pannonia and soon established Aquincum *(see pp162–3)* within the limits of the modern city. Little evidence remains of the next rulers, the Huns, who were followed by the Goths and the Longobards. For nearly three centuries, starting in around AD 600, the Avars were pre-eminent. In 896, the Magyars swept into the region and laid claim to what would later become the Hungarian state.

EXTENT OF THE CITY

⬛ *AD 300* ☐ *Today*

Bronze Decorations
In the 2nd century AD, Roman carts were often decorated with bronze plaques. This example depicts (from left): a satyr, Bacchus, god of wine and Pan, god of shepherds, under a palm frond. It was found in Somodor.

Workshops and shops, known as *tabernae*, were enclosed and faced onto the street.

The Sun God Mithras
The Persian god Mithras was adopted by the Eravi and his cult survived into the Roman period. This bronze image dates from 2nd–3rd centuries AD.

RECONSTRUCTION OF THE MACELLUM
This solidly built, square market hall was the focus for trade in the Roman town of Aquincum. At its centre was a courtyard with stalls, shops and workshops built around.

TIMELINE

10,000 BC Remains dating from the Palaeolithic era indicate the existence of a settlement in the Remeda Cave in Buda.	*Silver Celtic coin dating from the 4th century BC*	**c. 50 BC** Celtic Eravi settlement on Gellért Hill *(see pp88–9)*	**c. AD 10** The town of Aquincum established by the Roman
	800 BC Tombs with Iron Age urns at Pünkösdfürdö.	**400 BC** Scythians in the region	

10,000	**5000**	**1000**	**AD 1**

5000 BC Stone Age settlements in Talxina and along the Danube		**AD 89** Romans establish a permanent army camp in modern-day Óbuda
Scythian ornamental gold stag		**AD 106** Aquincum becomes the capital the Roman province of Lower Pannc

Sacrificial Altar
This altar, decorated with rams' heads, dates from the Neolithic era. It was found in Szeged.

Shell Necklace
Dating from the Neolithic era, some 5,000 years ago, this necklace was found in Kisköre. It provides evidence of the early migration of tribes and their developed trade activities.

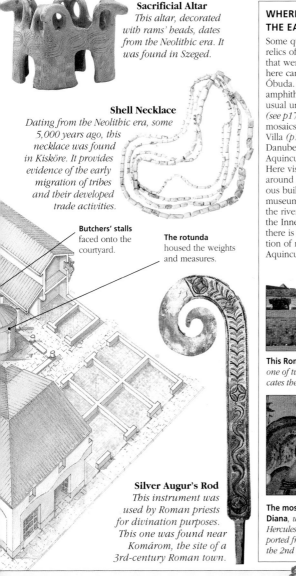

Butchers' stalls faced onto the courtyard.

The rotunda housed the weights and measures.

Silver Augur's Rod
This instrument was used by Roman priests for divination purposes. This one was found near Komárom, the site of a 3rd-century Roman town.

WHERE TO SEE THE EARLY CITY

Some quite considerable relics of the Roman legions that were once stationed here can be seen in modern Óbuda. The remains of an amphitheatre are near an unusual underground museum (*see p170*), while magnificent mosaics adorn the Hercules Villa (*p171*). Further up the Danube are the ruins of Aquincum itself (*pp162–3*). Here visitors can wander around the remains of various buildings and enter a museum. On the Pest side of the river, just to the north of the Inner City Parish Church, there is a small, open-air section of remains from Contra Aquincum (*p122*).

This Roman amphitheatre, *one of two in Aquincum, indicates the status of the town.*

The mosaic of Hercules and Diana, *which survives at the Hercules Villa, was probably imported from Alexandria during the 2nd or 3rd century AD.*

140–60 Two amphitheatres are built to serve Aquincum's growing population

409 The Huns, under Attila, conquer Aquincum

c. 600–896 The Avars rule the region

Ornate earring from the 7th century AD

200	400	600	800

194 Aquincum is promoted to the status of a Roman colony

294 Contra Aquincum is founded on the eastern bank of the Danube

453 Collapse of the Huns' domination

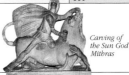

Carving of the Sun God Mithras

896 Magyar (Hungarian) tribes take over Pannonia

The Árpád Dynasty

Hair clasp from the 9th century

After a long journey beginning in the Urals region in Russia, nomadic tribes of Magyars eventually settled in Pannonia in AD 896. Following a period of internal disputes, the tribes made a blood-bonded alliance and chose one leader, Árpád. While Géza I made contact with missionaries, it was his son, István I, who accepted Christianity for his people. Their first crowned king, István organized the state according to the European, feudal model. Initially under the Árpáds, Esztergom *(see p164)* was the country's capital and later Székesfehérvár. The development of Buda, Pest and Óbuda began in the second half of the 12th century, but was interrupted by the Mongol invasion of 1241.

EXTENT OF THE CITY

▨ *1300*   ☐ *Today*

Christ is depicted twice in the middle section of the coat; in each case He is larger than the surrounding figures.

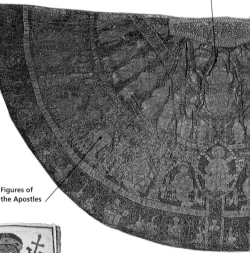

Figures of the Apostles

Trinity of Hungarian Saints
The figures of three saints, King István, his son Imre and Bishop Gellért, are presented on this colourful triptych in the Chapel of St Imre in Mátyás Church (see pp82–3).

King Géza
Géza I, the father of King István, is represented on an enamel plaque decorating the Crown of the Árpáds.

CORONATION COAT
This silk coronation coat was made in 1031 for the Árpád kings. It has a pearl-beaded collar and is embroidered with the figures of Christ, Mary, the Apostles and the Prophets.

TIMELINE

c.900 Árpád settles on Csepel Island (in modern-day Budapest) and his brother Kurszán in Óbuda

Sword of an Árpád king

850	900	950	1000	1050

973 King Géza invites missionaries into the region

1046 Revolt by pagans and the martyr's death of Bishop Gellért, thrown in a barrel into the Danube

Sculpture of King István I by Imre Varga

1001 Coronation of István (Stephen) I

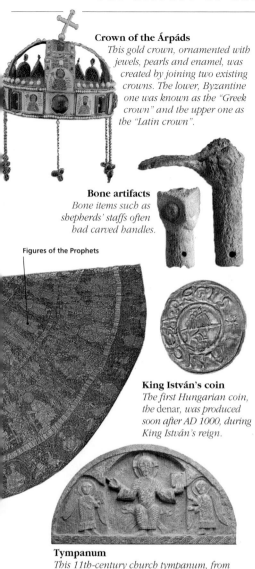

Crown of the Árpáds
This gold crown, ornamented with jewels, pearls and enamel, was created by joining two existing crowns. The lower, Byzantine one was known as the "Greek crown" and the upper one as the "Latin crown".

Bone artifacts
Bone items such as shepherds' staffs often had carved handles.

Figures of the Prophets

King István's coin
The first Hungarian coin, the denar, *was produced soon after AD 1000, during King István's reign.*

Tympanum
This 11th-century church tympanum, from Gyulafehérvár in modern Romania, is in the Hungarian National Gallery (see pp74–7).

WHERE TO SEE THE MEDIEVAL CITY

Only a few monuments survive from the Middle Ages. Among the notable ones that still remain are the crypts in Mátyás Church (*see pp82–3*), and the elevations and cellars of some historic houses in the Castle District (a few of which are now converted into wine bars). The reconstructed lower chambers of the Royal Palace (*pp70–71*) and parts of its fortifications also date from the medieval era.

*This **19th-century copy** of the Romanesque Ják Chapel (see p143) reveals how the Árpáds adopted European styles.*

Gothic niches can be seen by the entrances to many houses in the Old Town (see pp78–9).

1222 "Golden Bull" grants nobility privileges including tax exemption

1188 Béla III moves his headquarters to Óbuda and sets out on Frederick Barbarossa's crusade

1241 Mongol invasion

1247 Béla IV builds castle in Buda, which becomes capital of Hungary

1267 Béla IV announces new "Golden Bull"

1100	1150	1200	1250	1300

Magyar belt buckle dating from the 10th century

1244 The citizens of Pest are granted civic rights

1255 The citizens of Buda get civic rights

1301 Death of King András III, last king of the Árpád dynasty

Gothic and Renaissance Eras

Tabernacle of the Inner City Parish Church

As a result of the efforts of the Angevins and Sigismund of Luxembourg, the Gothic style reached Buda in the 14th century. Buda's palace and the summer palace in Visegrád were both extensively rebuilt. Shortly after defeat by the Turks at Varna, Hungary regained control of Belgrade and, for a while at least, halted their invasion. Mátyás Corvinus, the son of hetman János Hunyadi, the victor of Belgrade, became king. Under Mátyás's rule Hungary was turned into the greatest monarchy of Middle Europe, and, as a result of his marriage to Beatrice, a Neapolitan princess, the Renaissance began to blossom in the country.

EXTENT OF THE CITY

☐ *c. 1480*   ☐ *Today*

Illuminated letter from the Philostratus Codex
This letter depicts the son of King Mátyás I, Johannus Corvinus, after he took Vienna. It is housed in the Széchenyi National Library (see p72).

Castellan Ferenc Sárffy was the commander of Győr Castle.

Hungarian soldier

Royal Medallion
An unknown master from Lombardy commemorated King Mátyás I in this marble silhouette dating from the 1480s.

Gold Seal
This gold seal, which belonged to King Mátyás I, is indicative of the affluence enjoyed by Hungary while he was on the throne.

Ulrik Czettrich, an officer of the royal household, discovered the body of Louis II on the marshy bank of the Csele river.

TIMELINE

1355 Óbuda's citizens gain civic rights

Ciborium dating from the 14th century

1342 Louis I, "the Great", becomes king

1335 Treaty on co-operation and succession signed by the kings of Hungary, Poland and Czechoslovakia in Visegrád

1370 Louis I enters a political union and becomes king of Poland

1385 Sigismund of Luxembourg marries Maria

1395 University established in Óbuda

1387–1437 Rule of Sigismund of Luxembourg. He enlarges the Royal Palace (*see pp70–71*)

1382 After death of Louis I, one daughter, Maria, becomes queen of Hungary and another, Jadwiga, queen of Poland

1350	1375	1400	1425

Wine Cups

This pair of elaborate Renaissance wine cups, dating from the 16th century, is designed to fit together to form a covered receptacle.

Crest of King Mátyás Corvinus

Inscribed with the date 1470, this crest commemorates the building of significant additions to Mátyás Church (see pp82–3), which was then renamed after the king.

King Louis II

Hungarian knight

WHERE TO SEE THE GOTHIC AND RENAISSANCE CITY

The full bloom of the Gothic period took place in Hungary in the 14th century. Mátyás Church *(see pp82–3)* has portals that survive from this era. Renaissance art reached Hungary thanks to Italian masters brought by Mátyás's second wife, Beatrice. Both the Royal Palace *(pp70–71)* and the summer palace at Visegrád *(p164)* were outstanding pieces of Renaissance architecture. Since the storming of Buda by the Turks, only a few remnants of the former splendour have remained.

A royal chamber *from the period of Angevin rule can be seen in the Budapest History Museum (see p72).*

This portal of Mátyás Church *dates from the 14th century. In the 19th century, a Neo-Gothic porch was built around it.*

THE DISCOVERY OF LOUIS II'S BODY

At the Battle of Mohács, on 29 August 1526, King Louis II lost his life together with thousands of Hungarian and Polish knights. The tragic scene of the finding of his body was recreated by Bertalan Székely in 1859.

1440 Władysław III of Poland is Władysław I of Hungary	**1473** *Chronica Hungarorum*, the first book to be published in Hungary, is printed by András Hess	**1514** Peasant revolt under György Dózsa		Władysław *II (ruled 1490–1516)*	
	1456 Victory over Turks at the Battle of Belgrade				
1450	**1475**	**1500**	**1525**	**1550**
1458–1490 Reign of Mátyás Corvinus	**1478** Law is passed threatening landlords who fail to maintain their buildings with dispossession			**1526** Defeat by the Turks at the Battle of Mohács. King Louis II perishes during the fighting	
1444 Władysław I is killed during the Battle of Varna				*Shield of soldier in the army of Mátyás Corvinus*	

The Turkish Occupation

After the battle of Mohács, the Turks razed Buda, but they temporarily turned their attention elsewhere and did not return to occupy it until 1541. When they then moved into the Royal Palace *(see pp70–71)*, Buda became the capital of Ottoman Hungary, while eastern Hungary and Transylvania were feudal suzerains. The Ottomans soon converted the city's churches, including Mátyás Church, into mosques and also built numerous Turkish baths *(see pp50–53)*. The Habsburgs tried relentlessly to recover Buda during this period. Their sieges destroyed the city progressively and when, in 1686, the Christian armies eventually recovered it the scene was one of devastation.

Ottoman plate

EXTENT OF THE CITY

☐ 1630   ☐ Today

Turkish fortress on Gellért Hill

The Rudas and Rác Baths

The Liberation of Buda in 1686
After a bloody siege, the Christian army, led by Prince Eugene of Savoy, entered Buda and liberated it from the Turks. This painting by Gyula Benczúr, dating from 1896, depicts the event.

Ottoman Tombstones
A few inscribed Ottoman tombstones, topped by distinctive turbans, remain to this day in Tabán (see p94).

PEST AND BUDA IN 1617
Georgius Hurnagel's copperplate print shows the heavily-fortified towns of Pest and Buda in a period when much of Hungary was firmly under Turkish rule.

TIMELINE

1526–41 Turks conquer Buda on three occasions

1529 János I Szapolyai, the Hungarian monarch, pays homage to Sultan Süleyman I

1541–66 Reign of Sultan Süleyman I, "the Magnificent", who considered himself the Turkish king of Hungary

1602–3 Austrians, led by General Herman Russworm, fail in attempts to storm Pest and Buda

1525	1545	1565	1585	160

1530–40 János I Szapolyai rebuilds Buda

1542 The Austrians lay siege to Buda

Austrian siege of Buda

1594 Bálint Balassi, Hungary's first great lyric poet, is killed taking part in a battle against the Turks at Esztergom *(see p164)*

Campaign Tent
This Turkish leader's tent, decorated with appliqué work, was used during the siege of Vienna in 1683.

Mátyás Church *(see pp82–3)* was converted into a mosque.

Ottoman Coat
This 16th-century leather coat was supposedly taken from the battlefield of Mohács (see p25).

Ottoman Jug
Dating from the 17th century, this copper vessel was found in Buda during the reconstruction of the Royal Palace (see pp70–71).

WHERE TO SEE THE TURKISH CITY

Almost all Turkish buildings were razed by their successors, the Habsburgs, during or after the recapture of the city. Churches which the Turks had used as mosques were converted back again, although some *mihrabs*, the niches pointing towards Mecca, were left. These can be seen in the Inner City Parish Church *(see pp124–5)* and in the Capuchin Church *(p100)*. Among the few wonderful examples of classical Ottoman architecture to survive are the Rudas, Rác *(p95)* and Király Baths, and the Tomb of Gül Baba, a Turkish dervish *(p101)*.

The Király Baths, *built in the 16th century by Arshlan Pasha, remain an impressive Ottoman monument (see p101).*

The Rudas Baths *have an original Turkish dome covering their central chamber (see p93).*

Ottoman tablet with calligraphy

1634 György I Rákóczi, prince of Transylvania, joins an anti-Habsburg alliance with France and Sweden

1684 Start of ultimately successful siege of Buda by the Austrians

Viennese sword dating from the 17th century

| 1625 | 1645 | 1665 | 1685 |

1624 Signing of the Treaty of Vienna

1648 Death of György I Rákóczi

Gold five-ducat coin from 1603, showing the prince of Transylvania's crest

1686 Christian troops enter Buda. The end of Turkish rule in Hungary

Habsburg Rule

Order created by Maria Theresa

In order to gain control of Hungary, the Habsburgs encouraged foreign settlers, particularly Germans, to move into the country. This policy led to a national uprising in 1703–11, led by the prince of Transylvania, Ferenc II Rákóczi. Only in the second half of the 18th century, particularly under Empress Maria Theresa, did the reconstruction of Buda, Óbuda and Pest begin in earnest. This was accompanied by economic development and a further increase in the country's population. The university at Nagyszombat (now Trnava in the Slovak Republic) moved to Buda in 1777, and subsequently to Pest in 1784, and was an important factor in their expansion.

EXTENT OF THE CITY

■ 1770   □ Today

Maria Theresa holds the infant Joseph, the successor to her throne.

The Return of the Crown to Buda *(1790)*
A vast ceremonial procession of commissioners marked the arrival in Hungary of royal insignias from Vienna, a sign of peace between the two countries.

Ferenc II Rákóczi
This fine portrait by Ádám Mányoki depicts Ferenc II Rákóczi, the leader of the national uprising of 1703–11 and a figure much loved by the Hungarian people.

"VITAM ET SANGUINEM"
In 1741, the Hungarian states swore on "life and blood" their loyalty to the Habsburg Empress Maria Theresa. This copperplate print by Joseph Szentpétery depicts the scene of the oath-taking.

TIMELINE

1687 Under Austrian pressure, the Hungarian parliament gives up its right to elect a king and accedes to the inheritance of the throne by the Habsburgs

1702 The Jesuits open a college and theological seminary

1703 The Prince of Transylvania, Ferenc II Rákóczi, leads a rebellion by the Hungarians against the Habsburgs

1729 The start of the reconstruction of Pest's suburbs

1690

1705

1720

1735

1689 Bubonic plague devastates the population of Buda and Pest

Royal postal carriage

1711 Suppression of Rákóczi's rebellion; a second bubonic plague decimates the city

1724 The population of Buda and Pest reaches 12,000 people

1723 Great Fire of Buda

Triple-jug of the Andrássy family
These silver jugs are joined by a miniature of the castle belonging to the Andrássy family, at what is now Krásna Horka in the Slovak Republic.

Hungarian aristocrats swear on their lives to protect Maria Theresa's throne.

Dress *(c. 1750)*
This dress, typical of Hungarian style with its corset which was tightened by golden cords, was worn by a lady from the noble Majtényi family.

Ferenc II Rákóczi's Chair
Richly upholstered, this graceful 18th-century chair from Regéc Castle is typical of the style of the period.

WHERE TO SEE THE HABSBURG CITY

Having taken Buda and Pest from the Turks in the late 17th century, the Habsburgs set about rebuilding them in the 18th century, mainly in the Baroque style. Famous buildings from this era include the Municipal Council Offices, St Anne's Church *(see pp102–3)*, St Elizabeth's Church *(p101)* and the University Church *(p139)*.

St Anne's Church, *which was built between 1740–1805, astonishes visitors with its magnificent Baroque interior.*

The Municipal Council Offices *in the heart of Pest have a portico decorated with allegorical figures by Johann Christoph Mader (see p127).*

5–71 Building of the Habsburg Royal Palace

The magnificent Habsburg Royal Palace

1788 First Hungarian newspaper, *Magyar Merkurius*, begins printing

A hussar, or soldier

1778 Roman remains are discovered in Óbuda

1750	1765	1780	1795

1752 A regular postal service operates between Buda and Vienna

1766 A floating bridge links Buda and Pest

1792 Convocation of parliament and the coronation of Franz I

46–57 Construction of the Zichy Palace in Óbuda *(see p171)*

1777 University moves from Nagyszombat to Buda; later relocates to Pest

1784 Establishment of Ferenc Goldberger's textile factory in Óbuda

National Revival and the "Springtime of Revolutions"

Hungarian crest

The dynamic economic development of Buda and Pest began at the start of the 19th century. Pest, in particular, benefited from favourable circumstances for the grain trade and became, in the Napoleonic Wars, an important centre for the Habsburg monarchy. A national revival and rekindling of cultural life took place after the Napoleonic Wars. The Hungarian National Museum and many other public and private buildings were built at this time. Yet, Hungarian reformers were hampered by the Viennese royal court and an uprising erupted in the spring of 1848. This rebellion was suppressed by the Habsburgs, with the help of the Russian army, and a period of absolutism followed.

EXTENT OF THE CITY

■ *1848* □ *Today*

Count György Andrássy, offered 10,000 forints towards the building of the Hungarian Academy of Sciences.

The Advance of the Hussars

In this watercolour, painted in 1850, Mór Than depicts fighting in the Battle of Tápióbicske of 1849. The Hungarian side was led by a Polish general, Henryk Dembiński.

The Great Flood

This bas-relief, made by Barnabás Holló in 1900, shows a heroic rescue by Count Miklós Wesselényi during the Great Flood of 1838.

THE FOUNDING OF THE ACADEMY

In 1825, István Széchenyi put up 60,000 forints towards the building of Hungarian Academy of Sciences *(see p114),* a move which led to a national effort to collect funds for it. Barnabás Holló created this bas-relief depicting the major donors.

TIMELINE

1802 Count Ferenc Széchenyi donates collections which will form the basis for Széchenyi National Library *(see p72)* and Hungarian National Museum *(see pp130–33)*	**1809** Royal court moves from Vienna to Buda as Napoleon advances. Despite his offer of Hungarian independence, the Hungarians back the Habsburgs	**1817** First steamboat sails on Danube in the environs of Buda and Pest

1800	**1805**	**1810**	**1815**	**1820**

1808 Establishment of the Embellishment Commission, led by Governor Archduke Joseph

Boats on the Danube

Lajos Batthyány Eternal Flame
This lamp, designed by Móric Pogány, has burnt since 1926 in Liberty Square (see p110). It was there that the Austrians shot Lajos Batthyány, the first prime minister of liberated Hungary, on 6 October 1849.

Count István Széchenyi, an energetic force for change, is regarded as the one of the greatest Hungarians.

National Song
The 1848 uprising was sparked on 15 March when Sándor Petőfi recited his poem, Nemzeti Dal *(National Song), outside the Hungarian National Museum.*

WHERE TO SEE THE NEO-CLASSICAL CITY

In the early 19th century, the Embellishment Commission, set up by Archduke Joseph and led by architect János Hild, prepared a plan for the development of Pest in which its centre was redesigned on a pattern of concentric streets. Monumental Neo-Classical buildings were built here and to this day they form the heart and the character of this area. Structures to look for in particular include the Hungarian National Museum, the Chain Bridge and several houses located on József Nádor Square *(see p126).*

György Károlyi

The Hungarian National Museum, *which was built in 1837, is among Hungary's finest examples of Neo-Classical architecture* (see pp130–31).

Buda and Pest in 1838
Seen here in the year before the construction of the Chain Bridge, the Danube was an important means of transport.

The Chain Bridge, *the first permanent bridge over the Danube, was built by Adam Clark in 1839–49 (see p63).*

1825–48 Period of major projects: establishment of the Hungarian Academy of Sciences, Hungarian National Museum and National Theatre

Poet Sándor Petőfi (1823–49)

1840 Language Act: Hungarian takes over from Latin as the official language of the nation

15 March 1848 Uprising begins

1847 Death of Archduke Joseph, emperor's governor

| 1825 | 1830 | 1835 | 1840 | 1845 |

1830 István Széchenyi publishes his book, *On Credit.* It is seen as the manifesto for the fight for modern Hungary

The Great Flood

1838 Catastrophic Great Flood results in destruction of half of Pest's buildings

1846 First railway line in the city, linking Pest and Vác

1849 After stout resistance, the Russian army, under the command of General Ivan Paskievicz, suppresses uprising

Compromise and the Unification of Budapest

After suffering a defeat by Prussia in 1866, the Habsburgs realized the necessity of reaching an agreement with Hungary and the Compromise brokered in 1867 proved to be of tremendous importance for the future of Buda and Pest. The option of uniting the two cities had been considered since the opening of the Chain Bridge in 1849. It eventually came about in 1873 and Budapest soon found itself among Europe's fastest growing metropolises. In 1896, Városliget was the focal point for Hungary's Millennium Celebrations *(see p142).*

Maria Theresa

EXTENT OF THE CITY

■ *1873*   □ *Today*

The Citadel *(see p92)* on Gellért Hill

Castle District

Hungarian Wine Cup
This 19th-century wine cup is embellished with the Hungarian crest, which incorporates the Crown of the Árpáds (see p23).

Ferenc Deák
(1803–76)
A great statesman, Deák was an advocate of moderate reforms. He argued persuasively in favour of accepting the Compromise reached with the Habsburgs in 1867.

Today's Boráros tér, where goods were once traded.

Decorative Pipe *(1896)*
Made in the year of Hungary's Millennium Celebrations, this pipe of "heavenly peace" includes figures of the Árpád kings and Emperor Franz Joseph.

TIMELINE

1854 Martial law ends five years after 1848–9 uprising

1856 Tunnel *(see p100)* built by Adam Clark under Castle Hill

Entrance to the Tunnel

1875 Opening of the Franz Liszt Academy of Music *(see p129)*, with the composer as its principal

1850	1860	1870	1880

1859 Synagogue on Dohány utca *(see p134)* completed

1864 Opening of the Great Market Hall *(see p203)*

1873 The unification of Buda, Óbuda and Pest as one city, with a total of 300,000 inhabitants

1867 Compromise with Austria, giving Hungary independence in its internal affairs. Creation of the Dual Monarchy; Emperor Franz Joseph accepts the Hungarian crown

Monument to Hungarian Soldiers Killed in World War I
This bas-relief, by János Istók, commemorates the dead of World War I, in which Hungary fought on the German side. It is located next to the main entrance to the Servite Church (see p128).

"Handcuff" Bracelet
Following the defeat of the national uprising of 1848–9, Hungarians sought to symbolize their oppression even in pieces of jewellery.

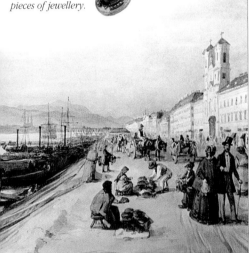

TRADING ON THE PEST EMBANKMENT
Completed in 1887, this painting by Antal Ligeti shows the Pest embankment at a time when the city was booming. Manufactured goods and grain were sent along the Danube for sale in Germany and the Balkans.

WHERE TO SEE THE HISTORICIST CITY
Historicism had a profound influence on the form of the rapidly developing metropolis at this time. A wonderful example of the style is the Hungarian Academy of Sciences. Among others are Parliament *(see pp108–9)*, St Stephen's Basilica *(pp116–17)*, the Museum of Fine Arts *(pp146–7)*, the New York Palace *(p129)* and many of the buildings that stand on Andrássy Street *(p144)*.

The Hungarian Academy of Sciences *is housed in this fine Neo-Renaissance palace dating from 1864 (see p114).*

St Stephen's Basilica *was built over a period of 60 years by three architects. It was finished in 1905 (see pp116–17).*

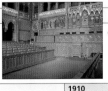

Old Upper House Hall in Parliament

1894 Body of Lajos Kossuth *(see p106)* is returned from Turin

1904 Grand opening of Parliament *(see pp108–9)*

1916 Franz Joseph dies and Charles IV becomes king of Hungary

| 1890 | 1900 | 1910 | 1920 |

1896 First metro line and several museums opened

1909 Airport opened in Rákos, now Kőbánya

1900 With a population of 773,000, Budapest is Europe's fastest growing city

1914 Hungary enters World War I on the German side

1918 Abdication of Charles IV marks end of the Austro-Hungarian Empire

Modern Budapest

Poster for
Unicum liqueur
(see p193)

Hungary paid a high price for its alliances first with Austria and later with Nazi Germany. Following defeat in both World Wars, the country had lost a large portion of its territory. As a result of the Yalta Agreement of 1945, it then found itself within the Soviet-controlled zone of Europe. Stalinism took on a particularly ruthless form here and led to the 1956 Uprising, which was brutally put down by Soviet tanks on the streets of Budapest. Efforts towards reform, undertaken by János Kádár, brought some changes but political opposition was not tolerated. In 1989, the Communists were ousted and Hungary at last regained control of its own affairs.

1944 Efforts to withdraw from World War II end with German troops entering the country. A ghetto is established in Budapest and the extermination of Hungarian Jews begins. As the Russian army approaches the city, all bridges across the Danube are blown up

1945 After a siege lasting six weeks, the Russian army takes Budapest

1946 Proclamation of Republic of Hungary. Smallholders' Party wins elections

1919 Communists take over government and declare the Hungarian Soviet Republic

1941 Hungary enters World War II on Germany's side

1947 After falsification of election results, Communists control the whole country

1939 Hungary neutral at beginning of World War II. Accepts refugees after capitulation of Poland

1957 János Kádár is first secretary of Hungarian Socialist Workers' Party

1922 Reopening of the State Opera House *(see pp118–19)* after World War I

1949 Stalinist terror prevails. Cardinal Mindszenty *(see p111)* goes on trial. László Rajk, secret police chief, sentenced to death by Moscow loyalists

1928 Budapest is a free port on Danube

1937 Sixth and last visit of author Thomas Mann

1920	1930	1940	1950

1920	1930	1940	1950

1935 Tabán *(see p94)* levelled and transformed into a park

1938 Eucharistic Congress

1953 The national football team beats England 6–3 at Wembley

1925 Radio Budapest broadcasts its first programme

1948 Mátyás Rákosi leads Hungarian Socialist Workers' Party, created by Communists

1919 Admiral Miklós Horthy enters Budapest; many killed in the period of "White Terror". Horthy becomes regent

1945–1 August 1946 Monetary reform. Banknotes valued at one billion pengő are printed during rampant inflation. There is not enough room for all the zeros to be shown on the notes

1918 Democratic revolution; Hungary declared a republic. Mihály Károlyi selected as the country's first president

1956 National uprising is suppressed through Soviet intervention

1958 The leader of the 1956 Uprising, Prime Minister Imre Nagy, is executed

60–66 Rebuilding of Castle District *(see pp68–85),* including Royal Palace, and the Danube bridges

October 1989 Republic of Hungary is proclaimed once more. The national emblem is changed

September 1989 Hungary opens its borders to allow refugees to flee from East Germany to the West

1991 Warsaw Pact is dissolved. Russian army leaves Hungary

1994 Election won by the Hungarian Socialist Party

1998 Election won by the Citizens' Party

2002 Election won by the Hungarian Socialist Party. Imre Kertész receives the Nobel prize for Literature

1981 Director István Szabó receives an Oscar for his film *Mefisto*

2004 Hungary becomes a member of the EU

1964 The Elizabeth Bridge *(see p63)* reopens to traffic, having been totally reconstructed

February 1989 Round-table talks between opposition parties and ruling socialist government

	1970	1980	1990	2000

	1970	1980	1990	2000

1968 Introduction of new economic system known as "goulash-Communism"

1987 UNESCO places the historic Castle District and the Banks of the Danube on its list of world heritage sights

June 1989 Ceremonial funeral for Imre Nagy and rehabilitation for other leaders of 1956 Uprising

1990 The Democratic Hungarian Forum wins free elections. József Antall becomes the first prime minister to be elected in a democratic process; Árpád Göncz is elected president

1993 Pope John Paul II visits Hungary

970 Opening of a new metro line

1991 Václav Havel, József Antall and Lech Walesa sign an agreement in Visegrád *(see p164)* between Czechoslovakia, Hungary and Poland

BUDAPEST AT A GLANCE

Often described as the "Little Paris of Middle Europe", Budapest is famous not only for the monuments reflecting its own 1,000-year-old culture, but also for the relics of others who settled here. Remains from both Roman occuption, and, much later, rule by the Turks can still be seen in the city. After Turkish rule, union with Austria had a particular influence on the city's form and style. Descriptions of nearly 150 places of interest can be found in the *Area by Area* section of the book. However, to help you make the most of your stay, the following 20 pages are a guide to the best Budapest has to offer. Museums and galleries, churches and synagogues, palaces and historic buildings, baths and pools are presented, together with the influence of Secession in the city. Each sight is is cross-referenced to its main entry. Below are the sights not to be missed.

BUDAPEST'S TOP TEN SIGHTS

Gellért Monument
See p93.

Gellért Baths
See pp90–91.

Váci Street
See p127.

Parliament
See pp108–9.

National Museum
See pp130–33.

State Opera House
See pp118–19.

Margaret Island
See pp172–3.

Danube and Chain Bridge
See p62.

Mátyás Church
See pp82–3.

National Gallery
See pp74–7.

◁ The Neo-Renaissance façade of the Cify Council Chamber *(see p138)* in the centre of Pest

Budapest's Best: Museums and Galleries

Unlike many other European cities – such as Paris with the Louvre and Madrid with the Prado – Budapest does not have a museum founded from a royal treasury because Hungary was for so long ruled by foreign powers. In the early 19th century, however, the modern aristocracy, backed by an increasingly affluent middle class, began to take an interest in preserving historic objects for the nation. Today, there are over 60 museums and galleries in Budapest, ranging from those with collections of international significance to others of much more local interest. For more information on museums and galleries see pages 40–41.

Museum of Military History
This museum has interesting displays illustrating the history of Hungarian weaponry.

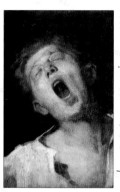

Hungarian National Gallery
The Hungarian art displayed here dates from the Middle Ages right through to the 20th century. The Yawning Journeyman *(1868), by the great Mihály Munkácsy, is among the highlights of the collection.*

North of the Castle

DANUBE

Castle District

Budapest History Museum
This Gothic work is one of the medieval treasures of the Budapest History Museum. The oldest exhibits are located in the original, lower-floor rooms of the Renaissance Royal Palace.

Gellért Hill and Tabán

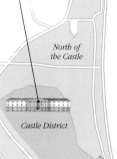

0 metres	500
0 yards	500

Semmelweis Museum of Medical History
Doctor Ignác Semmelweis, famous for his discovery of the cure for puerperal fever, was born in 1818 in the house where the museum is now situated.

Ethnographical Museum
Among the exhibits at this museum illustrating the material culture of the Hungarians is this jug, dating from 1864, made by György Mantl. There are also impressive displays concerning tribal societies in other parts of the world.

Museum of Fine Arts
The wonderful Portrait of a Man *(c.1565), by Paolo Veronese, is one of many Old Masters in this splendid collection of paintings and sculpture.*

Around Parliament

Around Városliget

Central Pest

Jewish Museum
Located in several rooms beside the Great Synagogue, this museum covers the Holocaust in this country and displays religious objects.

Hungarian National Museum
Beautiful frescoes by Károly Lotz and Mór Than decorate the elegant staircase of Hungary's oldest museum.

Museum of Applied Arts
Precious ceramics, porcelain and furnishings are housed in a building that is itself a work of art, surmounted by a magnificent, oriental-style dome.

Exploring the Museums and Galleries

Most of the city's museums and galleries are located in historic buildings. These include the spacious chambers of the restored Royal Palace, which in the 1970s and 1980s were designated as the premises of several museums, including the Hungarian National Gallery. The largest museums – including the Hungarian National Museum and Budapest History Museum – also stage temporary exhibitions that are popular with both locals and tourists.

Processional crucifix

Sculpture of Imre Varga at the gallery named after him *(see p171)*

HUNGARIAN PAINTINGS AND SCULPTURE

There are two important venues that should be on the itinerary of anyone interested in viewing the finest examples of Hungarian art.

At the **Hungarian National Gallery**, seven chronological sections present paintings and sculpture dating from the Middle Ages up until modern times. The sequence begins in the Lapidarium, where fragments of recovered medieval stone sculptures from the castles of the first Hungarian kings are exhibited.

As a rule, very few examples of Gothic and Renaissance art survive in Budapest because of the pillage inflicted by the Turks during their rule. However, a fine collection of altar retables from the 15th and 16th centuries are on display in the Hungarian National Gallery. In the 19th century, Hungarian painting developed and flourished, at the same time reflecting all the major international modern art movements. The Hungarian style can be seen particularly in the works of Pál Szinyei-Merse, Mihály Munkácsy and László Paál. For sculpture, meanwhile, the main names to look out for are István Ferenczy, Zsigmond Kisfaludi Stróbl and Imre Varga.

It is portraits, rather than paintings and sculpture, that are shown at the **Hungarian National Museum**. These provide a fascinating insight into the country's history.

The **Vasarely Museum** has a collection of 300 works by Hungarian-born artist Victor Vasarely. He moved to Paris in 1930 and became famous as one of the main exponents of the Op Art movement.

EUROPEAN PAINTINGS AND SCULPTURE

Masterpieces by the finest European artists, from medieval times to the modern day, are also divided between two museums in Budapest.

The **Museum of Fine Arts** has a magnificent collection of Italian paintings, dating from the 14th century up to the Baroque period, by masters such as Titian, Antonio Correggio, Paolo Veronese, Giambattista Tiepolo and Jacopo Tintoretto. However, it is the *Esterházy Madonna* (1508) by Raphael, that is the jewel of the Italian collection. Equally splendid is the exhibition of Spanish paintings, which is one of the largest in the world. Works by Goya include *The Water Carrier* (c.1810). There are seven canvases by El Greco and others by Francisco de Zurbarán and Bartolomé Esteban Murillo. Other galleries within the museum represent artists of the Netherlands and Germany, as well as British, French and Flemish masters. The museum also owns more than 100,000 drawings and engravings by the Old Masters, while its modern art collection includes some notable works.

Modern European paintings can also be viewed in the **Ludwig Museum of Contemporary Art.** All the canvases belong to the Peter Ludwig Foundation of Germany. Highly prized works here include two paintings by Pablo Picasso, *Mother and Child* and *Musketeer*.

Pablo Picasso's *Musketeer* (1967), in the Ludwig Collection

The Jewish Museum, located beside the Great Synagogue

HISTORY

The history of Budapest, and that of Hungary as a whole, is illustrated in several museums. Relics from the Roman era can be found at the **Aquincum Museum** and at a handful of museums, including the **Roman Camp Museum**, in Óbuda.

The most important national historic treasures are housed in the **Hungarian National Museum**. The Coronation Mantle, dating back to the 11th century, is included in this collection.

Medieval seals and Gothic statuary are among the exhibits at **Budapest History Museum**. At the **Museum of Military History**, displays chart various Hungarian struggles for liberty, including the 1956 Uprising (see p34).

The **Jewish Museum** has a room covering the Holocaust, as well as many ritual objects. The collection of the **Lutheran Museum**, situated next to the Lutheran Church, includes a copy of Martin Luther's will.

MUSIC

Two of the museums featured in this book, the **Franz Liszt Museum** and the **Zoltán Kodály Museum**, are dedicated to internationally renowned composers. In each case, the setting is the apartment where the composer lived and worked, and on display are the instruments they played, musical scores and photographs.

A more general view of Hungarian music is on offer at the **Museum of Musical History**, located in a Baroque palace on Mihály Táncsics Street. Displays feature the development of instruments and music in the 18th and 19th centuries; a special section is dedicated to Béla Bartók.

ETHNOGRAPHY AND ORIENTAL CRAFTS

Lavish folk costumes, as well as many other everyday items that belonged to the people of the region, can be viewed in the beautiful interiors of the **Ethnographical Museum**. The museum also has a section that focuses on the primitive tribes of Africa, America and, particularly, Asia. It is in Asia that the Hungarians seek their roots as it is from there that the Magyars are thought to have come.

This fascination with the Orient has led to the foundation of two other museums displaying Eastern artefacts. The **Ferenc Hopp Museum of Far Eastern Art** has assorted Indian objects; its Chinese and Japanese collections are displayed at the **Rath György Museum.**

DECORATIVE ARTS

Housed in an extraordinary building designed by Ödön Lechner (see p56), the **Museum of Applied Arts** gives an impressive overview of the development of crafts from the Middle Ages onwards. Meissen porcelain is exhibited alongside oriental carpets and

Stained-glass window at the Museum of Applied Arts

Hungarian pieces. The display relating to the Secession (see pp54–7) is striking. The museum's permanent collection was founded in 1872. Major exhibitions tend to change each year, while smaller national and foreign displays change monthly.

SPECIALIST MUSEUMS

The **Semmelweis Museum of Medical History** explores the work of a doctor called Ignác Semmelweis, who discovered the cure for puerperal fever. This affliction had previously been a serious threat for women who had recently given birth. The **Golden Eagle Pharmacy Museum** is situated in a building that first opened as a pharmacy in 1681. Many original fixtures are intact and pharmaceutical exhibits are displayed.

Railway enthusiasts of all ages will not fail to appreciate the **Transport Museum** on Hermina Street, with its enormous collection of model trains, as well as exhibits on the evolution of air, sea, road and rail transport.

Budapest's Best: Churches and Synagogues

There are very few medieval and Renaissance churches still standing in Budapest. This is mainly due to the fact that the Turks, during their 150-year rule, turned all churches into mosques, which were later destroyed during the attacks on Buda and Pest by the Christians. The reconstruction of old churches and the building of new ones started in the late 17th century, hence the prevalence of Baroque and Neo-Classical styles.

Capuchin Church
Two Turkish windows remain from the time when this church was used as a mosque, alongside fragments of its medieval walls.

St Anne's Church
Built in the mid-18th century, this is one of the most beautiful Baroque churches in the city. The joined figures of St Anne and Mary decorate the centre of its façade.

North of the Castle

Castle District

Mátyás Church
Romanesque and Gothic styles are both evident in the coronation church of the Hungarian kings. The Neo-Gothic altar dates from the 19th century.

Gellért Hill and Tabán

Rock Church
In the rocky interior of St István's Cave, on the south side of Gellért Hill, the priests of the Pauline order established a church in 1926. It was designed to imitate the holy grotto at Lourdes.

| 0 metres | 500 |
| 0 yards | 500 |

DANUBE

St Stephen's Basilica

A bas-relief by Leó Feszler, representing the Virgin Mary surrounded by Hungarian saints, decorates the main tympanum of St Stephen's Basilica. This imposing church was built between 1851–1905.

Lutheran Church

This Neo-Classical church was completed by Mihály Pollack in 1808. The impressive façade was added half a century later by József Hild.

Around Városliget

Around Parliament

Central Pest

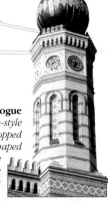

Great Synagogue

Two Moorish-style minarets, each topped by an onion-shaped dome, dominate the exterior of the largest synagogue in Europe.

Franciscan Church

The magnificent 19th-century paintings that decorate the interior of this Baroque church are by Károly Lotz.

Inner City Parish Church

Dating from 1046, this church is Pest's oldest building. A figure of St Florian, the patron saint of fire fighters, was placed on the wall beside the altar after the church survived the great fire of 1723.

Exploring the Churches and Synagogues

Detail on St Elizabeth's Church

Most of the city's churches are found around the centres of Buda and Pest. Only a few sacred buildings of architectural interest are situated on the outskirts of the city. The greatest period of construction took place in the 18th century, after the final expulsion of the Turks. Another phase occurred in the second half of the 19th century, producing two of Budapest's grandest places of worship: St Stephen's Basilica and the Great Synagogue. Religious buildings were neglected after World War II, but thanks to restoration some have now regained their former splendour.

Reconstructed Gothic window of the Church of St Mary Magdalene

MEDIEVAL

Both **Mátyás Church** and the **Inner City Parish Church** date originally from the reign of Béla IV in the 13th century. Glimpses of their original Romanesque style can be seen, although each church was subsequently rebuilt in the Gothic style. After being sacked by the Turks in 1526,

Mátyás Church was given a Baroque interior by the Jesuits who had at that time taken it over. Finally, the church was returned to a likeness of its medieval character between 1874–96, when all Baroque elements were systematically removed and it was given a Neo-Gothic shape.

The **Church of St Mary Magdalene**, built in 1274 in the Gothic style, was almost completely destroyed in 1945. All that remains intact today is the 15th-century tower with its two chapels. A Gothic window has also been rebuilt.

St Michael's Church, founded in the 12th century on Margaret Island, was completely destroyed by the Turks. However, in 1932 it was reconstructed from its original Romanesque plans.

BAROQUE

In the 18th century, 17 churches were built in Pest, Buda and Óbuda, all of them in the Baroque style. The influence of the Italian architectural school is visible in many of them, although only

University Church was built by an Italian architect, Donato Allio. Under Habsburg rule, the leading architects working in the city, András Meyerhoffer, Mátyás Nepauer and Kristóf Hamon, often chose to follow Austrian examples.

University Church and **St Anne's Church** are generally considered to be the most beautiful buildings in the city dating from this era. The former astonishes visitors with its beautifully carved stalls and pulpit, and with the paintings by Johann Bergl adorning its vaults. St Anne's Church has a magnificent Baroque façade and reveals the influence of southern German Baroque in its oval floor plan. Inside, there is a lavish altar and pulpit designed by Károly Bebó.

The **Franciscan Church**, which is situated in the centre of Budapest and dates from 1758, has a wide Baroque nave and a main altar created by Antal Grassalkovich.

The interior of the Servite Church (1725), with its Baroque altar

SPIRES AND DOMES

The Gothic spire belonging to the Church of St Mary Magdalene and the Neo-Gothic spire of Mátyás Church are among Budapest's main landmarks. The twin Baroque towers of St Anne's Church and the soaring spire of the Calvinist Church rise above the Danube in Buda. On the Pest side, the dome of St Stephen's Basilica and the minarets of the Great Synagogue dominate.

Gothic spire of the Church of St Mary Magdalene

Baroque towers of St Anne's Church

Neo-Gothic spire of the Calvinist Church

NEO-CLASSICAL AND HISTORICIST

In 1781, Joseph II passed an edict permitting the building of Protestant churches. The city already had many Catholic churches and Protestant communities now started to build their own places of worship in the prevailing style of the time, Neo-Classicism.

One of the first to go up was the **Lutheran Church**, on Deák Ferenc tér, completed in 1808 by Mihály Pollack, a gifted master of Neo-Classical architecture. The white, ascetic interior of the church, with its two-floor gallery, was ideally suited to the nature of this place of worship. The majesty and simplicity of the Neo-Classical style corresponded with the more austere nature of Protestant belief. József Hild, another master of the style, later extended the church. He added the portico with its Doric columns, linking the church with the presbytery and a school. The complex as a whole is one of the best examples of Neo-Classical architecture in Budapest.

On a more modest scale is the **Calvinist Church**, built in the Neo-Gothic style between 1893–6.

When plans for it were drawn up by József Hild in 1845, **St Stephen's Basilica** was intended to be the pinnacle of Neo-Classical architecture. However, several delays, including the collapse of its dome at one point, meant

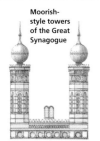

Baptismal font at the Lutheran Church

that the realization of the original design was impossible. Following Hild's death in 1867, Miklós Ybl continued the project. He departed from Hild's plan, incorporating Renaissance-style features. The Basilica was finally completed by a third architect, József Kauser, in 1905.

LATE 19TH- AND 20TH-CENTURY

The two most stunning synagogues in Budapest were designed by Viennese architects in the second half of the 19th century.

Ludwig Förster constructed the **Great Synagogue** in Byzantine-Moorish style in 1859 and Otto Wagner, an important Secession architect *(see pp54–7)*, realized one of his first projects in 1872. This was the **Orthodox Synagogue** on Rumbach utca, which also incorporated Moorish ideas.

Closely linked to the Secession style is the Hungarian National Style, based on an idiosyncratic combination of ethnic motifs and elements from folk art. This style is most visible in two churches by Hungarian architects. Ödön Lechner, the originator of the Hungarian National Style, completed **Kőbánya Parish Church**, on the outskirts of Budapest, in 1900. Meanwhile, Aladár Árkay built **Városliget Calvinist Church** in 1913. These two churches display a striking combination of

The Byzantine-Moorish interior of the Great Synagogue

colourful ceramics, Eastern-style ornamentation and also Neo-Gothic elements.

WHERE TO FIND THE CHURCHES AND SYNAGOGUES

Moorish-style towers of the Great Synagogue

Dome of the eclectic St Stephen's Basilica

Budapest's Best: Palaces and Historic Buildings

Detail on the façade of Károly Palace

Budapest boasts historic buildings and palaces in a broad range of architectural styles. The majority represent the Neo-Classicism, Historicism and Secession of the 19th and early 20th centuries, when a dynamic development of the capital took place. All but a few Gothic and Renaissance details were lost in the destruction of Buda and Pest by Christian troops in 1686, but some examples of its Baroque heritage remain. This map gives some highlights, with a more detailed look on pages 48–9.

Royal Palace
This palace has a turbulent history dating back to the 13th century. Its present form, however, reflects the opulence of the 19th century. Today the palace houses some of the city's finest museums.

Houses on Vienna Gate Square
This charming row of four houses was built in the late 18th and early 19th centuries on the ruins of medieval dwellings. The houses are adorned with decorative motifs in the Baroque, Rococo and Neo-Classical styles.

Sándor Palace
The original friezes that decorated this 19th-century palace were recreated by Hungarian artists as part of its restoration. The palace is now the headquarters of the President of the Republic of Hungary.

North of the Castle

Castle District

DANUBE

Gellért Hill and Tabán

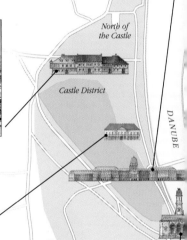

Várkert Casino
This Neo-Renaissance pavilion was built by Miklós Ybl (see p119) as a pump house for the Royal Palace. It now houses the luxurious Várkert Casino.

Hungarian Academy of Science

The façade of the academy is adorned with statues by Emil Wolff and Miklós Izsó, symbolizing major fields of knowledge: law, natural history, mathematics, philosophy, linguistics and history.

Gresham Palace

Now housing a Four Seasons Hotel, this splendid example of Secession design was built in 1905–7 by Zsigmond Quittner.

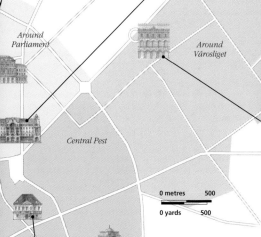

Around Parliament

Around Városliget

Central Pest

0 metres 500

0 yards 500

Pallavicini Palace

Gustáv Petschacher built this Neo-Renaissance mansion on Kodály körönd in 1882. The inner court-yard was copied from the Palazzo Marini in Milan.

Ervin Szabó Library

The grand, Neo-Baroque palace that now houses this library was originally built in 1887 for the Wenckheims, a family of rich industrialists.

Péterffy Palace

This plaque, commemorating a flood of 1838, was placed on one of the few Baroque mansions that remain in Pest. The house was built in 1756.

Exploring the Palaces and Historic Buildings

Little more than fragments remain of Budapest's Gothic and Renaissance past. However, some Baroque buildings have survived in Buda's Castle District and Víziváros. Neo-Classicism, on the other hand, has a much wider presence; there are many apartment buildings, palaces and secular monuments built in this style, especially around the old fortification walls of Pest on the eastern side of the Danube. Historicism dominated the architecture of the second half of the 19th century. It played a vital role in the enlargement of the city as it expressed and celebrated the optimism of the era.

Façade of the Gross Palace, built by Jószef Hild in 1824

BAROQUE PALACES AND BUILDINGS

Many buildings in the Castle District and neighbouring Víziváros, around Fő utca, have retained their original Baroque façades. The main entrance of the **Hilton Hotel**, formerly a 17th-century Jesuit college, is a fine example.

Other outstanding instances of this style are the four houses on **Vienna Gate Square, the Batthyány Palace** on Parade Square and the **Erdődy Palace** on Mihály Táncsics Street, now the Museum of Musical History.

The **Zichy Palace** in Óbuda is a splendid Baroque edifice, and the buildings of the former **Trinitarian Monastery**, now the Kiscelli Museum, stand as significant models of the style.

There are only two Baroque monuments remaining in Pest. The **Péterffy Palace**, a mansion that stands below the current street level, dates from 1755. Pest's other Baroque edifice was, however, the first to be built in either Buda or Pest. The huge complex of the **Municipal County Offices**, formerly a hospital for veterans of the Turkish wars, was constructed by the Italian master Anton Erhard Martinelli. It was greatly admired by Empress Maria Theresa, who declared it to be more beautiful than the Schönbrunn Palace in Vienna.

NEO-CLASSICAL PALACES AND BUILDINGS

Neo-classicism, influenced by ancient Greco-Roman design, was popular in the first half of the 19th century as it reflected the confidence of this period of national awakening and social reform. Many monumental Neo-Classical structures were produced, including the Chain Bridge, built in 1839–49. The leading Neo-Classical architect was Mihály Pollack, who built the **Hungarian National Museum**.

Two stunning Neo-Classical palaces deserve particular mention – **Sándor Palace** in Buda and **Károlyi Palace** in Pest. The first stands on Castle Hill, by the top of the funicular railway, and impresses visitors with its harmonious elegance. The second, now housing the Petőfi Literary Museum, gained its present form in 1834 after considerable reconstruction.

A group of particularly attractive Neo-Classical houses is situated on **József Nádor Square**. Some of their features, such as the pillars, projections and tympanums, merit individual attention.

In 1808, the Embellishment Commission was set up by the Austrian architect János Hild to develop Pest. He and his son, József Hild, who built the **Gross Palace** in 1824, were both involved in the general restoration of the city. Having studied architecture in Rome, they created many splendid Italianate buildings.

The outstanding Baroque façade of Erdődy Palace, Museum of Musical History

HISTORICIST PALACES AND BUILDINGS

In the second half of the 19th century, Historicism took precedence over Neo-Classicism. After the unification of Buda, Óbuda and Pest in 1873, Historicism had a significant influence on the city's architectural development. In this period Budapest gained an eclectic mix of new apartment buildings and palaces, as Historicist architects sourced different genres for inspiration. Miklós Ybl, whose work includes the **State Opera House** and the expansion of the **Royal Palace**, looked to the Renaissance, while Imre Steindl designed a Neo-Gothic **Parliament** (to which a Neo-Renaissance dome was added). Frigyes Schulek's **Fishermen's Bastion** features

Sculptures on the Vigadó façade

Neo-Gothic and Neo-Romanesque designs.

The **Vigadó**, a concert hall built by Frigyes Feszl between 1859 and 1864, is often thought of as the most magnificent Historicist building, with its façade richly decorated with relief sculptures and busts of the great Hungarians. However, the complex of three French-style, Neo-Renaissance palaces, Festetics, Károly and Esterházy, in **Mihály Pollack Square**, is also considered by many to be a fine example.

The **Drechsler Palace** in Andrássy út is a marvellous model of Neo-Renaissance design, while the **Divatcsarnok** department store features Lotz's Hall, stunningly decorated with paintings and gold. The twin apartment buildings known as the **Klotild Palaces** incorporate Spanish-Baroque motifs and

Beautiful Neo-Baroque interior of the New York Palace

can be admired near the Elizabeth Bridge. Perhaps one of the most extravagant of all the examples of Historicism in the city is the Neo-Baroque **New York Palace** by Alajos Hauszmann, which has a luxurious interior of marble columns and rich colour.

DECORATIVE FEATURES

The façades of many palaces and buildings still display the rich sculptural decoration characteristic of the various styles of architecture prevalent in the city. These features include coves, cartouches, finials, relief sculptures and ornamental window frames.

Regrettably, almost no original Gothic detail remains in Budapest, but niches or pointed arches decorating old apartment buildings can be spotted in the Old Town.

Baroque elements are still evident in fine buildings such as the Zichy Palace and the Erdődy Palace. Decorative Neo-Classical features,

such as borders and tympanums, are visible on many buildings from the first half of the 19th century.

A finial with cartouche on the Neo-Classical Károlyi Palace

Relief on the Hungarian National Bank (1905)

Cove detail on the façade of the Staffenberg House

Ornate window frame adorning the house at 21 József Nádor utca

Budapest's Best: Baths and Pools

Budapest is one of the great spa cities of Europe. Numerous natural hot springs pour out over 80 million litres (18 million gal) of richly mineralized water every day. The greatest concentrations of natural springs are situated in Óbuda, near Gellért Hill, on the Buda embankment near Margaret Bridge and on Margaret Island itself. Baths have existed here since Roman times, but it was the Turks who best exploited Budapest's natural resources. Today there is a wide choice of therapeutic and recreational baths and pools.

Palatinus Strand
With seven swimming pools, hot springs, water slides and a restful location on Margaret Island, this spa is perhaps the most beautiful in Europe.

Hajós Olympic Pool
The pool was designed by Alfréd Hajós, who won Hungary's first Olympic gold medal for swimming in 1896, and on the walls of the swimming hall hang gold-engraved marble plaques citing Hungary's numerous Olympic champions.

DANUBE

North of the Castle

Castle District

Gellért Hill and Tabán

Lukács Baths
These 19th-century thermal pools are open all year round, and attract both tourists and the locals of Budapest.

Király Baths
Dating from 1566, these baths were built by the Turks and have many authentic Ottoman features.

Rác Baths
The original Ottoman pool and cupola are hidden behind a 19th-century façade.

Dagály Strand
Half a century ago, it was discovered that the water in a pond on this site was beneficial to health. Now a huge open-air complex of swimming pools, children's pools and a hydrotherapy and fitness centre is located here.

Széchenyi Baths
This spa has the hottest thermal baths in Budapest and the added attraction of magnificent Neo-Baroque architecture. The warmth of the water is such that these baths are popular even during the winter season.

Around Városliget

Around Parliament

Central Pest

Rudas Baths
The most famous of the Turkish baths were constructed during the 16th century. They still have an original Ottoman cupola and octagonal pool.

Gellért Baths
The main indoor swimming pool of this popular Buda spa delights bathers with its beautiful Secession interior, marble columns and colourful mosaics.

| 0 metres | 500 |
| 0 yards | 500 |

Exploring Budapest's Baths and Pools

Heated deep inside the earth, the waters of the mineral-rich hot springs which bubble up through fractures in the rocky hills of Buda and Óbuda have given the city a Turkish-influenced bathing culture which has survived even the rigours of Communism. A total of 31 spa-water pools and thermal baths, with entrance fees kept low by generous government subsidies, make taking the waters an unmissable treat for visitors to Budapest.

THE TURKISH INFLUENCE

Although the ruins of Roman thermal baths dat-ing from the 2nd century AD have been found in Óbuda, it was only under the Ottoman occupation of the 16th–17th centuries (see pp 26–7), that the bathing culture really took hold in Budapest.

Four stunning Turkish-built baths, some of the few rema-ining examples of Ottoman architecture in Budapest, are still in operation. The **Rudas**, the **Rác**, the **Király** and the **Komjády** (formerly known as Császár) were all built in the 16th century, and are con-structed on a single model. A marble staircase leads into a chamber containing a dome-topped, octagonal thermal pool, which is surrounded by smaller dome-covered pools at temperatures ranging from icily cold to roastingly hot. The most beautiful are almost certainly the Rudas Baths, followed closely by the Király Baths. The Rác Baths have undergone extensive restoration work and will re-open in 2006 as a spa and

hotel complex. The Császár Baths have been absorbed into the Lukács Baths complex (see below).

Many of the city's newer baths are for both men and women. The Turkish baths, however, remain resolutely single-sex, though the Rudas Baths are open to men during the week and women at weekends; and the Rác and the Király Baths open to men and women on alternate days. There is no need to wear a bathing suit, as a small apron is provided.

AFTER THE TURKS

The late 19th and early 20th century was a new golden age for Budapest (see pp32–3), and saw the building of a number of splendid baths. Many have spring-water swim-ming pools attached.

Opened in 1894 the Neo-Classical **Lukács Baths** offer two outdoor swimming pools as well as the 16th-century Császár thermal pool. The **Széchenyi Baths**, opened 20 years later on the Pest side of the river, make up the biggest

bathing complex in Europe. In addition to the usual indoor thermal pools, they also boast outdoor thermal and swimming pools, complete with sun terraces. With the hottest spa-water in the city, the outdoor thermal pool is popular even in the depths of winter.

As well as the thermal pools, Budapest's bathing establish-ments also include a steam room and sauna. Professional massages are almost always available for a small fee. Some places offer medicinal mud and sulphur baths. You will be invited to take a shower, and a short nap in the rest room before you leave.

Swim in style at the Gellért Hotel

SPA HOTELS

Nestling at the foot of Gellért Hill, the beautiful **Gellért Hotel and Baths Complex** is the oldest and most famous of a handful of luxury hotels in Budapest offering swimming and thermal pools, steam rooms, sauna and massage. The renowned Gellért Baths were opened to the general public in 1927, and include a fabulous, marble-columned indoor swimming pool, a labyrinth of thermal baths (one set for men and one for women), single-sex nudist sun-bathing areas and an outdoor swimming pool. A hugely popular wave machine is switched on in the latter for ten minutes in every hour.

A second wave of spa-hotels were built in the 1970s and '80s. Set on Margaret Island, the modern, squeaky-clean and extremely luxurious **Thermal Hotel Margitsziget**, is linked by an underground passage to the older **Grand Hotel Margitsziget**. In addition to the usual range of baths and pools, services on offer here

Outdoor pool at the Gellért Hotel and Baths Complex

include manicure, pedicure and a solarium. The late 1980s saw the arrival of two new spa hotels, the **Thermal Hotel Helia** not far from the Pest riverbank and, on the Buda side, the **Corinthia Aquincum**, facing north towards Óbuda. Both make use of the hot springs on Margaret Island, and offer gyms, bars and restaurants as well as swimming pools and thermal baths.

Széchenyi Baths, the biggest bathing complex in Europe

THE HEALING WATERS

The citizens of Budapest are great believers in the social, psychological and medical benefits of the thermal baths. Office workers will often visit the public baths as early as 6am, to prepare for the day. Others like to visit at the end of the day, at 6pm, to relax, recharge and work up an appetite. Most of the baths employ staff who can offer advice on the most appropriate pools and special treatments for a particular ailment. The warm, mineral-rich spa waters are extremely good for general relaxation. They can also be helpful in the relief of a number of specific complaints, including post-traumatic stress, joint and muscle damage, rheumatism and menstrual pain. Budapest's public baths are also extremely good value for money. Admission is usually no more than 500 forints, and a 15-minute massage costs the same. All baths employ expert masseurs.

An ornamental tap, typical of the architectural detail found in Budapest's historic baths

SWIMMING AS SPORT

Many Hungarians are excellent swimmers, and the country has chieved great success in competitive water sports. In addition to Budapest's many recreational pools, sports pools include the **Hajós Olympic Pool** complex on Margaret Island. The complex consists of three sports pools, two outdoor, including one at full Olympic size, and one indoor. The pools are used for professional training, but are also open to the public. Together with the Komjádi Béla Swimming Stadium on Árpád Fejedelem útja, the Hajós Olympic Pool is the place to go to see professional swimming, diving or water polo.

Sculpture at the Római Strand

A DAY AT THE STRAND

Designed as a complete bathing day out, the strands of Budapest are a phenomenon not to be missed. A total of 12 strands in the city testifies to their popularity. Outdoor swimming and thermal pools are surrounded by grassy sun-bathing areas. Trampolines and ping-pong and pool tables offer a change from the water, while ice creams, beers and hot dogs add to the summer-holiday atmosphere.

The lovely **Palatinus Strand**, set in a large area of

parkland on Margaret Island, boasts seven outdoor pools, some thermal and some for swimming, complete with water slides and wave machines. Just east of the Pest river bank is the vast, modern **Dagály Strand** complex. Built after World War II, it includes 12 pools, with space for up to 12,000 people. Other strands worth visiting include **Római Strand** in Óbuda in the north of the city. Three pools have been carefully rebuilt here, on the site of some Roman baths, together with a not-so-Roman water chute. To the north of the city at Csillaghegy on the HÉV suburban train line, **Csillaghegy Strand** consists of four pools set in picturesque grounds, and includes a popular south-facing nudist beach.

Budapest's Best: the Secession

Decoration on a house on Áldás utca

Visitors to Budapest are often impressed by its wonderful late 19th and early 20th century buildings. The majority of these are found in central Pest and around Városliget; Buda was already developed at this stage and so boasts few examples. The movement started among groups of avant-garde artists in Paris and Vienna, from where the term Secession comes. In Budapest, the Secession style was also the inspiration for the development of the Hungarian National Style. Further details are given on pages 56–7.

The School on Rose Hill
Károly Kós and Dezső Zrumeczky used motifs from village houses in Transylvania to give this building on Áldás utca its character.

Woman with a Birdcage (1892)
This painting by József Rippl-Rónai has an atmosphere of mystery and intimacy typical of Hungarian art of the period. It hangs in the Hungarian National Gallery (see p77) today.

North of the Castle

Castle District

D A N U B E

Ironwork Gates of Gresham Palace
Two peacocks, a classic Secession motif, decorate the wrought-iron gates of the Four Seasons Gresham Palace hotel. The building was built by Zsigmond Quittner and the Vágó brothers between 1905–7.

Gellért Hill and Tabán

Gellért Hotel and Baths Complex
Supported by flattened arches, a glass roof adds to the tranquil appeal of this hall in the famous spa at the Gellért Hotel. The Secession interiors created here are among the most splendid to be found in Budapest.

Post Office Savings Bank
The main staircase of this building by Ödön Lechner is embellished by fine balusters, rounded lamps and decorative windows.

Entrance to the Zoo
Kornel Neuschloss made ingenious use of elements of Hindu architecture when he created this amusing gate guarded by two elephants.

Around Parliament

Around Városliget

Central Pest

Sipeky Balázs Villa
Built between 1905–6, this fanciful villa is perhaps the most representative example of the Secession style in Budapest. It was designed by Ödön Lechner.

Philanthia Florist's
This extraordinary florist's is on Váci utca. The interior of the shop is in the Secession style, while the building itself is Neo-Classical.

| 0 metres | 500 |
| 0 yards | 500 |

Apartments on Bartók Béla utca
Ödön Lechner was the leading exponent of the Hungarian National Style. He built this apartment block, with a studio for himself on the fourth floor, in 1899. The block is at 40 Bartók Béla utca.

Exploring Secession Budapest

Secession ornament

The Secession movement crossed artistic boundaries, influencing painting and the decorative arts as well as architecture. Colourful, sometimes fantastical designs are instantly recognizable hallmarks of the style. The Hungarian National Style drew heavily on this general trend, incorporating motifs from old Hungarian architecture, particularly that of Transylvania, folk art and even oriental features.

Vase designed by István Sovának, in the Museum of Applied Arts

József Rippl-Rónai's *Woman in White-Spotted Dress* (1899), in the Hungarian National Gallery

PAINTINGS AND DRAWINGS

The main exponents of Secession art in Hungary were József Rippl-Rónai, János Vaszary and Lajos Gulácsy.

Rippl-Rónai spent many years in Paris, at the time when the Art Nouveau movement was beginning to flourish. *Lady in Red*, which he painted in 1899, was the first Hungarian painting in the Secession style. Many of Rippl-Rónai's works are on show in the **Hungarian National Gallery**. There is also a tapestry version of *Lady in Red* in the **Museum of Applied Arts**.

The work of János Vaszary was heavily influenced by both German and English art. His finest pictures, which include *Gold Century* and the mysterious *Adam and Eve*, can be admired in the Hungarian National Gallery. Lajos Gulácsy was influenced by the Pre-Raphaelite movement and his pictures are often symbolic. Many of his paintings, too, can now be viewed in the Hungarian National Gallery.

The artists' colony based at Gödöllő was an important centre for painters working in the new Secession style. Its founder, Aladár Körösfői-Kriesch, created numerous works, including a fresco entitled *The Fount of Youth* which decorates the **Franz Liszt Academy of Music**.

DECORATIVE ARTS

New ideas in the decorative arts at this time were closely related to architectural developments. Ödön Lechner

began to make use of colourful ceramic tiles, acquired from his father-in-law's brickyard in Pécs in southern Hungary, not only to cover roofs but also as a decorative element.

The owner of this brickyard, Vilmos Zsolnay, discovered an innovative method of glazing tiles and ceramics. This proved so successful that the the brickyard was turned into a factory specializing in their production. Zsolnay's factory eventually made most of the vivid and distinctive ceramic tiles covering the Secession buildings in the city.

Zsolnay also employed leading designers to create ranges of dinner services, vases and candlesticks. For these he was awarded the Gold Medal of the Legion of Honour at the World Fair in Paris. And at an exhibition organized in 1896, to mark the millennial anniversary of the Hungarian Kingdom, the

---

ODON LECHNER (1845–1914)

The most influential architect of the Hungarian Secession, Ödön Lechner trained in Berlin before completing his apprenticeship by working in both Italy and France. His quest was to create an identifiable Hungarian National Style, by combining Secession motifs with elements from Hungarian folk art and Hindu designs. The colourful ceramics that he often used

Portrait of Lechner

became his signature. Among the buildings that Budapest owes to him are the Museum of Applied Arts, the Post Office Savings Bank and the Institute of Geology. Behind the ingenious and fantastical exteriors, Lechner's buildings have wonderfully simple, functional and superbly lit interiors.

factory introduced its most beautiful pieces.

Gresham Palace and the **Gellért Hotel and Baths Complex** are among the many buildings in the city that are embellished by ornamental wrought-iron gates, gratings and banisters that incorporate Secession motifs.

INTERIOR DECORATION

Among the interiors of the era, those of the **New York Palace** *(see p129)* are a real jewel. Decked out in the best materials, including bronze and marble, they retain the splendour of their original, Neo-Baroque form.

Also worth visiting are the **Hungarian National Bank** and the **Post Office Savings Bank**, with their furnished secure rooms and ornate door and window frames. The interior of Philanthia, a florist's shop, is another wonderfully

A Secession cabinet, displayed in the Museum of Applied Arts

Window created by Miksa Róth, at the Hungarian National Bank

preserved example of decor from the Secession.

Exhibitions of attractive Secession furniture are a feature of both the Museum of Applied Arts and also the **Nagytétény Palace.**

ARCHITECTURE

Hungarian architecture of the *fin de siècle* is characterized not only by decorative forms using glazed ceramics, but, more fundamentally, by the implementation of modern technical solutions. Reinforced concrete, steel and glass were used together, and large, light-filled interiors were often achieved. The central hall of the Museum of Applied Arts is a fine example of this.

Aside from Ödön Lechner, the most important of the Hungarian Secession architects, others who contributed significant buildings in the prevailing style included Béla Lajta, Aladár Árkay, Károly Kós and István Medgyaszay.

Béla Lajta, a pupil of Lechner, designed the **Rózsavölgyi Building**, with its distinctive geometrical ornamentation, on Martinelli tér. Also among his buildings is the extraordinary former **Jewish Old People's Home**, at No. 57 Amerikai út. With sophisticated ornamental details based on folk designs, **Városliget Calvinist Church** was the creation of Aladár Árkay.

Károly Kós was a highly original member of this set. Fascinated by the traditional architecture of Transylvania, he trawled the whole of that region, making drawings of the village churches and manor houses he encountered. Motifs from these buildings were later transferred to the aviary at Budapest's **Zoo** and the houses of the **Wekerle Estate.**

Frieze on the Rózsavölgyi Building

DECORATIVE MOTIFS

Stylized folk motifs derived from embroidery and also oriental patterns were often employed in Budapest's decorative arts during this period. Secession motifs such as feline forms, based on Viennese and Parisian examples, also feature.

Sunflower motif adorning the Post Office Savings Bank

Secession lettering on the sign of Philanthia Florist's

Colourful mosaic at No. 3 Aulich utca

BUDAPEST THROUGH THE YEAR

Set in the middle of Hungary, Budapest enjoys a continental climate with sharply defined seasons, each of which brings its own attractions, from traditional feast days to cultural and sporting events. Historically a centre of cultural, and especially musical, activity, Budapest continues the tradition with many musical events including the

Spring Festival logo

Spring Festival, an international celebration of classical music and ballet, and the smaller Budapest Contemporary Music Weeks, devoted to contemporary classical music. Many hotels and tourist offices provide a programme of the events taking place in the city, as do the English-language weeklies.

SPRING

Spring makes a welcome return to the city in March, with sunshine and fresh, warm days. Budapest turns green and the Spring Festival sees the arrival of some of the year's first tourists.

MARCH

The Spring Uprising *(15 Mar)*. A public holiday marks the day in 1848 when the youth of Buda, led by the poet Sándor Petőfi, rebelled against the Habsburg occupation of Hungary *(see pp30–31)*. Thousands of people take to the streets to lay wreaths and light eternal flames, wearing the national colours of red, white and green. There are speeches and street theatre, especially in front of the Hungarian National Museum *(see pp130–33)*.
Spring Festival *(the last two weeks of Mar– mid-Apr)*. www.festivalcity.hu

Parade in the Castle District during the Spring Festival

Top national and international musicians gather for several weeks of music and dance in churches and concert halls all over the city. The emphasis of the festival is on the classical tradition, but also in evidence are folk music and dance, as well as pop and jazz

APRIL

Easter is an important religious event in Hungary and the Easter service is well worth attending in one of the city's many churches. On the

morning of Easter Monday young men spray their female friends and relatives with perfume or water, a ritual which is said to keep the recipients beautiful until the following year. Painted eggs are given in return.
World Dance Festival *(end Apr)*. The National Dance Theatre and the Association of Hungarian Dance Artists organize this festival every year, with participation from top Hungarian dance groups and foreign guest artists. Castle Theatre, Erkel Theatre, the Light Opera Theatre and the Hungarian State Opera House hold the events.
Horse Racing *(Sun, Apr–Oct)*. April sees the beginning of the flat-racing season. Place your bets at the busy and charmingly down-at-heel Kincsem Park race course on Albertirsai út.
Budapest International Book Festival. Organised in co-operation with the Frankfurt Book Fair, this festival is the most important event in Hungary's publishing year, both for the publishing industry and for the general public. It is held in the Budapest Congress Centre.

MAY

May Day *(1 May)*. No longer a compulsory display of patriotism, May Day celebrations take place in public parks all over the city and involve craft markets, street performers and sausage and beer tents. A dip in the local thermal bath or swimming pool *(see pp50–53)*, is another popular May Day activity.

Springtime magnolia blossom on Margaret Island

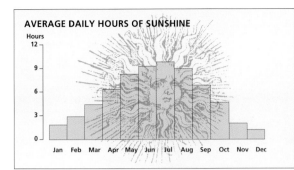

AVERAGE DAILY HOURS OF SUNSHINE

Hours

12

9

6

3

0

Jan Feb Mar Apr May Jun Jul Aug Sep Oct Nov Dec

Sunshine Chart
*Budapest enjoys some
of the sunniest weather
in Europe, with an
average of eight hours
of sunshine each day
from April to September.
During the sticky
months of high summer
(June, July and August),
the Buda hills provide a
welcome refuge from
the heat of the city.*

SUMMER

The long hot days of summer
are made for relaxing on
Margaret Island or sun-bathing
at some of the city's twelve
open-air pools.

JUNE

Open-Air Theatre Festival
(Jun–Aug). **www**.szabadter.hu
Margaret and Óbuda Islands
provide two of the major
venues for this summer-long,
open-air arts festival.
Budapesti Búcsú *(last weekend
in Jun).* **www**.festivalcity.hu
A mixture of music, dance
and theatre celebrates the
departure from Hungary of
Soviet troops in 1991.
Danube Carnival International Cultural Festival.
www.dunaart.hu
Various venues host music
and dance events.

Formula One racing in the Hungarian Grand Prix

JULY

Hungarian Grand Prix *(end
Jul).* **www**.hungaroring.hu
The biggest event in the
Hungarian sporting calendar
takes place east of the city, at
Mogyoród race track.
Chain Bridge Festival
(weekends in Jul & Aug).
www.budapestinfo.hu
A lively series of free events
including concerts and dance,

traditional arts and crafts,
street theatre, parades and
activities for children.
**Concerts in St Stephen's
Basilica** *(Jul–Aug).* Monday
evening organ concerts in
the city's largest church *(see
pp116–17)* provide a perfect
opportunity to study the lavish interior decoration of this
extraordinary building.
**Budapest Summer Opera and
Ballet Festival** *(Jul or Aug).*
Look out for the ten-day
series of shows that makes up
the summer season at the State
Opera House *(see pp118–19).*

AUGUST

St István's Day *(20 Aug).*
St István, the patron saint of
Hungary, is celebrated with
mass in St Stephen's Basilica
followed by a huge procession.
The day ends with fireworks
on Gellért Hill *(see pp88–9)*
and along the Danube.
Sziget Festival *(Aug).* Ten
stages and a camp site are set
up on Óbuda Island for this
popular week-long festival of
rock, folk and jazz.
Budapest Parade *(end Aug).*
A carnival on Andrássy Street
and Hősök tere.

Fireworks on Gellért Hill to celebrate St István's Day

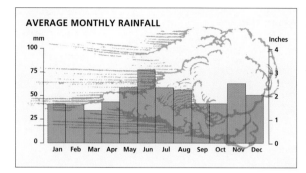

AVERAGE MONTHLY RAINFALL

Rainfall Chart
Budapest is a fairly dry city. Typically, it rains very heavily for two days or so, then is dry for several weeks. June is the wettest month, with May, July, August and November only slightly drier. Autumn is usually the dryest season, while there is some snowfall in the winter months.

AUTUMN

One of the many treats of autumn in Budapest is a visit to one of the city's fruit and vegetable markets, where you can feast your eyes on a vast array of jewel-coloured vegetables and fruit.

SEPTEMBER

Budapest Wine Festival *(2nd week of Sep)*. After the late-August grape harvest, wine makers set up their stalls for wine tastings and folk dancing on Buda's Castle Hill *(see p69)* and in squares around the city.

Jewish Summer Cultural Festival. This multicultural festival includes a Jewish book fair, an Israeli film festival, art exhibitions, and cuisine presentations.

OCTOBER

Plus Budapest International Marathon and Running Festival *(Oct)*. There is a marathon, a relay race, a mini-marathon and a family running competition for participants. Concerts and events are held for spectators.
Autumn Festival *(mid-Oct)*. Several weeks of contemporary film, dance and theatre at venues across the city.

A colourful food stall in one of Budapest's covered markets

Vienna-Budapest Super Marathon Running Competition. This competition aims, through sport, to strengthen ties between central European countries, particularly those of Austria and Hungary, and celebrates open European borders.
www.szupermarathon.hu
Remembrance Day *(23 Oct)*. This is a national day of mourning to remember the 1956 Uprising, when 30,000 people were killed by Soviet tanks and 200,000 fled the country. Wreaths are laid in Municipal Cemetery *(see pp158–9)*, on the grave of the executed leader Imre Nagy *(see p34)*.

NOVEMBER

Budapest Christmas Fair *(26 Nov–24 Dec)*. The Budapest Christmas Market transforms Vörösmarty Square into a festive marketplace, where Hungarian artists and craftsmen display their work and national dishes are served.
www.budapestinfo.hu

Performers take part in the Open-Air Theatre Festival

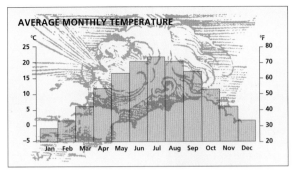

Temperature Chart
Seasons in Budapest are sharply defined. Daytime temperatures rise rapidly from March onwards. By June, the thermometer often reaches 30°C (90°F) and more. September sees cooler weather, with temperatures falling rapidly to lows of well below freezing in January.

WINTER

Despite the cold weather, winter can be an exciting time to visit Budapest. Open-air ice-skating takes place from November, roast-chestnut sellers appear on the streets and a Christmas tree is erected in Mihály Vörösmarty Square.

DECEMBER

Budapest Christmas Fair *(26 Nov–24 Dec)* continues.
Silver and Gold Sunday *(2nd-to-last Sunday before Christmas)*. All the city's shops stay open for this Sunday of serious Christmas shopping.
Mikulás *(6 Dec)*. On *Mikulás*, or St Nicholas Day, children leave their shoes on the window sill for Santa Claus to fill.
Christmas *(25–26 Dec)*. The city shuts down for two days. Celebrations begin with a family meal of carp on 24 Dec.
Szilveszter *(31 Dec)*. Budapest celebrates in style on New Year's Eve, with music in Vörösmarty and Nyugati Squares until dawn, and fireworks. Public transport is free and runs all night.

Seeing in the New Year, a stylish affair in Budapest

Christmas tree in Mihály Vörösmarty Square

JANUARY

New Year's Gala Concert *(1 Jan)*. This cheerful occasion is an excellent way to start the new year. Outstanding Hungarian and foreign artists perform excerpts from European opera and musicals, providing a lively evening of music.

FEBRUARY

Hungarian Film Festival *(early Feb)*. This two-day celebration of Hungarian film has been run by the *Magyar Filmszemle* since 1969, to attract funding to a hard-pressed industry. Many films are subtitled.
Masked-Ball Season *(Feb)*. Budapest forgets the cold weather to welcome the coming of spring, and the arrival of the *farsang*, or fancy dress masked-ball season. The climax of the season is the spectacular Opera Ball and a masked procession, on the last Saturday and Sunday before Lent, respectively.
www.operabal.com

Shopping for Christmas

PUBLIC HOLIDAYS

Public holidays mainly follow the Christian calendar. Two days mark cataclysmic events in Magyar history, while one, May Day, is a reminder of the country's socialist past.

New Year's Day *(1 Jan)*
Spring Uprising *(15 Mar)*
Easter Sunday *(variable)*
Easter Monday *(variable)*
Whit Monday *(variable)*
May Day *(1 May)*
St István's Day *(20 Aug)*
Remembrance Day *(23 Oct)*
All Saints' Day *(1 Nov)*
Christmas Day *(25 Dec)*
Boxing Day *(26 Dec)*

Margaret Bridge to Elizabeth Bridge

Crown on Elizabeth Bridge

A trip on a river boat along the Danube provides a unique panorama of the city. Most major cities have a river at their heart. However, the Danube historically played a different role in this case, for centuries dividing the separate towns of Buda and Pest. Several road bridges today link the two halves of the modern city. All had to be reconstructed this century after being destroyed by the retreating Nazi army towards the end of World War II.

Centenary Monument
This monument was erected in 1973 to commemorate the centenary of the joining of Buda, Óbuda and Pest as Budapest. It stands on Margaret Island (see pp172–3), close to Margaret Bridge.

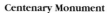

St Elizabeth's Church
This Baroque church was built for an order of nuns, with its front facing away from the Danube. The hospital and hostel run by the sisters face the river (see p101).

BATTHYÁNY TÉR

Mátyás Church
With medieval origins, the tower of this church has been rebuilt several times. It overlooks the Hilton Hotel and the Fishermen's Bastion (see pp82–3).

St Anne's Church
can be recognized by its twin, slender Baroque towers.

Chain Bridge was built between 1839–49 at the inititiative of Count István Széchenyi *(see p31)*. It was designed by Englishman William Tierney Clark and built by the unrelated Scot, Adam Clark. The bridge extends for 380 m (1,250 ft), supported by two towers – a major feat of engineering at the time.

KEY

 Metro

 River boat boarding point

Margaret Bridge was built by the French engineer Ernest Gouin, at the point where the Danube becomes a single body once more after dividing to flow around Margaret Island. The bridge is distinguished by its unusual chevron shape. It was erected in 1872–6, and between 1899–1900 access from the bridge onto the island was added. Sculptures by Adolphe Thabart decorate its columns.

Parliament

The magnificent, high dome of the Parliament building is visible from every point along the Danube in central Budapest (see pp108–9).

Much of the eastern bank of the river is characterized by fairly uniform architecture. Variation is provided here by the dome and towers of St Stephen's Basilica *(see pp116–17).*

0 metres	300
0 yards	300

Hungarian Academy of Sciences

Elizabeth Bridge, constructed in 1897–1903, was at that time the longest suspension bridge in the world. Destroyed in 1945, it was rebuilt in its current form by Pál Sávolya.

The bridgehead of Chain Bridge is guarded by two vast stone lions sculpted by János Marschalkó. According to an anecdote János was heartbroken because he forgot to give the lions any tongues, so he drowned himself in the river. In fact the lions do have tongues, but they are not easily visible.

VÖRÖSMARTY
TÉR
M

FERENCIEK
TERE
M

ZSÉBET HÍD

Piers, from which passenger cruises operate daily in summer, are spaced frequently along the Danube in central Budapest.

Elizabeth Bridge to Lágymányosi Bridge

Like Paris, Budapest has fully exploited
the opportunities given by its river. The
most important and beautiful buildings
of Buda and Pest crowd along the
banks of the Danube. These include the
Royal Palace, churches, historic palaces
and houses, and Hungary's Parliament.

Royal Palace
*The monumental Habsburg Royal Palace that once
occupied this spot was destroyed during World War II,
then reconstructed to reveal defensive walls and royal
chambers that date from the Middle Ages (see pp70–71).*

**Inner City Parish
Church**
*This church was built in
the 12th century on the
ruins of Roman Contra
Aquincum's walls. The
spot was, from early
times, an important
place for crossing the
river (see pp124–5).*

**Gellért Hotel and
Baths Complex**
*The architects of this hotel
maximized its river façade
to make it as imposing as
possible (see pp90–91).*

Technical University
*The campus of Hungary's
largest educational institution occupies almost
the entire space between
Liberty Bridge and Petőfi
Bridge (see p157).*

The embankment walk near Petőfi Bridge extends along the length of the Danube on the Pest side. It is a favourite place to meet or to go for a stroll, and is lined by smart hotels and restaurants.

Little Princess (1989), perched by the tram rails on the Pest side of the Danube, was so liked by Charles, Prince of Wales, on his visit here that he invited its designer, László Marton, to exhibit in London.

KALVIN
TÉR
M

Liberty Bridge was built between 1894–9 by Hungarian engineer János Feketeházy. Opened by Emperor Franz Joseph, it initially took his name. All its original features were retained when it was rebuilt after World War II: on top of the bridge there are legendary Hungarian *turul* birds and royal crests.

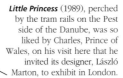

Corvinus University
Formerly a customs' headquarters, this building has an elegant façade decorated with ten allegorical figures. These are the work of German sculptor August Sommer (see p138).

PETŐFI HÍD

Lágymányosi Bridge, Budapest's most modern and southernmost bridge, is pictured here under construction. Opened in 1996, it is designed to carry traffic on a ring road bypassing the city centre.

LÁGYMÁNYOSI HÍD

BUDAPEST AREA BY AREA

CASTLE DISTRICT

The hill town of Buda grew up around its castle and Mátyás Church from the 13th century onwards. At 60 m (197 ft) above the Danube, the hill's good strategic position and natural resources made it a prize site for its earliest inhabitants. In the 13th century, a large settlement arose when, after a Tartar invasion, King Béla IV decided to build his own defensive castle and establish his capital here. The reign of King Mátyás Corvinus in the 15th century was an important period in the evolution of

Bas-relief on the Eugene of Savoy monument

Buda, but it suffered neglect under Turkish rule during the next century and was then destroyed by Christian troops. The town was reborn, however, and assumed an important role during the 18th and 19th centuries under the Habsburgs. By the end of World War II, the Old Town had been almost utterly destroyed and the Royal Palace burnt to the ground. Since the war the Royal Palace and Old Town have been reconstructed, restoring the original allure of this part of the city.

SIGHTS AT A GLANCE

Churches
Buda Lutheran Church **17**
Church of St Mary Magdalene **18**
Mátyás Church pp82–3 **11**

Museums and Galleries
Budapest History Museum **1**
Golden Eagle Pharmacy Museum **8**
House of Hungarian Wines **10**
Hungarian National Gallery pp74–7 **4**

Labyrinth **22**
Museum of Military History **20**
Széchenyi National Library **2**

Historic Streets and Squares
András Hess Square **14**
Holy Trinity Square **9**
Lords' Street **21**
Mihály Táncsics Street **15**
Parade Square **5**
Parliament Street **19**
Vienna Gate Square **16**

Palaces, Historic Buildings and Monuments
Castle Theatre **7**
Fishermen's Bastion **12**
Hilton Hotel **13**
Mátyás Fountain **3**
Sándor Palace **6**

GETTING THERE
Castle Hill and the Old Town are largely pedestrianized, but there are a couple of car parks where cars and coaches can park for a fee, allowing visitors to walk to the area. Bus 16 runs from Clark Ádám tér to Dísz tér, and a funicular railway (Sikló) connects Clark Ádám tér to Szent György tér. There is also a minibus (Várbusz) that arrives at this square from Moszkva tér to the north.

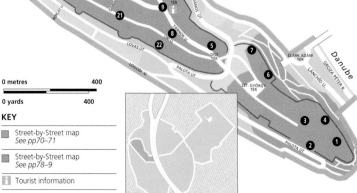

0 metres   400

0 yards   400

KEY

◾ Street-by-Street map
See pp70–71

◾ Street-by-Street map
See pp78–9

ℹ Tourist information

◁ **Fountain on Tárnok utca in the Old Town**

Street-by-Street: The Royal Palace

The Royal Palace has borne many incarnations
during its long life. Even now it is not known
exactly where King Béla IV began building his
castle, though it is thought to be nearer the site of
Mátyás Church *(see pp82–3)*. The Holy Roman
Emperor Sigismund of Luxembourg built a Gothic
palace on the present site, from which today's
castle began to evolve. In the 18th century, the
Habsburgs built their monumental palace here.
The current form dates from the rebuilding
of the 19th-century palace after its destruction in February 1945. During this work,
remains of the 15th-century Gothic palace
were uncovered. Hungarian archeologists
decided to reveal the recovered defensive
walls and royal chambers in the reconstruction.

An ornamental gateway,
dating from 1903, leads
from the Habsburg Steps
to the Royal Palace. Nearby, a bronze sculpture of
the mythical turul bird
guards the palace. This
statue marks the millen-
nium anniversary of the
Magyar conquest in 896.

★ Mátyás Fountain
*In the northwest courtyard of the Royal
Palace stands the Mátyás Fountain. It
was designed by Alajos Stróbl in 1904
and depicts King Mátyás Corvinus and
his beloved Ilonka* ❸

Lion Gate, leading to a
rear courtyard of the Royal
Palace, gets its name from
the four lions that watch
over it. These sculptures
were designed by János
Fadrusz in 1901.

TIMELINE					
1255 First written document, a letter by King Béla IV, refers to building a fortified castle	**c.1400** Sigismund of Luxembourg builds an ambit-ious Gothic pal-ace on this site	**1541** After capturing Buda, the Turks use the Royal Palace to stable horses and store gunpowder	**1719** The building of a small palace begins on the ruins of the old palace, to a design by Hölbling and Fortunato de Prati	**1881** Miklós Ybl *(see p119)* begins programme to re-build and expand the Royal Palace	
1200	**1400**	**1600**	**1800**		
c.1356 Louis I builds a royal castle on the southern slopes of Castle Hill		**1686** The assault by Christian soldiers leaves the palace completely razed to the ground	**1849** Royal Palace is destroyed again, during an un-successful attack by Hungarian insurgents	Turul *bird*	
1458 A Renaissance palace evolves under King Mátyás		**1749** Maria Theresa builds a vast palace comprising 203 chambers			

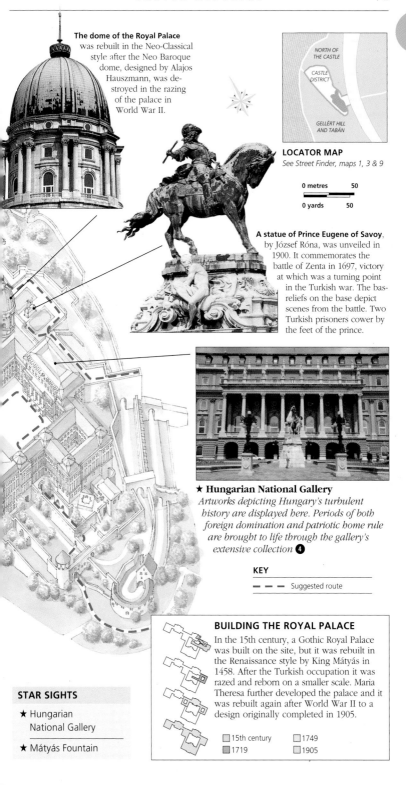

The dome of the Royal Palace was rebuilt in the Neo-Classical style after the Neo Baroque dome, designed by Alajos Hauszmann, was destroyed in the razing of the palace in World War II.

LOCATOR MAP
See Street Finder, maps 1, 3 & 9

| 0 metres | 50 |
| 0 yards | 50 |

NORTH OF THE CASTLE

CASTLE DISTRICT

GELLÉRT HILL AND TABÁN

A statue of Prince Eugene of Savoy, by József Róna, was unveiled in 1900. It commemorates the battle of Zenta in 1697, victory at which was a turning point in the Turkish war. The bas-reliefs on the base depict scenes from the battle. Two Turkish prisoners cower by the feet of the prince.

★ **Hungarian National Gallery**
Artworks depicting Hungary's turbulent history are displayed here. Periods of both foreign domination and patriotic home rule are brought to life through the gallery's extensive collection ④

KEY

– – – Suggested route

BUILDING THE ROYAL PALACE
In the 15th century, a Gothic Royal Palace was built on the site, but it was rebuilt in the Renaissance style by King Mátyás in 1458. After the Turkish occupation it was razed and reborn on a smaller scale. Maria Theresa further developed the palace and it was rebuilt again after World War II to a design originally completed in 1905.

☐ 15th century ☐ 1749
☐ 1719 ☐ 1905

STAR SIGHTS

★ Hungarian National Gallery

★ Mátyás Fountain

Renaissance majolica floor from the 15th century, uncovered during excavations on Castle Hill and displayed at the Budapest History Museum

Budapest History Museum ❶

BUDAPESTI TÖRTÉNETI MÚZEUM

Szent György tér 2. **Map** 3 C1 (9 B4). *Tel* 225 78 16. 🚌 5, 16, 78, Várbusz. ⭕ Mar–Oct: 10am–6pm daily (Tue Mar–May & Sep–Oct); Nov–Feb: 10am–4pm Wed–Mon. 🖼 ♿ www.bhm.hu

Since the unification of Budapest in 1873, historic artifacts relating to Hungary's capital have been collected. Many are now on show at the Budapest History Museum (also called the Castle Museum).

During the rebuilding that followed the destruction suffered in World War II, chambers dating from the Middle Ages were uncovered in the south wing (wing E) of the Royal Palace. They provide an insight into the character of a much earlier castle within today's Habsburg reconstruction.

These chambers, including a tiny prison cell and a chapel, were recreated in the basement of the palace. They now house an exhibition, the Royal Palace in Medieval Buda, which displays authentic weapons, seals, tiles and other early artifacts.

On the ground floor, Budapest in the Middle Ages illustrates the evolution of the town from its Roman origins to a 13th-century Hungarian settlement. Also on this level are reconstructed defensive

walls, gardens, a keep, and Gothic Statues from the Royal Palace dating from the 14th and 15th centuries. The statues were uncovered by chance in the major excavations of 1974. On the first floor, Budapest in Modern Times traces the history of the city from 1686 to the present.

Széchenyi National Library ❷

NEMZETI SZÉCHENYI KÖNYVTÁR

Szent György tér 6. **Map** 3 C1 (9 B4). *Tel* 224 37 00. 🚌 5, 16, 78, Várbusz. ⭕ 9am–9pm Tue–Fri, 10am–8pm Sat. ⭘ Sun. www.oszk.hu

A magnificent collection of books has been housed, since 1985, in wing F of the Royal Palace, built in 1890–1902 by

Corviniani illuminated manuscript in the Széchenyi National Library

Alajos Hauszmann and Miklós Ybl (see p119). Previously, the library was part of the Hungarian National Museum (see pp130–33).

Among the library's most precious treasures is the *Corviniani*, a collection of ancient books and manuscripts that originally belonged to King Mátyás Corvinus (see p24–5). His collection was one of the largest Renaissance libraries in Europe. Also of importance are the earliest surviving records in the Hungarian language, dating from the early 13th century.

The library was established by Count Ferenc Széchenyi in 1802. He endowed it with 15,000 books and 2,000 manuscripts. The collection now comprises five million items; everything that has been published in Hungary, in the Hungarian language or that refers to Hungary is here.

Crest on the Mátyás Fountain in a courtyard at the Royal Palace

Mátyás Fountain ❸
MÁTYÁS KÚT

Royal Palace. **Map** 1 C5 (9 B3). 🚌 5, 16, 78, Várbusz.

The ornate fountain in the northwest courtyard of the Royal Palace (situated between wings A and C) was designed by Alajos Stróbl in 1904. The statue is dedicated to the great Renaissance king, Mátyás, about whom there are many popular legends and fables.

The Romantic design of the bronze sculptures takes its theme from a 19th-century ballad by the poet Mihály Vörösmarty. According to the tale, King Mátyás, while on a hunting expedition, meets a beautiful peasant girl, Ilonka, who falls in love with him. This representation shows King Mátyás disguised as hunter, standing proudly with his kill. He is accompanied by his chief hunter and several hunting dogs in the central part of the fountain. Beneath the left-hand columns sits Galeotto Marzio, an Italian court poet, and the figure of the young Ilonka is beneath the columns on the right.

In keeping with the romantic reputation of King Mátyás, a new tradition has grown up concerning this statue. The belief is that anyone wishing to revisit Budapest should throw some coins into the fountain to ensure their safe return.

The western elevation of the Neo-Classical Sándor Palace

Hungarian National Gallery ❹

MAGYAR NEMZETI GALÉRIA

See pp 74–7.

Batthyány Palace on Parade Square retains its original Baroque façade

Parade Square ❺

DÍSZ TÉR

Map 1 B5 (9 A3). 🚌 *Várbusz.*

Parade Square is named after the military parades that were held here in the 19th century. At the northern end of the square is the Honvéd Monument, built in 1893 by György Zala. It honours and commemorates those who died during the recapture of Buda from Austria in the 1848 revolution.

The house at No. 3 was built between 1743–8, by József Giessl. This two-floor Baroque palace was the home of the Batthyány family until 1945. Although the building has been frequently remodelled, the façade remains intact.

A few houses on Parade Square incorporate medieval remains. Such houses can be seen at Nos. 4–5 and No. 11, built by Venerio Ceresola. The former has seat niches dating from the 13th century.

Sándor Palace ❻

SÁNDOR PALOTA

Szent György tér 1–3. **Map** 1 C5 (9 A3). 🚌 *5, 16, 78, Várbusz.* 🚫 *to the public.*

By the top of the cog-wheel railway stands the grand Neo-Classical mansion, Sándor Palace. It was commissioned in 1806 by Count Vincent Sándor from architects Mihály Pollack and Johann Aman.

The bas-reliefs that decorate the palace are the work of Richárd Török, Miklós Melocco and Tamás Körössényi. The decoration on the western elevation depicts Greek gods on Mount Olympus. The southern elevation shows Count Sándor being knighted and the northern elevation features a 1934 sculpture of Saint George by Zsigmond Kisfaludi Stróbl.

Sándor Palace functioned as the prime minister's official residence from 1867 to 1944,

when it was severely damaged in World War II. The building has been completely restored, and it is now the official residence of the President of Hungary.

Castle Theatre ❼

VÁRSZÍNHÁZ

Színház utca 1–3. **Map** 1 C5 (9 A3). **Tel** 201 44 07 or 375 86 49. 🚌 *5, 16, 78, Várbusz.* **Box Office** 🕐 *1–6pm Mon–Sun.* **www**.nemzetitancszinhaz.hu

An unlikely assortment of institutions have stood on the site now occupied by the Castle Theatre. The church of St John the Evangelist, founded by King Béla IV, stood here in the 13th century. This church was then used as a mosque under Ottoman rule, and in 1686 it was demolished by the Christian armies that retook the city. In 1725 the Carmelite order built a Baroque church in its place, and it is this building that was first converted into a theatre in 1786, during the reign of Emperor Joseph II. Farkas Kempelen, a famous Hungarian designer added a Rococo façade and seats for 1,200 spectators. The first plays were in German and it was not until 1790 that any work was staged in Hungarian. Beethoven's concert of 1800 is commemorated by a plaque.

The building was damaged in World War II and restored in 1978. The National Dance Theatre now performs here.

Hungarian National Gallery 4

Established in 1957, the Hungarian National Gallery houses a comprehensive collection of Hungarian art from medieval times to the 20th century. Gathered by various groups and institutions since 1839, these works had previously been exhibited at the Hungarian National Museum *(see pp130–33)* and the Museum of Fine Arts *(see pp146–9)*. The collection was moved to the Royal Palace (wings B, C and D) in 1975. There are now six permanent exhibitions, presenting the most valuable and critically acclaimed Hungarian art in the world.

Sisters by Erzsébet Schaár

St Anne Altarpiece
(c.1520)
Elaborately decorated, this folding altarpiece from Kisszeben is one of the Gothic highlights in the gallery.

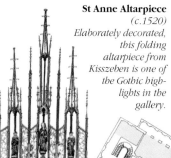

First floor

Madonna of Toporc
(c. 1420)
This is a captivating example of medieval wood sculpture in the Gothic style. It was originally crafted for a church in Spiz (now part of Slovakia).

Madonna of Bártfa
(1465–70)
This painting of a Madonna and Child is from a church in Bártfa (now in Slovakia). It is thought to have been painted in Cracow, Poland.

Ground floor

Main entrance

★ **The Visitation** *(1506)*
This painting by Master MS is a delightful example of late Gothic Hungarian art. It is a fragment of a folding altarpiece from a church in Selmecbánya in modern-day Slovakia.

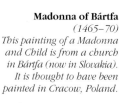

STAR EXHIBITS

★ The Visitation

★ Picnic in May

KEY

☐ Stone sculptures and artifacts
☐ Gothic works
☐ Late Gothic altarpieces
☐ Renaissance and Baroque works
☐ 19th-century works
☐ Early 20th-century works
☐ Temporary exhibitions

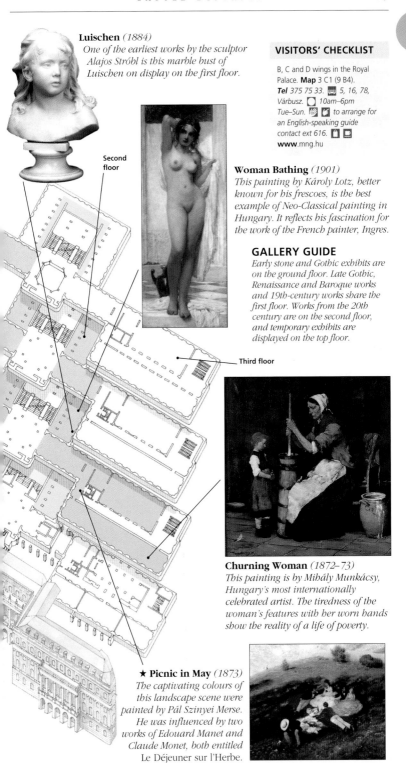

Luischen (1884)
One of the earliest works by the sculptor Alajos Stróbl is this marble bust of Luischen on display on the first floor.

Second floor

Woman Bathing (1901)
This painting by Károly Lotz, better known for his frescoes, is the best example of Neo-Classical painting in Hungary. It reflects his fascination for the work of the French painter, Ingres.

GALLERY GUIDE
Early stone and Gothic exhibits are on the ground floor. Late Gothic, Renaissance and Baroque works and 19th-century works share the first floor. Works from the 20th century are on the second floor, and temporary exhibits are displayed on the top floor.

Third floor

Churning Woman (1872–73)
This painting is by Mihály Munkácsy, Hungary's most internationally celebrated artist. The tiredness of the woman's features with her worn hands show the reality of a life of poverty.

★ Picnic in May (1873)
The captivating colours of this landscape scene were painted by Pál Szinyei Merse. He was influenced by two works of Edouard Manet and Claude Monet, both entitled Le Déjeuner sur l'Herbe.

Exploring the Hungarian National Gallery

Secession poster

The works are displayed in six permanent exhibitions and give a thorough insight into Hungarian art from the early Middle Ages to the present day. Although one-and-a-half centuries of Turkish occupation and wartime destruction interrupted the development of Hungarian art, the birth of national pride in the 19th century allowed a new indigenous style to develop. Among the most interesting are the Hungarian paintings of the late 19th century, when a greater diversity of styles came to the fore.

The Habsburg Crypt, with the sarcophagus of Palatine Archduke Joseph

THE LAPIDARIUM

On the ground floor, to the left of the main entrance, is a display of stone objects discovered during the reconstruction of the Royal Palace *(see p70)*. Called the Lapidarium, it includes sculptures and fragments of architectural features, such as balustrades and windows, that decorated the royal chambers during the Angevin and Jagiełło eras *(see p18)*. The most valuable exhibit, however, is a sculpture of King Béla III's head, which dates from around 1200.

Also in this first section are two marble bas-reliefs of King Matthias and his wife Beatrice, by an unknown Renaissance master from Lombardy.

The second section exhibits late Gothic and Renaissance artifacts from other palaces in Hungary. There are pillars and balustrades from the palace at Visegrád and bas-reliefs from a chapel in Esztergom.

GOTHIC WORKS

A collection of painted panels, sculptures and fragments of altar decoration is opposite the Lapidarium. Note, however, the image of the *Madonna of Bártfy*, which is a rare complete example from the Gothic period.

The sculptures of the "Beautiful Madonnas" are executed in the Soft Style. This style

King's head sculpted from red marble

is characterized, as its name suggests, by the sentimental and gentle imagery of the Madonna playing with the Christ child.

The Annunciation, a magnificent late Gothic work by Master GH, is, in fact, only the main section of an altar; the other pieces are now in Esztergom *(see p164).*

RENAISSANCE AND BAROQUE WORKS

The exhibition begins with a still life by Jakab Bogdány (1660–1724) and portraits by Ádám Mányoki (1673–1757) *(see p28),* who actually settled outside Hungary. As a result of the powerful influence of the Habsburgs during this period *(see pp28–9),* Baroque art was overwhelmingly dominated by Austrian artists. Painters such as Joseph Dorfmeister and Franz Anton Maulbertsch and sculptors Georg Raphael Donner and Philipp Jakob Straub were the acknowledged masters. Jan Kupetzky's portraits are also exemplary models of this era.

The sculptures by Donner and the sacred paintings of Dorfmeister conclude this section of the gallery.

LATE GOTHIC ALTARPIECES

One of the star exhibits of this collection is the imposing late Gothic altarpiece. Arranged in the Great Throne Room, the majority of these vast altarpieces date from the 15th and early 16th centuries.

The Great Throne Room, displaying the collection of folding altarpieces

Architecturally these altarpieces are pure Gothic, while adorned with sculptures and paintings revealing a Renaissance influence. This is evident in the altars of St Anne and St John the Baptist from a church in Kisszeben (now Sabinov in Slovakia), which date from 1510–16. The most recent altarpiece dates from 1643 and is from the church of Our Lady Mary in Csíkmenaság.

Christmas (1903) by Jozsef Rippl-Ronai, a leading Hungarian artist

Bertalan Székely's *Women of Eger* (1867), depicting the Turkish wars

19TH-CENTURY WORKS

The wonderful collection of works from this period reflects the rise of fine art in Hungary in the 19th century.

Historicist art developed during this period. Among those distinguishing themselves in particular were Gyula Benczúr and Bertalan Székely, who produced the epic works *The Return of Buda in 1686* (1896) and *Women of Eger* (1867) respectively. The latter depicts the women of the town defending the Castle of Eger against the Turks.

Viktor Madarász's work *The Mourning of László Hunyadi* (1859) refers to the execution of László Hunyadi by the Habsburgs in 1457. It alludes, too, to the execution of many Hungarians after the crushing of the uprising against Austria in 1849 *(see pp30–31)*.

European developments in fine art can also be seen in Hungarian painting from the late-19th century. The influence of Impressionism, for example, is best seen in Pál Szinyei Merse's *Picnic in May* (1873).

Hungarian Realism is expressed in the work of László Paál and Mihály Munkácsy, the latter being widely regarded as the country's greatest artist. Paintings by Munkácsy which deserve particular attention are *The Yawning Traveller* (1869), *Dusty Road* (1874), the still life *Flowers* (1881), and – most notably – *Woman Carrying Brushwood* (1870), which was painted at the zenith of his career.

It is also worth spending a few moments seeing the paintings of the Neo-Classical artists. The work of Károly Lotz, who is perhaps better known for his frescoes that can be seen on walls and ceilings around Budapest, is exhibited here.

20TH-CENTURY WORKS

Examples of work from the Secession era through to Expressionism and Surrealism, and even contemporary art are exhibited here. They provide a comprehensive review of 20th-century Hungarian art.

József Rippl-Rónai studied in France with Gaugin and Toulouse-Lautrec. His work shows the influence of the Secession style in *The Palace in Körtyvélyes* and *Woman with a Birdcage*. But one of the most engaging artists from the early-20th century is Károly Ferenczy whose *The Painter* (1923) exemplifies the serene qualities of his work.

Tivadar Kosztka Csontváry is an artist whose work did not follow any conventional style but was greatly admired, even by Pablo Picasso. One of his paintings in particular, the *Ruins of the Greek Amphitheatre in Taormina* (1905), captures his abstract interpretation of the world.

The Eight, a group of artists who set up the first Hungarian avant-garde school, were active between the two world wars. Notable examples of their work are *Young Girl with a Bow* by Béla Czóbel, *Woman Playing a Doublebass* by Róbert Berény, *The Oarsmen* by Ödön Marffy, *Walking by the Water Tower* by István Farkas and *Riders at the Edge* by Károly Kernstok.

The best works of Hungarian Expressionism can be seen in the paintings *Along the Tracks*, *For Bread* and *Generations*, by Gyula Derkovits.

Among the sculptures on display, the most interesting are *Raising Oneself* and *The Sower*, by Ferenc Medgyessy, and *Standing Girl*, by Béni Ferenczy. The exhibition is completed by a section on contemporary artists.

The Painter by Károly Ferenczy (1923), a typically peaceful work

Street-by-Street: the Old Town

Bas-reliefs on a house on Fortuna utca

Buda's old town has been a barometer of Hungary's changing fortunes. It developed, to the north of the Royal Palace, from the 13th century. Under kings such as Sigismund, it flourished, and wealthy German merchants set up shops in Lords' Street (Úri utca) to supply the court. The area was later destroyed by the Turks and again by their evictors. It was most recently rebuilt after World War II, but genuine relics can be hunted out in its cobbled streets and squares.

Mihály Táncsics Street
During the Middle Ages, this street was inhabited by Jews. A museum at No. 26, on the site of an old synagogue, displays finds such as tombstones ⓯

The State Archive of Historic Documents, located in a Neo-Romanesque building, houses items that were transferred to Buda in 1785 from the former capital of Hungary, Bratislava.

Surviving tower of the Church of St Mary Magdalene

Labyrinth
This 1,200-metre long system of dungeons, springs, caves and cellars that runs beneath Castle Hill also includes exhibitions on early Hungarian history and legend ㉒

Defensive walls

0 metres 50
0 yards 50

★ Lords' Street
Once the homes of aristocrats and merchants, the houses on Úri utca have medieval foundations. Many have Gothic details and peaceful courtyards ㉑

KEY

– – – Suggested route

★ Mátyás Church
Although with much earlier parts, this church is mainly a Neo-Gothic reconstruction dating from 1874–96. A picturesque vestibule on the church's southern façade covers an original Gothic portal dating from the 14th century **⑪**

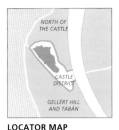

LOCATOR MAP
See Street Finder, maps 1 & 9

This statue of St Stephen, or István, the first crowned king of Hungary (*see pp22–3*), was erected in 1906. Its pedestal includes a bas-relief showing scenes from the king's life.

Fishermen's Bastion
Designed by Frigyes Schulek in 1895, this fantastical structure never had the role of a defensive building, despite its name. It serves instead as a viewing terrace. The conical towers are an allusion to the tribal tents of the early Magyars **⑫**

Holy Trinity Square
In 1713, after an epidemic of the plague was overcome, a column representing the Holy Trinity was raised in this square **⑨**

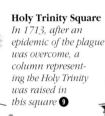

Golden Eagle Pharmacy Museum
From the 18th century a pharmacy called "Under the Golden Eagle" traded in this medieval house, now a museum **⑧**

e House of
ngarian Wines
rs wine-tasting
rs detailing the
e-growing
ions of Hungary.

STAR SIGHTS

★ Lords' Street (Úri utca)

★ Mátyás Church

Golden Eagle Pharmacy Museum 🔟

ARANYSAS PATIKAMÚZEUM

Tárnok utca 18. **Map** 1 B5 (9 A2).
Tel *375 97 72.* 🚌 *16, Várbusz.*
⬛ *Mid-Mar–Oct: 10:30am–6pm
Tue–Sun; Nov–mid-Mar: 10:30am–
4pm Tue–Sun.*

This pharmacy was opened
in 1688 by Ferenc Ignác
Bösinger and traded under the
name the "Golden Eagle" from
1740. It moved to this originally
Gothic building, with its Baroque interior and Neo-Classical
façade, in the 18th century. The
museum opened here in
1974. It displays pharmaceutical items from the Renaissance
and Baroque eras.

Holy Trinity Square 🟨

SZENTHÁROMSÁG TÉR

Map 1 B4 (9 A3).
🚌 *Várbusz from Moszkva tér.*

This square is the central
point of the Old Town.
It takes its name from the
Baroque Holy Trinity Column,
originally sculpted by Philipp
Ungleich in 1710–13, and restored in 1967. The column
commemorates the dead of
two outbreaks of the plague,
which struck the inhabitants
of Buda in 1691 and 1709.

The pedestal of the column
is decorated with bas-reliefs
by Anton Hörger. Further up
are statues of holy figures and
at the summit is a magnificent
composition of the figures of

the Holy Trinity. The
central section of the column
is decorated with angelic
figures surrounded by clouds.

Buda's Old Town Hall, a
large Baroque building with
two courtyards, was also built
on the square at the beginning
of the 18th century. It was
designed by the imperial court
architect, Venerio Ceresola,
whose architectural scheme
incorporated the remains of
medieval houses. In 1770–74
an east wing was built, and
bay windows and a stone
balustrade with Rococo urns,
by Mátyás Nepauer, were also
added. The corner niche,
opposite Mátyás Church,
houses a small statue by Carlo
Adami of Pallas Athene.

At No. 6 is the House of
Hungarian Wines with an
extensive selection of wines
to sample and buy.

House of Hungarian Wines 🔟

MAGYAR BAROK HÁZA

1014 Szentháromság tér 6.
Map 1 B4 (9A2). ***Tel*** *212 10 31.*
🚌 *Várbusz from Moszkva tér.*
⬛ *noon–8pm daily.* 🏷
www.magyarborokhaza.hu

At No. 6 on the square,
opposite the Hilton Hotel, the
House of Hungarian Wines
represents all 22 of the
country's wine-producing
regions and stocks
approximately 700 different
wines. Some 55 of these
are made available to
visitors for tasting. The
wider aim of the
House is to stock the
complete range of

wines produced in Hungary
in a single location, to aid
appreciation and unders-
tanding. The House also aims
to raise the profile of
Hungarian wines both
nationally and internationally.

Mátyás Church 🔟

MÁTYÁS TEMPLOM

See pp82–3.

A statue of St István stands in
front of the Fishermen's Bastion

Fishermen's Bastion 🔟

HALÁSZBÁSTYA

Szentháromság tér. **Map** 1 B4 (9 A2).
🚌 *Várbusz from Moszkva tér.*
⬛ *9am–10pm daily.* 🏷 *Mar–Oct.*

Frigyes Schulek designed this
Neo-Romanesque monument
to the Guild of Fishermen in
1895. It occupies the site of
Buda's old defensive walls
and a medieval square where
fish was once sold. The bastion
is a purely aesthetic addition
to Castle Hill and boasts
beautiful views of the Danube
and Pest. In front of it stands
a statue of St István, the king
who introduced Hungary
to Christianity.

Buda's Old Town Hall, its clock tower crowned with an onion-shaped dome, on Holy Trinity Square

Bas-relief depicting King Mátyás on the façade of the Hilton Hotel

Hilton Hotel ⑬

HILTON SZÁLLÓ

Hess András tér 1–2. **Map** 1 B4 (9 A2).
Tel 889 66 00. 🚌 Várbusz. ♿
www.hilton.com

Built in 1976, the Hilton Hotel is a rare example of modern architecture in the Old Town. Controversial from the outset, the design by the Hungarian architect Béla Pintér combines the historic remains of the site with contemporary materials and methods.

From 1254 a Dominican church, to which a tower was later added, stood on this site, followed by a late-Baroque Jesuit monastery. The remains of both these buildings are incorporated into the design. For example, the remains of the medieval church, uncovered during excavations in 1902, form part of the Dominican Courtyard, where concerts and operettas are staged during the summer season.

The main façade comprises part of the façade of the Jesuit monastery. To the left of the entrance is St Nicholas's Tower. In 1930, a replica of the 15th-century German bas-relief of King Mátyás, considered to be his most authentic likeness, was added to this tower.

András Hess Square ⑭

HESS ANDRÁS TÉR

Map 1 B4 (9 A2).
🚌 Várbusz from Moszkva tér.

This square is named after the Italian-trained printer who printed the first Hungarian book, *Chronica Hungarorum*, in a printing works at No. 4 in 1473. The house was rebuilt at the end of the 17th century as an amalgamation of three medieval houses, with quadruple seat niches, barrel-vaulted cellars and ornamental gates.

The former inn at No. 3 was named the Red Hedgehog in 1696. This one-floor building has surviving Gothic and Baroque elements.

The square also features a statue by József Damkó

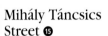

Hedgehog on the façade of No. 3 András Hess Square

of Pope Innocent XI, who was involved in organizing the armies who recaptured Buda from the Turks. It was built to mark the 250th anniversary of the liberation, in 1936.

Mihály Táncsics Street ⑮

TÁNCSICS MIHÁLY UTCA

Map 1 B4 (9 A2). 🚌 Várbusz.
Museum of Musical History
Tel 214 67 70. 📷 For reconstruction.

Standing at No. 7 is Erdődy Palace, built in 1750–69 for the Erdődy family by Mátyás Nepauer, the leading architect of the day. It features outstanding Baroque façades on its Danube, courtyard and street sides. Like many houses on this street, it was erected on the ruins of medieval houses.

In 1800, Ludwig van Beethoven, who was then giving concerts in Budapest, resided here for a short period.

The palace now houses the Museum of Musical History and the Béla Bartók archives. A permanent exhibition illustrates musical life in Budapest from the 18th to 20th centuries, and includes the oldest surviving Hungarian musical instruments.

The Royal Mint stood on the site of No. 9 during the Middle Ages, and, in 1810, the Joseph Barracks were built here. These were later used by the Habsburgs to imprison leaders of the 1848–9 uprising, including Mihály Táncsics himself.

An original mural has survived on the façade of the house at No. 16, which dates from around 1700. It depicts Christ and the Virgin Mary surrounded by saints. The bas-reliefs on the gateway are, however, from a Venetian church.

Relics of Buda's Jewish heritage can be found at Nos. 23 and 26. The remains of a 15th-century synagogue stand in the garden of the mansion at No. 23. During archeological excavations, tombs and religious items were also found in the courtyard of No. 26.

The Museum of Musical History on Mihály Táncsics Street

Mátyás Church ⓫

The Parish Church of Our Lady Mary was
built on this site between the 13th and
15th centuries. Some of the existing
architectural style dates from the reign of
Sigismund of Luxembourg, but its name
refers to King Mátyás Corvinus, who
greatly enlarged and embellished the
church. Much of the original detail was
lost when the Turks´converted the church
into the Great Mosque in 1541. During the
liberation of Buda the church was almost
totally destroyed, but was rebuilt in the
Baroque style by Franciscan Friars. The
church sustained more damage in 1723,
and was restored in the Neo-Gothic style
by Frigyes Schulek in 1873–96. The crypt
houses the Museum of Ecclesiastical Art.

Rose Window
*Frigyes Schulek faithfully repro-
duced the medieval stained-glass
window that was in this position
during the early Gothic era.*

Béla Tower
*This tower is named after
the church's founder,
King Béla IV. It has
retained several of its
original Gothic features.*

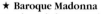

★ Baroque Madonna
*According to legend, the original
statue was set into a wall of the
church during the Turkish occupation. When the church was virtually
destroyed in 1686, the Madonna
made a miraculous appearance. The
Turks took this as an omen of defeat.*

Main Portal
*Above the arched west
entrance is a 19th-
century bas-relief of
the Madonna and
Child, seated between
two angels. The work
is by Lajos Lantai.*

STAR FEATURES

★ Baroque Madonna

★ Mary Portal

★ Tomb of King
Béla III and Anne
de Châtillon

★ **Tomb of King Béla III and Anne de Châtillon**

The remains of this royal couple were transferred from Székesfehérvár Cathedral to Mátyás Church in 1860. They lie beneath an ornamental stone canopy in the Trinity Chapel.

VISITORS' CHECKLIST

Szentháromság tér 2. **Map** 1 B4 (9 A2). *Tel* 355 56 57. Várbusz. ☐ 9am–5pm Mon–Fri, 9am–1pm Sat, 1–5pm Sun. **Museum** ☐ 9am–5pm Sun–Fri.

The roof is decorated with multicoloured glazed tiles.

Pulpit

The richly decorated pulpit includes the carved stone figures of the four Fathers of the Church and the four Evangelists.

The main altar was created by Frigyes Schulek and based on Gothic triptychs.

Stained-Glass Windows

Three arched windows on the south elevation have beautiful 19th-century stained glass. They were designed by Frigyes Schulek, Bertalan Székely and Károly Lotz.

★ **Mary Portal**

This depiction of the Assumption of the Blessed Virgin Mary is the most magnificent example of Gothic stone carving in Hungary. Frigyes Schulek reconstructed the portal from fragments.

TIMELINE

c.1387 Church redesigned as Gothic hall-church by Sigismund of Luxembourg	**1458** Thanksgiving mass following the coronation of Mátyás Corvinus	**1686** After liberation of Buda from Turkish rule, church is almost destroyed. New church built with a Baroque interior	
	1541 Turks convert church into a mosque	*Holy figures on the pulpit*	

1250	1350	1450	1550	1650	1750	1850	1950

1309 Coronation of the Angevin king Charles Robert		**1526** Cathedral burnt in the first attack by Turks		**1896** Frigyes Schulek completes the reconstruction of the church in the Neo-Gothic style		**1970** Final details are completed in post-war rebuilding programme	
1255 Church originally founded by King Béla IV after the Mongol invasion		**1470** Mátyás Tower is completed after its collapse in 1384		**1945** Church is severely damaged by German and Russian armies			

Vienna Gate, rebuilt in 1936, commemorating the liberation of Buda

Vienna Gate Square **⑯**
BÈCSI KAPU TÉR

Map 1 B4.
🚌 Várbusz from Moszkva tér.

The square takes its name from the gate that once led from the walled town of Buda towards Vienna. After being damaged several times, the old gate was demolished in 1896. The current gate, based on a historic design, was erected in 1936 on the 250th anniversary of the liberation of Buda from the Turks.

The square has a number of interesting houses. Those at Nos. 5, 6, 7 and 8 were built on the ruins of medieval dwellings. They are Baroque and Rococo in design and feature sculptures and bas-reliefs. The façade of No. 7 has medallions with the portraits of Classical philosophers and poets; Thomas Mann, the German novelist, lodged here between 1935–6. No. 8, meanwhile, is differentiated by its bay windows, attics and the restored medieval murals on its façade.

On the left-hand side of the square is a vast Neo-Romanesque building with a beautiful multicoloured roof, built in 1913–20 by Samu Pecz. This building houses the National Archive, which holds documents dating from before the battle of Mohács in 1526 and others connected with the Rákóczi and Kossuth uprisings (see pp 25, 31 and 38).

Behind the Vienna Gate Square is a monument built in honour of Mihály Táncsics, the leader of the Autumn Uprising. It was unveiled in 1970.

Buda Lutheran Church **⑰**
BUDAVÁRI EVANGÉLIKUS TEMPLOM

Bécsi kapu tér. **Map** 1 B4.
Tel 356 97 36. 🚌 Várbusz. ♿

Facing the Vienna Gate is the Neo-Classical Lutheran church, built in 1896 by Mór Kollina. A plaque commemorates pastor Gábor Sztéhló, who saved 2,000 children during World War II.

At one time, a painting by Bertalan Székely, called *Christ Blessing the Bread*, adorned the altar, but it was unfortunately destroyed during the war.

Church of St Mary Magdalene **⑱**
MÁRIA MAGDOLNA TEMPLOM TORNYA

Kapisztrán tér 6. **Map** 1 A4.
🚌 Várbusz.

Now in ruins, this church was built in the mid-13th century. During the Middle Ages, Hungarian Christians worshipped here because Mátyás Church was only for use by the town's German population. The church did not become a mosque until the second half of the Turkish occupation, but it was severely damaged in 1686, during the liberation of Buda from the Turks. An

order of Franciscan monks subsequently took possession and added a Baroque church and tower.

After World War II, all but the tower and the gate were pulled down. These now stand in a garden, together with the reconstructed Gothic window.

Parliament Street **⑲**
ORSZÁGHÁZ UTCA

Map 1 A4 & 1 B4.

This street was once inhabited by the Florentine artisans and craftsmen who were working on King Mátyás' Royal Palace (see pp70–71), and it was known for a time as Italian Street. Its present name comes from the building at No. 28, where the Hungarian parliament met from 1790–1807. This building was designed in the 18th century by the architect Franz Anton Hillebrandt as a convent for the Poor Clares. However, Emperor Joseph II dissolved the order before the building was completed.

Numerous houses on Parliament Street have retained attractive Gothic and Baroque features. No. 2, now with a Neo-Classical façade, is the site of the Alabárdos Étterem (see p196), but its history dates back to the late 13th century. In the 15th century, Sigismund of Luxembourg built a Gothic mansion here and some details, such as the colonnade around the courtyard and the murals on the second floor, have survived until the present day. The entrance to No. 9 features the Gothic traceried seat niches that were popular in Buda at this time. In front of the Neo-Classical house at No. 21 is a statue of Márton Lendvay (1807–58), who was a famous Hungarian actor and member of the National Theatre.

The reconstructed Baroque tower of the Church of St Mary Magdalene

Museum of Military History ⑳

HADTÖRTÉNETI MÚZEUM

Tóth Árpád Sétány 40. **Map** 1 A4.
Tel 356 95 22. 🚌 *Várbusz.*
🗋 *Apr–Sep: 10am–6pm daily;*
Oct–Mar: 10am–4pm daily.
⬤ *Monday.* 🖳 **www**.hm-him/hu

The museum is located in a wing of the former Palatine barracks. It houses a wide range of military items relating to the skirmishes and wars that have afflicted Budapest from before the Turkish occupation to the 20th century. Uniforms, flags, weapons, maps and ammunition from as far back as the 11th century give an insight into the long, turbulent history of Budapest.

Of particular interest is the exhibit concerning the 1956 Uprising. Photographs illustrate the 13 days of demonstrations that ended in a Soviet invasion. and a huge civilian death toll.

Lords' Street ㉑

ÚRI UTCA

Map 1 A4, 1 B4 and 1 B5 (9 A2).
🚌 *Várbusz.* **Telephone Museum**
Tel 201 81 88. 🗋 *10am–4pm*
Tue–Sun.

The buildings in Lords' Street were destroyed first in 1686 and again in 1944. Reconstruction in 1950–60 restored much of their original medieval character. Almost all have some remnant of a Gothic gateway or hall, while the façade is Baroque or Neo-Classical.

An excellent example of a Gothic façade can be seen on Hölbling House at No. 31. Enough of its original features survived the various wars and renovations to enable architects to reconstruct the façade in considerable detail. The first-floor window is a particularly splendid Gothic feature. The houses opposite are also examples of this restoration work.

The building at No. 53 was rebuilt between 1701–22 as a Franciscan monastery, but in 1789 it was used for use by Emperor Joseph II. In 1795, Hungarian Jacobites, led by Ignác Martinovics, were

imprisoned here; a plaque records this event. A well featuring a copy of a sculpture of Artemis, the Greek goddess of hunting, by Praxiteles, was set in front of the house in 1873.

There are two museums located on Lords' Street. The Telephone Museum, at No. 49, is a former telephone exchange and one of the most fun and interactive museums in the city. At No. 9 is the entrance to the Labyrinth (*see below*), a relatively new attraction.

Labyrinth ㉒

LABIRINTUS

Úri utca 9 & Lovas út 4. **Map** 1 B5.
Tel 489 32 81, 212 02 87.
🚌 *Várbusz.* 🗋 *9:30am–7:30pm*
daily; oil lamps lit 6–7:30pm. 🖳
English, German; personal tours from
8pm. 🖳 **www**.labirintus.com

The haunt of prehistoric man some half a million years ago, the Labyrinth of Buda Castle comprises a 1,200-metre (1,000-yard) section of the impressive complex of caves, cellars, dungeons and springs that run beneath Castle Hill to a depth of several storeys. The complex, which was created by the action of hot spring water on calcareous rock, has been used variously

One of many tufa-clad caves in the ancient, subterranean Labyrinth

as a storage area, a refuge and a secret military installation. Now it contains a series of imaginative and unusual themed exhibits. "Prehistoric Labyrinth" contains copies of the most celebrated cave paintings in Europe; "Historical Labyrinth" is populated by figures from Hungarian myth and legend; and "Gallery" is a collection of reconstructions and representations of labyrinths from various ages and cultures. From 6pm, oil lamps are lit. Personal tours, conducted in the dark, "for those who are not afraid of themselves", can be arranged.

Lords' Street, which runs the full length of the Old Town

GELLÉRT HILL AND TABÁN

Carving on the altar in the Cave Church

Rising steeply beside the Danube, Gellért Hill is one of the city's most attractive areas. From the top, at a height of 140 m (460 ft), a beautiful view of the whole of Budapest unfolds. The Celtic Eravi, who preceded the Romans, formed their settlement on the hill's northern slope *(see p94)*. Once called simply Old Hill, many superstitions and tales are connected with it. In 1046, heathen citizens threw a sealed barrel containing Bishop Gellért, who was trying to convert them to Christianity, from the hill to his death. Afterwards, the hill was named after this martyr. Gellért Hill bulges out slightly into the Danube, which narrows at this point. This made the base of the hill a favoured crossing place, and the settlement of Tabán evolved as a result.

SIGHTS AT A GLANCE

Museums
Semmelweis Museum of Medical History **12**

Churches
Rock Church **2**
Tabán Parish Church **10**

Historic Buildings
Citadel **4**
Golden Stag House **13**

Hotels and Baths
Gellért Hotel and Baths Complex pp90–91 **1**
Rác Baths **9**
Rudas Baths **6**

Districts, Squares and Monuments
Liberation Monument **3**
Miklós Ybl Square **11**
Queen Elizabeth Monument **7**
Statue of St Gellért **5**
Tabán **8**

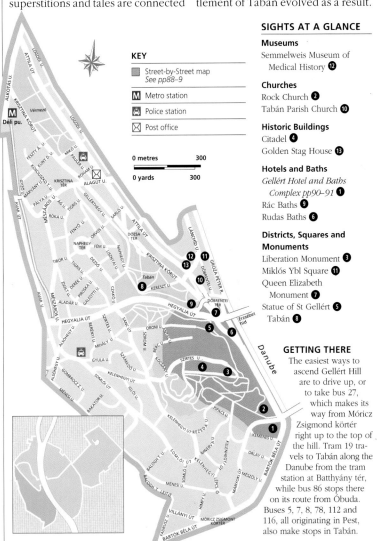

KEY

	Street-by-Street map See pp88–9
M	Metro station
	Police station
	Post office

0 metres   300

0 yards   300

GETTING THERE
The easiest ways to ascend Gellért Hill are to drive up, or to take bus 27, which makes its way from Móricz Zsigmond körtér right up to the top of the hill. Tram 19 travels to Tabán along the Danube from the tram station at Batthyány tér, while bus 86 stops there on its route from Óbuda. Buses 5, 7, 8, 78, 112 and 116, all originating in Pest, also make stops in Tabán.

◁ **The Statue of St Gellért, dedicated to a murdered 11th-century bishop**

Street-by-Street: Gellért Hill

The hill to the south of Castle hill was long regarded as a notorious spot. In the 11th century, Prince Vata, brother of King István, incited a heathen rebellion here that resulted in the death of Bishop Gellért. During the Middle Ages, witches were even reputed to celebrate their sabbath here. Under the Turks, a small stronghold was first built on the hill to protect Buda. In 1851, the Austrians placed their own bleak and intimidating Citadel at the summit. Not until the end of the 19th century did the popular image of Gellért Hill begin to change, when it became a venue for picnicking parties. In 1967, the area around the Citadel was made into an attractive park.

★ Statue of St Gellért

Blessing the city with his uplifted cross, the martyred Bishop Gellért is the patron saint of Budapest **5**

Queen Elizabeth Monument
Close to the entrance to Elizabeth Bridge stands this statue of Emperor Franz Joseph's wife, who was popular with the Hungarians **7**

HEGYALJA ÚT

Citadel
Once a place to inspire terror, the Citadel now hosts a hotel, restaurant and wine bar, where people can relax and enjoy the view **4**

0 metres	500
0 yards	500

KEY

– – – Suggested route

Liberation Monument
At the foot of the Liberation Monument, towering above the city, are two sculptures, one representing the battle with evil **3**

STAR SIGHTS

★ Rock Church

★ Statue of St Gellért

Rudas Baths

These famous Turkish baths, which date from the 16th century, have a characteristic Ottoman cupola ❻

The observation terraces on Gellért Hill provide those who climb up to them with a beautiful panorama over the southern part of Buda and the whole of Pest.

LOCATOR MAP
See Street Finder, maps 3, 4 & 9

THE RESERVOIR

In 1978, a reservoir for drinking water was established close to the Uránia Observatory on Gellért Hill. The surface of the reservoir is covered over and provides a point from which to observe the Royal Palace *(see pp70–71)* to the north. A sculpture by Márta Lessenyei decorates the structure.

Sculpture by Márta Lessenyei on Gellért Hill's reservoir

★ **Rock Church**
This church was established in 1926 in a holy grotto. Under the Communists, the Pauline order of monks was forced to abandon the church, but it was reopened in 1989 ❷

SZENT GELLÉRT RAKPART

Gellért Hotel and Baths Complex
One of a number of bath complexes built at the beginning of the 20th century, this magnificent spa hotel was erected here to exploit the natural hot springs ❶

Gellért Hotel and Baths Complex ❶

Stained-glass window by Bózó Stanisits

Between 1912–18, this hotel and spa was built in the modernist Secession style (*see pp54–7*) at the foot of Gellért Hill. The earliest reference to the existence of healing waters at this spot dates from the 13th century, during the reign of King András II and in the Middle Ages a hospital stood on the site. Baths built here by the Ottomans were referred to by the renowned Turkish travel writer of the day, Evliya Çelebi. The architects of the hotel were Ármin Hegedűs, Artúr Sebestyén and Izidor Sterk. Destroyed in 1945, it was rebuilt and modernized after World War II. The hotel has several restaurants and cafés. The baths include an institute of water therapy, set within Secession interiors, but with modern facilities.

Outdoor Wave Pool
An early swimming pool with a wave mechanism, built in 1927, is situated at the back of the complex, looking towards Gellért Hill behind.

★ **Baths**
Two separate baths, one for men and one for women, are identically arranged. In each there are three plunge pools, with water at different temperatures, a sauna and a steam bath.

Balconies
The balconies fronting the hotel's rooms have fanciful Secession balustrades that are decorated with lyre and bird motifs.

★ **Entrance Hall**
The interiors of the hotel, like the baths, have kept their original Secession decor, with elaborate mosaics, stained-glass windows and statues.

Sun Terraces
Situated in the sunniest spot, these terraces are a popular place for drying off in the summer.

VISITORS' CHECKLIST

Szent Gellért tér. **Map** 4 E3.
Tel 466 61 66. 🚌 7, 7A, 86.
🚃 18, 19, 47, 49. Ⓟ ♿ 🅿
🍴 🏠 **Baths** Kelenhegyi út.
🕐 6am–5/6pm daily. 📷 Ⓟ ♿
www.budapestspas.hu

Hot pool with
medicinal
spa water

Eastern-Style Towers
The architects who designed the hotel gave its towers and turrets a characteristically oriental, cylindrical form.

Main Staircase
The landings of the main staircase have stained-glass windows by Bózó Stanisits, added in 1933. They illustrate an ancient Hungarian legend about a magic stag, recorded in the poetry of János Arany.

Restaurant Terrace
From this first-floor terrace, diners can appreciate a fine view of Budapest. On the ground and first floors of the hotel there are a total of four cafés and restaurants.

★ Main Façade
Behind the hotel's imposing façade are attractive recreational facilities and a health spa that is also open to non-guests. The entrance to the baths is around to the right from the main entrance, on Kelenhegyi út.

STAR FEATURES

★ Baths

★ Entrance Hall

★ Main Façade

Gellért Hotel and Baths Complex ❶
GELLÉRT SZÁLLÓ ÉS FÜRDŐ

See pp90–91.

Rock Church ❷
SZIKLATEMPLOM

Gellért rakpart 1a. **Map** 4 E3.
Tel 385 15 29. 🕘 9am–8pm daily.
🚃 7, 7A, 86. 🚋 18, 19, 47, 49.

On the southern slope of
Gellért Hill, the entrance to
this grotto church is a short
walk from the Gellért Hotel
and Baths Complex. Based on
the shrine at Lourdes, the
church, designed by Kálmán
Lux, was established in 1926.
   The church was intended
for the Pauline order of monks,
which was founded in the
13th century by Eusebius of
Esztergom. In 1934, 150 years
after Joseph II had dissolved
the order in Hungary, 15
friars arrived back in the city
from exile in Poland. However,
their residence lasted only
until the late 1950s, when the
Communist authorities suspended the activities of the
church, accusing the monks
of treasonable acts, and sealed
the entrance to the grotto.
   The church and adjoining
monastery were reopened on
27 August 1989, when a papal
blessing was conferred on its
beautiful new granite altar,
designed by Győző Sikot. To
the left within the grotto is a
copy of the *Black Madonna of
Czestochowa* and a depiction
of a Polish eagle. Visitors will
also see a painting of St Kolbe,

a Polish monk who gave his
life to protect other inmates at
Auschwitz concentration
camp. A memorial plaque lists
the names of the camps
where Polish soldiers were
interned during World War II,
together with the towns and
schools where Polish refugees
were sheltered in those years.
   At the entrance to the church
stands a statue of St István. The
monastery can be reached
through the Chapel of St István
inside. Here, it is worth
pausing to look at Béli Ferenc's
exquisite wooden sculptures.

Liberation Monument ❸
FELSZABADULÁSI EMLÉKMŰ

Map 4 D3. 🚃 27.

Positioned high on Gellért
Hill, this imposing monument
towers over the rest of the
city. It was designed by the
outstanding Hungarian sculptor
Zsigmond Kisfaludi Stróbl and
set up here to commemorate
the liberation of Budapest by
the Russian army in 1945 *(see
p34)*. The monument was
originally intended to honour
the memory of István, son of
the Hungarian Regent Miklós
Horthy, who disappeared in
1943 on the eastern front.
However, after the liberation
of the city by Russian troops,
Marshal Klimient Woroszyłow
spotted it in the sculptor's
workshop and reassigned it to
this purpose.
   The central figure on the
monument is a woman holding

The Liberation Monument, standing
at the top of Gellért Hill

aloft a palm leaf. Standing on
its pedestal, this reaches a
height of 14 m (46 ft). At the
base of the monument there
are two allegorical compositions, representing progress
and the battle with evil.
   The arrival of the Russians
in Budapest was a liberation
but also the beginning of
Soviet rule. After Communism's
fall, a figure of a Russian
soldier was removed from
the monument to Statue
Park *(see p160)*.

Citadel ❹
CITADELLA

Map 4 D3. 🚃 27. 🕘 *daily.*
🏨 **Hotel Citadella** *Tel* 466 57 94.
Citadella Restaurant *Tel* 386 48
02. 🕘 *11am–11pm daily.*
www.citadellarestaurant.com

After the suppression of the
uprising of 1848–9 *(see
pp30–31)*, the Habsburgs
decided to build a fortification
on this strategically important
site. Constructed in 1850–54,
the Citadel housed 60 cannons,
which could, in theory, fire on
the city at any time. In reality,
from its very inception the
Citadel did not fulfil any real
military requirements, but
served rather as a means of
intimidating the population.
   The Citadel is some 220 m
(720 ft) long by 60 m (200 ft)
wide, and has walls 4 m (12 ft)
high. After peace was agreed
with the Habsburgs, Hungarian
society continually demanded
the destruction of the Citadel,
but it was not until 1897 that
the Austrian soldiers left their
barracks here. A section of its

Entrance to the Rock Church, run by the Pauline order of monks

entrance gateway was then symbolically ripped out.

After much discussion in the early 1960s, the Citadel was converted into a leisure complex. A restaurant *(see p196)*, hotel *(see p182)* and even a nightclub now attract customers up Gellért Hill. From the old defensive walls of the Citadel there is a spectacular panorama of the city.

Statue of St Gellért ❺

SZENT GELLÉRT EMLÉKMŰ

Map 4 E3. 🚌 *27. (And a long walk. Go via the steps by Elizabeth Bridge.)*

In 1904 a vast monument was established on the spot where Bishop Gellért was supposedly murdered in the 11th century. It is said the bishop was thrown into the Danube in a barrel, by a mob opposed to the adoption of Christianity. St Gellért holds a

The main plunge pool at the Rudas Baths, covered by a Turkish cupola

cross in his outstretched hand and a Hungarian convert to Christianity kneels at his feet.

The statue was designed by Gyula Jankovits; the semicircular collonade behind it is by Imre Francsek. A spring that bubbles up here was used to create the fountain.

Overlooking the Elizabeth Bridge, the monument can be seen from throughout the city.

Rudas Baths ❻

RUDAS GYÓGYFÜRDŐ

Döbrentei tér 9. **Map** 4 D2 (9 C5). **Tel** *356 13 22.* **Spa Baths** 🕐 *6am– 6pm Mon–Fri, 6am–noon Sat & Sun.* **Swimming pool** 🕐 *6am–6pm Mon–Fri, 6am–1pm Sat & Sun.* **www**.budapestspas.hu

Dating originally from 1550, these baths were greatly extended in 1566 by Sokoli Mustafa, an Ottoman pasha. The main part of the baths dates from this period. In this section there are an octagonal plunge pool and four small corner pools with water of varying temperatures.

In more recent years the baths have been extensively modernized and now include a covered swimming pool. The pool is mixed, but the warm, healing spa water is reserved for men during the week.

Queen Elizabeth Monument ❼

ERZSÉBET KIRÁLYNÉ SZOBRA

Döbrentei tér. **Map** 4 D2 (9 C5).

This monument to Queen Elizabeth, wife of Habsburg Emperor Franz Joseph, was created by György Zala.

The statue was erected in its present location in 1986. It stands close to the Elizabeth Bridge *(see p63)*, which was also named after the empress, who showed great friendship to the Hungarians. The statue stood on the opposite side of the river from 1932 until 1947, when the Communists ordered it to be taken down.

The landmark Gellért Monument overlooking the Elizabeth Bridge

Tabán ❽

Map 3 C1, C2, C3 (9B5). 🚋 18, 19.
🚌 5, 78, 112.

The Tabán now consists of a pleasant park and a few historic buildings, but was once very different. In the early 20th century this district, nestling in between Castle Hill and Gellért Hill, was a slum which was cleared as part of a programme to improve the city. Only a few buildings, including Tabán Parish Church, escaped the demolition.

Natural conditions ensured that this was one of the first places in the area where people chose to live. The Celtic Eravi were the first to make a settlement here, while the Romans later built a watchtower from which they could observe people using a nearby crossing point over the river. The first reference to bathing in thermal waters in Tabán dates from the 15th century. The Turks took advantage of this natural asset and built two magnificent baths here, the Rác Baths and the Rudas Baths *(see p93)*, around which a blossoming town was established. Apart from the baths, virtually everything was destroyed in the recapture of Buda in 1686 *(see p26)*.

In the late 17th century, a large number of Serbs, referred to in Hungarian as Rácami, moved into the Tabán after fleeing from the Turks. They were joined by Greeks and Gypsies. Many of the inhabitants of the Tabán at this stage were tanners or made their living on the river. On the hillside above grapevines were cultivated. By the early 20th century, though picturesque, the district was still without proper sanitation. The old, decaying Tabán, with its numerous bars and gambling dens, was demolished and the present green space established in its place.

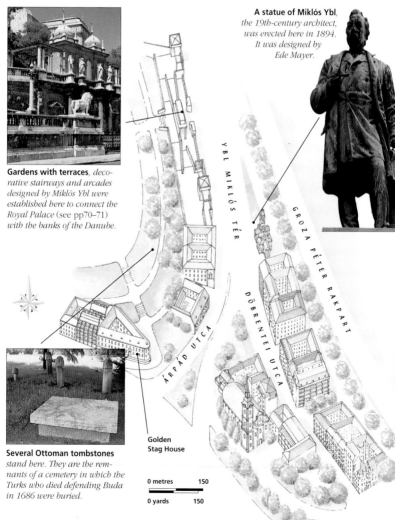

Gardens with terraces, *decorative stairways and arcades designed by Miklós Ybl were established here to connect the Royal Palace (see pp70–71) with the banks of the Danube.*

A statue of Miklós Ybl, *the 19th-century architect, was erected here in 1894. It was designed by Ede Mayer.*

YBL MIKLÓS TÉR

GROZA PÉTER RAKPART

DÖBRENTEI UTCA

ÁRPÁD UTCA

Golden Stag House

Several Ottoman tombstones *stand here. They are the remnants of a cemetery in which the Turks who died defending Buda in 1686 were buried.*

| 0 metres | 150 |
| 0 yards | 150 |

Rác Baths ❾

RÁC GYÓGYFÜRDŐ

Hadnagy utca 8–10. **Map** 4 D2 (9 B5).
🚋 18, 19. ⬜ Re-opening 2006

Taking their name from the
Serbian, or Rác, people who
once lived here, the baths date
back to the Turkish era *(see
pp26–7)*. This is not clear
from the outside, as the baths
were redeveloped in 1869 to
a design by Miklós Ybl. Inside,
however, original Ottoman
features include an octagonal
pool and cupola. Many locals
take the waters for their
believed therapeutic benefits.
If planning to visit the baths
in 2006, check first to ensure
that renovation works are
complete and they are open.

The façade of the Rác Baths

Tabán Parish Church ❿

TABÁNI PLÉBÁNIATEMPLOM

Attila út 11. **Map** 4 D1 (9 C5). *Tel*
375 54 91. 🚋 18, 19.

A temple is thought to have
stood on this site even in the
reign of Prince Árpád. In the
Middle Ages a church was
built here, which was converted into a mosque by the
Turks and subsequently destroyed. In 1728–36, after the
Habsburgs had taken control
of the city, a second church
was erected to a design by
Keresztély Obergruber. Mátyás
Nepauer added the tower in
the mid-18th century. In 1881
the façade was extended and
the tower crowned by a Neo-
Baroque dome.
    Inside the church, on the
right-hand side under the
choir gallery, is a copy of a

**Tabán Parish Church, with its Neo-
Baroque domed tower**

12th-century carving entitled
Christ of Tabán; the original
is now in the collection of the
Budapest History Museum
(see p72). The altar, pulpit and
several paintings adorning the
walls of the church all date
from the 19th century.

Miklós Ybl Square ⓫

YBL MIKLÓS TÉR

Map 4 D1 (9 C4). 🚋 19.

It is no coincidence that the
important architect Miklós Ybl
(see p119) is commemorated
by a statue in this square, close
to many of his buildings.
Among Ybl's most monumen-
tal projects were the State
Opera House *(see pp118–19)*,
St Stephen's Basilica *(see
pp116–17)* and also a large-
scale rebuilding of the Royal
Palace *(see pp70–71)*.
    The Várkert Kiosk, on the
square, was also built by Ybl.
Initially it pumped water up
to the Royal Palace, but in
1903 it was converted into a
café. Since 1992 the building
has contained the Casino-
Valentine Restaurant.

Semmelweis Museum of Medical History ⓬

SEMMELWEIS ORVOSTÖRTÉNETI MÚZEUM

Apród utca 1–3. **Map** 4 D1 (9 B4).
Tel 375 35 33. 🚋 18, 19.
⬜ 10:30am–5:30pm Tue–Sun.
🎦 📷 🚫

This museum is located in the
18th-century house where Dr
Ignáz Semmelweis was born
in 1818. He is renowned for
his discovery of an antiseptic-
based treatment for puerperal
fever, a fatal condition
common among women who
had recently given birth.
    The history of medicine from
ancient Egypt onwards is portrayed in the museum, which
includes a replica 19th-century
pharmacy. Semmelweis's
surgery can also be seen with
its original furniture. In the
courtyard is a monument called
Motherhood by Miklós Borsos.

Golden Stag House ⓭

SZARVAS HÁZ

Szarvas tér 1. **Map** 3 C1 (9 B4).
Tel 375 64 51. 🚋 19.

Standing at the foot of
Castle Hill is this distinctive
early 19th-century house. It
received its name from the inn
that opened here called
"Under the Golden Stag" –
above the entrance you will
see a bas-relief depicting a
golden stag pursued by two
hunting dogs. The building still
accommodates a restaurant of
that name, Aranyszarvas,
which specializes in game
dishes. There is also a
separate wine bar located
in the cellar.

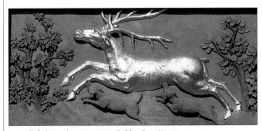

Bas-relief above the entrance to Golden Stag House

NORTH OF THE CASTLE

Between Castle Hill and the western bank of the Danube, extending north from the Chain Bridge towards Margit körút, is the area known as Víziváros or Water Town. This area gained its name in the Middle Ages due to constant flooding. It was originally an area inhabited by artisans and fishermen who, consequently, remained poorer than their neighbours on Castle Hill. Today,

Decoration on the Millachera well

the church towers of Víziváros create a wonderful vista along the western bank of the Danube.

In the Middle Ages and during the 150 years of Turkish occupation this area north of Castle Hill was fortified by a system of walls. A short section of these walls still exists by No. 66 Margit körút, and is commemorated by a plaque. The tomb of Gül Baba, a Turkish dervish, is in the north of the area. It is one of the few surviving Ottoman monuments.

SIGHTS AT A GLANCE

Churches
Calvinist Church ❸
Capuchin Church ❷
St Anne's Church pp102–3 ❹
St Elizabeth's Church ❻

Historic Buildings and Monuments
Tomb of Gül Baba ❽
Tunnel ❶

Squares
Batthyány Square ❺

Baths
Király Baths ❼
Lukács Baths ❾

GETTING THERE
This area is well served by public transport. Buses 4, 16, 86 and 105 run to Clark Ádám tér (next to the Chain Bridge). Tram 19, metro line M2 (red) and the HÉV suburban train converge at Batthyány tér. The tram and HÉV run parallel with the Danube, the tram from the south, the HÉV from the north. The M2 metro links the area with Pest to the east.

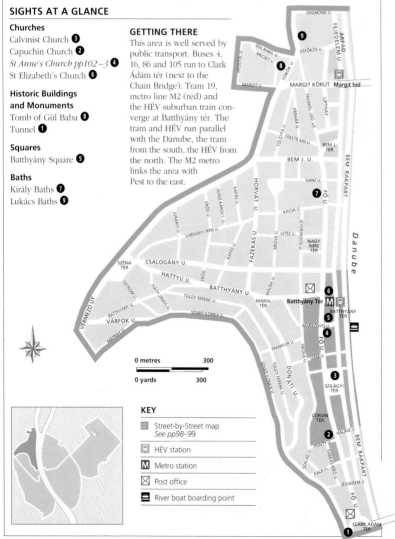

KEY

	Street-by-Street map See pp98–99
🚊	HÉV station
M	Metro station
✉	Post office
🚢	River boat boarding point

◁ The Calvinist Church, viewed from the Danube, beautifully illuminated at night

Street-by-Street: Víziváros

Fő Utca, the main street of Víziváros (Water Town), runs the length of the neighbourhood. Numerous cafés and restaurants, spectacular Baroque monuments, and a promenade along the Danube give this area a charming atmosphere. A fine array of churches, in an interesting assortment of architectural styles, reflect the history of the area as far back as the Middle Ages. From the Danube promenade the panorama of Pest opposite, with Parliament *(see pp108–9)* in the foreground, can best be viewed.

★ St Elizabeth's Church
The Baroque pulpit in this church was carved by the Franciscans, for whom the church was built in the mid-18th century ❻

BATTHY
TÉR

The Hikisch House was built on top of medieval walls. The façade, dating from 1795, features bas-reliefs of cherubs carrying out different tasks. Other reliefs depict allegories of the four seasons.

The White Cross Inn, one of Budapest's earliest inns, was established in 1770. Its asymmetrical façade was created by joining two houses together. Among those reputed to have stayed here are Emperor Joseph II and also Casanova.

0 metres   100

0 yards   100

STAR SIGHTS

★ Batthyány Square

★ St Anne's Church

★ St Elizabeth's Church

★ Batthyány Square
A monument to Ferenc Kölcsey (1790–1838) overlooks this square. He was a literary critic and political commentator of the early 19th century, and also wrote the prayer Lord, Bless Hungary, *which is used as the lyrics for the Hungarian national anthem* ❺

KEY

- - - Suggested route

★ St Anne's Church
Characteristic of the late Baroque period, the interior of this church is quite stunning. The main portal is decorated with allegorical sculptures of Faith, Hope and Charity ❹

LOCATOR MAP
See Street Finder, maps 1 & 9

Calvinist Church
The roof of this church, built in 1893–6, is covered with colourful ceramic tiles from the Zsolnay factory (see p56). They are a strong focal point in the panorama of Buda ❸

A Monument to Samu Pecz
stands beside one of his most important buildings, the Calvinist Church. Pecz was a follower of the Neo-Gothic movement and constructed many other important buildings in the city.

Capuchin Church
In its original medieval form, this church underwent conversion into a mosque at the hands of the Turks. Many Gothic elements have survived, however. Its present structure dates from 1854–6 ❷

To Clark Ádám tér and the Chain Bridge

Kapisztory House,
at No. 20 Fő utca, was built in 1811 for the Greek merchant, Joseph Kapisztory. Its unusual turretted cylindrical window is an attractive feature of this street.

The imposing entrance to the Tunnel on Clark Ádám tér

Tunnel ❶

ALAGÚT

Clark Ádám tér. **Map** 1 C5 (9 B3).
16, 86.

The Scottish engineer Adam Clark settled in Hungary after completing the Chain Bridge *(see p62)*. One of his later projects, in 1853–7, was building the Tunnel that runs right through Castle Hill, from Clark Ádám tér to Krisztin-aváros. The Tunnel is 350 m (1,150 ft) long, 9 m (30 ft) wide and 11 m (36 ft) in height.

The entrance on Clark Ádám tér is flanked by two pairs of Doric columns. This square is the city's official centre because of the location here of the Zero Kilometre Stone, from which all distances from Budapest are calculated.

The Tunnel's western entrance was originally orna-mented with Egyptian motifs. However, it was rebuilt with-out these details after it was damaged in World War II.

Capuchin Church ❷

KAPUCINUS TEMPLOM

Fő utca 32. **Map** 1 C4 (9 B2). *Tel* 201 47 25. by arrangement.

The origins of this church date from the 14th century, when the mother of Louis I, Queen Elizabeth, decided to establish a church here. Frag-ments of walls on the northern façade survive from this time.

During the Turkish occupa-tion *(see pp26–7)*, the church was converted into a mosque. Features from this period, such

as the window openings and and the doorway on the south-ern façade, have remained despite the fighting of 1686.

Between 1703–15 the church was rebuilt, following a Baroque design created by one of the Capuchin Fathers.

In 1856 the church was again restyled, by Ferenc Reitter and Pál Zsumrák, who linked the differently styled façades har-moniously together. The statue of St Elizabeth on the mid-19th-century Romantic façade also dates from 1856.

The altar of the Capuchin Church

Calvinist Church ❸

REFORMÁTUS TEMPLOM

Szilágyi Dezső tér 3. **Map** 1 C4 (9 B2). *Tel* 201 37 25.

One of Budapest's more unusual churches, the Calvinist Church was built by Samu Pecz between 1893–6 on the site of a former medieval mar-ket. It is one of the major ex-amples of his work.

Despite the use of modern tiles on the roof, the church is

Neo-Gothic in style. It is also interesting to note that Pecz used this traditional design of medieval Catholic churches for a Calvinist church, which has very different liturgical and ecclesiastical needs.

St Anne's Church ❹

SZENT ANNA TEMPLOM

See pp102–3.

Batthyány Square ❺

BATTHYÁNY TÉR

Map 1 C3 (9 B1). M *Batthyány tér.*

Batthyány Square is one of the most interesting squares on the Danube's west-ern bank. Beautiful views of Parliament and Pest on the op-posite bank unfold from here.

In 1905, the square was renamed after Count Lajos Batthyány, the prime minister during the Hungarian uprising of 1848–9 *(see pp30–31)*, who was shot by the Austrian army.

The square features buildings in many different styles. The Hikisch House, at No. 3, dating from the late 18th century, is late Baroque. It is notable for the bas-reliefs on its façade depicting the four seasons. The White Cross Inn, at No. 4, also late Baroque, features Rococo decoration. On the western side of the square is the first covered market in Buda, dating from 1902. Though damaged in World War II, it is now fully restored.

The Hikisch House, with bas-reliefs representing the four seasons

St Elizabeth's Church ❻

ERZSÉBET APÁCÁK TEMPLOMA

Fő utca 41–43. **Map** 1 C3 (9 B1).
Tel 201 80 91. Ⓜ Batthyány tér.

In 1731–57 a church was built for the Franciscan order on the ruins of a former mosque, to a design by Hans Jakab. In 1785, after he had dissolved the Franciscan order, Emperor Joseph II gave the church to St Elizabeth's Convent.

The Baroque interior is adorned with late 19th-century frescoes, including one of St Florian protecting Christians from a fire in 1810. Their resonance is due to their recent restoration. The original pulpit and pews, carved by the friars, have remained intact.

In the early 19th century, a hospital and hostel were built adjacent to the church. These were run by the Elizabeth Sisters.

Király Baths ❼

KIRÁLY GYÓGYFÜRDŐ

Fő utca 84. **Map** 1 C2.
Tel 201 43 92. Ⓜ Batthyány tér.
🕐 7am–6pm Mon, Wed, Fri (women); 9am–8pm Tue, Thu, Sat (men). 🎫

The Ottoman Király Baths are one of the city's four remaining Turkish baths *(see p50–53)*. Built from 1566–70, with 19th-century neo-classical additions, they retain many original features, the most beautiful being the central cupola hall with its octagonal pool. From here radiate out the smaller pools of different temperatures, the steam rooms and saunas.

At the end of Fő utca, in the square that bears his name is the monument to the Polish general József Bem. The hero of the 1848–9 uprisings, he is depicted with his arm in a sling. It was in this state, in the front line of the Battle of Pisk, that he inspired the Hungarian troops to attack the bridge and achieve victory over the Habsburg armies. Memorable words, which he uttered during the battle, are engraved on the base of the monument.

Tiles on the Tomb of Gül Baba

Tomb of Gül Baba ❽

GÜL BABA TÜRBÉJE

Mecset utca 14. **Map** 1 B1. 🚌 91.
🕐 Jan–Apr: 10am–6pm daily;
May–Dec: 10am–4pm (sometimes 5pm or 6pm) Tue–Sun. 🎫

Gül Baba was a Muslim dervish and member of the Bektashi order, who died in 1541, just after the capture of Buda. He was one of the few Turks who was respected and revered by the people of Hungary. His remains now lie in a tomb built between 1543 and 1598.

According to legend, it was Gül Baba who introduced roses to Budapest. From this came both the name of this area, Rózsadomb, meaning Rose Hill, and Gül Baba's own name, which in English means Father of Roses. Fittingly, the tomb of Gül Baba is surrounded by a lovely rose garden.

A 400-year-old dome covers the octagonal tomb. Inside, the sarcophagus is draped in green cloth with gold citations from the Koran. Pictures, religious items and beautiful rugs also adorn the tomb.

Lukács Baths ❾

LUKÁCS GYÓGYFÜRDŐ

Frankel Leo út 25–9. **Map** 1 C1.
Tel 326 16 95. 🕐 6am–7pm
Mon–Fri; 6am–5pm Sat & Sun. 🎫
🚊 17. www.budapestspas.hu

This famous spa is named after St Luke. Although the Neo-Classical complex was established in 1894, the baths are one of a number still operating in the city *(see pp50–53)* that date back to the period of Turkish rule.

Set in peaceful surroundings, the complex comprises the 16th-century Komjády (Császár) thermal baths and two outdoor swimming pools. Natural hot springs keep these pools heated all year round; bathing is comfortable even in winter.

It is also worth entering the overgrown courtyard to see a statue of St Luke, dating from 1760, and the plaques inscribed with thanks by bathers from around the world who benefited from the healing waters.

Lukács Baths, with beautiful old plane trees growing outside

St Anne's Church ❹

Budapest is home to many churches, but the twin-towered parish church of Vízíváros is one of its most beautiful Baroque examples. Initially a Jesuit church, the architect who first designed it is unknown. Building was begun in 1740 by Kristóf Hámon and completed after his death by Mátyás Nepauer. In 1763 an earthquake seriously damaged the building and the dissolution of the Jesuit order ten years later further delayed the completion of the church. Thus it remained unconsecrated until 1805. The rectory now houses the Angelika café.

Crucifix on the St Cross altar

The twin towers are crowned by magnificent Baroque spires.

Façade

Buda's coat of arms appears in the centre of the tympanum. The symbol of the Trinity is above this, between two kneeling angels.

★ Pulpit

This magnificent, late Baroque pulpit was created by Károly Bebó in 1773. It features gilded details and angels that embody theological virtues. The reliefs were added at a later date.

Main entrance

Organ

The organ case from a former Carmelite church on Castle Hill was transferred to St Anne's Church in the late 18th century, after the dissolution of the order by Emperor Joseph II.

★ Painted Ceiling
The painted ceiling in the cupola of the chancel depicts the Holy Trinity. It was painted in 1771 by Gergely Vogl. There are also Neo-Baroque frescoes in the nave dating from 1938.

★ High Altar
The sculptures depict Mary, as a child, being brought into the Temple of Jerusalem by St Anne, her mother. Completed in 1773, it is regarded as one of the most beautiful works of Károly Bebó.

Church Pew
The choir pews are decorated with intricately carved wooden panels which feature figurative scenes.

Baptismal Font
Concealed behind a pillar, this baptismal font has a carved pedestal and a simply, but beautifully, decorated cover.

Side Altar
This late Baroque altar of St Francis the Saviour, like the altar of St Cross on the opposite side of the church, is the work of Antal Eberhardt and dates from 1768. The picture in the centre was, however, executed by Franz Wagenschön.

STAR FEATURES

★ High Altar
─────────────
★ Painted Ceiling
─────────────
★ Pulpit

AROUND PARLIAMENT

Towards the end of the 18th and throughout the 19th century Pest underwent a series of huge changes. In 1838 a flood destroyed most of the rural dwellings that had occupied the area until that time. The unification of Budapest in 1873 and the 1,000-year anniversary, in 1896, of the Magyar conquest also boosted the city's development. The medieval walls that originally marked Pest's limits were crossed as the area was gradually urbanized. This period produced a number of the most important buildings in Hungary, including St Stephen's Basilica, Parliament and the Hungarian Academy of Sciences, which were built in a variety of revivalist styles. Many Neo-Classical residences were also built, particularly on Nádor utca, Akadémia utca and Október 6 utca.

An ornate lantern on the Parliament

SIGHTS AT A GLANCE

Historic Buildings and Palaces
Central European University **6**
Drechsler Palace **12**
Gresham Palace **8**
Hungarian Academy of Sciences **9**
Ministry of Agriculture **3**
Parliament pp108–9 **1**
Post Office Savings Bank **5**
Radisson Béke Hotel **13**

Museums
Ethnographical Museum **2**

Squares
Liberty Square **4**
Roosevelt Square **7**

Theatres
Budapest Operetta Theatre **14**
State Opera House pp118–19 **11**

Churches
St Stephen's Basilica pp116–17 **10**

GETTING THERE

The M2 metro line (red) runs to Kossuth Lajos tér and the M3 metro line (blue) runs to Arany János utca. Tram 2 runs north along the Danube and terminates past Parliament at Margaret Bridge. Trolley buses 70 and 78 also serve this area.

KEY

▨	Street-by-Street map *See pp106–7*
▨	Street-by-Street map *See pp112–13*
M	Metro station
⊠	Post office
🛈	Tourist information

◁ Neo-gothic spires, flying buttresses and stained-glass windows on Hungary's Parliament

Street-by-Street: Kossuth Square

Brigadier Woroniecki

This square expresses well the pomp and pride with which Pest was developed during the 19th and early 20th centuries. Parliament dominates the square on the Danube side, but equally imposing are the Ministry of Agriculture and the Ethnographical Museum on the opposite side. Several monuments commemorate nationalist leaders and provide a visual record of Hungary's recent political history.

★ **Ethnographical Museum**
Among 170,000 exhibits amassed in the museum's collection is a captivating collection of folk costumes representing the various nationalities and ethnic groups in Hungary **2**

★ **Parliament**
This building has become the recognized symbol of democracy in Hungary, despite the dome being crowned by a red star during the Communist period **1**

Attila József was a radical poet whose work sensitively explored the human condition. In 1937 he committed suicide, aged 32. This statue by László Marton dates from 1980.

LAJOS KOSSUTH (1802 – 94)

The popularity of Lajos Kossuth among the Hungarian people is immense. He led the 1848–9 uprising against Austrian rule *(see pp30–31)*, and was one of the most outstanding political figures in Hungary. He was a member of the first democratic government during the uprising, and briefly became its leader before being exiled after the revolt was quashed in 1849.

Stained-glass window depicting Lajos Kossuth

BALASSI BÁLINT U

| 0 metres | 150 |
| 0 yards | 150 |

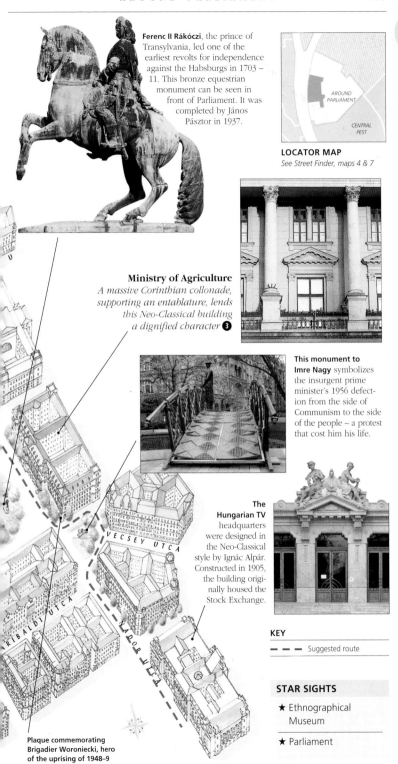

Ferenc II Rákóczi, the prince of Transylvania, led one of the earliest revolts for independence against the Habsburgs in 1703 – 11. This bronze equestrian monument can be seen in front of Parliament. It was completed by János Pásztor in 1937.

LOCATOR MAP
See Street Finder, maps 4 & 7

Ministry of Agriculture
A massive Corinthian colonnade, supporting an entablature, lends this Neo-Classical building a dignified character ❸

This monument to Imre Nagy symbolizes the insurgent prime minister's 1956 defection from the side of Communism to the side of the people – a protest that cost him his life.

The Hungarian TV headquarters were designed in the Neo-Classical style by Ignác Alpár. Constructed in 1905, the building originally housed the Stock Exchange.

KEY

– – – Suggested route

STAR SIGHTS

★ Ethnographical Museum

★ Parliament

Plaque commemorating Brigadier Woroniecki, hero of the uprising of 1948–9

Parliament ❶

One of the pair of lions at the main entrance

Hungary's Parliament is the country's largest building and has become a symbol of Budapest. A competition was held to choose its design, the winner being Imre Steindl's rich Neo-Gothic masterpiece built between 1884–1902. Based on the Houses of Parliament in London, completed by Charles Barry in 1835–6, it is 268 m (880 ft) long and 96 m (315 ft) high, and comprises 691 rooms.

Aerial View
The magnificent dome marks the central point of the Parliament building. Although the façade is elaborately Neo-Gothic, the ground plan follows Baroque conventions.

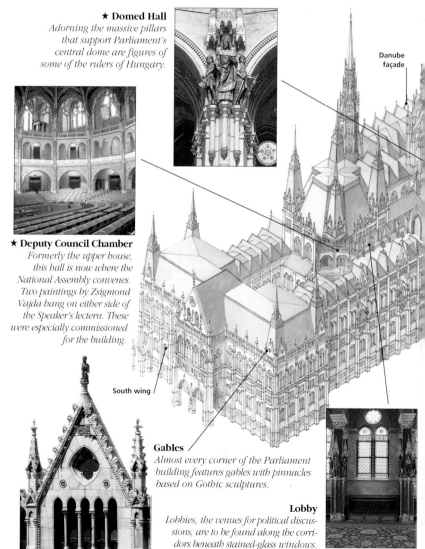

★ Domed Hall
Adorning the massive pillars that support Parliament's central dome are figures of some of the rulers of Hungary.

Danube façade

★ Deputy Council Chamber
Formerly the upper house, this hall is now where the National Assembly convenes. Two paintings by Zsigmond Vajda hang on either side of the Speaker's lectern. These were especially commissioned for the building.

South wing

Gables
Almost every corner of the Parliament building features gables with pinnacles based on Gothic sculptures.

Lobby
Lobbies, the venues for political discussions, are to be found along the corridors beneath stained-glass windows.

Dome
The ceiling of the 96-m (315-ft) high dome is covered in an intricate design of Neo-Gothic gilding combined with heraldic decoration.

VISITORS' CHECKLIST

Kossuth Lajos tér. **Map** 2 D3 (9 C1). **Tel** 441 49 04. 2, 2A. Kossuth tér. 70, 78. English 10am, noon, 1pm, 2pm. non-EU. www.parliament.hu

Gobelin Hall
This hall is decorated with a Gobelin tapestry illustrating Prince Árpád, with seven Magyar leaders under his command, signing a peace treaty and blood oath.

North wing

Old Upper House Hall
This vast hall is virtually a mirror image of the National Assembly Hall. Both halls have public galleries running around a horseshoe-shaped interior.

The Royal Insignia, excluding the Coronation Mantle (see p132), are kept in the Domed Hall.

The main entrance on Kossuth Lajos tér

STAR FEATURES

★ Domed Hall

★ Deputy Council Chamber

Main Staircase
The best contemporary artists were invited to decorate the interior. The sumptuous main staircase features ceiling frescoes by Károly Lotz and sculptures by György Kiss.

The magnificent façade of the
Ethnographical Museum

Parliament **●**
ORSZÁGHÁZ

See pp108–9.

Ethnographical Museum **②**
NÉPRAJZI MÚZEUM

Kossuth Lajos tér 12. **Map** 2 D3 (9
C1). **Tel** 473 24 41. Ⓜ *Kossuth Lajos
tér.* ◯ *10am– 6pm Tue–Sun.* 🖼 🎫
🖥 www.neprajz.hu

This building, designed by
Alajos Hauszmann and con-
structed between 1893–6,
was built as the Palace of
Justice and, until 1945, served
as the Supreme Court.

The building's design links
elements of Renaissance,
Baroque and Classicism. The
façade is dominated by a vast
portico crowned by two towers. It also features a gable
crowned by the figure of the
Roman goddess of justice in a
chariot drawn by three horses,
by Károly Senyei. The grand
hall inside the main entrance
features a marvellous staircase
and frescoes by Károly Lotz.

The building was first used
as a museum in 1957, housing
the Hungarian National Gallery
(see pp74–7), which was later
transferred to the Royal Palace.
The Ethnographical Museum
has been here since 1973.

The museum's collection was
established in 1872 in the Department of Ethnography at the
Hungarian National Museum
(see pp130–33). There are
now around 170,000 exhibits,

although most are not on
display. The collection
includes artifacts reflecting the
rural folk culture of Hungary
from the prehistoric era to the
20th century. A map from
1909 shows the settlement of
the various communities who
came to Hungary. Ethnic
items relating to these communities, as well as primitive
objects from North and South
America, Africa, Asia and
Australia, can also be seen.

The museum has two very
informative permanent displays: Traditional Culture of
the Hungarian Nation, and
From Primeval Communities
to Civilization.

Ministry of Agriculture **❸**
FÖLDMŰVELÉSÜGYI MINISZTÉRIUM

Kossuth Lajos tér 11. **Map** 2 D3 (9
C1). Ⓜ *Kossuth Lajos tér.*

On the southeast side of
Kossuth Square is this huge
building, bordered by streets
on all its four sides. It was
built for the Ministry of
Agriculture by Gyula Bukovics
at the end of the 19th century.

The façade is designed in
a manner typical of late
Historicism, drawing heavily
on Neo-Classical motifs. The
columns of the colonnade are
echoed in the fenestration
above the well-proportioned
pedimented windows.

On the wall to the right of
the building two commemo-
rative plaques can be seen.
The first is dedicated to a
commanding officer of the
Polish Legion, who was also
a hero of the 1848–9 uprising
(see p30–31). Brigadier M

Woroniecki, who was renowned for his bravery, was shot
down on this spot by the
Austrians in October 1849.

The second plaque honours
Endre Ságvári, a Hungarian
hero of the resistance movement, who died in the fighting
against the Fascists in 1944.

The two sculptures in front
of the building are by Árpád
Somogyi. The *Reaper Lad* dates
from 1956 and the *Female
Agronomist* from 1954.

Liberty Square **❹**
SZABADSÁG TÉR

Map 2 E4 (10 D1). Ⓜ *Kossuth Lajos
tér, Arany János utca.*

After the enormous Neuge
bäude Barracks were
demolished in 1886, Liberty
Square was laid out in its
place. The barracks, built for
the Austrian troops, once
dominated the southern part of
Lipótváros (Leopold Town).
It was here that Hungary's
first independent prime
minister, Count Lajos Batthyány
was executed on 6 October
1849. Since 1926, an eternal
flame *(see p31)* has been
burning at the corner of Aulich
utca, Hold utca and Báthory
utca to honour all those
executed during the uprising.

Two particularly impressive
buildings by Ignác Alpár are on
opposite sides of the square.
The former Stock Exchange,
now the Hungarian TV headquarters (Magyar Televízió
székháza), dates from 1905
and shows the influence of the
Secession style. The Hungarian
National Bank (Magyar Nemzeti Bank) is decorated in a
pastiche of Historicist styles
and also dates from 1905.

Bas-reliefs on the former the Stock Exchange

Beautiful Secession interior of the Post Office Savings Bank

tendrils and icons taken from nature. The bees climbing up the gable walls represent the bank's activity and the pinnacles, which look like hives, represent the accumulation of savings. These features were intended to be accessible to the people who banked here.

The building is not officially open to the public, but it is possible to see the Cashiers' Hall during office hours.

Central European University ❻
KÖZÉP-EURÓPAI EGYETEM

Nádor utca 9. **Map** 2 E5 (10 D2). **Tel** 327 30 00. Ⓜ Kossuth Lajos tér www.ceu.hu

This Neo-Classical palace on Nádor utca, in the direction of Roosevelt Square, was built in 1826 by Mihály Pollack for Prince Antal Festetics. Since 1993 it has housed the Central European University.

Founded by the American millionaire George Soros, who was born in Budapest, this international educational establishment is open to students from central and eastern Europe and the former USSR.

The university offers post-graduate courses in subjects ranging from history and law to political and environmental sciences. In Budapest, the Soros Foundation finances numerous other ventures and it has branches in all the central European countries.

An obelisk by Károly Antal stands at the northern end of the square commemorating the Red Army soldiers who died during the siege of Budapest in 1944–5. A second statue is to the US general Harry Hill Bandholtz. He led the allied forces that thwarted the Romanian troops looting the Hungarian National Museum.

Post Office Savings Bank ❺
POSTATAKARÉK PÉNZTÁR

Hold utca 4. **Map** 2 E4 (10 D1). Ⓜ Kossuth Lajos tér.

A masterpiece by Ödön Lechner, the former Post Office Savings Bank was built between 1900–1901. Chiefly a Secession architect, Lechner (see p56) combined the curvilinear motifs of that style with motifs from Hungarian folk art to produce a unique visual style for his work.

Approaching the Post Office Savings Bank, one can see glimpses of the details that

have made this building one of Pest's most unusual sights. The construction methods, interior design and exterior detailing of the building are remarkable. Lechner commissioned the tiles used in the design, including the vibrant roof tiles, from the Zsolnay factory (see p56). The façades are decorated with floral

THE AMERICAN EMBASSY

This beautiful house, at No. 12 Liberty Square, was designed by Aladár Kálmán and Gyula Ullmann and built between 1899–1901. The façade is decorated with bas-reliefs featuring motifs typical of the Secession style.

By the entrance to the embassy is a plaque with an image of the Catholic Primate, Cardinal Joseph Mindszenty, who was part of the movement seeking to liberate Hungary from the Communists after World War II. He was imprisoned by the regime in 1949 and was mistreated for many years. Released during the 1956 uprising, he asked for political asylum in the embassy. He lived here for 15 years in internal exile until, in 1971, the Vatican finally convinced him to leave Hungary.

Plaque commemorating Joseph Mindszenty

Street-by-Street: Roosevelt Square

In 1867, a cermonial mound was made of earth from all over the country to celebrate the coronation of Franz Joseph as king of Hungary. Today, the historic earth has been dug into the ground where Roosevelt Square now stands. At the head of the Chain Bridge on the eastern bank of the Danube, it features many of Pest's most beautiful buildings, such as the Hungarian Academy of Sciences, to the north of the square, and Gresham Palace, to the east. The square was named after American president Franklin D Roosevelt in 1947.

No. 1 Akadémia utca was built in the Neo-Classical style by Mátyás Zitterbarth the younger, in 1835. A plaque shows that in November 1848 General József Bem *(see p101)* stayed here when it was the Prince Stephen Hotel.

★ **Gresham Palace**
One of the most expressive examples of Secession architecture in Budapest, now a Four Seasons hotel **8**

House designed by József Hild in 1836

★ **Hungarian Academy of Sciences**
The debating hall of the Hungarian Academy of Sciences is decorated with sculptures by Miklós Izsó and ceiling paintings by Károly Lotz **9**

The Chain Bridge *(see p62)* was built between 1839–49 and was the city's first permanent river crossing. It was destroyed by the German forces in World War II and was reopened in 1949, 100 years after it was first finished.

ROOSEVELT TÉR

AKADÉMIA UTCA

NÁDOR UTCA

The Pichler House is an unusual building. It was completed by Ferenc Wieser between 1853–7 in the style of a Venetian Gothic palace.

LOCATOR MAP
See Street Finder, maps 2, 9 & 10

★ **St Stephen's Basilica**
The interior of this church was decorated by leading Hungarian artists, such as Alajos Stróbl and Károly Lotz. It was seriously damaged in World War II, and renovation began in the 1980s **⑩**

No. 7 Nádor utca is a Neo-Classical building completed in 1830. It has a modest but well-balanced façade accented by pilasters with decorative capitals, and the large first-floor windows are crowned with elegant arches.

No. 8 József Attila utca, an impressive five-floor office building, was erected in 1898 by Artúr Meinig. It is an attractive example of the use of the Secession style *(see pp54–7)*.

0 metres   100

0 yards   100

KEY

– – –   Suggested route

STAR SIGHTS

★ Gresham Palace

★ Hungarian Academy of Sciences

★ St Stephen's Basilica

Monument to Ferenc Deák, dating from 1887, in Roosevelt Square

Roosevelt Square ❼

ROOSEVELT TÉR

Map 2 D5 (9 C3). 🚋 16. 🚎 2.

Previously, Roosevelt Square was known by several different names – Franz Joseph Square and Unloading Square among others – but it received its current title in 1947. It is located at the head of the Pest side of the Chain Bridge, and is home to many beautiful and important buildings.

At the beginning of the 20th century the square was lined with various hotels, the Diana Baths and the Lloyd Palace designed by József Hild. The only building from the previous century still standing today is the Hungarian Academy of Sciences. The other buildings were demolished and replaced by the Gresham Palace and the Bank of Hungary, on the corner of Attila József utca. Two large modern hotels, the Sofitel Atrium (see p184) and the InterContinental (see p186), stand on the southern side of the square.

There is a statue to Baron József Eötvös (1813–71), a reformer of public education, in front of the Inter-Continental. Situated in the centre of the square are monuments to two politicians who espoused quite different ideologies: Count István Széchenyi (1791–1860), the leading social and political reformer of his age, and Ferenc Deák (1803–76), who was instrumental in the Compromise of 1867, which resulted in the Dual Monachy (see p32).

Gresham Palace ❽

GRESHAM PALOTA

Roosevelt tér 5–7. **Map** 2 D5 (9 C3). *Tel* 268 60 00. 🚋 16. 🚎 2. **www**.greshampalace.com

This Secession palace aroused both controversy and praise from the moment it was built. One of Budapest's most distinctive pieces of architecture, it was commissioned by the London-based Gresham Life Assurance Company from Zsigmond Quittner and the brothers József and László Vágó, and completed in 1907.

This enormous edifice enjoys an imposing location directly opposite the Chain Bridge. The crumbling façade features characteristic Secession motifs (see pp54–7), such as curvilinear forms and organic themes. The ornately carved window surrounds appear as though they are projecting from the walls, blending seamlessly with the architecture. The bust by Ede Telcs, at the top of the façade, is of Sir Thomas Gresham. He was the founder of the Royal Exchange in London and of Gresham's Law: "bad money drives out good".

On the ground floor of the palace there is a T-shaped arcade, covered by a multi-coloured glazed roof, which is occupied by shops and a restaurant. The entrance to the arcade is marked by a beautiful wrought-iron gate with peacock motifs. Still the original gate, it is widely regarded as one of the most

Bust of Sir Thomas Gresham on the façade of the Gresham Palace

splendid examples of design from the Secession era. Inside the building, the second floor of the Kossuth stairway has a stained-glass window by Miksa Róth, featuring a portrait of Lajos Kossuth (see p106).

In 2004 the palace opened as a Four Seasons Hotel, the second in Central Europe, and the first in Hungary. Visitors can wander in and admire its many splendours.

Miklós Izsó's sculptures inside the Hungarian Academy of Sciences

Hungarian Academy of Sciences ❾

MAGYAR TUDOMÁNYOS AKADÉMIA

Roosevelt tér 9. **Map** 2 D4 (9 C2). *Tel* 411 61 00. 🚋 16. ⬜ 11am– 4pm Mon–Fri. **www**.mta.hu

Built between 1862–4, this Neo-Renaissance building was designed by the architect Friedrich August Stüler.

The statues adorning the façade represent six disciplines of knowledge – law, history, mathematics, sciences, philosophy and linguistics – and are the works of Emil Wolf and Miklós Izsó. On the Danube side are allegories of poetry, astronomy and archeology, and on the corners of the building are statues of renowned thinkers including Newton, Descartes and Révay. The interior features more statues by Miklós Izsó, and the library, on the ground floor, has a priceless collection of academic books.

The Neo-Renaissance façade of the Drechsler Palace

St Stephen's Basilica ❿

SZENT ISTVÁN BAZILIKA

See pp116–17.

State Opera House ⓫

MAGYAR ÁLLAMI OPERAHÁZ

See pp118–19.

Drechsler Palace ⓬

DRECHSLER PALOTA

Andrássy út 25. **Map** 2 F4 (10 E2). Ⓜ Opera.

Soon to be a 5-Star hotel, and formerly the State Ballet Institute, the Drechsler Palace was originally built as Neo-Renaissance apartments for the Hungarian Railways Pension Fund in 1883. It was designed by Gyula Pártos and Ödön Lechner to harmonize with the façade of the State Opera House *(see pp118– 19)*.

Its name derives from the Drechsler Café, which occupied the ground floor of this building towards the end of the 19th and in the early 20th century.

Radisson SAS Béke Hotel ⓭

BÉKE RADISSON SAS HOTEL

Teréz körút 43. **Map** 2 F3. *Tel*. 889 39 00. Ⓜ Oktogon. **www**.danubiushotels.wm/beke

This elegant, historic hotel was built in 1896 as an apartment building, and in 1912 was restyled by Béla Malmai as the Hotel Brittania. A mosaic, created by György Szondi, was added to the façade at this time.

In 1978 the hotel was taken over by the Radisson group, which restored the rich interiors. Notable features are the stained-glass windows in the Szondi Restaurant, by Jenő Haranghy, which illustrate the works of Richard Wagner. The Romeo and Juliet conference room and the Shakespeare Restaurant are named after the murals that decorate them. The Zsolnay Café serves cake and coffee on porcelain from the Pécs factory *(see p56)*.

Budapest Operetta Theatre ⓮

BUDAPESTI OPERETT SZÍNHÁZ

Nagymező utca 17. **Map** 2 F4 (10 F1). *Tel* 472 20 30. ▦ 4, 5, 6. **www**.operettszinhaz.hu

Budapest has a good reputation for musical entertainment, and its operetta scene *(see p216)* is over 100 years old. Operettas were first staged on this site in the Orfeum Theatre, designed in the Neo-Baroque style by the Viennese architects Fellner and Helmer, in 1898. The project was financed by the impressario Károly Singer-Somossy.

In 1922, the American entrepreneur Ben Blumenthal redeveloped the building and opened the Capital Operetta Theatre, which then specialized in the genre. After 1936, this theatre became the only venue for operetta in Budapest.

The repertoire of the theatre includes the works of both international and Hungarian composers of this genre, including Imre Kálmán, Ferenc Lehár and Pál Ábrahám, who wrote the *Csárdás Princess*.

Entrance to the Budapest Operetta Theatre on Nagymező utca

St Stephen's Basilica ⑩

St István's coronation

Dedicated to St Stephen, or István, the first Hungarian Christian king *(see p22)*, this church was designed by József Hild in the Neo-Classical style, using a Greek cross floor plan. Construction began in 1851 and was taken over in 1867 by Miklós Ybl *(see p119)*, who added the Neo-Renaissance dome after the original one collapsed in 1868. József Kauser completed the church in 1905. It received the title of Basilica Minor in 1938, the 900th anniversary of St István's death.

Dome
Reaching 96 m (315 ft), the dome is visible from all over Budapest.

St Matthew
St Matthew is one of the four Evangelists represented in the niches on the exterior of the dome. They are all the work of the sculptor Leó Feszler.

Observation point

Tower
A bell, weighing 9,144 kg (9 tons) is housed in this tower. It was funded by German Catholics to compensate for the original bell, which was looted by the Nazis in 1944.

Main Portal
The massive door is decorated with carvings depicting the heads of the 12 Apostles.

Mosaics
The dome is decorated with mosaics designed by Károly Lotz.

VISITORS' CHECKLIST

Szent István tér. **Map** 2 E4 (10 D2). **Tel** 317 28 59. **M** Deák Ferenc tér. **Treasury** 🕙 9am–5pm daily (winter: 10am–2pm). 🈸 🚻 ✝

★ Main Altar
In the centre of the altar there is a marble statue of St István by Alajos Stróbl. Scenes from the king's life are depicted behind the altar.

★ Holy Right Hand
Hungary's most unusual relic is the mummified forearm of King István. It is kept in the Chapel of the Holy Right Hand.

Figures of the 12 Apostles, by Leó Feszler, crown the exterior colonnade at the back of the church.

St Gellért and St Emeryka
This portrayal of St Gellért and his pupil, St Emeryka, is the work of Alajos Stróbl.

★ Painting by Gyula Benczúr
This image shows King István, left without an heir, dedicating Hungary to the Virgin Mary, who became Patrona Hungariae, the country's patron.

STAR FEATURES

★ Main Altar

★ Holy Right Hand

★ Painting by Gyula Benczúr

State Opera House ⓫

Decorative lamp with putti

Opened in September 1884, the State Opera House in Budapest was built to rival those of Paris, Vienna and Dresden. Its beautiful architecture and interiors were the life's work of the great Hungarian architect, Miklós Ybl. The interior also features ornamentation by Hungarian artists, including Alajos Stróbl and Károly Lotz. During its lifetime, the State Opera House has seen some influential music directors, including, Ferenc Erkel, composer of the Hungarian opera *Bánk Bán*, Gustav Mahler and Otto Klemperer.

Façade
The decoration of the symmetrical façade follows a musical theme. In niches on either side of the main entrance there are figures of two of Hungary's most prominent composers, Ferenc Erkel and Franz Liszt (see p144). Both were sculpted by Alajos Stróbl.

Murals
The vaulted ceiling of the foyer is covered in magnificent murals by Bertalan Székely and Mór Than. They depict the nine Muses.

★ Foyer
The foyer, with its marble columns, gilded vaulted ceiling, murals and chandeliers, gives the State Opera House a feeling of opulence and grandeur.

Main entrance
Wrought-iron lamps illuminate the wide stone staircase and the main entrance.

★ Main Staircase
Going to the opera was a great social occasion in the 19th century. A vast, sweeping staircase was an important element of the opera house as it allowed ladies to show off their new gowns.

Chandelier

The main hall is decorated with a bronze chandelier that weighs 3,050 kg (3 tons). It illuminates a magnificent fresco, by Károly Lotz, of the Greek gods on Olympus.

Central Stage

This proscenium arch stage employed the most modern technology of the time. It featured a revolving stage and metal hydraulic machinery.

The side entrance has a loggia that reflects the design of the main entrance.

★ Royal Box

The royal box is located centrally in the three-storey circle. It is decorated with sculptures symbolizing the four operatic voices – soprano, alto, tenor and bass.

MIKLOS YBL (1814 – 91)

The most prominent Hungarian architect of the second half of the 19th century, Miklós Ybl had an enormous influence on the development of Budapest. He was a practitioner of Historicism, and tended to use Neo-Renaissance forms. The State Opera House and the dome of St Stephen's Basilica are examples of his work. Ybl also built apartment buildings and palaces for the aristocracy in this style. A statue of the architect stands on the western bank of the Danube, in Miklós Ybl Square (*see p95*).

Bust of Miklós Ybl

STAR FEATURES

★ Foyer

★ Main Staircase

★ Royal Box

CENTRAL PEST

At the end of the 17th century much of Pest was in ruins and few residents remained. Within the next few decades, however, new residential districts were established, which are today's mid-town suburbs. In the 19th century, redevelopment schemes introduced grand houses and apartment blocks, some with shops and cafés, as well as secular and municipal buildings. Perhaps the most prominent example of this work is the Hungarian National Museum. At this time Pest surpassed Buda as a centre for trade and industry. This was partly due to the area's Jewish community, who played an active role in its development.

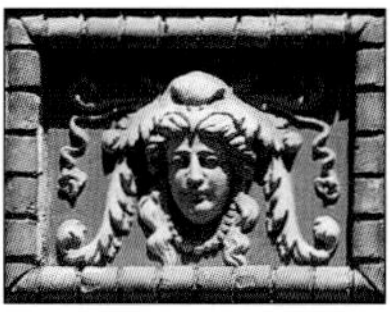

Bas-relief on the façade of the City Council Chamber

SIGHTS AT A GLANCE

Churches
Calvinist Church 22
Chapel of St Roch 18
Franciscan Church 31
Great Synagogue 17
Inner City Parish Church pp124–5 1
Lutheran Church 11
Serbian Church 26
Servite Church 10
University Church 28

Museums
Hungarian National Museum pp130–33 20
Museum of Applied Arts pp136–7 23

Streets and Squares
Jewish Quarter 16
József Nádor Square 3
Mihály Pollack Square 19
Mihály Vörösmarty Square 4
Váci Street 5
Vigadó Square 2

Historic Buildings and Monuments
City Council Chamber 25
Danube Fountain 12
Ervin Szabó Library 21
Franz Liszt Academy of Music 14
Károlyi Palace 29
Klotild Palaces 6
Lóránd Eötvös University 27
Municipal Council Offices 8
New Theatre 13
New York Palace 15
Pest County Hall 7
Turkish Bank 9
University Library 30
University of Economics 24

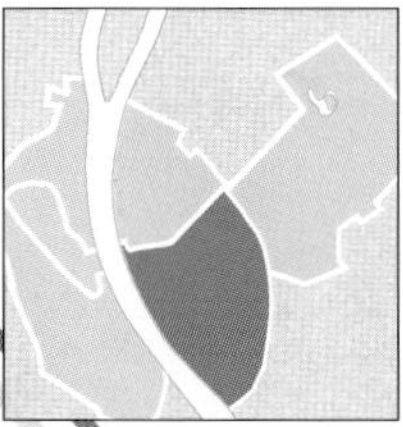

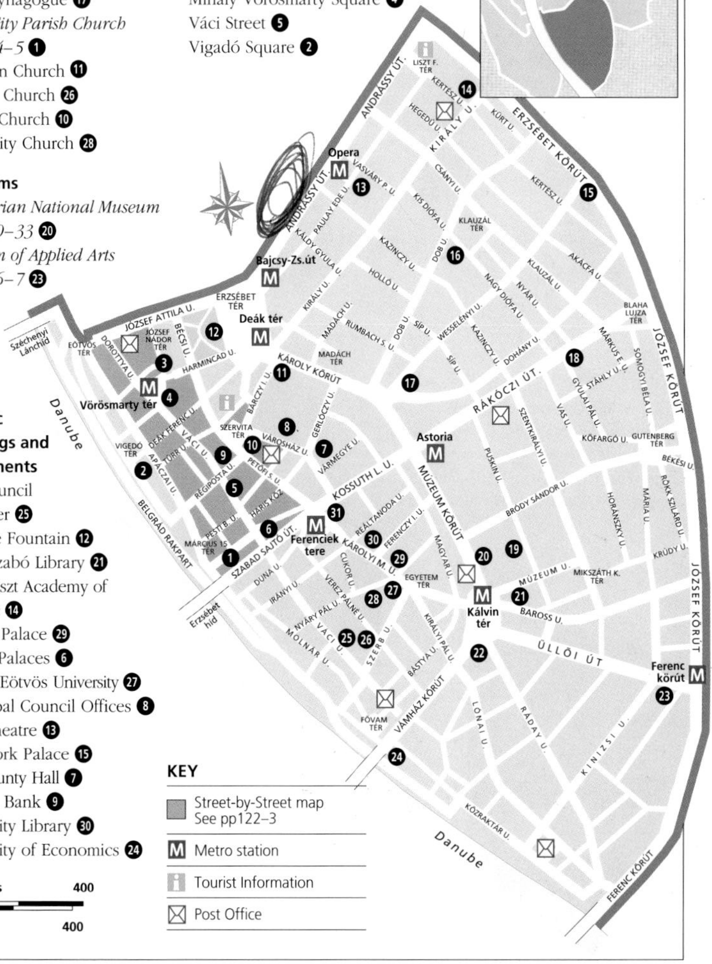

KEY
Street-by-Street map See pp122–3
Metro station
Tourist Information
Post Office

0 metres 400
0 yards 400

◁ **The well of Danaid, who was condemned to carry water to a leaking barrel, in Szomory Dezső tér**

Street-by-Street: Around Váci Street

The nothern section of Váci Street has been Budapest's
fashionable area for walking, meeting in cafés and
shopping in elegant boutiques since the early 19th century. Its attractive promenade is an enjoyable place for
an evening stroll, when it is stylishly illuminated.

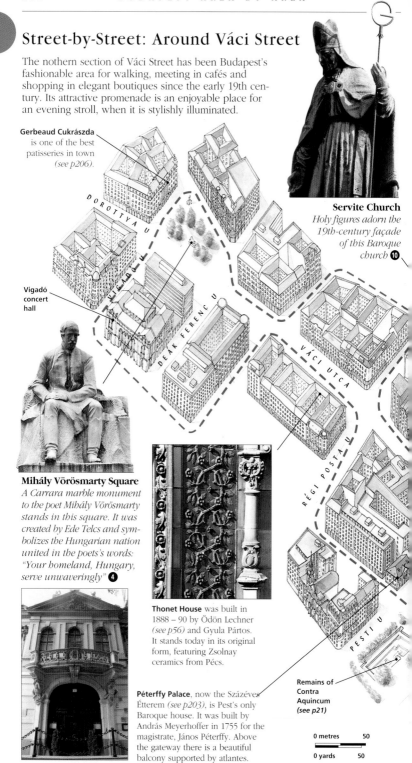

Gerbeaud Cukrászda
is one of the best
patisseries in town
(see p206).

D O R O T T Y A   U

L I G A D O

**Vigadó
concert
hall**

Servite Church
*Holy figures adorn the
19th-century façade
of this Baroque
church* **10**

D E Á K   F E R E N C   U

V Á C I   U T C A

R É G I   P O S T A   U

P E S T I   U

Mihály Vörösmarty Square
*A Carrara marble monument
to the poet Mihály Vörösmarty
stands in this square. It was
created by Ede Telcs and symbolizes the Hungarian nation
united in the poet's words:
"Your homeland, Hungary,
serve unwaveringly"* **4**

Thonet House was built in
1888 – 90 by Ödön Lechner
(see p56) and Gyula Pártos.
It stands today in its original
form, featuring Zsolnay
ceramics from Pécs.

Péterffy Palace, now the Százéves
Étterem *(see p203)*, is Pest's only
Baroque house. It was built by
András Meyerhoffer in 1755 for the
magistrate, János Péterffy. Above
the gateway there is a beautiful
balcony supported by atlantes.

**Remains of
Contra
Aquincum
*(see p21)***

0 metres   50

0 yards   50

LOCATOR MAP
See Street Finder, maps 2, 7, 8, 10

★ Váci Street
Budapest's most elegant promenade and shopping area is lined with fashion boutiques, cafés, fountains and statues. Off the street there are old courtyards and shopping arcades ❺

Párizsi Udvar *(see p212)* is found on the corner of Kígyó utca and Petőfi Sándor utca. The arcade, which features shops, bookshops and a cafe, is decorated with beautiful wrought-iron work.

★ Klotild Palaces
This beautifully decorated block is one of two buildings, which together form a magnificent gateway to the Elizabeth Bridge ❻

KEY

— — — Suggested route

STAR SIGHTS

★ Inner City Parish Church

★ Klotild Palaces

★ Váci Street

★ Inner City Parish Church
This white limestone and red marble tabernacle, in the church, dates from the early 16th century ❶

Inner City Parish Church ❶

This church is the oldest building in Pest. It was first established during the reign of St István, the first king of Hungary *(see pp22–3)*, on the burial site of the martyred St Gellért. In the 14th century, a large Gothic church was built, which was used as a mosque under the Turks. Damaged by the Great Fire of 1723, the church was partly rebuilt in the Baroque style by György Pauer in 1725–39. The interior also features Neo-Classical elements by János Hild, as well as some 20th-century works.

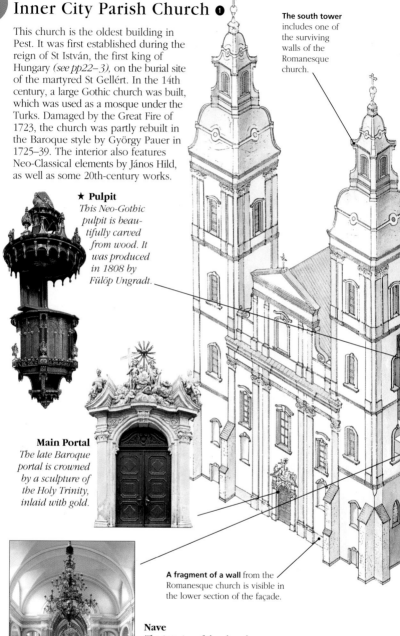

The south tower includes one of the surviving walls of the Romanesque church.

★ **Pulpit**
This Neo-Gothic pulpit is beautifully carved from wood. It was produced in 1808 by Fülöp Ungradt.

Main Portal
The late Baroque portal is crowned by a sculpture of the Holy Trinity, inlaid with gold.

A fragment of a wall from the Romanesque church is visible in the lower section of the façade.

Nave
The interior of the church reflects the Gothic and Baroque periods in which it was built. The nave, in the western section of the church, is Baroque in design.

STAR FEATURES

★ Fresco

★ Gothic Chapel

★ Pulpit

★ **Fresco**
This fragment of a 15th-century Italianate fresco depicts the crucifixion of Christ. It was transferred from the cloister to its current location in the choir.

VISITORS' CHECKLIST

Március 15 tér 2. **Map** 4 E1 (10 D5). **Tel** 318 31 08.
Ⓜ *Ferenciek tere.*
🕐 *9am–7pm daily.* ✝ *daily.*

Reconstructed Gothic tabernacle

Main Altar
The original altar was destroyed in World War II, and the current one, by Károly Antal and Pál C Molnár, dates from 1948.

Turkish Prayer Niche
One of the few remnants of the Turkish occupation (see pp26–7) is this mihrab, or prayer niche, indicating the direction of Mecca.

★ **Gothic Chapel**
This vaulted chapel is entered through a painted archway. It features recreated tracery windows.

Crest of Pest
The crest of Pest adorns the pedestal of a Renaissance tabernacle, which was commissioned by Pest's city council in 1507. It is the work of a 16th-century Italian artist.

HISTORICAL FLOORPLAN OF THE CHURCH

Nothing remains of the first church: the oldest sections date from the 12th-century Romanesque church.

KEY

▮	Romanesque church
▯	Gothic church
▯	Baroque church

The opulent façade of the Vigadó concert hall, decorated with figures
and busts of statesmen, leaders and other prominent Hungarians

Inner City Parish Church ❶

BELVÁROSI PLÉBÁNIA TEMPLOM

See pp124–5.

Vigadó Square ❷

VIGADÓ TÉR

Map 4 D1 (10 D4). 🚊 2. ⊙ For
refurbishment.

The Vigadó concert hall
(closed until 2006) dominates
the square with its mix of
eclectic forms. It was built by
Frigyes Feszl in 1859–64 to
replace a predecessor de-
stroyed by fire during the uprising of 1848–9 (see pp30–
31). The façade includes
features such as folk motifs,
dancers on columns and busts
of former monarchs, rulers and
other Hungarian personalities.
An old Hungarian coat of arms
is also visible in the centre.

The Budapest Marriott Hotel
(see p185), located on one side
of the square, was designed
by József Finta in 1969. It was
one of the first modern hotels
to be built in Budapest.

On the Danube promenade
is a statue of a childlike figure
on the railings: Little Princess
(see p65), by László Marton.
The square also has craft stalls,
cafés and restaurants.

József Nádor Square ❸

JÓZSEF NÁDOR TÉR

Map 2 E5 (10 D3). Ⓜ Vörösmarty tér.

Archduke József, after whom
this square is named, was
appointed as the emperor's

Palatine for Hungary in 1796
at the age of 20. He ruled the
country for 51 years until his
death in 1847. One of the few
Habsburgs sympathetic to the
Hungarian people, he was
instrumental in the development of Budapest
and, in 1808, he initi-
ated the Embellishment
Commission (see p30).

A statue of Archduke
József, by Johann
Halbig, stands in the
middle of the square.
It was erected in 1869.

Some of the houses
on the square are worth
individual mention. The
Neo-Classical Gross
Palace at No. 1 (see
p48) was built in 1824
by József Hild. Once a
café, it now houses a
bank. The building at Nos.
5–6, which overlooks the

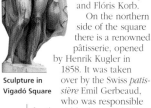

Sculpture in
Vigadó Square

southern end of the square,
dates from 1859 and was built
by Hugó Máltás. At No. 11 is
a shop run by the Herend
company (see p212). Its factory in southwest Hungary
has produced world-renowned
porcelain for almost 200 years.

Mihály Vörösmarty Square

VÖRÖSMARTY MIHÁLY TÉR ❹

Map 2 E5 (10 D3). Ⓜ Vörösmarty tér.

In the middle of the square
stands a monument depicting
the poet Mihály Vörösmarty
(1800–55). Unveiled in 1908,
it is the work of Ede Telcs.

Behind the monument,
on the eastern side of
the square, is the Luxus
department store (see
p213). It is located in
a three-floor corner
building dating from
1911 and designed
by Kálmán Giergl
and Flóris Korb.

On the northern
side of the square
there is a renowned
pâtisserie, opened
by Henrik Kugler in
1858. It was taken
over by the Swiss patis-
sière Emil Gerbeaud,
who was responsible
for the richly decorated interior which survives to this day.

The elegant interior of the Gerbeaud pâtisserie, on Mihály Vörösmarty Square

A tempting selection of coffee, cakes, pastries and desserts are on offer. In summer, these can be taken on a terrace overlooking the square.

Thonet House, decorated with Zsolnay tiles, at No. 11 Váci Street

Váci Street ❺

VÁCI UTCA

Map 4 E1–F2 (10 E5).
Ⓜ *Ferenciek tere.*

Once two separate streets, which were joined at the beginning of the 18th century, Váci still has two distinct characters. Today, part of the southern section is open to traffic, while the northern end is pedestrianized and has long been a popular commercial centre. Most of the buildings lining the street date from the 19th and early 20th centuries. More recently, however, modern department stores, banks and shopping arcades have sprung up among the older original buildings.

Philantia, a Secession style florist's shop opened in 1905, now occupies part of the Neo-Classical block at No. 9, built in 1840 by József Hild. No. 9 also houses the Pest Theatre, where classic plays by Anton Chekhov, among others, are staged. The building was once occupied by the Inn of the Seven Electors, which had a large ballroom-cum-concert hall. It was here that a 12-year-old Franz Liszt performed.

Thonet House, at No. 11, is most notable for the Zsolnay tiles *(see p56)* from Pécs, which decorate its façade.

No. 13 is the oldest building on Váci Street and was built in 1805. In contrast, the post-modern Fontana department store at No. 16, was built in 1984. Outside the store there is a bronze fountain with a figure of Hermes, dating from the mid-19th century.

The Nádor Hotel once stood at No. 20 and featured a statue of Archduke Palatine József in front of the entrance. Today the Taverna Hotel *(see p183)*, designed by József Finta and opened in 1987, stands here.

In a side street off Váci Street, at No. 13 Régiposta utca, is a building from the Modernist period. An unusual sight in Pest, this Bauhaus-influenced building dates from 1937 and is by Lajos Kozma.

Klotild Palaces ❻

KLOTILD PALOTÁK

Szabadsajtó utca. **Map** 4 E1 (10 E5).
Ⓜ *Ferenciek tere.*

Flanking Szabadsajtó utca, on the approach to the Elizabeth Bridge, stand two massive apartment blocks built in 1902. The buildings were commissioned by the daughter-in-law of Palatine József, Archduchess Klotild, after whom they were named.

They were designed by Flóris Korb and Kálmán Giergl in the Historicist style, with

One of the twin Klotild Palaces, from 1902, by the approach to the Elizabeth Bridge (see p63)

elements of Rococo decoration. Once all rented apartments, now only the upper floors remain residential. The ground floor is occupied by shops, a café and the Budapest Gallery with its exhibition space.

Pest County Hall ❼

PEST MEGYEI ÖNKORMÁNYZAT

Városház utca 7. **Map** 4 F1 (10 E4).
Tel 485 68 00. Ⓜ *Ferenciek tere.*
Ⓞ 8am–6pm Mon–Fri.

Built in several stages, this is one of Pest's most beautiful, monumental Neo-Classical civic buildings. It was erected during the 19th century, as part of the plan for the city drawn up by the Embellishment Commission.

A seat of the Council of Pest has existed on this site since the end of the 17th century. By 1811, however, the building included two conference halls, a prison and a prison chapel. In 1829–32, a wing designed by József Hofrichter was added on Semmelweis utca, which was used to accommodate council employees.

In 1838 another redevelopment programme was begun, this time employing designs by Mátyás Zitterbarth Jr, a highly regarded exponent of Neo-Classical architecture. Completed in 1842, it included an impressive façade, which overlooks Városház utca. This features a portico with six Corinthian columns supporting a prominent tympanum.

Pest County Hall was destroyed in the course of World War II. During post-war rebuilding it was enlarged, with the addition of three internal courtyards, the first of which is surrounded by atmospheric cloisters. Due to the excellent acoustics, concerts are often held here during the summer.

Between Pest County Hall and the Municipal Council Offices building *(see p128)*, in the small Kamermayer Károly tér, there is a monument to the first mayor of Budapest. Károly Kamermayer (1829–97) took office in 1873 after the unification of Óbuda, Buda and Pest. The aluminium monument was designed in 1942 by Béla Szabados.

Municipal Council Offices ❽

FŐVÁROSI ÖNKORMÁNYZAT

Városház utca 9–11. **Map** 4 E1 & F1 (10 E4). **Tel** 327 10 00. Ⓜ Ferenciek tere. ◯ 8am–6pm Mon, 8am–4:30pm Tue–Thu, 8am–12:30pm Fri.

The largest Baroque building in Budapest, this edifice was completed in 1735 to a design by the architect Anton Erhard Martinelli. It was originally a hospital for veterans of the war between the Christians and Turks at the end of the 17th century (see pp26– 7).

In 1894 the city authorities bought the building in order to convert it into council offices. Ármin Hegedűs was commissioned to refurbish the building.

Most notable are the bas-reliefs decorating the gates on the Városház utca side of the building. The scenes depicted in the bas-reliefs commemorate a victory of Charles III (see p19) and Prince Eugene of Savoy's role in the war against the Turks (see p71). These are thought to be the work of the Viennese sculptor Johann Christoph Mader.

Turkish Bank ❾

TÖRÖK BANKHÁZ

Szervita tér 3. **Map** 4 E1 (10 D4). Ⓜ Deák Ferenc tér.

Dating from 1906 and designed by Henrik Böhm and Ármin Hegedűs, the building that formerly housed the Turkish Bank is a wonderful example of the Secession style.

The exterior used modern construction methods to create the glass façade, which is set in reinforced concrete. Above the fenestration, in the gable, is a magnificent colourful mosaic by Miksa Róth. Entitled Glory to Hungary, it depicts Hungary paying homage to the Virgin Mary, or Patrona Hungariae (see p117). Angels and shepherds surround the Virgin, along with figures of Hungarian political heroes, such as Prince Ferenc Rákóczi (see p28), István Széchenyi (see pp30– 31) and Lajos Kossuth (see p106).

Glory to Hungary, the mosaic on the façade of the Turkish Bank

Servite Church ❿

SZERVITA TEMPLOM

Szervita tér 7. **Map** 4 E1 (10 D4). Ⓜ Deák Ferenc tér.

This Baroque church was built between 1725–32 to a design by János Hölbling and György Pauer. In 1871, the façade was rebuilt and the tower was covered with a new roof, designed by József Diescher.

Above the doorway there are figures of St Peregrin and St Anne, and above them sit St Philip and St Augustine. To the right of the entrance there is a bas-relief by János Istók, dating from 1930. It is dedicated to the heroes of the VIIth Wilhelm Hussar Regiment who gave their lives in World War I.

Lutheran Church ⓫

EVANGÉLIKUS TEMPLOM

Deák tér 4. **Map** 2 E5 (10 E3). **Tel** 317 34 13. Ⓜ Deák Ferenc tér. ♿ **National Lutheran Museum Tel** 235 02 07. ◯ 10am–6pm Tue– Sun. 📷 ✓ by arrangement.

Mihály Pollack designed this Neo-Classical church, built between 1799–1808. A portico, which features a tympanum supported by Doric columns, was added to the façade in 1856 by József Hild.

The church's simplicity is typical of early Neo-Classicism.

It also reflects the notion of minimal church decoration, which was upheld by this branch of Protestantism. Above the modest main altar is a copy of Raphael's Transfiguration by Franz Sales Lochbihler, made in 1811. Organ recitals are often held in the church, which has excellent acoustics.

Another Neo-Classical building by Mihály Pollack adjoins the church. Constructed as a Lutheran school, it is now the National Lutheran Museum. The museum illustrates the history of the Reformation in Hungary, with the most interesting exhibit being a copy of Martin Luther's last will and testament. The original document, dating from 1542, is held in the Lutheran Archives.

Neo-Classical main altar in the Lutheran Church

The Danube Fountain, built in 1880–83 by Miklós Ybl

Danube Fountain ⑫

DANUBIUS KÚT

Erzsébet tér. **Map** 2 E5 (10 D3). Ⓜ Deák Ferenc tér.

This fountain, which once stood in Kálvin tér, was designed and built by Miklós Ybl (*see p94*) in 1880–83. It is decorated with copies by Dezső Győri of original sculptures, by Béla Brestyánszky and Leó Feszler, which were damaged in World War II.

The figure at the top of the fountain is Danubius, representing the Danube. The three female figures below symbolize Hungary's three principal rivers after the Danube: the Tisza, the Dráva and the Száva.

New Theatre ⑬

ÚJ SZÍNHÁZ

Paulay Ede utca 35. **Map** 2 F4 (10 E2). **Tel** 269 60 21. Ⓜ Opera.

Originally completed in 1909, this building has undergone many transformations. It was designed by Béla Lajta in the Secession style, and, as the home of the cabaret troupe Parisian Mulató, became a shrine to frivolity.

In 1921 it was completely restyled by László Vágó, who turned it into a theatre. After World War II, the theatre gained a glass-and-steel façade, and a children's theatre company was based here.

Between 1988–90 the building was returned to its original form using Lajta's plans. Gilding, stained glass and marble once more adorn this unusual building. Hungary's New Theatre is now in residence.

Franz Liszt Academy of Music ⑭

LISZT FERENC ZENEAKADÉMIA

Liszt Ferenc tér 8. **Map** 7 A1 (10 F2). **Tel** 462 46 00. 🚋 4, 6 to Király utca.

The academy is housed in a late Historicist palace, built between 1904–7 by Kálmán Giergl and Flóris Korb. Above the main entrance there is a statue of Franz Liszt, by Alajos Stróbl. The six bas-reliefs above its base are by Ede Telcs, and depict the history of music.

The Secession interiors of this building have remained intact and deserve particular attention. The *Fount of Youth* fresco, in the first floor foyer, is by Aladár Körösfői-Kriesch, who was a member of the Gödöllő school. The academy has two auditoriums. The first seats 1,200 people and features allegories of musical movements. The second seats 400 and is used for chamber music.

New York Palace ⑮

NEW YORK PALOTA

Erzsébet körút 9–11. **Map** 7 B2. **Tel** 413 14 00. Ⓜ Blaha Lujza tér. 🍴 🖥 www.newyorkpalace.hu

Built between 1891–5 to a design by the architect Alajos Hauszmann, the building was initially the offices of an American insurance firm.

This five-floor edifice displays an eclectic mix of Neo-Baroque and Secession motifs. The decorative sculptures that animate the façade are the work of Károly Senyei.

On the ground floor is the renowned New York Café. The beautiful, richly gilded Neo-Baroque interior, with its chandeliers and marble pillars, now attracts tourists, just as it once attracted the literary and artistic circles in its heyday. Following refurbishment, the hotel reopened in 2006 with 107 rooms, a luxurious spa, and a restaurant serving international haute cuisine.

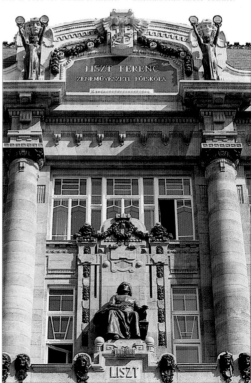

Statue of Franz Liszt above the entrance to the Academy of Music

Hungarian National Museum ⓴

Seal from Esztergom

The Hungarian National Museum is the country's richest source of art and artifacts relating to its own turbulent history. Founded in 1802, the museum owes its existence to Count Ferenc Széchényi, who offered his collection of coins, books and documents to the nation. The museum's constantly expanding collection of art and documents is exhibited in an impressive Neo-Classical edifice built by Mihály Pollack.

Placing the Cornerstone *(1864)*
This painting by Miklós Barabás shows the ceremony that marked the beginning of construction of the Chain Bridge (see p62) in 1842.

Campaign Chest
This carved Baroque campaign chest features the prince regent's decoration and the Hungarian crest. It dates from the insurrection led by Ferenc II Rákóczi (see p28).

Armchair
Adorned with multicoloured fruit and floral ornamentation, this armchair dates from the early 18th century. It is the work of Ferenc II Rákóczi, who learnt carpentry during his exile in Turkey.

★ **Coronation Mantle**
This textile masterpiece, made of Byzantine silk, was donated to the church in Székesfehérvár by St Stephen in 1031. It became the Coronation Mantle in the 12th century.

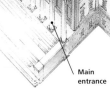

Main entrance

KEY

☐	Coronation Mantle
☐	Archaeological exhibition
☐	11th–17th-century exhibition
☐	18th–19th-century exhibition
☐	20th-century exhibition

MUSEUM GUIDE
On the first floor is the Coronation Mantle and the archaeological exhibition. Second floor exhibits comprise Hungarian artifacts from 11th – 20th centuries. The Roman Lapidary is found in the basement.

★ **Funeral Crown**
*This magnificent 13th-century golden
crown was found in the ruins of the
Dominican Church and Convent on
Margaret Island in the Danube
(see pp172–3).*

VISITORS' CHECKLIST

Múzeum körút 14–16. **Map** 7 A4
(10 F5). **Tel** *338 21 22 (327 77 73
for guided tours in English).*
47, 49. **M** *Kálvin tér, Astória.*
9, 15. *10am–6pm Tue–Sun.*
www.hnm.hu

Second
floor

Pelisse
*This short jacket is typical of
Hungarian national costume.
It belonged to Gábor Bethlen, a
prince of Transylvania, and
dates from around 1620.*

First
floor

Gothic Well
*These recon-
structed fragments are
part of a well from
the Royal Palace at
Visegrád (see
p164). The well
dates from the 14th-
century rule of the
Angevin dynasty.*

★ **Golden Stag**
*This hand-forged Iron Age figure dates
from the 6th century BC. It was originally
part of a Scythian prince's shield.*

STAR EXHIBITS

★ Coronation Mantle

★ Funeral Crown

★ Golden Stag

Exploring the Museum's Collection

A 13th-century seal

The steps of the Hungarian National Museum were the scene of a major event in Hungary's history. It was from these steps that, in 1848, the poet Sándor Petőfi first read his *National Song*, which sparked the uprising against Habsburg rule *(see p30–31)*. This moment is commemorated each year on 15 March, when the museum is decorated in the national colours and a re-enactment is performed. Items from the museum's rich collection, including works of art and craft, historical documents and photographs, vividly illustrate this and other events from Hungary's varied and fascinating past.

Remarkably, the royal insignia, which includes a sceptre and golden crown, have survived Hungary's dramatic history. Discovered by the American forces during World War II, they were removed and stored in Fort Knox before being returned to Hungary in 1978.

In 2000, these other treasures of the royal insignia were transferred to the Domed Hall of Parliament *(see pp108–9)*, where they can also be visited.

Monument to poet János Arany in front of the Neo-Classical façade

MUSEUM BUILDING

Built between 1837–47, according to a design by Mihály Pollack, this imposing Neo-Classical building is one of the finest manifestations of that architectural epoch.

The façade is preceded by a monumental portico, which is crowned by a tympanum designed by Raffael Ponti. The composition depicts the figure of Pannonia *(see p20)* among personifications of the arts and sciences.

In the gardens surrounding the museum there are a number of statues of prominent figures from the spheres of literature, science and art. A monument to the poet János Arany, author of the *Toldi Trilogy*, stands in front of the main entrance. This bronze

and limestone work dates from 1893 and is by Alajos Stróbl. The notable features of the interior include the magnificent paintings by Mór Than and Károly Lotz in the main staircase.

CORONATION MANTLE

One of the most important Hungarian treasures, the Coronation Mantle *(see pp22–3)*, is currently on display in a separate hall of its own in the museum. Made of Byzantine silk, it was originally donated to the church by St Stephen in 1031. The magnificent gown was then refashioned in the 13th century. The now much faded cloth features an intricate embroidered design of fine gold thread and pearls.

ARCHAEOLOGICAL EXHIBITION

The archaeological display was opened in 2002 to celebrate the 200th anniversary of the museum's foundation. The visitor is taken through a display of Hungary's heritage, spanning the period between 400 BC and AD 804, from the first inhabitants of the country at Vértesszőlős until the end of the Early Medieval period, immediately preceeding the Hungarian Conquest.

The exhibition presents some of the latest and important archaeological finds, and abounds in authentic reconstructions of the past.

11TH–17TH-CENTURY EXHIBITION

The exhibition begins in the Árpád era and features one of the museum's most valuable exhibits, the crown of Constantine IX Monomachus, decorated with enamel work. Also on display in this section are the funeral decorations of

Carved base of a chalice dating from the 15th century

Béla III, Romanesque sacred vessels, weapons and an interesting collection of coins.

The period of Angevin rule *(see p18)* coincided with the birth of the Gothic style, which is represented here by some excellent examples of gold work. The next two halls explore the reign of Sigismund of Luxembourg *(see p24)* and the achievements of János Hunyadi *(see p24)*. On display here are copies of portraits of King Sigismund by Albrecht Dürer and a richly decorated ceremonial saddle. There are also several platinum and gold pieces, illuminated manuscripts and documents. The lifestyle of peasants from this era is illustrated, as well as the history of the royal court.

The reign of Mátyás Corvinus *(see pp24–5)* and the Jagiełło dynasty *(see p18)* marks the decline of the Gothic period and the birth of the Renaissance. Exhibits from this era include a 15th-century glass goblet belonging to King Mátyás, late Gothic pews from a church in Bártfa, armour and weapons, as well as a 16th-century dress belonging to Maria Habsburg.

Magnificent examples of sculpture, art and artifacts from the 16th and 17th centuries follow. Of interest are items that survived the Turkish occupation *(see pp26–7)*, especially the everyday objects and weapons.

A separate hall is dedicated to the Transylvanian dukedom and the important historical role that it played. Exhibited here are vessels and jewellery elaborately crafted in gold, 17th-century costumes, and original ceramics produced by the people of Haban, who settled there in the early 17th century. This last section of the exhibition ends in 1686, at the time of the liberation of Buda by the Christian armies after the Turkish occupation. In this part of the museum there are also portraits of influential Hungarians from the period, and an interesting exhibition of jewellery dating from the 17th century.

Printing press used in 1848 to print nationalist propaganda

18TH–19TH-CENTURY EXHIBITION

This part of the museum covers Habsburg rule, a period of great civil unrest. The exhibition begins with artifacts connected to the Rákóczi insurrection of 1703–11 *(see pp28–9)*. Weapons, as well as furniture from Ferenc II Rákóczi's palace, are exhibited here. One item of particular interest is the armchair produced by Rákóczi himself. The next hall is dedicated to 18th-century Hungarian art and culture.

The following rooms portray the Hungarian history of the first half of the 19th century. Artworks, including magnificent portraits and historic paintings, such as *Placing the Cornerstone of the Chain*

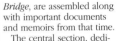

Brooch from the 18th-century

Bridge, are assembled along with important documents and memoirs from that time.

The central section, dedicated to the uprising of 1848–9 *(see pp30–31)*, features a printing press on which were printed leaflets outlining the 12 demands in Hungary's fight for independence from Austria.

The exhibits from the second half of the 19th century include collections of masonic items, official decorations, coins and historic manuscripts. Items relating to the coronation of Franz Joseph in 1867 and the Millennium Celebrations of 1896 are also displayed here.

20TH-CENTURY EXHIBITION

Reflecting the technical developments of this century, Hungary's recent history is presented in a documentary style. Photographs, and documents are widely used to illustrate this period. Artifacts relating to World War I and the era of revolution between the wars, and shocking documents from World War II can be found here. The post-war history of Hungary is depicted mainly from a political perspective. Emphasis is placed on significant episodes, such as the uprising of 1956 and the events of 1989, which signalled the end of Communism in Eastern Europe *(see p35)*.

Guild chest
from the 20th century

Jewish Quarter ⑯

ZSIDÓ NEGYED

Király utca, Rumbach Sebestyén utca, Dohány utca & Akácfa utca. **Map** 2 F5 & 7 A2 (10 F3). Ⓜ *Deák Ferenc tér.*

Jews first came to Hungary in the 13th century and settled in Buda and Óbuda. In the 19th century, a larger Jewish community was established outside the Pest city boundary, in a small area of Erzsébetváros.

In 1251, King Béla IV gave the Jews of Buda certain privileges, including freedom of

HOLOCAUST MEMORIAL

This sculpture of a weeping willow, designed by Imre Varga, was unveiled in 1991 in memory of the 600,000 Hungarian Jews killed by the Nazis in World War II. It was partly funded by the Hungarian-American actor Tony Curtis.

Window of the Great Synagogue

religion. The Jewish community became well integrated into Hungarian society, until in 1941, a series of Nazi anti-Semitic laws were passed and the wearing of the Star of David was made compulsory. In 1944, a ghetto was created in Pest and the deportation of thousands of Jews to camps, including Auschwitz, was implemented. After heavy fighting between the Russian and German armies, the Soviet Red Army liberated the ghetto on 18 January 1945. In total, 600,000 Hungarian Jews were

victims of the Holocaust. This fact is commemorated by a plaque at the Orthodox Synagogue on Rumbach utca.

In the late 19th century, three synagogues were built and many Jewish shops and workshops were established. Kosher establishments, such as the Hanna Étterem (*see p200*) in the courtyard of the Orthodox Synagogue, and the butcher at No. 41 Kazinczy utca, were a common feature. Shops are now being reconstructed to recreate the pre-ghetto character of the Jewish Quarter.

Great Synagogue ⑰

ZSINAGÓGA

Dohány utca 2. **Map** 4 F1 (10 F4). **Tel** *342 89 49.* Ⓜ *Astoria.* **Jewish Museum** ☐ *May–Oct: 10am–5pm Mon–Thu, 10am–2pm Fri & Sun; Nov–Apr: 10am–3pm Mon–Thu, 10am–2pm Fri & Sun.* 🖾 🖍

This synagogue is the largest in Europe. It was built in a Byzantine-Moorish style by the Viennese architect Ludwig Förster between 1854–9. It has three naves and, following orthodox tradition, separate galleries for women. Together the naves and galleries can accommodate up to 3,000 worshippers. Some features, such as the position of the reading platform, reflect elements of Judaic reform. The interior has valuable decorative fittings, particularly those on the Ark of the Law, by Frigyes Feszl. In 1931, a

museum was established; a vast collection of historical relics, Judaic devotional items and everday objects, from ancient Rome to the present

day, has been assembled. It includes the book of Chevra Kadisha from 1792. There is also a moving Holocaust Memorial Room.

A large rose window is the façade's main ornamentation. It is located between two richly decorated towers crowned with distinctive onion domes.

The façade is composed of white and red brick and intricately designed ceramic friezes.

A Hebrew inscription from the second book of Moses is situated under the rose window.

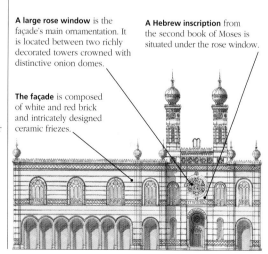

Chapel of St Roch

SZENT RÓKUS KÁPOLNA

Gyulai Pál u 2. **Map** 7 A3. **Tel** 338
35 15. Ⓜ *Astoria or Blaha Lujza tér.*

Pest town council built this
chapel in what was then an
uninhabited area. It was dedicated to St Roch and St Rozali,
who were believed to provide
protection against the plague,
which afflicted Pest in 1711.

In 1740 the chapel was extended to its present size, and
a tower was added in 1797.
The façade is decorated with
Baroque figures of saints,
although the originals were
replaced with copies in 1908.

Inside, on the right-hand wall
of the chapel's nave, is a painting of the Virgin Mary from
1740. A painting by Jakab
Warsch, depicting the Great
Flood of 1838, is in the oratory.

Mihály Pollack Square

POLLACK MIHÁLY TÉR

Map 7 A4 (10 F5). Ⓜ *Kálvin tér.*
Festetics Palace Tel 266 52 22.
📷 *by prior arrangement.*

At the rear of the Hungarian
National Museum *(see pp130–
33)* is a square named after
Mihály Pollack, the architect of
several Neo-Classical
buildings such as the museum
and Sándor Palace *(see p73)*.

In the late 19th century, three
palaces were built side by side
on this square for the aristocratic elite of Hungary: Prince
Festetics, Prince Eszterházy and
Count Károlyi. The beautiful
façades makes this one of the
city's most captivating squares.

Miklós Ybl *(see p94)* built
the French-Renaissance style
palace at No. 6 for Lajós
Károlyi, in 1863–5. The façade
is decorated with sculptures by
Károly Schaffer. There is also
a covered driveway for carriages. Next door, at No. 8, is a
small palace, which was built
in 1865 for the Eszterházy
family by Alájos Baumgarten.
At No. 10 is the palace built
for the Festetics family in 1862,
again by Miklós Ybl. The
interior, especially the Neo-
Baroque staircase, is splendid.

Magnificent staircase inside the Festetics Palace on Mihály Pollack Square

Hungarian National Museum

NEMZETI MÚZEUM

See pp130–33.

Ervin Szabó Library

SZABÓ ERVIN KÖNYVTÁR

Szabó Ervin tér 1. **Map** 7 A4 (10 F5).
Tel 411 50 00. Ⓜ *Kálvin tér.*
🕐 *10am–8pm Mon–Fri, 10am–
4pm Sat.*

In 1887, the wealthy
industrialist Wenckheim
family commissioned the
architect Artur Meining to build
a Neo-Baroque and Rococo
style palace. The result was
the former Wenckheim Palace,
regarded as one of the most
beautiful palaces in Budapest.
The magnificent wrought-iron

Spiral staircase in one of the
rooms of the Ervin Szabó Library

gates, dating from 1897, are the
work of Gyula Jungfer. Also
worth particular attention are
the richly gilded salons on the
first floor, as well as the dome
above an oval panel of reliefs.

In 1926, the city council
acquired the building and
converted it into a public
lending library, whose collection focuses on the city itself
and the social sciences.

The Ervin Szabó Library was
named after the politician and
social reformer Ervin Szabó
(1877–918), who was the
library's first director. It has
over a hundred branches
throughout Budapest and
some three million books.

Calvinist Church

REFORMÁTUS TEMPLOM

Kálvin tér 7. **Map** 4 F2.
Tel 217 67 69. Ⓜ *Kálvin tér.* 🕐
6pm Thu; 10am, 11:30am, 6pm Sun.

This single nave church was
designed by József Hofrichter
and built between 1816–30.
In 1848 József Hild designed
the four-pillared façade and
tympanum, and a spire was
added in 1859. Inside the
church, the pulpit and choir
gallery were designed by Hild
in 1831 and 1854 respectively.
The stained-glass windows
are the work of Miksa Róth.
Sacred artefacts from the 17th
and 18th centuries are kept in
the church treasury.

Museum of Applied Arts ㉓

Opened in 1896 by Emperor Franz Joseph
as part of the Millennium Celebrations, this
collection is housed not within a Neo-
Classical building, but within an outstanding
Secession building designed by Gyula Pártos
and Ödön Lechner *(see p56)*. The exterior incorporated elements inspired by the Orient
as well as the Zsolnay ceramics characteristic of Lechner's work. Damaged in 1945
and again in 1956, the building only recently regained its original magnificence. The
collection, founded in 1872, includes many
examples of arts and crafts workmanship.

A Lalique
pendant

Silver Plate
*This magnificent Baroque
plate depicts the Battle
of Vezekény. It was
crafted in 1654 in
Augsburg by Philip
Jacob Drentwett.*

**Pendant with Amphitrite
and Triton**
*This elaborate example of
gold work is decorated with
enamelwork, pearls and
precious stones. It was
made in around 1600.*

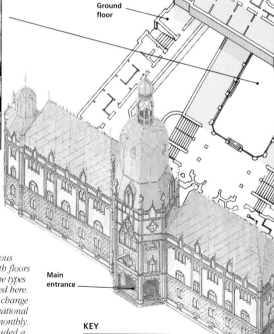

Ground
floor

Inner Courtyard
*This courtyard, covered
by a glazed roof, is sur-
rounded by cloisters with
arcades designed in an
Indian-Oriental style.*

MUSEUM GUIDE

*The museum is home to various
temporary exhibitions on both floors
of the building. Examples of the types
of items on show are illustrated here.
The major exhibitions tend to change
each year, whilst the smaller national
and foreign displays change monthly.
Recent exhibitions have included a
wonderful display of glass and an
exploration of clocks and time.
The library, dating from 1872, is
located on the first floor and
contains around 50,000 books.*

Main
entrance

KEY

☐	Library
☐	Temporary exhibitions
☐	Non-exhibition space

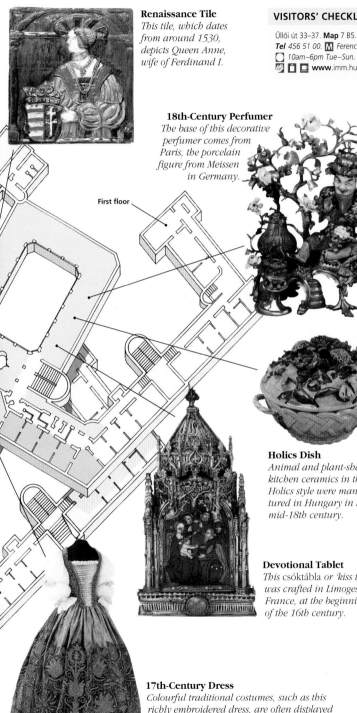

Renaissance Tile
This tile, which dates from around 1530, depicts Queen Anne, wife of Ferdinand I.

VISITORS' CHECKLIST

Üllői út 33–37. **Map** 7 B5.
Tel 456 51 00. **M** Ferenc körút.
10am–6pm Tue–Sun.
www.imm.hu

18th-Century Perfumer
The base of this decorative perfumer comes from Paris, the porcelain figure from Meissen in Germany.

First floor

Holics Dish
Animal and plant-shaped kitchen ceramics in the Holics style were manufactured in Hungary in the mid-18th century.

Devotional Tablet
This csóktábla *or 'kiss tablet' was crafted in Limoges, France, at the beginning of the 16th century.*

17th-Century Dress
Colourful traditional costumes, such as this richly embroidered dress, are often displayed in temporary exhibitions.

University of Corvinus ㉔

CORVINUS EGYETEM

Fővám tér 8. **Map** 4 F3.
Tel 216 18 50. 2, 2A, 47, 49.
www.bke.hu

Facing the Danube, this Neo-Renaissance edifice was designed by Miklós Ybl *(see p94)* and built as the Main Customs Office in 1871–4.

The façade is 170 m (560 ft) long and features a colonnade supporting a balcony. On the balustrade stand ten allegorical figures by August Sommer.

In 1951, this building opened as a university specializing in economics and management. There is a statue of Karl Marx, after whom the university was once named, in the atrium.

Façade of the University of Corvinus, designed by Miklós Ybl

Decorative element on the façade of the City Council Chamber

City Council Chamber ㉕

ÚJ VÁROSHÁZA

Váci utca 62–64. **Map** 4 F2 (10 E5).
Deák tér. **Tel** 235 17 00.

This three-floor edifice was built between 1870–75 as offices for the newly unified city of Budapest *(see p32)*. Its architect, Imre Steindl, was also responsible for designing Parliament *(see pp108–9)*.

The building is a mix of styles. The exterior is a Neo-Renaissance design in brick, with grotesques between the windows, while the interior

features cast-iron Neo-Gothic motifs. The Great Debating Hall is decorated with mosaics designed by Károly Lotz.

Many antiquarian bookshops and galleries have now opened around here. Fashionable bars, restaurants and cafés, and the recent pedestrianization, make this a very charming area.

Serbian Church ㉖

SZERB TEMPLOM

Szerb utca 2–4. **Map** 4 F2 (10 E5).
Kálvin tér. 8am–7pm daily.

Serbs settled in the now largely residential area around the church as early as the 16th century. The end of the 17th century brought a new wave of Serb immigrants, and by the early 19th century Serbs comprised almost 25 per cent of Pest's home-owners.

In 1698, the Serb community replaced an earlier church on the site with this Baroque one. The church gained its final appearance after a rebuilding project that lasted until the mid-18th century, which was probably undertaken by András Meyerhoffer.

The interior of the church is arranged according to Greek Orthodox practice. A section of the nave, which is entered from the vestibule, is reserved for women. This area is divided

Ceramic tile from the Serbian Church

from the men's section by a partition, and the division is further emphasized by the floor, which has been lowered by 30 cm (1 ft). The choir gallery is enclosed by an iconostasis that divides it from the sanctuary. This iconostasis dates from around 1850. The carving is by the Serb sculptor Miahai Janich and the Italian Renaissance-influenced paintings are the work of the Greek artist Károly Sterio.

Lóránd Eötvös University ㉗

EÖTVÖS LÓRÁND TUDOMÁNY EGYETEM KÖZPONTJA

Egyetem tér 1–3. **Map** 4 F2 (10 E5).
Ferenciek tere, Kálvin tér.
Tel 411 65 00. www.elte.hu

In 1635, Cardinal Péter Pázmány, the leader of the Counter-Reformation, established a university in Nagyszombat (now Trnava in Slovakia). It moved to Buda in 1777, nearly a century after the end of the Turkish occupation *(see pp26–7)*, during the reign of Maria Theresa. Emperor Joseph II transferred the university to Pest, to the environs of the Pauline Church, now called the University Church. It was not until 1889 that the university was endowed with a permanent home. This Neo-Baroque building, now the Law Faculty, was designed by architects including Sándor Baumgarten and Fülöp Herzog.

The university is named after the noted physicist Lóránd Eötvös (1848–1919).

University Church ❷

EGYETEMI TEMPLOM

Papnövelde utca 9. **Map** 4 F2 (10 E5). **Tel** 318 05 55. Ⓜ Kálvin tér. ⭘ 7am–7pm daily.

This single-nave church is considered one of the most impressive Baroque churches in the city. It was built for the Pauline Order in 1725–42, and was probably designed by András Meyerhoffer. The tower was added in 1771. The Pauline Order, founded in 1263 by Canon Euzebiusz, was the only religious order to be founded in Hungary.

The magnificent exterior features a tympanum and a row of pilasters that divide the façade. Figures of St Paul and St Anthony flank the emblem of the Pauline Order, which crowns the exterior. The carved-wood interior of the main vestibule is also worth particular mention.

Inside the church a row of side chapels stand behind unusual marble pilasters. In 1776 Johann Bergl painted the vaulted ceiling with frescoes depicting scenes from the life of Mary. Sadly, these frescoes are now in poor condition.

The main altar dates from 1746, and the carved statues behind it are the work of József Hebenstreit. Above it is a copy of the painting *The Black Madonna of Czestochowa*, which is thought to date from 1720. Much of the Baroque interior detail of the church is the work of the Pauline monks, for example the balustrade of the organ loft, the confessionals and the carved pulpit on the right.

Tympanum adorning the façade of the University Library

Károlyi Palace ❷

KÁROLYI PALOTA

Károlyi Mihály utca 16. **Map** 4 F2 (10 E5). **Tel** 317 31 43. Ⓜ Ferenciek tere, Kálvin tér. **Petőfi Exhibition** ⭘ 10am–6pm Tue–Sun. 🖾 317 36 11.

In 1696 there was a small Baroque palace on this site, which was extended by András Meyerhoffer between 1759–68. Subsequent rebuilding, which gave the palace a Neo-Classical appearance, was undertaken between 1832–41 by Anton Riegl. It is named after Mihály Károlyi, leader of the 1918–19 Hungarian Republic (see p34), who was born here in 1875.

The palace now houses the Hungarian Museum of Literature and the Petőfi Exhibition, which is dedicated to the poet Sándor Petőfi (see p31). Other Hungarian poets remembered here include Atilla József, Endre Ady and Mór Jókai.

University Library ❸

EGYETEMI KÖNYVTÁR

Ferenciek tere 6. **Map** 4 F1 (10 E5). **Tel** 266 58 66. Ⓜ Ferenciek tere, Kálvin tér. ⭘ 9am–3:30pm Mon–Fri.

This Neo-Renaissance Edifice, by Antal Szkalniczky and Henrik Koch, was built from 1873–6. It is distinguished by the dome on the corner tower. The library's two million works include 11 *Corviniani (see p72)* and 160 medieval manuscripts and miniatures. The reading room has sgraffiti by Mór Than and frescoes by Károly Lotz.

Franciscan Church ❸

BELVÁROSI FERENCES TEMPLOM

Ferenciek tere 9. **Map** 4 F1 (10 E4). **Tel** 317 33 22. Ⓜ Ferenciek tere. ⭘ 7am–8pm daily. 🔔 noon–4pm.

A Franciscan church and monastery have stood on this site, beyond the old city walls, since the 13th century. In 1541 the Turks rebuilt the church as the Mosque of Sinan, but after the liberation (see pp26–7) the monks regained the building. Between 1727–43 they remodelled the church in the Baroque style, which it still retains today.

The façade features a magnificent portal incorporating sculptures of Franciscan saints, and the Franciscan emblem crowned by a figure of Mary being adored by angels.

The interior of the church is decorated with frescoes, dating from 1894–5, by Károly Lotz and paintings by Victor Tardo Kremer, from 1925–6. The jewel of this church is the Baroque main altar with sculptures that date from 1741 and 1851. The side altars and the pulpit date from 1851–2.

Sculptures decorating the pulpit in the University Church

AROUND VÁROSLIGET

Városliget, or City Park, was once an area of marshland, which served as a royal hunting ground. Leopold I gave the land to the town of Pest, but it was in the mid-18th century, under Maria Theresa, that the area was drained and planted. Today's park was designed towards the end of the 19th century in the English style, which was the fashion of the

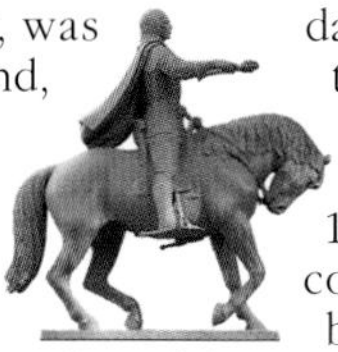

Statue of János Hunyadi

day. Városliget was chosen as the focus of the Millennium Celebrations in 1896 *(see p142)*, which marked the 1,000-year anniversary of the conquest of the Carpathian basin by the Magyars. A massive building programme was undertaken, which included the Museum of Fine Arts, Vajdahunyad Castle and the impressive monument in Heroes' Square.

SIGHTS AT A GLANCE

Museums
Ferenc Hopp Museum
of Far Eastern Art **6**
Franz Liszt Museum **2**
House of Terror Museum **1**
*Museum of Fine Arts
pp146–9* **9**
Műcsarnok Palace of Art **8**
Zoltán Kodály Museum **4**

Parks and Zoos
Funfair **12**
Zoo **11**

Streets and Monuments
Hermina Street **14**
Millennium Monument **7**
Városligeti Avenue **5**

Historic Buildings
University of Fine Art **3**
Erkel Theatre **15**
Széchenyi Baths **13**
Vajdahunyad Castle **10**

GETTING THERE
The M1 metro line runs under Andrássy út from Bajcsy-Zs Út to Hősök tere, while bus 4 runs along the street above. Trams, buses and the metro operate in the south of the area, around Thököly út.

KEY

▨	Street-by-Street map *See pp142–3*
Ⓜ	Metro station
⊠	Post office
🚆	Train station

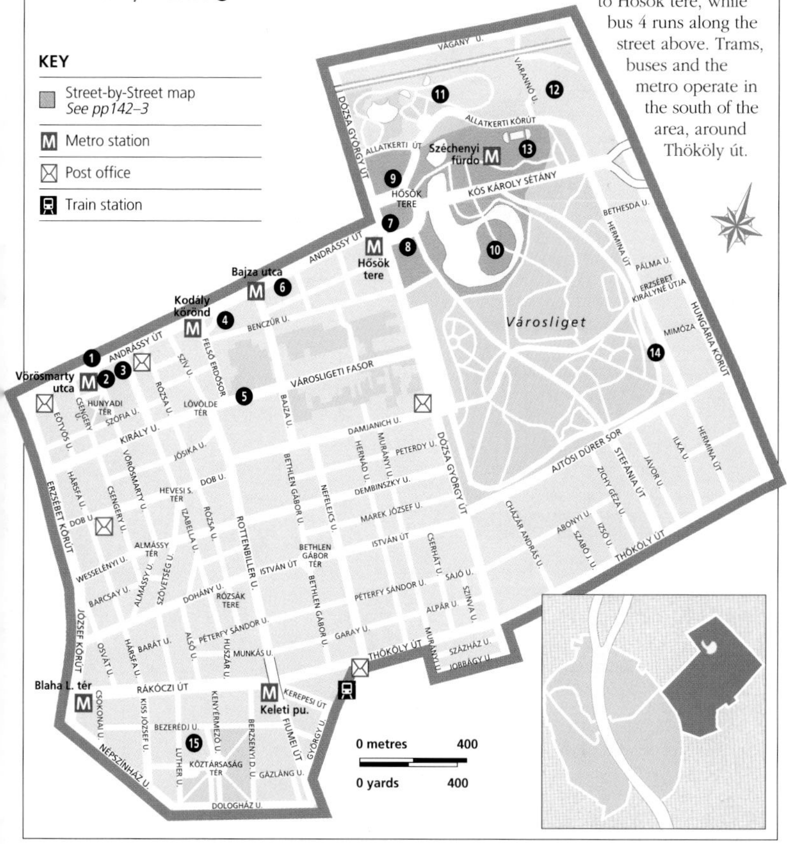

Városliget

Street-by-Street: Around Heroes' Square

Árpád, leader of
the Magyars

Heroes' Square is a relic of a proud era in Hungary's history. It was here that the Millennium Celebrations opened in 1896. A striking example of this national pride is the Millennium Monument. Its colonnades feature statues of renowned Hungarian leaders and politicians, and the grand central column is crowned by a figure of the Archangel Gabriel. Vajdahunyad Castle was built in Városliget, or City Park, adjacent to the square. Probably the most flamboyant expression of the celebrations, it is composed of elements of the finest architectural works found throughout Hungary.

★ **Museum of Fine Arts**
This monumental museum building has an eight-pillared portico supporting a tympanum ❾

Entrance
to the Zoo

Millennium Monument
Dominating Heroes' Square, this monument includes a figure of Rydwan, the god of war, by György Zala.

**Műcsarnok
Palace of Art**
The crest of Hungary decorates the façade of this building – the country's largest venue for artistic exhibitions ❽

Secession
pavilion

THE HUNGARIAN MILLENNIUM CELEBRATIONS

The Millennium Celebrations in 1896 marked a high point in the development of Budapest and in the history of the Austro-Hungarian monarchy. The city underwent modernization on a scale unknown in Europe at that time. Hundreds of houses, palaces and civic buildings were constructed, gas lighting was introduced and continental Europe's first underground transport system was opened.

Archangel
Gabriel

0 metres		200
0 yards		200

KEY

– – – Suggested route

★ **Széchenyi Baths**
This is the largest complex of spa baths in Europe. Its hot springs, discovered in 1876, bubble up from a depth of 970 m (3,180 ft) and are reputed to have considerable healing properties ⑬

LOCATOR MAP
See Street Finder, maps 5 & 6

Városliget

Ják Chapel
This chapel faithfully reproduces the portal of a Benedictine chapel, dating from 1214, which can be found in the area of Ják, near the border with Austria. It is part of the Vajdahunyad Castle complex.

Statue of Anonymous
Completed in 1903 by Miklós Ligeti, this is one of Budapest's most famous monuments.

★ **Vajdahunyad Castle**
This Baroque section of the castle houses the Museum of Agriculture ⑩

STAR SIGHTS

★ Museum of Fine Arts

★ Széchenyi Baths

★ Vajdahunyad Castle

The former headquarters of the secret police on Andrássy Avenue

House of Terror Museum ➊

TEROR HÁZA MÚZEUM

Andrássy út 60. **Map** 2 F5 (10 E2). *Tel* 374 26 00. Ⓜ Vörösmarty utca, 4,6 to Oktogon. ☐ 10am–6pm Tue–Fri, 10am–7:30pm Sat & Sun. www.terrorhaza.hu

The museum is located in the former headquarters of the secret police of both the Nazi and Communist governments. It records the grim events and practices of the "double occupation" of Hungary at the end of World War II.

Franz Liszt Museum ➋

LISZT FERENC EMLÉKMÚZEUM

Vörösmarty út 35. **Map** 5 A5. *Tel* 322 98 04. Ⓜ Vörösmarty utca. ☐ 10am–6pm Mon–Fri, 9am–5pm Sat. www.lisztmuzeum.hu

This Neo-Renaissance corner house was designed in 1877 by Adolf Lang. Above the windows of the second floor are bas-reliefs depicting famous composers – J S Bach, Wolfgang Amadeus Mozart, Joseph Haydn, Ferenc Erkel,

Ludwig van Beethoven, and Franz Liszt himself. Liszt not only lived in this house, but also established an Academy of Music in the city *(see p129)*.

In 1986, 100 years after Franz Liszt's death, this museum was established in his house. Various items were assembled here, including documents, furniture and two pianos on which he composed and practised his work.

University of Fine Art ➌

KÉPZŐMŰVÉSZETI EGYETEM

Andrássy út 69–71. **Map** 5 A5. *Tel* 342 17 38. Ⓜ Vörösmarty utca. **Barcsay Gallery** ☐ 10am–6pm Mon–Fri, 10am–1pm Sat. www.mke.hu

The university began as a drawing school, later becoming a Higher School of Art. Since 1876, it has occupied these adjacent buildings on Andrássy Street.

The two-floor Neo-Renaissance building at No. 71 was designed in 1875, by Lajos Rauscher. Its façade is decorated with sgraffiti by Robert Scholtz. The Italianate Renaissance exterior of No. 69, designed by Adolf Lang from 1875–7, is distinguished by Corinthian pilasters and a full-length balcony. The entrance hall and first-floor corridor feature frescoes by Károly Lotz. Only the Barcsay Gallery is open to visitors, but the interior can be glimpsed from here.

Sgrafitto by Robert Scholtz

Zoltán Kodály Museum ➍

KODÁLY ZOLTÁN EMLÉKMÚZEUM

Kodály Körönd 1. **Map** 5 B5. *Tel* 342 84 48. Ⓜ Kodály Körönd. ☐ 10am–4pm Wed, 10am–6pm Thu–Sat, 10am–2pm Sun. ● Mon, Tue. www.kodaly.hu/muzeum.htm

Zoltán Kodály (1881–1967) was one of the greatest Hungarian composers of the 20th century. His profound knowledge of Hungarian folk music allowed him to use elements of it in his compositions, which reflected the fashion for Impressionism and Neo-Romanticism in music.

This museum was established in 1990 and occupies the house where he lived and worked from 1924 until his death in 1967. A plaque set into one of the walls of the house bears testimony to this fact. The museum consists of three rooms that have been preserved in their original style, and a fourth room that is used for exhibitions. An archive has also been created here, for the composer's valuable handwritten music scores and correspondence.

Worthy of attention are the composer's piano in the salon and a number of folklore ceramics which Kodály collected in the course of his ethnographical studies. Portraits and busts of Kodály by Lajos Petri can also be viewed.

Városligeti Avenue ➎

VÁROSLIGETI FASOR

Map 5 C5. Ⓜ Hősök tere.

This beautiful street, lined with plane trees, leads from Lövölde tér to Városliget.

At the beginning of the avenue is a Calvinist church built in 1912–13 by Aladár Árkay. This stark edifice is virtually bereft of any architectural features. However, stylized, geometric folk motifs

Original furnishings in the salon in the Franz Liszt Museum

Chinese gate at the Ráth György Museum on Városligeti Avenue

have been used as ornamentation and harmonize with the interior Secession decoration.

In front of the church is the Ráth György Museum, part of the Ferenc Hopp Museum of Far Eastern Art, displaying artifacts from China and Japan collected in the 19th century.

Further along the avenue is a Lutheran church. It was constructed between 1903–5 to a Neo-Gothic design by Samu Pecz, who also designed the interior detail. Worthy of note is the painting on the high altar, by Gyula Benczúr, entitled *The Adoration of the Magi*.

Ferenc Hopp Museum of Far Eastern Art **❻**

HOPP FERENC KELET-ÁZSIAI MŰVÉSZETI MÚZEUM

Andrássy út 103. **Map** 5 B4. **Tel** 322 84 76. Ⓜ Bajza utca. ◯ 10am–6pm Tue–Sun. For guided tours call 456 51 00. **Ráth György Museum** Városligeti Fasor 12. **Tel** 342 39 16. ◯ 10am–6pm Tue–Sun.

Ferenc Hopp (1833–1919), a wealthy merchant and the proprietor of an opthalmic shop, was the first great Hungarian traveller, amassing a collection of more than 20,000 items from countries such as India, China and Vietnam.

The collection's smaller examples of art and handicrafts

can be seen in his former home, while its garden features large stone sculptures and architectural fragments.

The Chinese and Japanese collection is displayed in the **Ráth György Museum**.

Millennium Monument **❼**

MILLENIUMI EMLÉKMŰ

Map 5 C4. Ⓜ Hősök tere.

This monument was designed by György Zala and Albert Schikedanz to commemorate Hungary's Millennium Celebrations in 1896, but was not completed until 1929.

At the centre of the monument is a 36-m (120-ft) high Corinthian column, upon which stands the Archangel Gabriel holding St István's crown and the apostolic cross. These objects signify Hungary's conversion to Christianity under King István *(see p22)*. At the base of the column there are equestrian statues of Prince Árpád and six of the conquering Magyar warriors.

A stone tile set in front of the column marks the Tomb of the Unknown Soldier.

The column is embraced by two curved colonnades, featuring allegorical compositions at both ends. Personifications of War and Peace are nearest the column, while Knowledge and Glory crown the far end of the right-hand colonnade, and Labour and Prosperity crown the far end of the left. Statues of great Hungarians, including statesmen and monarchs, are arranged within the colonnades.

The right-hand colonnade of the Millennium Monument on Heroes' Square, completed in 1929

Museum of Fine Arts ❾

The origins of the Museum of Fine Arts' comprehensive collection date from 1870, when the state bought a magnificent collection of paintings from the artistocratic Esterházy family. The museum's collection was enriched by donations and acquisitions, and in 1906 it moved to its present location.

Grimani jug

The building, by Fülöp Herzog and Albert Schickedanz, is Neo-Classical with Italian-Renaissance influences. The tympanum crowning the portico is supported by eight Corinthian columns. It depicts the Battle of the Centaurs and Lapiths, and is copied from the Temple of Zeus at Olympia, Greece.

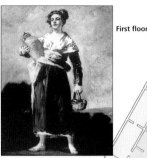

First floor

The Water Carrier *(c. 1810)*
La Aquadora *demonstrates the full range of Francisco de Goya's artistic talent.*

Satyr and Peasants *(c. 1620)*
The Flemish artist, Jacob Jordaens, worked alongside van Dyck and was Rubens' principal associate.

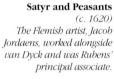

★ Esterházy Madonna *(c. 1508)*
This unfinished picture by Raphael is so named because it became the property of the Esterházy family at the beginning of the 19th century.

Lower ground floor

KEY

- ☐ Egyptian artefacts
- ☐ Classical artefacts
- ☐ German art
- ☐ Dutch art
- ☐ Flemish art
- ☐ Italian art
- ☐ Spanish art
- ☐ French and English art
- ☐ Drawings and graphic art
- ☐ 19th- and 20th-century works
- ☐ Temporary exhibitions

St James Conquers the Moors *(1750)*
Giambattista Tiepolo portrayed the miraculous appearance of the saint during a battle at Clavijo in 844.

View of Amsterdam

(c. 1656)
Jacob van Ruisdael was a master of Dutch realist landscape painting. He greatly influenced the development of European landscape painting in the 19th century.

Mother and Child

(1905)
The rare subtlety of this intensely intimate picture, by Pablo Picasso, is achieved using watercolour.

Second floor

★ **St John the Baptist's Sermon** *(1566)*
In this wonderful painting, Pieter Bruegel the Elder, a renowned observer of daily life, depicts a preacher addressing a group of peasants from Flanders.

Ground floor

These Women in the Refectory *(1894)*

This pastel sketch by the artist Henri de Toulouse-Lautrec, an observer and protagonist in the Parisian demi-monde, depicts prostitutes in a bar.

MUSEUM GUIDE

As a result of restoration work on the museum, begun in 1997, not all the rooms are currently open to the public. The works displayed are being moved as restoration work progresses.

STAR PAINTINGS

★ Esterházy Madonna

★ St John the
  Baptist's Sermon

Exploring the Museum of Fine Arts

The museum's collection encompasses international art dating from antiquity to the 20th century. As well as Egyptian, Greek and Roman artifacts, the museum houses galleries dedicated to a variety of modern art. Alongside its interesting collection of sculptures, there are priceless drawings and works of graphic art. Over the next few years the museum will be undergoing a process of redevelopment. In spite of this, exhibits will continue to be open to the public throughout the duration of the restoration work. Individual collections will simply be moved to different locations as building work progresses.

Egyptian head (c. 1200 BC)

Albrecht Dürer's simple yet beautiful *Portrait of a Young Man*

EGYPTIAN ARTEFACTS

Egyptian artefacts have been exhibited in the museum since 1939. Principally, they are the result of 19th-century excavations that involved Hungarian archaeologists.

The rich collection includes stone sculptures from each historic period, from the Old Kingdom to the Ptolemy dynasty. A nobleman's head of a votive statue dates from the New Kingdom and is a particularly beautiful example.

Also worthy of note is the collection of small bronze figures, which also date mainly from the New Kingdom, together with domestic objects that illustrate everyday life.

CLASSICAL ARTEFACTS

The collection of Classical artefacts is rather varied. It encompasses works of Greek, Etruscan, and Roman works.

Detail of a hunting scene on a 3rd-century AD Greek sarcophagus

The collection of Greek vases ranks as one of the best of its kind in Europe. A black-figure amphora by Exekias and a kylix from the studio of the painter Andokides are very fine examples of this work.

Bronze work, which dates from various epochs, including the famous Grimani jug from the 5th century BC, gold jewellery, and marble and terracotta sculptures are all exquisite artefacts from this era.

SCULPTURE

Undoubtedly the most valuable element of this collection is a small bronze sculpture by Leonardo da Vinci (1452–1519). This is an unusually dynamic representation of King François I of France on his horse. Other superb examples of Italian sculpture, by masters such as Andrea Pisano of the Ronni family, can also be seen.

Leonardo da Vinci's figure of François I

GERMAN ART

Among the most valuable works in the collection are the *Portrait of a Young Man*, by Albrecht Dürer, and the carefully composed painting of *The Dormition of Mary*, by Hans Holbein. The work of such masters as Hans Baldung Grien and Lucas Cranach are worth seeing, as is the collection of German and Austrian Baroque painting, which includes work by Franz Anton Maulbertsch.

DUTCH AND FLEMISH ART

The museum's Dutch and Flemish collection features works by the finest masters, including influential landscape artist, Jacob van Ruisdael, with *View of Amsterdam (see p147)*. The subtle *Nativity* by Gerard David and Pieter Bruegel's detailed masterpiece *St John the Baptist's Sermon (see p147)*, depicting Flemish peasants listening to the saint's words, are exemplary exhibits.

The museum also boasts canvases attributed to Rembrandt, including *St Joseph's Dream*, portraits by Frans Hals and Jan Vermeer's *Portrait of a Lady*. Not to be missed are the magnificent 17th-century Dutch paintings by artists including Adrian van Ostade, Jacob Ruisdael, Jan Steen and others.

The highlight of the Flemish collection is the 17th-century *Mucius Scaevola before Porsenna* by Peter Rubens and his then assistant, Anthony van Dyck. The latter was responsible for the picture of St John the Evangelist, also on display.

Also important are the paintings of Adam and Eve and *Satyr with Peasants* by Jacob Jordaens, who also worked as an assistant to Rubens.

ITALIAN ART

This valuable collection of Italian art, which was the core of the Esterházy family's collection, is often considered the museum's biggest attraction. All the schools of Italian painting, from the 13th to the 18th centuries, are on display here. The Renaissance period is perhaps the best represented.

Of particular note is the captivating *Esterházy Madonna (see p146)*, an unfinished painting by Raphael. Another great work by this outstanding artist is the *Portrait of Pietro Bembo*.

There is no shortage of work by famous 16th-century Venetian artists among the paintings collected here. Important works by Titian, Bonifazio Veronese, Antonio Correggio, Jacopo Tintoretto, Giorgione and Giovanni Boltraffio are all exhibited here. An excellent example of Baroque art is Giambattista Tiepolo's vast late 18th-century painting, *St James Conquers the Moors (see p146)*.

Giovanni Boltraffio's *Madonna and Child* (c. 1506)

SPANISH ART

The most important features of this collection are seven paintings by El Greco, including *The Annunciation, Christ in the Garden of Gethsemane* and *The Penance of St Mary Magdalene*, a subtle though fully expressive work.

The dramatic *Martyrdom of St Andrew* by Jusepe de Ribera should not be missed, nor the work of artists such as Diego

El Greco's *The Penance of St Mary Magdelene* (c. 1576)

Velázquez, Bartolomé Murillo and Francisco Zurbarán. Francisco de Goya's observations of daily life produced paintings such as *The Water Carrier (see p146)*, which also deserves special attention.

FRENCH AND ENGLISH ART

Works by French and English artists are not as numerous as Italian works, for example, but represent the various styles of the two countries.

French works include the well-composed *Resting on the Journey to Egypt* by Nicolas Poussin, *Villa in the Roman Countryside* by Claude Lorrain, and *Satyr and Peasants*, by the Flemish artist Jacob Jordaens *(see p146)*.

The collection of English paintings includes portraits by artists of the calibre of Joshua Reynolds, William Hogarth and Thomas Gainsborough.

DRAWINGS AND GRAPHIC ART

The collection of drawings and graphic art combines the work of old masters, including drawings by Leonard da Vinci, Raphael, Albrecht Dürer and Rembrandt, with pieces from artists of the 19th and 20th centuries. The collection is one of Europe's best.

19TH- AND 20TH-CENTURY WORKS

French painting makes up the largest constituent of the collection of 19th- and 20th-century art. The visitor can admire works by all the major painters of the time, including Pablo Picasso's *Mother and Child (see p147)*, Henri de Toulouse-Lautrec's *These Women in the Refectory (see p147)*, Gustave Courbet's *Wrestlers*, Edouard Manet's *Woman with a Fan* and Camille Pissarro's *Pont-Neuf*. Paul Gauguin's *Black Pigs*, one of his first Tahitian canvases, is also on display here. To complete the collection, the likes of Eugène Delacroix, Claude Monet, Pierre Bonnard, Pierre Renoir and Paul Cézanne are also represented.

Austrian and German 19th- and 20th-century art is represented with works by Waldmüller, Amerling, Lenbach, Leibl and Menzel.

Paul Cézanne's still life, *Credenza*, dating from 1874–7

The façade of the Palace of Art, featuring a six-columned portico

Műcsarnok Palace of Art ⑧

MŰCSARNOK

Hősök tere. **Map** 5 C4. *Tel* 363 26 71. Ⓜ *Hősök tere.* ◯ 10am–6pm Tue–Sun noon–8pm Thu. 🖼 ♿ ☑

Situated on the southern side of Heroes' Square, opposite the Museum of Fine Arts *(see pp146–9)*, is Hungary's largest exhibition space. Temporary exhibitions of mainly contemporary painting and sculpture are held here.

The imposing Neo-Classical building, which was designed by Albert Schickedanz and Fülöp Herzog in 1895, is fronted by a vast six-columned portico. The mosaic, depicting St István as the patron saint of fine art, was added to the tympanum between 1938–41. Behind the portico is a fresco in three parts by Lajos Deák Ébner: *The Beginning of Sculpture, The Source of Arts* and *The Origins of Painting*.

Museum of Fine Arts ⑨

SZÉPMŰVÉSZETI MÚZEUM

See pp146–9.

Vajdahunyad Castle ⑩

VAJDAHUNYAD VÁRA

Városliget. **Map** 6 D4. *Tel* 363 19 73. **Museum of Agriculture** *Tel* 343 05 73. ◯ Mid-Mar–Oct: 10am–5pm Tue, Fri & Sun, 10am–6pm Sat; Nov–mid-Mar: 10am–4pm Tue, Fri & Sun, 10am–5pm Sat. ◯ Mon. 🖼 ♿ ☑ **www.**mmgm.hu

This fairytale-like building is located among the trees at the edge of the lake in Városliget. Not a genuine castle but a complex of buildings reflecting various architectural styles, it was designed by Ignác Alpár for the 1896 Millennium Celebrations *(see p142)*.

Alpár's creation illustrated the history and evolution of architecture in Hungary. Originally intended as temporary exhibition pavilions, the castle proved so popular with the public that, between 1904–6, it was rebuilt using brick to create a permanent structure.

The pavilions are grouped in chronological order of style: Romanesque is followed by Gothic, Renaissance, Baroque and so on. The individual styles were linked together to give the impression of a single, cohesive

design. Each of the pavilions use authentic details copied from Hungary's most important historic buildings or are a looser interpretation of a style inspired by a specific architect of that historic period.

The Romanesque complex features a copy of the portal from a chapel in Ják *(see p143)* as well as a monastic cloister and palace. The details on the Gothic pavilion have been taken from castles like those in Vajdahunyad and Segesvár (both now in Romania). The architect Fischer von Erlach was the inspiration for the Renaissance and Baroque complex. The façade copies part of the Bakócz chapel in the cathedral at Esztergom *(see p164)*.

The Museum of Agriculture can be found in the Baroque section. It has exhibits on cattle breeding, wine-making, hunting and fishing.

The entire complex reflects more than 20 of Hungary's most renowned buildings. The medieval period, often considered the most glorious time in Hungary's history, is given greatest emphasis, while the controversial Habsburg era is pushed into the background.

Zoo ⑪

FŐVÁROSI ÁLLAT-ÉS NÖVÉNYKERT

Állatkerti körút 6–12. **Map** 5 C3. *Tel* 363 37 10. Ⓜ *Széchenyi fürdő.* ◯ Mar–Oct: 9am–6pm daily; Nov–Feb 9am–4pm daily. 🖼 **www.**zoobudapest.com

Budapest's zoo is one of the city's great attractions. It was established in 1866 by the Hungarian Academy of Sciences *(see p114)*. In 1907 it was bought by the State and totally redeveloped,

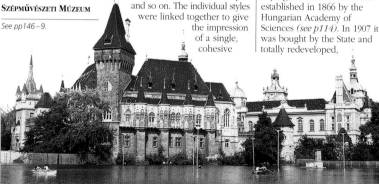

View across the lake of the Gothic (left) and Renaissance (right) sections of Vajdahunyad Castle

between 1909–11, by Károly Kós and Dezső Zrumeczky.

The animals are housed in enclosures most of which strive to mimic their natural habitat. The elephant house, however, by Kórnel Neuschloss-Knüsli, is a fine example of Secession style. Károly Kós, on the other hand, adopted a folk style for the aviary, in which a wide variety of birds fly freely.

One of the outdoor pools at the beautiful Széchenyi Baths

Funfair ⑫

VIDÁMPARK

Állatkerti körút 14–16. **Map** 6 D2.
Tel 363 83 10. Ⓜ Széchenyi fürdő.
Ⓞ Apr–Sep: 10am–8pm daily.
www.vidampark.hu

In 1878 there was already a carousel here, along with games and theatrical shows.

Today it is a charmingly un-sophisticated amusement park with an assortment of old-fashioned rides. Next door is a smaller funfair for toddlers.

There are numerous kiosks, bars and restaurants serving food, so it is easy to spend the entire day here. The circus is also close by *(see p219)*.

Széchenyi Baths ⑬

SZÉCHENYI STRANDFÜRDŐ

Állatkerti körút 11. **Map** 6 D3.
Tel 363 32 10. Ⓜ Széchenyi fürdő.
Ⓞ May–Sep: 6am–7pm daily;
Oct–Apr: 6am–5pm daily.
www.budapestspas.hu

A statue stands at the main entrance to the Széchenyi Baths depicting geologist Vilmos Zsigmond, who dis-covered a hot spring here while drilling a well in 1879.

The Széchenyi Baths are the deepest and hottest baths in Budapest – the water reaches the surface at a temperature of 74–5° C (180° F). The springs, rich in minerals, are distinguished by their alleged healing properties. They are recommended for treating rheumatism and disorders of the nervous system, joints and muscles. The spa, housed in a

Neo-Baroque building by Győző Cziegler and Ede Dvorzsák, was constructed in 1909–13. In 1926, three open-air swimming pools were added. The pools are popular all year due to the high temperature of the water. Bathing caps are required.

Hermina Street ⑭

HERMINA ÚT

Map 6 E3, 6 E4 & 6 F4. 🚌 70.
Transport Museum *Tel* 273 38 40.
Ⓞ Jan–Apr: 10am–4pm Tue–Thu,
10am–5pm Sat & Sun; May–Sep:
10am–5pm Tue–Sun; Oct–Dec:
10am–5pm Sat & Sun. Ⓜ Year-round:
Mon; Jan–Apr: Mon & Fri.

This beautiful street is worth walking along to experience the romantic atmosphere of the historic, elegant villas in this area. Particularly notable is the unusual Secession building at No. 47, Sipeky Balázs Villa *(see p55)*, built in 1905–6 by architects Ödön Lechner, Marcell Komor and Dezső Jakab. The asymmetric design of the villa's façade includes features

A steam train exhibited at the Transport Museum, just off Hermina Street

such as a domed glass conser-vatory, an ironwork porch and a tall, narrow side tower. The villa's exterior decoration is inspired by national folk art.

Hermina Chapel at No. 23, by József Hild, was built in 1842–6 in memory of Palatine József's daughter, Hermina Amália, who died in 1842.

Backing onto Hermina Street, at No. 11 Városligeti körút, is the Transport Museum with exhibits on the evolution of air, sea, road and rail trans-port. Among the trains, helicopters and aeroplanes are some pre-World War II right-hand-drive cars.

Poster for a gala ballet
performance at the Erkel Theatre

Erkel Theatre ⑮

ERKEL SZÍNHÁZ

Köztarsaság ter 30. **Map** 7 C3.
Tel 333 01 08. Ⓜ Keleti pu.

An alternative venue of the National Opera Company, this is the largest theatre in Hungary, seating 2,500 people. Designed in 1911 by Marcell Komor, Dezső Jakab and Géza Márkus, its current form dates from the 1950s. Concerts and operas are performed here.

FURTHER AFIELD

Budapest is a sprawling city and several sights on its periphery are well worth a visit. North from the centre of Buda are the fascinating ruins of Aquincum, a town founded by the Romans in approximately AD 100. To the west, the city is skirted by wooded hills, which offer walks around beautiful nature reserves and exciting cave visits. Out

Roman urn from Aquincum

to the east of Pest is Kerepesi Cemetery, where a host of famous Hungarians are buried. To the south of the city is the Nagytétény Palace, one of the most beautiful Baroque palaces in Hungary. The new setting for Socialist-era statues, the Park of Monuments, is not far from the palace. All the sights can be reached easily using public transport.

SIGHTS AT A GLANCE

Museums
Aquincum **25**
Gizi Bajor Theatre Museum **19**
Palace of Arts **10**

Historic Buildings and Monuments
Geology Institute **4**
Ludovika Academy **9**
Nagytétény Palace Museum **23**
Raoul Wallenberg
  Monument **1**
Statue Park **21**
Technical University **16**
Törley Mausoleum **22**
Wekerle Estate **15**

Parks and Recreation Areas
Buda Hills **24**
Congress and World Trade
  Centre **18**
Eagle Hill Nature Reserve **20**
Ferenc Puska's Stadium **5**
Railway History Park **11**
Szemlő-hegy and Pál-völgy
  Caves **2**
University Botanical Gardens **8**

Cemeteries
Jewish Cemetery **14**
Kerepesi Cemetery **6**
Municipal Cemetery **13**

Churches
Cistercian Church of St Imre **17**
Józsefváros Parish Church **7**
Kőbánya Parish Church **12**
Újlak Parish Church **3**

KEY

▨	City centre
▢	Greater Budapest
✈	Airport
🚉	Train station
▬	Motorway
▭	Main road
—	Railway

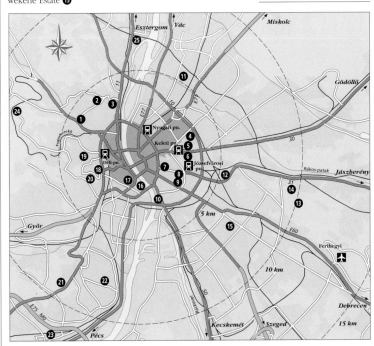

◁ The huge 19th-century Catholic cathedral at Esztergom, overlooking the Danube *(see p164)*

Raoul Wallenberg Monument **❶**

RAOUL WALLENBERG SZOBOR

Szilágyi Erzsébet fasor.
🚊 56.

Tucked away at the junction of Szilágyi Erzsébet fasor and Nagyajtai utca, is this monument to an heroic but little known figure of World War II. Raoul Wallenberg was a Swedish diplomat who used his position to save over 20,000 Hungarian Jews from the extermination camps. He set up safe houses in the city and obtained fake Swedish documents for them.

Following the liberation of Budapest by the Soviet army, Wallenberg disappeared. It is thought he was arrested by the KGB and sent to a prison camp where he died. The memorial, by sculptor Imre Varga, was erected in 1987.

Szemlő-hegy and Pál-völgy Caves **❷**

SZEMLŐ-HEGYI-BARLANG ÉS
PÁL-VÖLGYI-CSEPPKŐBARLANG

Szemlő-hegy Cave Pusztaszeri út 35. **Tel** 325 60 01. 🚌 29. ◯ 10am–4pm Wed–Mon. 🖼 ♿ 📷
Pál-völgy Cave Szépvölgyi út 162. **Tel** 325 95 05. 🚌 65. ◯ 10am–4pm Tue–Sun. 🖼 📷

To the north of Budapest lies the Pilis mountain range, formed of limestone and dolomite. Natural geological processes which occur within these mountains have created some picturesque caves, two of which are unusual tourist attractions.

Szemlő-hegy Cave features extraordinary formations called "cave pearls", produced when hot spring waters penetrate its limestone walls. There are guided tours every hour.

In Pál-völgy Cave, strange formations protruding from the rock face resemble animals.

It is a good idea to wear warm clothes when visiting the caves as they are cold and damp. Some claim, however, that the atmosphere in the caves has a therapeutic effect on the respiratory system.

The Baroque interior of Újlak Parish Church, dating from 1756

Újlak Parish Church **❸**

ÚJLAKI PLÉBÁNIATEMPLOM

Bécsi út 32.
🚊 17.

Bavarian settlers first built a small church here early in the 18th century. The present church, designed by Kristóf Hamon and Mátyás Nepauer, was finished in 1756. Its tower was added some years later.

In the Baroque interior there is a depiction of the Madonna, a gift from the inhabitants of Passau to the church. The main altar, dating from 1798, also includes

a painting entitled *The Visitation*, which was the work of Francis Falkoner.

Not far away, at Zsigmond tér, stands the Holy Trinity Column, built in 1691 as a memorial to the city's earliest plague epidemic. The Baroque monument is the work of two Italian sculptors, Venerio Cresola and Bernard Feretti, and was moved from central Buda to Újlak in 1712.

Geology Institute **❹**

FÖLDTANI INTÉZET

Stefánia út 14. **Map** 8 F1. **Tel** 251 09 99. 🚊 75, 77. **Museum** ◯ 10am–4pm Thu, Sat & Sun. 📷

This beautiful and unusual building, housing the Geology Institute, dates from 1898–9 and was designed by Ödön Lechner *(see p56)*.

Lechner's very individual Secession style, also known as the Hungarian National Style, is on show here including motifs drawn from Hungarian Renaissance architecture.

On the picturesque elevations and gables of the building pale yellow plaster walls form a striking contrast to the brick-work quoins and window frames. Here and there Zsolnay blue glazed ceramic ornaments adorn the walls and harmonize with the blue roof tiles. The central pitched roof is topped by three

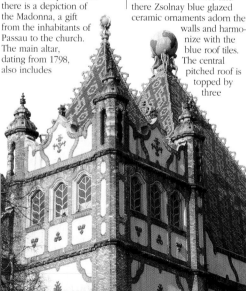

The Geology Institute, with its stunning blue ceramic roof

human figures bent under the weight of a large globe.

Inside the Geology Institute, there is a small museum with rock and mineral exhibits. Lechner's Secession interiors have been carefully preserved in their original condition. The central hall, which is particularly magnificent, can be seen when visiting the museum or on its own with the caretaker's permission.

Ferenc Puska's Stadium ❺

PUSKA'S FERENC STADION

Kerepesi út. **Map** 8 F1. *Tel* 471 43 21. 23, 24, 36. 8am–2pm Mon–Thu, 8am–noon Fri.

Hungary's biggest sports stadium was recently renamed after a national football hero. It was built between 1948–53, to a design by Károly Dávid. The roofless structure seats 78,000, but generally only fills to capacity when a major pop group plays. The entrance is at the end of the "Avenue of Youth", which is lined with Stalinist-era statues, depicting various sports, by well-known Hungarian sculptors including Imre Varga and István Tar.

Kerepesi Cemetery ❻

KEREPESI TEMETŐ

Fiumei út 16–20. **Map** 8 E3. 23, 24, 36.

For more than 150 years since it was established in 1847, the Kerepesi Cemetery has provided the resting place for many of Hungary's most prominent citizens. Fine tombstones mark the graves of some, while others were interred here inside monumental mausoleums.

The mausoleum of the leader of the 1848–9 uprising, Lajos Kossuth (*see p106*) is by Alajos Stróbl, while that of Lajos Batthyány, the first prime minister of Hungary (*see p31*) is the work of Albert Schickedanz.

Ferenc Deák, who formulated the Compromise with Austria (*see p32*), is among the other statesmen buried here.

Also at the cemetery are the graves of poets Endre Ady and Attila József (*see p106*), writers Kálmán Mikszáth Zsigmond Móricz and actors such as Lujza Blaha, whose tomb is particularly beautiful. Sculptors, painters and composers are buried close to great architects, including Alajos Stróbl, Ödön Lechner and Alajos Hauszmann.

Hungarian Communists, including László Rajk (*see p34*), who were sentenced to death in the show trials of 1949, were buried in a separate part of the cemetery. Their funerals inspired a revolutionary spirit which, a few years later, led to the 1956 Uprising (*see p34*).

Józsefváros Parish Church ❼

JÓZSEFVÁROS PLÉBÁNIATEMPLOM

Horváth Mihály tér 7. **Map** 7 C4. *Tel* 313 61 26. 83. 9, 17.

The building work on this Baroque church began in 1797. It was not completed until 1814, by Fidél Kasselik. At the end of 19th century further additions were made to the structure.

The main altar is by József Hild. A formidable architectural composition, it is based on a triumphal arch. This frames a magnificent painting, *The*

The late Baroque façade of Józsefváros Parish Church

Apotheosis of St Joseph, by Leopold Kupelwieser, an Austrian artist. The church also has two beautiful, late Baroque side altars.

University Botanical Gardens ❽

EGYETEMI BOTANIKUS KERT

Illés utca 25. **Map** 8 D5. *Tel* 314 05 35. Klinikák. **Garden** Nov–Mar: 9am–4pm; Apr–Oct: 9am–5pm. **Glasshouses** noon–1pm.

Gardens were first established on this 3-ha (8-acre) site by the Festetics family. Their modest, early Neo-Classical villa is now the administration centre for the botanical gardens. It was built in 1802–3, most probably to a design by Mihály Pollack. The smoking room in the villa houses a huge collection of tropical plants. These include the striking *Victoria regia*, which flowers once a year. The Hungarian author Ferenc Molnár (1878–1952) used the gardens as a setting in his novel, *The Paul Street Boys*, although the lake mentioned in the book no longer exists. Not far away are Pál utca (Paul Street) and Mária utca, the scene of a battle the boys fought (prior to the invasion of tenement blocks).

BLAHA LUJZA 1850 — 1926.

The tomb of actress Lujza Blaha at Kerepesi Cemetery

Ludovika Academy ❾

LUDOVIKA AKADÉMIA

Ludovika tér 2–6. Ⓜ *Klinikák.*
Tel 210 10 85. ◯ *10am–5pm
Wed–Mon.* **Natural History
Museum** ◯ *10am–6pm Wed–
Mon.* 🎫 ♿ **www**.nhmus.hu

The huge Ludovika Academy
is in district IX, east of the
city centre. It was designed in
the 1830s by Mihály Pollack,
the famous architect of the
Hungarian National Museum
(see pp130–33). A military
academy until 1945, it is an
impressive example of Neo-
Classical style, with many
original features intact. It is
now home to the city's
Natural History Museum.

The impressive open-space interior of
the Palace of Arts, a cultural hub

Palace of Arts ❿

MŰVÉSZETEK PALOTÁJA

Komor Marcell utca 1. 🚊 *1, 2, 2A,
24.* **Tel** *555 30 00, 333 33 01 or
555 33 00* ◯ *10am–10pm daily.*
www.mupa.hu **Ticket Office** *(for
all events)* ◯ *1–6pm Mon–Sat,
10am–6pm Sun.* **www**.jegyelado.hu

The Palace of Arts in the
Millennium City Centre,
located on the Pest side of
the Danube between the
Lágymányos bridge and the
new National Theatre, brings
together the different
branches of the arts under
one roof. Permanent residents
include the Ludwig Museum
of Contemporary Art, the
National Philharmonic
Orchestra and the National
Dance Theatre.

Railway History Park ⓫

VASÚTTÖRTÉNETI PARK

Tatai út 95. Ⓜ *Klinikák.* **Tel** *450 14
97.* ◯ *Mid–end Mar: 10am–3pm
Tue–Sun; Apr–Sep: 10am–6pm;
Nov–Dec: 10am–3pm Tue–Sun.*
⬤ *Mon, 19 Dec–mid-Mar.* 🎫 ♿
www.mavnosztalgia.hu

This open-air museum of
railway history is one of
Europe's largest. Set in a large
park, it boasts around 100
locomotives – most fully
functioning – dating from the
early days of steam to
modern times. Visitors have
the opportunity to drive a
steam train, play with a
model railway and ride in a
line-inspection car. Every
year, the legendary *Orient
Express* makes several visits
here. The park is popular with
families as well as enthusiasts,
and there is a full programme
of events for children.

Kőbánya Parish Church ⓬

KŐBÁNYAI PLÉBÁNIATEMPLOM

Szent László tér. 🚋 *13, 28.*
🚌 *17, 32, 62, 185.* ♿

An industrial suburb on the
eastern side of Pest, Kőbánya
is the unexpected home of the
beautiful Kőbánya Parish
Church. Designed by Ödön
Lechner *(see p56)* in the 1890s,
the church makes magnificent
use of the architect's favourite
materials, including vibrant
roof tiles developed and
produced at the now-
famous Zsolnay factory in
the town of Pécs. Like
much of Lechner's
work, including the
Museum of Applied
Arts *(see pp136–7)*,
the church com-
bines motifs and
colours from
Hungarian folk
art with Neo-
Gothic elements.
Inside the church,
both the altar and
the pulpit are
superb examples
of early 20th-
century wood

Gleaming ceramic tiles on the
roof of Kőbánya Parish Church

carving. Somehow surviving
heavy World War II bombing,
a number of Miksa Roth's
original stained-glass windows
are still in place.

Municipal Cemetery ⓭

RÁKOSKERESZTÚR

See pp158–9.

Jewish Cemetery ⓮

ZSIDÓ TEMETŐ

Kozma út. 🚌 *37.*

Next door to the Municipal
Cemetery is the Jewish
Cemetery, opened in 1893.
The many grand tombs here
are a vivid reminder of the
vigour and success
of Budapest's pre-war
Jewish community. At
the end of the 19th
century, nearly a
quarter of the city's
inhabitants were
Jewish. Tombs
to look out for
as you stroll
among the
graves include
that of the
Wellisch family,
designed in
1903 by Arthur
Wellisch, and
that of Konrád
Polnay, which

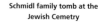

Schmidl family tomb at the
Jewish Cemetry

was designed five years later by Gyula Fodor. Perhaps the most eyecatching of all belongs to the Schmidl family. The startlingly flamboyant tomb, designed in 1903 by architects Ödön Lechner and Béla Lajta, is covered in vivid turquoise ceramic tiles. The central mosaic in green and gold tiles represents the Tree of Life.

Wekerle Estate

WEKERLE TELEP

Kós Károly tér. Ⓜ Határ út, then 194.

Out in district XIX, the Wekerle Estate was built between 1909 and 1926, and represents a bold and successful experiment in 20th-century social planning. Named after Prime Minister Sándor Wekerle, the estate was originally known as the Kispest Workers and Clerks Settlement and was built to provide better housing for local workers.

Designed by a group of young architects, students of Ödön Lechner, the buildings have a uniquely Hungarian style. Seeking inspiration from medieval peasant buildings, the architects would visit rural locations, gathering together architectural details in the same way that Béla Bartók and Zoltán Kodály *(see p144)*

Façade of the Technical University, as seen from the Danube

collected folk songs. Other key influences were the English Arts and Crafts movement, and early English new towns such as Hampstead Garden Suburb in London.

Conceived as a self-contained village, the estate enjoys many of its own amenities, including a Catholic church, several schools, a cinema and a police station. Fanning out around Kós Károly tér, 16 types of family house and apartment block are separated by tree-lined streets. Wooden gables and balconies, and sharply pitched, brightly tiled roofs, contribute to the estate's lively and eclectic atmosphere.

Rents on the Wekerle Estate are now high, though the area manages to retain much of its working-class spirit.

Technical University ⑯

BUDAPESTI MŰSZAKI EGYETEM

Műegyetem rakpart 3. **Map** 4 F4.
Tel 463 11 11. 🚊 4, 6, 18, 19, 47, 49. 🚌 7, 86.

Founded in 1857, the city's Technical University moved to its present site in 1904. Built on reclaimed marshland, the imposing building over-looks the Danube just south of Gellért Hill *(see pp88–9)*. Extended at the end of World War II, it is now the largest higher education establishment in Hungary. Former students include Imre Steindl, the architect of the Parliament building *(see pp108–9)*, and the richest and most widely known graduate to date, Ernő Rubik, inventor of the Rubik Cube.

Cistercian Church of St Imre ⑰

CISZTERCITA SZENT IMRE PLÉBÁNIATEMPLOM

Villányi út 25. **Map** 3 C4. 🚊 61. 🚌 27, 40. 🅰

Not far from the Technical University is the Cistercian Church of St Imre. The vast Neo-Baroque structure with its double tower was built in 1938 and is typical of the grand and rather sombre architecture in vogue in Budapest during the inter-war years.

Inside the church are relics of St Imre, canonized at the end of the 11th century. Other patron saints of the Cistercian order are depicted above the church's main entrance.

A police station on the early 20th-century Wekerle Estate

Municipal Cemetery ⑬

A new, historic significance was gained
by the Municipal Cemetery following the
1956 Uprising *(see p35)*. Here, at
Budapest southeastern limits, the leaders
and victims of this bloody revolution
against the oppressive Stalinist government
were secretly buried in mass graves. During the 1970s, the country's democratic
opposition began placing flowers on the
site, at the far side of the cemetery. In
1990, after the fall of Communism, the
revolutionary heroes were given a ceremonial funeral and reburied, and several
memorials were set up to them.

View of Plot 300
*Until 1989, the state militia guarded
access to a thicket which covered the
communal graves of the heroes of
the 1956 Uprising.*

Campanile
*A wooden campanile is the type of decoration
often found in old Hungarian cemeteries.
It stands in front of panels listing the names
of over 400 victims of the 1956 Uprising,
giving the exact locations of their graves.*

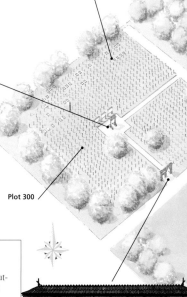

Plot 300

PLAN OF THE CEMETERY

In 1886, the city authorities opened a vast, new
municipal cemetery in Rákoskeresztúr, on the outskirts of town. It became the largest cemetery in
Budapest, occupying 30 sq km (12 sq miles).

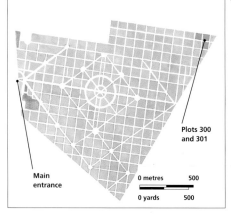

Plots 300
and 301

Main
entrance

0 metres	500
0 yards	500

★ **Transylvanian Gate**
*The 1956 Uprising Combatants'
Association erected the carved
Transylvanian Gate which stands
at the beginning of one of the paths
leading into plot 300. It is inscribed
with the words: "Only a Hungarian
soul may pass through this gate".*

★ **Imre Nagy's Grave**
A marble slab bears the modest inscription: "Imre Nagy, Prime Minister of Hungary, 1956". Arrested after the uprising, Nagy was interned and shot dead on 16 June 1956 in Budapest, following a bogus political trial.

NAGY IMRE
MAGYARORSZÁG
MINISZTERELNÖKE
1 9 5 6

VISITORS' CHECKLIST

Kozma utca 8–10, Kőbánya.
95 from Zalka Máté tér.
Plots 300 and 301 *30 mins walk from the main gate.*
Fee charged for cars.

Plot 301

Christ the Sorrowful
A figure of Christ the Sorrowful is traditionally placed in a plot containing Protestant graves.

★ **Heroes' Monument**
This simple monument symbolizes the passage through purgatory. It was created by the leading modern Hungarian sculptor, György Jovánovics.

Protestant Graves
The tradition of Hungarian Protestants is to place a simple wooden post to mark each grave.

STAR SIGHTS

★ Heroes' Monument

★ Imre Nagy's Grave

★ Transylvanian Gate

View from Eagle Hill Nature Reserve, down across the smart residential quarter below

Congress & World Trade Centre ⓲

KONGRESSZUSI ÉS VILÁGKERESKEDELMI KÖZPONT

Jagelló út 1–3. **Tel** 372 57 00.
📷 61. 🔲 For events. www.bc.hu

Opened in 1975, this large arts complex houses a concert hall, a cinema, conference rooms and several restaurants. It host international conferences and events, as well as the annual Hungarian Film Festival (see p61). It was designed, with the neighbouring Novotel Budapest Congress (see p189), by the architect József Finta. The *Tree of Life* decorating the main wall of the Congress Hall is by József Király.

Gizi Bajor Theatre Museum ⓳

BAJOR GIZI SZÍNÉSZMÚZEUM

Stromfeld Aurél út 16.
Tel 356 42 94. 📷 105.
🔲 2–6pm Thu–Sun. 📷 📷

This museum was opened in 1952, in a garden villa which once belonged to Gizi Bajor, a leading Hungarian actress of her day. Its exhibits, which include furniture, portraits, theatrical props, fans and velvet gloves, transport visitors to the world of the theatre in the 19th century.
In 1990, the 200th anniversary of theatre in Hungary, the museum's collection was further extended, to include mementoes of well-known contemporary Hungarian

actors, after whom some of the museum's rooms are named.
The garden features the busts of several writers together with a number of other leading figures in Hungary's cultural history.

Eagle Hill Nature Reserve ⓴

SASHEGY TERMÉSZETVÉLDEMI TERÜLET

Tájék utca 26. **Tel** 319 67 89.
📷 8, 8A. 🔲 Mid-Mar–mid-June & Sep–mid-Oct: 10am–4pm Sat & Sun.
📷 compulsory.

A nature reserve more or less in the centre of a city of two million inhabitants is a remarkable phenomenon.
Access to the summit of this steep, 266-m (872-ft) high hill to the west of Gellért Hill (see pp88–9) is strictly regulated to protect the extremely rare animal and plant species found here. A smart residential quarter, which lies on the lower slope of Eagle Hill, extends almost to the fence of the reserve and the craggy 30-ha wilderness that it encloses.
It is well worth taking a guided walk, particularly in spring or early autumn. Only here is it possible to see *centaurea sadleriana*, a flower resembling a cornflower but much bigger. The reserve is also home to a type of spider not found anywhere else in the world, as well as to extraordinary, colourful butterflies and to *ablebharus kitaibeli*, a rare lizard.

Statue Park ㉑

SZOBOR PARK

Balatoni út & Szabadkai utca.
Tel 424 75 00. 📷 50. 🔲 10am–dusk daily. 📷 www.szoborpark.hu

In 1991, Budapest's City Council decided to gather in one place 41 Communist monuments which had formerly occupied prestigious locations in the city. The park where they can be viewed is now a popular attraction for visitors to the city who are curious about its recent past.
The competition for the design of the park was won by architect Ákos Eleöd and it opened to the public in 1993. Behind a red-brick wall, six rings of monuments are arrayed on the site. Statues of Karl Marx, Friedrich Engels, VI Lenin and Hungarian Communist heroes stand side by side, headed by the leader of the 1919 revolution in Hungary (see p34), Béla Kun. A statue of a Russian soldier removed from the Liberation Monument (see p92) can also be seen in the park.
The park has its own shop which sells books, posters and other paraphenalia connected with the Communist era.

Cubist-style statues of Marx and Engels in the Statue Park

The marble Törley Mausoleum

Törley Mausoleum ㉒
TÖRLEY MAUZOLEUM

Sarló utca 6. 🚋 3.

Until 1880 Budafok had a number of vineyards, but their cultivation was destroyed in that year by a plague of phylloxera (American aphid). It was then that József Törley, who had studied wine-making in Reims, started to produce sparkling wine in Budafok using the French model (*see p194*). His wines sold well abroad and he quickly expanded his enterprise, storing the wines in the local cellars.

József Törley died in 1900 and was laid to rest in this monumental mausoleum designed by Rezső Vilmos Ray. Constructed of white marble, it is adorned with Eastern motifs and bas-reliefs by József Damkó.

Nagytétény Palace Museum ㉓
NAGYTÉTÉNYI KASTÉLY MÚZEUM

Kastélypark utca 9–11. *Tel 207 00 05 ext. 105.* 🚋 41. ⏱ 10am–6pm Tue–Sun. 📷 🎫 In period costume, by arrangement. **www**.nagytetenyi

This is one of the best known Baroque palaces in Hungary. Nagytétény Palace was built in the mid-18th century, incorporating the remains of a 15th-century Gothic building. The work was started by György Száraz and completed by his son-in-law,

József Rudnyánszky, acquiring its final shape in 1766. Based on the typical Baroque layout, it includes a main block and side wings. The coping features the Száraz and Rudnyánszky family crests.

The palace suffered severe damage during World War II, but the original wall paintings and furnishings survived. In 1949, the palace was rebuilt and turned into an interior design museum. Now it is a department of the Museum of Applied Arts (*see pp136–7*). On display are fine pieces of Hungarian and European furniture from the 15th–18th centuries, early 19th-century paintings and more functional items, such as tiled stoves.

Standing close to the palace is an 18th-century Baroque church, built on the remains of a medieval church. Original Gothic features incorporated in it include the window openings in its tower and three supports on the outer wall of the presbytery.
In 1760, the Austrian artist Johann Gfall created the painting in the dome which features illusory galleries. The altars, pulpit and baptistries also date back to the mid-18th century.

Buda Hills ㉔
BUDAI-HEGYSÉG

Ⓜ *Moszkva tér, then* 🚌 *56, then cog-wheel railway and chair lift.*

To the west of the city centre are the wooded Buda Hills where Budapesters come to walk and relax.

The first station of a cog-wheel railway, built in 1874, is on Szilágyi Erzsébet fasor. This runs up Sváb Hill – named after the Germanic Swabians, who settled here under the Habsburgs (*see p28*) – and then Széchenyi Hill.

From Széchenyi Hill a narrow-gauge railway covers a 12-km (7-mile) route to the Hűvös Valley. As in the days of the Soviet Young Pioneers movement, the railway is entirely staffed by children, apart from the adult train drivers. At the top of János Hill stands the Erzsébet Look-Out Tower, designed by Frigyes Schulek in 1910. A chair lift also connects the summit of János Hill with Zugligeti út and is a good way of making the descent.

Aquincum ㉕
AQUINCUM

See pp162–3.

The Erzsébet Look-Out Tower at the summit of János Hill

Aquincum 🄯

The remains of the Roman town of Aquincum *(see p20–21)* were excavated at the end of the 19th century. Visitors are free to stroll along its streets, viewing the outlines of temples, shops, baths and houses, in what was once the centre of the town. This civilian town was founded at the beginning of the 2nd century AD, a couple of decades after a legionary fortress *(see pp170–71)* was established to its south. In the centre of the site there is a Neo-Classical museum displaying the most valuable Roman archaeological finds. On the other side of the road are the remains of an amphitheatre, where Aquincum's inhabitants once sought entertainment.

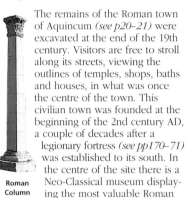

Roman Column

View Towards the Museum
The area opened to visitors is only a fragment of a much bigger town.

★ Public Baths
The walls of the thermal baths are immaculately preserved. Visiting the baths was a social event for the Romans.

Central Heating System
Archaeologists have here unearthed the Roman version of central heating, an under-floor system in which hot air was circulated under mosaic floors.

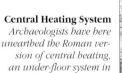

★ Macellum
This was the covered market hall. Having stalls positioned around a cool inner courtyard kept the produce fresh and made shopping comfortable all year round (see pp20–21).

STAR SIGHTS

★ Macellum

★ Museum

★ Public Baths

★ Museum
This Neo-Classical Lapidarium is part of the museum, which houses an exhibition of objects found at Aquincum and at other Roman sites nearby. These include weapons and inscribed stone monuments.

VISITORS' CHECKLIST

Szentendrei út 139. **Tel** 250 16 50.
🚉 Aquincum. ⬭ 9am–5pm Tue–Sun. 🖼 **Museum** ⬭ 10am–5pm Tue–Sun. 🌑 Mid-Oct–mid-Apr. 🖼 📷 www.aquincum.hu

Thoroughfare
Paving stones can still be seen on the network of streets that run across the town at right angles.

Double Baths
Built mainly of stone, the baths were once richly decorated. Traces of wall paintings and mosaics can still be seen in some

Drain Cover
Aquincum had a water supply system. Carefully crafted drain covers, such as this one, cut into the stone paving slabs, provided the required drainage.

Peristyle House
Surrounded by a colonnade, this courtyard once stood at the centre of a large town

Excursions from Budapest

Budapest is ten times bigger than any other Hungarian city. Sleepy and charming, the towns and villages on these pages are ideal for day or overnight trips. Coaches *(see p234)* and trains *(see p239)* are cheap and reliable. Esztergom, Visegrád and Szentendre to the north of the city can all be reached by boats *(see p235)*, which run throughout the summer along this beautiful stretch of the Danube. More off the beaten track, the towns and villages to the south offer a fascinating glimpse of traditional life.

Esztergom ❶

46 km (28 miles) NW of Budapest.
🏠 *30,000.* 🚌 *from Árpád híd.*
🚆 *from Nyugati pu.* 🚢 *from Vigadó tér (summer only).* 🛈 *Lőrinc utca.* **Cathedral** *Szent István tér 1.*
***Tel** (0633) 41 18 95.* ⏰ *Apr–Oct: 8am–6pm; Nov–Apr: 8am–4pm.* ♿
Treasury *Tel (0633) 40 23 54.*
⏰ *Mar–Oct: 9am–4:30pm daily; Nov–Dec: 11am–3:30pm Tue–Sun.*
📷 🏰 **Castle *Tel** (0633) 41 59 86.*
⏰ *Apr–Oct: 10am–6pm Tue–Sun; Nov–Mar: 10am–4pm Tue–Sun.* 📷

St István, Hungary's first Christian King, was baptized in Esztergom and crowned here on Christmas Day 1000 AD. Almost completely destroyed by the Mongol invasion 250 years later, the city was gradually rebuilt in the 18th and 19th centuries.

Esztergom today is still the country's most sacred city, the seat of the archbishop of Hungary. Dominating the skyline is the huge Catholic **cathedral**, built in the early 19th century. By the southern entrance, built by 16th-century Florentine craftsmen, is the red marble Bakócz burial chapel. On the northern side is the **treasury** containing a collection of ecclesiastical treasures

Overlooking the Danube, the vast cathedral at Esztergom

rescued from the ruins of the 12th-century church that existed on the cathedral site.

Below the cathedral are the remains of the 10th-century **castle**, rebuilt several times. It features a 12th-century chapel. The picturesque old town is also well worth exploring. At its heart is the town square, home to several cafés.

SIGHTS AT A GLANCE

Esztergom ❶
Fót ❺
Gödöllő ❻
Kecskemét ❼
Kiskunfélegyháza ❽

Martonvásár ❿
Ráckeve ❾
Szentendre ❸
Vác ❹
Visegrád ❷

KEY

🟦 City centre
⬜ Greater Budapest
═══ Motorway
▬▬▬ Main road

25 kilometres = 15 miles

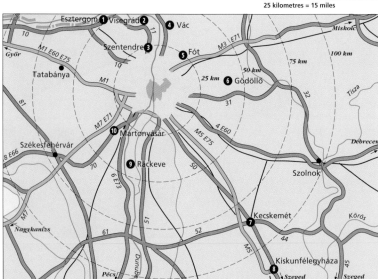

Visegrád ❷

40 km (25 miles) N of Budapest.
🏛 *1,800.* 🚌 *from Árpád híd.*
🚢 *from Vigadó tér (summer only).*
ℹ *Rév utca 15.* **Tel** *(0626) 39 81 60.*
Castle **Tel** *(0626) 39 81 01.*
🕐 *Mar–Sep: 9:30am–6pm
Mon– Sun; Oct–Nov: 9:30am–4pm
Mon–Sun; Dec–Feb: 9:30am–4pm
Sat & Sun.* 📷 ♿
Mátyás Museum & Visegrád Palace
Tel *(0626) 39 80 26.* 🕐 *9am–5pm
Tue–Sun.* 📷 📷 *by arrangement.*

Set on the narrowest stretch of the Danube, the village of Visegrád is a popular tourist destination, thanks to its spectacular ruined **castle**.

A 25-minute walk, or a short bus or taxi ride will take you up to the castle from Visegrád. Built in the 13th century by King Béla IV, this was once one of the finest royal palaces ever built in Hungary. The massive outer walls are still intact, and offer stunning views over the surrounding countryside.

Halfway down the hill, in the Salamon Tower, is the **Mátyás Museum**, a collection of items excavated from the ruins of the **Visegrád Palace**. Built by King Béla IV at the same time as the castle, the palace was renovated two centuries later, in magnificent Renaissance style, by King Mátyás Corvinus *(see pp24– 5)*. Destroyed in the 16th century after the Turkish invasion, then buried in a mud slide, the ruins were not rediscovered until 1934, when the excavations took place here.

Szentendre ❸

25 km (16 miles) N of Budapest.
🏛 *20,000.* 🚇 *from Batthyány tér.*
🚌 *from Árpád híd.* 🚢 *from Vigadó
tér (summer only).* ℹ *Dumtsa Jenő
utca 22.* **Tel** *(0626) 31 79 66.*
Belgrade Cathedral *Pátriárka utca 5.*
Tel *(0626) 31 23 99.* ♿
Museum of Serbian Art *Pátriárka
utca 5.* **Tel** *(0626) 31 23 99.*
🕐 *May–Sep: 10am–6pm Tue–Sun;
Oct–Apr: 10am–4pm Tue–Sun;
Jan–Feb: 10am–4pm Fri–Sun.* 📷 📷
Margit Kovács Museum
Vastaggyörgy utca 1. **Tel** *(0626) 31
07 90.* 🕐 *9am–5pm Tue–Sun.* 📷
📷 📷 *by arrangement.*
Hungarian Open Air Museum
Sztaravodai u. Pf 63. **Tel** *(0626) 50
25 11.* 🕐 *Apr–Nov: 9am–5pm
Thu–Sun.* 📷 *Sat–Wed.*

Only 25 km (16 miles) outside Budapest, Szentendre is a town built and inhabited by a

Blagovestenska church in Fő tér, Szentendre's main square

succession of Serbian refugees. Most of Szentendre's older buildings date from the 18th-century.

Orthodox religious tradition lies at the heart of the town, which contains many Orthodox churches. The western European façades hide Slavic interiors filled with incense, icons and candlelight. **Blagovestenska Church** on Fő tér, is just one example. Look out for the magnificent iconostasis that separates the sanctuary from the nave. Also of interest is Sunday mass at **Belgrade Cathedral**.

Next door is a **Museum of Serbian Art**, full of icons and other religious artefacts. Since the 1920s, Szentendre

has been home to an ever increasing number of artists and the town contains many galleries exhibiting the work of local artists.

Margit Kovács Museum shows the work of one of Hungary's best-known ceramic artists. Margit Kovács (1902–77) drew inspiration from Hungarian mythology and folk traditions.

To the west of town is the **Hungarian Open Air Museum**, an ethnographical museum, illustrating the different Hungarian regions and their rural architecture and culture across the social groups, from the 18th to the 20th century. The museum is set in a pleasant park.

Vác ❹

40 km (25 miles) N of Budapest.
🏛 *36,000.* 🚇 *from Nyugati pu.*
🚌 *from Árpád híd.* ℹ *Március 15
tér 17.* **Tel** *(0627) 31 61 60.*

Vác has stood on the eastern bank of the Danube since 1000 AD. Destroyed by war in the late 17th century, the town was rebuilt and today its centre, built around four squares, dates from the early 18th century. At its heart is Március 15 tér, where the **Town Hall** and **Fehérek Church** are located. At the northernmost end of the old town, on Köztársaság út, is Hungary's only **Arc de Triomph**. This was built in 1764, after a visit from the Habsburg Empress, Maria Theresa.

***Arc de Triomph** in Vác, built in honour of Empress Maria Theresa*

Exterior of Fót's Church of the Immaculate Conception

Fót ❺

25 km (15 miles) NE of Budapest.
🏛 *16,000.* 🚆 *Nyugati pu.* 🚌
Árpád hid. ℹ️ *Vörösmarty tér 3.* ***Tel***
(0627) 53 82 60. **Károlyi Palace and
park** *Vörösmarty tér 2.* ⏱ *by appt.*
Tel *(0627) 35 80 22.* 🖼 🚻 *ground
floor only.* 📷 *obligatory.* **Church of
the Immaculate Conception**
Vörösmarty út 2. 📷

Just outside Budapest is the
small town of Fót. Its main
attraction is the **Károlyi
Palace**, birthplace of the
country's first president, Mihály
Károlyi *(see p34).* The palace
was built in the 1830s, with a
pavilion added on each side a
decade later. Also worth a
visit is the town's attractive
19th-century **Church of the
Immaculate Conception**,
with its impressive many-
columned nave.

Gödöllő ❻

35km (20 miles) NE of Budapest.
🚆 *Hév from Örs vezér tere.*
Grassalkovich Mansion ⏱
*Apr–Oct: 10am–6pm Tue–Sun;
Nov–Mar: 10am–5pm Tue–Sun.*
Tel *(0628) 41 01 24.* 🖼 🚻 📷

Gödöllő is most famous for its
restored Baroque palace, the
Grassalkovich Mansion. Built
in 1741, it was the favourite
residence of Queen Elizabeth,
wife of Franz Joseph. The
permanent exhibition in the
Royal Museum incorporates
the Ceremonial Hall and royal
suites, and details the life of the
Austro-Hungarian monarchy.

Kecskemét ❼

86km (52 miles) SE of Budapest.
🏛 *110,000.* 🚆 *Nyugati pu.*
🚌 *Népstadion.* ℹ️ *Kossuth tér 1.*
Tel *(0676) 48 10 16.* **Town Hall**
Kossuth tér 1. ***Tel*** *(0676) 51 35 13.*
⏱ *7:30am–4pm Mon– Thu, 7:30am–
1pm Fri.* 📷 *by appointment.* **Cifra
Palace** *Rákóczi utca 1.* ***Tel*** *(0676) 48
07 76.* ⏱ *10am–5pm Tue–Sat,
1–5pm Sun.* 🖼 🚻 📷

Spreading out in a vast sweep
around Budapest is the Great
Hungarian Plain, or *Alföld*,
which covers nearly half of
modern Hungary. For
hundreds of years, Kecskemét
has been the major market
town of the central-southern
plain. Distributing and pro-
cessing the products of the
surrounding rich farmland,
Kecskemét grew affluent, particularly towards the end of
the 19th century. As a result,
the town today boasts many
gracious squares and splendid
19th and early 20th century
buildings. The most famous is
Ödön Lechner's massive **Town
Hall**. Built between 1893–6,
the building is a combination
of both Renaissance and
Middle-Eastern influences.
The flamboyant **Cifra Palace**
(Ornamental Palace), built
as a casino in 1902, is a
uniquely Hungarian vari-
ation of the Secession
style *(see pp54–7).*

**Kecskemét Town Hall, designed
by Ödön Lechner**

Kiskunfélegyháza ❽

110 km (66 miles) SE of Budapest.
🏛 *40,000.* ℹ️ *Szent János tér 2.*
Tel *(0676) 56 14 20.* 🚆 *Nyugati pu.*
🚌 *Népstadion.* **Kiskunsági
National Park (office)** *Liszt Ferenc
utca19.* ***Tel*** *(0676) 48 26 11.*
⏱ *8am–3pm Mon–Thu, 8am–1pm
Fri (park open permanently).* **House
of Nature Visitor Centre.**
Tel *(0676) 50 15 96* ⏱ *9am–4pm
Tue–Fri, 10am–2pm Sat.* 📷 **Kiskun
Museum** *Dr Holló Lajos utca 9.* ***Tel***
(0676) 46 14 68. ⏱ *late Mar–Oct:
9am–5pm Wed–Sun.* 🖼 📷

Much of the Great Hungarian
Plain is now used to grow
maize and vines. Small areas,
however, have been
preserved as national
parks. About 10 km
(6 miles) to the east of

Detail of the ornate Town Hall façade at Kiskunfélegyháza

Kiskunfélegyháza is the **Kiskunsági National Park**. Many rare native animals and birds can be seen here, as well as the traditional way of life of the plains herdsman.

The poet Sándor Petőfi was born in Kiskunfélegyháza, and his childhood home is now part of the **Kiskun Museum**. The **Town Hall** is a masterpiece, combining influences of the Secession style *(see pp54–7)* with motifs from Hungarian folk art.

Ráckeve ❾

43 km (26 miles) SW of Budapest.
🚶 *8,500.* 🚉 *Soroksári út.*
🚌 *Stadion.* ⓘ *Kossuth Lajos út 51.* **Tel** *(0624) 42 97 47.*

The village of Ráckeve is built on Csepel Island, which extends 54 km (34 miles) south along the middle of the Danube from Budapest. Ráckeve (Rác means Serb in Hungarian) was founded in the 15th century by Serbs from Keve, who fled Serbia after the Turkish invasion *(see pp26–7)*.

The oldest building in the village is the **Orthodox church**, built by some of the first of the Serbian refugees. Dating back to 1487, this is the oldest Orthodox church in Hungary. Its walls are covered in well-preserved frescos, the first telling the story of the Nativity and the last showing the Resurrection. The church also boasts a beautiful iconostasis separating the sanctuary from the nave.

Ráckeve's peaceful and convenient situation made it the country home of one of Europe's greatest military strategists, Prince Eugene of Savoy *(see p26)*. Credited with the expulsion of the Turks from Hungary at the end of the 17th century, Prince Eugene built himself a country **mansion** on what is now Kossuth Lajos utca. Now used as a hotel, the interior of the house has been modernized, but the elegant façade has been preserved. The formal gardens can be seen from the river.

Well-preserved frescoes in the Orthodox church at Ráckeve

Martonvásár ❿

30 km (18 miles) SW of Budapest.
🚶 *4,900.* ⓘ Buda út 13. **Tel** *(0622) 46 00 16.* 🚉 *Déli pu.*
Brunswick Palace Brunswick utca 2.
⏰ *8am–dusk daily (park only).* 📷
Beethoven Museum ⏰ *10am–noon, 2–6pm Tue–Sun.* 📷 📷
www.martonvasar.hu

The village of Martonvásár has existed here since medieval times, but its principal tourist attraction is now the **Brunswick Palace**. Towards the end of the 18th century the whole village was bought by the German Brunswick family, and the original palace was built for Anton Brunswick in grand Baroque style. A century later, in 1875, the palace was totally rebuilt, this time in the Neo-Gothic style. Little evidence of the original palace remains today, among the flamboyant turrets and pinnacles. The magnificent parklands, however, are open to the public and are much as they always have been. The estate's church, built in 1775, also remains largely unaltered. The interior of the church is decorated with well-preserved frescoes.

Ludwig van Beethoven was a regular visitor to the original palace. He gave music lessons to the daughters of the house, Thérèse and Josephine, with whom he is said to have fallen in love. Some of the palace rooms have been converted into a small **Beethoven Museum**. The Beethoven festival is held in the gardens during the summer months.

The Neo-Gothic Brunswick Palace at Martonvásár

THREE GUIDED WALKS

Budapest is a city made for exploring on foot. From Turkish bathhouses to Baroque palaces, evidence of the city's past is visible at every turn. These guided walks take you through three fascinating areas: Óbuda to the north of the city centre, once the site of a Roman garrison and now a residential district; Margaret Island, a park in the middle of the Danube; and the historic stretch that extends from Buda

Anchor at the Vasmacska restaurant

across Chain Bridge and into Pest. Óbuda has yielded some of the oldest archeological finds in Hungary. This walk takes in the ruins of a Roman amphitheatre, as well as more modern attractions. The walk around car-free Margaret Island includes an exotic landscaped garden. The third excursion encompasses the lovely old buildings of Buda's Castle District, an underground labyrinth and Pest's lively Central Market.

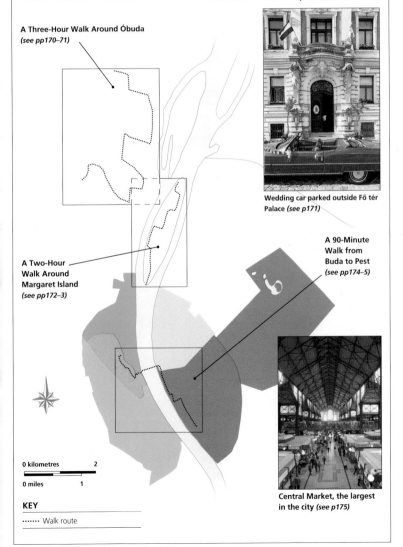

A Three-Hour Walk Around Óbuda
(see pp170–71)

Wedding car parked outside Fő tér Palace *(see p171)*

A Two-Hour Walk Around Margaret Island
(see pp172–3)

A 90-Minute Walk from Buda to Pest *(see pp174–5)*

Central Market, the largest in the city *(see p175)*

0 kilometres 2

0 miles 1

KEY

······ Walk route

◁ Statue of a young girl in Margaret Island's landscaped Japanese Garden *(see p173)*

A Three-Hour Walk Around Óbuda

At first glance Óbuda today seems little more than a concrete jungle of tower blocks and flyovers. Behind the grey façade, however, there is a strong local identity and clues to the area's long and colourful past abound. Arriving here in AD 89, the Romans built a garrison in this district shortly before founding the civilian town of Aquincum *(see pp162–3)* to the north. After the departure of Romans in the 5th century AD, successive waves of invaders, including the Magyars *(see pp22–3)* all left their mark on Óbuda (literally "Old Buda"). By the end of the 16th century, Óbuda was a thriving market town, eventually forming part of the city of Budapest in 1873.

A section of Óbuda's impressive Roman amphitheatre ①

The elegant, Neo-Baroque Fő tér Palace with its sentry box ⑪

From the Roman Amphitheatre to the Roman Camp Museum

Begin the walk at the corner of Bécsi utca and Pacsirtamező út, which is dominated by the remains of a very fine Roman amphitheatre ①. The Romans arrived in the region soon after the time of Christ, building this impressive amphitheatre in the middle of the 2nd century AD, by which time Aquincum was the thriving capital of the province of Lower Pannonia *(see pp20–21)*. Originally used by the Roman soldiers from the nearby garrison, it became a fortress in the 9th century for the invading Magyar army. Not much remains of its once huge walls, but the scale of the theatre, which

was designed to seat 14,000, is still awe inspiring. From the amphitheatre, continue along Pacsirtamező út to No. 63, the Roman Camp (Táborváros) Museum ②. In the 1950s, this modern residential district, built on top of a Roman military camp complex, was found to be enormously rich in Roman artifacts. The museum (open Sundays and public holidays) houses Roman finds from the area, including ceramics, glassware and household tools.

Old Óbuda Synagogue to Flórián Tér

Retrace your steps and turn left down Perc utca, up Mókus utca, then Jós utca, turning left into Lajos utca. At No. 163 is the former Óbuda Synagogue ③, now a television studio. Built in the early 1820s to serve the area's growing Jewish community, this is a Neo-Classical building with a six-columned portico. Also on Lajos utca, at No. 168, is Óbuda Parish Church ④. Constructed in 1744–9 on the site of the Roman military camp, the church has survived since then largely unchanged. The interior includes a magnificently

carved pulpit showing the Good Shepherd and Mary Magdalene. Turning left up Óbudai utca, you will pass the house where the popular novelist, bon viveur and local character, Gyula Krúdy once lived ⑤. Writing in the early 20th century, much of

The former home of novelist and colourful local figure, Gyula Krúdy ⑤

Krúdy's work looks back at an idealized rural Hungary and is extremely popular in his country. From here, turn right along Tanuló utca and pass the ruins of the 14th-century St Clare's Nunnery ⑥. Then turn left towards Flórián tér. As you

KEY

••• Walk route

🚉 HÉV railway station

0 metres   400

0 yards   400

Zichy Palace, built in the 18th century for an aristocratic family ⑩

pass Kálvin köz, on the left at No. 2 is the 18th-century Óbuda Calvinist Church ⑦. Next door is the presbytery, built in 1909 to a design by Károly Kós, better known for his work on the Wekerle Estate *(see p157)*. No. 4 is home to a collection of folk crafts. Walk back up to busy Flórián tér, where in 1778 Roman thermal baths were discovered. Hidden in the underpasses beneath the square are the Roman Baths Museum and the Roman Settlement Museum ⑧.

Szentlélek Tér and Fő Tér

Tavasz utca, off to the right from north of Flórián tér, leads to Szentlélek tér. In the south wing of the Zichy Palace, on Szentlélek tér, is the Vasarely Museum ⑨. The 20th-century artist Victor Vasarely is remembered as the founder of the Op-Art movement,

producing work full of bright colours and optical illusions. The crumbling Zichy Palace ⑩ itself was built for the Zichy family in 1757. Continue north up to Fő tér, one of the few areas of 18th- and 19th-century architecture remaining in Óbuda. On one side of the square stands the Neo-Baroque Fő tér Palace ⑪, its entrance still guarded by an 18th-century sentry box.

Imre Varga Gallery to the Hercules Villa

From Fő tér Palace walk up Laktanya utca, where there is a group of statues, *Women with Umbrellas*, by contemporary sculptor Imre Varga ⑫. At No. 7 Laktanya utca is the Imre Varga Gallery ⑬, where further examples of the sculptor's work can be seen. Finally, make your way up to Szentendrei út and cross it at an underpass. Turn right into Kerék ut (if you miss this, take the next right up Szél utca), then left into Herkules utca then onto Meggyfa utca to finish the walk at No. 21, the ruins of the Hercules Villa ⑭. Once a lavish Roman home, it takes its name from some stunning mosaics *(see p21)*. Near the villa are the remains of the *cella trichora*, an early Christian chapel dating from the fourth century AD.

One of several *Women with Umbrellas* by Imre Varga ⑫

TIPS FOR WALKERS

Starting point: *Pacsirtamezõ út.*
Getting there: *Bus 60 or tram 17.*
Length: *3 km (1.8 miles).*
Stops: *The Kéhli Restaurant (see p199) on Mókus utca, or the Régi Sipos Étterem (see p199) on Lajos utca for the city's freshest fish.*

A Two-Hour Walk Around Margaret Island

Historically inaccessible in the middle of the Danube, Margaret Island was a retreat for religious contemplation from at least the 11th century onwards. Relics of the island's past include the remains of two monastic churches and also the ruins of the convent home of Princess Margit, daughter of King Béla IV, who gave the island its name. Opened to the public in 1869, Margaret Island is today Budapest's most beautiful park, a car-free haven of greenery in the middle of the city and the ideal location for a peaceful stroll. On the western shore, the Palatinus Strand bathing complex makes use of the mineral-rich hot springs rising on the island.

The Water Tower ⑤

A relief of Archangel Michael on St Michael's Church ⑧

Centenary Monument to Palatinus Strand

The walk begins amid the peace and greenery of the southern tip of Margaret Island. Proceeding to the north, the first landmark is the Centenary Monument ① (*see p62*), which stands in front of a sizable fountain. Designed by István Kiss, the monument was made in 1973, to commemorate the centenary of the unification of the towns of Buda, Óbuda and Pest (*see p32*). At night the fountain is dramatically illuminated. You can also rent four-wheel family bikes here called *Bringóhintó*. Taking a left turn ahead, the Hajós Olympic Pool Complex (*see p53*) ② is soon reached. Built in 1930, the complex was designed by the multi-talented Alfréd Hajós. He won gold medals in swimming

events in the 1896 Olympic Games and was also a member of the Hungarian football team. Continuing northwards, there is a rose garden to the right before the ruins of the early 14th-century Franciscan Church ③ come into view. Constructed in the Gothic style of the time, the church was originally attached to a monastery. Visible in the west wall is the doorway which once led to the organ loft, as well as a spiral staircase and fine arched window. Further on is the busy Palatinus Strand ④ (*see p53*). In front of the entrance to its pools stands a statue by French sculptor Emile Guilleaume.

Water Tower to St Michael's Church

Clearly visible to the northeast of Palatinus Strand, is the 57-m (187-ft) high Water Tower ⑤. Built in 1911 and now protected by UNESCO, this graceful tower is currently used as an exhibition space for a variety of previously unexhibited modern crafts and artworks, ranging from puppets to paintings. At the foot of the Water Tower is the Summer Theatre, a large modern amphi-theatre seating 3,500 people, which hosts a summer season of operatic performances. To the southeast of the Water Tower are the ruins of a 13th-century Dominican Church and Convent ⑥.

Ruins of the 14th-century Franciscan Church ③

HAJÓS ALFRÉD SÉTÁNY

Danube

Danube

Margithíd

Margit híd
250 metres / 300 yards

The latter was once home to Princess Margit, after whom the island is named. King Béla IV *(see p23)* swore that if he succeeded in repelling the Mongol invasion of 1241 that he would offer his daughter to God. He kept his oath, building the church and convent, to which the 9-year-old Princess Margit was sent in 1251. She led a godly and ascetic life and died here at the age of 29. Nearly 300 years later, in 1541, the nuns of the convent fled to Pozsony (now Bratislava, capital of the Slovak Republic) in the face of the Turkish invasion, *(see pp26–7)*, leaving the church and the convent to be destroyed. Severe floods in 1838 led to the discovery of the ruined church and its underground vaults. The tomb of the now-canonized Margit was also excavated here 20 years later. Just to the north of the Dominican Church and Convent, near to the Water Tower, is the beginning of Artists' Avenue ⑦. A collection of contemporary busts of Hungarian writers, painters and musicians lines this promenade leading up to the Grand Hotel Margitsziget. A little way before the hotel is

Bust of Zsigmond Móricz on Artists' Avenue ⑦

KEY

••• Walk route

🚤 River boat boarding point

🚉 HÉV railway station

0 metres 500

0 yards 500

Stepped pathway through the lush foliage of the Japanese Garden ⑪

St Michael's Church ⑧. Originally built by members of the Premonstratensian Order, this is the oldest building on the island. In addition, the foundations of an 11th-century chapel have been excavated inside the 12th century church. Destroyed by the invading Turks in 1541, the church was eventually reconstructed in the 1930s, using materials from the original building. In the bell tower hangs a bell which, unusually, survived the Turkish invasion. Probably buried by the monks at the time of the invasion, the bell dates from the early 15th century. It was discovered in 1914 when its walnut-tree hiding place was uprooted during a violent storm.

Grand Hotel Margitsziget to Árpád Bridge

The Grand Hotel Margitsziget ⑨ *(see p185)* was designed in 1872 by Miklós Ybl *(see p119)*. For many years it was the most fashionable hotel in Budapest, known simply as "The Grand". After World War II, the hotel was modernized and called the Danubius Grand, and in the 1970s the luxurious Thermal Hotel Margitsziget ⑩ was built nearby. The two hotels are joined by an underground walkway and offer thermal baths and a variety of spa treatments *(see p52)*. Heading west from the Danubius Thermal Hotel, the final stretch of the walk passes beside the Japanese Garden ⑪. A variety

of exotic plants, a rock garden, waterfalls and streams crossed on rustic bridges all add to the garden's atmosphere. The final stopping point on the walk is an unusual musical well, known as the Bodor Well ⑫. The original well was designed and constructed by Transylvanian Péter Bodor in 1820 and stood in the town of Marosvásárhely (modern-day Tirgu Mures, in Romania), which was then part of the Austro-Hungarian Empire. In 1936 this copy was built on Margaret Island. Continuing past the well, at the northern tip of Margaret Island the Árpád Bridge provides another link from the island to the city.

The musical Bodor Well ⑫

TIPS FOR WALKERS

Starting point: Southern end of Margaret Island, reached from Margaret Bridge.
Getting there: Bus 26. Tram 4, 6.
Length: 3.3 km (2 miles).
Stops: There are numerous take-away kiosks and several cafés on Margaret Island, selling drinks, snacks and ice creams in summer. The Danubius Grand Hotel and Danubius Thermal Hotel also have restaurants and cafés.

A 90-Minute Walk from Buda to Pest

Buda and Pest were unified in 1873, an act made possible by the construction of the monumental Chain Bridge some 20 years earlier. Before that, the two areas had shared a relatively common history, but they always retained separate identities. Even today, Buda remains more regal and relaxed than commercial, dynamic Pest. This walk reveals such differences, while highlighting the bond that makes Budapest's whole greater even than the sum of its sublime parts.

views of the Royal Palace and the unmistakable Neo-Gothic silhouette of Mátyás Church.

Roosevelt tér to Váci utca
Facing the Pest side of the river there are rewarding vistas too: of Budapest's peerless Parliament building

The terrace and conical towers of Fishermen's Bastion ②

(see page 73) and the Honvéd Monument ③. The monument was raised in honour of those who died in the Hungarian revolution of 1848–49.

Head south out of the square, along stately Szinház utca to Sándor Palace ④ (see p73), one of Buda's finest buildings and the residence of the Hungarian president. Past the terminus of the Sikló, the funicular that links the Royal Palace to the embankment below, an extravagantly ornamental gateway ⑤ (see p70) leads from the Habsurg Steps to the Royal Palace. A wide path meanders in front of the palace and offers more fine views of Pest.

The Castle District
The walk begins at the 13th-century Mátyás Church ① (see pp82–3), one of the oldest buildings in Buda, and coronation church of the Hungarian kings. Directly behind are the ramparts of Fishermen's Bastion ② (see p80), from where there are famous views across the Danube to Pest. Return past the main portal of Mátyás Church and onto Tárnok utca, running the gauntlet of its myriad souvenir shops, before arriving at Dísz tér

Across the Danube into Pest
The path leads down through well-kept terraces to Clark Ádam tér, named after the Scottish engineer Adam Clark, who built the awe-inspiring Chain Bridge and the Neo-Classical Alagút tunnel ⑥, which channels traffic underneath the Royal Palace. In the centre of the square is the Kilometre 0 Stone ⑦, from which the official distance from Budapest to Vienna is measured. Walk to the centre of Chain Bridge ⑧ (see p112) and look back towards the Castle District. On a clear day there are glorious

(see p106); and of the city's grandest hotel, the Four Seasons Gresham Palace ⑨ (see p114), on the far side of Roosevelt tér. The hotel's astonishingly opulent foyer is well worth a visit.

From Roosevelt tér, a walkway runs south alongside the tram lines on Belgrád Rakpart. After a short walk, the Budapest Marriott hotel ⑩, a modernist masterpiece, appears on the left. Nearby, on the right, perched on the railings next to the tram line, is László Morton's charming

TIPS FOR WALKERS

Starting point: Mátyás Church, Moszkva tér.
Getting there: Várbusz from Moszkva tér.
Length: 3.8km (2 miles).
Stops: Gresham Palace Kavehaz on Roosevelt tér, Corso Etterem at Vigado tér 2, or 1000 Tea at Váci utca 6.

View from Buda to the Parliament Building in Pest

The striking architecture of Vigadó Concert Hall on Vigadó tér ⑬

sculpture of a little boy, oddly entitled *Little Princess* ⑪. Passing the small pier at Vigadó tér ⑫ (*see p126*), you cannot miss the eclectic architecture of Vigadó Concert Hall ⑬ on the square's eastern side.

Continuing along the embankment, take a left turn just before Petfi tér onto Régiposta utca. Next, a sharp right turn onto Apáczai utca leads to the Roman remains of Contra Aquincum ⑭ (*see p122*), and the Inner City Parish Church ⑮ (*see pp124–5*), now sadly hemmed in by the approach to the Elizabeth Bridge.

Turn left at the church, and, with the Danube at your back, head towards Vaci utca to the point where it crosses the busy Szabadsajtó utca. Here, the Klotild Palaces ⑯ (*see p127*), massive twin apartment blocks built on either side of the road, provide a splendid gateway to the bridge.

Cafés and the Central Market

The southern part of Váci utca ⑰ (*see p127*) is less charming and more commercial than its northern counterpart, but on summer afternoons it is thronged with people, many of whom stop to enjoy coffee or something

Street tram and the *Little Princess* by László Morton ⑪

stronger on its many terraces. Halfway along on the right is the hapless St Michael City Church ⑱, built around 1230, devastated by the Turks in 1541, rebuilt in 1701, and finally completely renovated from 1964–8. Its unimpressive exterior belies a rich interior.

From here, more cafés and bars lead along a widening street to Central Market ⑲ (*see p211*). The largest market in the city, its stalls sell fruit and vegetables, fish, meat and cheese, and Hungarian crafts.

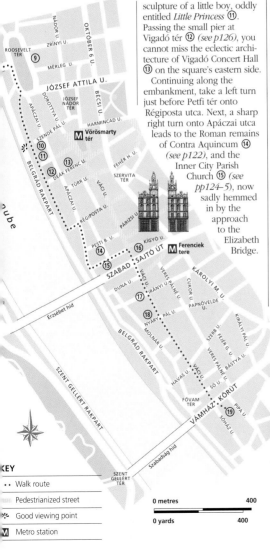

The shops and busy terrace cafés of Váci utca ⑰

KEY

• • Walk route

▬ Pedestrianized street

⚜ Good viewing point

Ⓜ Metro station

0 metres 400

0 yards 400

TRAVELLERS' NEEDS

WHERE TO STAY

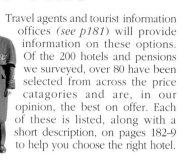

Budapest has a broad range of accommodation from top-class hotels, some with spa facilities, and private apartments to campsites and hostels. The larger hotels often belong to well-known groups and meet international standards, but are more expensive. Cheaper accommodation can be found in hostels or bed and breakfasts, or outside the city centre. Travel agents and tourist information offices (see p181) will provide information on these options. Of the 200 hotels and pensions we surveyed, over 80 have been selected from across the price catagories and are, in our opinion, the best on offer. Each of these is listed, along with a short description, on pages 182–9 to help you choose the right hotel.

The exterior of the Kempinski Corvinus Hotel (see p186)

WHERE TO LOOK

When deciding on accommodation, first choose the general location: Buda or Pest, or maybe even the picturesque suburbs further afield. In low-lying Pest, many hotels are literally only a few steps away from most of the major tourist attractions, while visitors who choose to stay in hilly Buda can enjoy cool, fresh air and quiet surroundings.

Good value for money can be found by renting a room in one of the small pensions or private hotels in and around Budapest. The more exclusive hotels offer a luxurious stay, but at a much greater price – as much as 40,000 Hungarian forints and above per night.

Most luxury hotels, such as the Sofitel Atrium Budapest (see p184), are set along the eastern bank of the Danube. Others, such as the Marriott (see p185) or the Kempinski

Corvinus (see p186) are situated nearer to the centre of Pest, close to the theatres and shops. Those located further out of town are usually an easy journey from the city centre, particularly since hotels are often situated close to metro stations.

Tourinform (see p181) is a chain of tourist offices in Budapest that provide information (in Hungarian, English, French, German, Russian, Spanish and Italian) on accommodation and places to eat, as well as on tourist and cultural events. Maps can be found on sale here, as well as free booklets and pamphlets.

The offices are open daily, including during the winter months. Should visitors need information to supplement this guide, Tourinform offices can offer details on alternative accommodation – from hotels to campsites – car rental, sightseeing, and purchasing tickets to cultural and spectator sports events.

The Sofitel Atrium (see p184), with its suspended model plane

Reception desk at the Hilton Hotel (see p182) in the Castle District

HOTEL AND PENSION CLASSIFICATION

Hotels are classified in five categories from one to five stars and there are two categories of pension.

At the luxury end of the scale – the five-star and four-star hotels – all rooms have a bathroom, a telephone, a TV, a radio and a refrigerator, and many will be air-conditioned. The majority of these hotels will also offer business and fitness facilities. Three-star hotels have at least one restaurant and one bar, and staff are expected to speak at least one foreign language. Two thirds of the rooms in two-star hotels have their own shower or bath, while rooms in one-star hotels simply have wash-basins with hot and cold running water.

Pensions have a standard minimum room size, and every room has a shower or a bath. The accommodation is clean and simple, and all the necessary services and amenities should be provided by friendly and helpful staff.

The Radisson SAS Béke Hotel (see p184), featuring György Szondi's mosaic

HOTEL PRICES

Room tariffs reflect the hotel classification, but it is always wise to double check the price at the time of booking. Accommodation in a centrally located, higher category hotel will be much more expensive than in an out-of-town, lower category hotel. Relatively cheap rooms can be found in pensions and hostels. Hotel prices usually include breakfast, which in hotels with three stars or more typically means a self-service buffet. Pensions also offer good value, substantial meals.

Many luxury hotels, such as the Corinthia Aquincum (see p189), offer substantial weekend reductions in the low season (mid-September to mid-March). During this period a three-night stay would cost the same as one-night stay during the high season.

In spa hotels, such as the Gellért (see p183), which offer hydrotherapy, the fee for using the pools and sauna is included in the room price. However, any treatments, such as massage, will incur an extra charge. Check these details with the hotel in advance.

Prices in Budapest's hotels and pensions are invariably quoted in Euros.

HIDDEN EXTRAS

Both VAT and resort tax are included in the price of the room (resort tax is charged because Budapest is classed as a health resort), but there are often hidden surcharges that can greatly increase the overall cost of a stay. For example, a number of hotels have currency ex-change desks, but these offer a poor rate of exchange. It is better to change money at a bank or *bureau de change* where rates tend to be much more favourable.

Telephone calls, particularly international calls, cost almost twice as much when made from hotel rooms as opposed to public telephones. There are plenty of these in Budapest, although it may be necessary to buy a phone card (see p230).

Most hotels have their own car parks. Some, such as the InterContinental (see p183), the Sofitel Atrium Budapest (see p184) or the Victoria (see p183), offer off-street or garage parking, for which a modest fee may be charged.

HOW TO BOOK

The Budapest tourist season starts in the middle of June and lasts until the end of September. During this period, as well as around New Year and the Hungarian Grand Prix weekend (see p59), hotels become fully booked very quickly.

It is advisable to book at least two weeks ahead. Most hotels will accept bookings made by e-mail or fax and will reply in the same way. Guests should confirm their reservations with a follow-up phone call a few days before they arrive.

It is possible to find accom-modation without booking in advance, but rooms may be harder to come by, especially in the high season. Bookings can be made in the tourist offices at Ferihegy airports 1 and 2 (see pp232–3) and at Nyugati pu, the city's western train station (see p234–5).

Stained-glass window in the Gellért Hotel (see p183)

The entrance to the Grand Hotel Margitsziget *(see p189)*, Margaret Island

SERVICE

The services and amenities offered by each hotel will vary according to price. As in most other countries, hotel rooms are cleaned regularly, and most higher category hotels offer 24-hour service, including meals that can be brought to the room. This usually incurs an extra charge, but tips are always welcome.

Most reception personnel will speak some foreign languages, most commonly English and German. They are happy to help make sightseeing suggestions.

TRAVELLING WITH CHILDREN

Most hotels welcome children and offer free accommodation to those up to the age of four travelling with their parents. Additional beds can often be provided for older children in the parents' room for a small extra charge. Many hotels also offer a child-minding service.

DISABLED TRAVELLERS

Budapest is trying to make up for the neglect that disabled travellers to the city have suffered. Specialist facilities are gradually being introduced throughout the city. For example, most recently built hotels have facilities enabling disabled guests to have as pleasant and easy a stay as able-bodied people. Such hotels will display information about their facilities for disabled guests. Further information can be obtained from tourist information offices and travel agents.

SELF-CATERING

A few hotels in Budapest, especially those in the embassy district, such as the Radio Inn *(see p186)*, offer accommodation in suites with kitchenettes. This type of accommodation is particularly good for families as it gives them the option of eating "at home", rather than taking every meal at a restaurant. Another advantage is, of course, the extra space, which allows greater freedom of movement; often hotel suites are equal in size to an apartment.

There are also some specially converted buildings that consist solely of self-catering apartments. The **Charles Apartment House** is a good example of this type of accommodation; the apartments are spacious and well equipped.

HOSTELS

Budapest has a few hostels that stay open all year. For visitors on a tight budget, these provide good, if basic, low-cost accommodation. **Travellers' Hostels Universitás** and the **Citadella** *(see p182)*, which is situated in the Citadel *(see pp92–3)* on Gellért Hill, are just some examples. Hostels often provide guests with a choice of staying in a dormitory or a single or double room.

SEASONAL HOSTELS

The closest thing to youth hostels that Budapest has are the college halls of residence, which are only available during the summer vacation in July and August. Many students' halls of residence are turned into hostels, adding approximately 4,000 beds to Budapest's accommodation list and providing tourists with a convenient and inexpensive place to stay.

Given their popularity, it is advisable to book a room in advance. This is best done on the Internet via the **Mellow Mood Travel Agency**, or via tourist offices and travel bureaux. International Youth Hostels Organisation membership will enable guests to get a discount on room rates.

The interior of the Astoria Hotel *(see p185)*

STAYING IN PRIVATE ROOMS AND APARTMENTS

Some visitors choose to stay in a private home. Accommodation usually consists of a separate bedroom and use of a kitchen and bathroom. The price depends on the facilities and the area, and varies from 2,000–5,000 Hungarian forints per day for a double room and upwards of 2500 forints for a single. **TO-MA Tour** and **Ibusz** are reputable agencies through which this type of accommodation can be booked.

Renting an apartment is probably the most economical way of having a longer stay in Budapest. As well as using agencies to find private apartments, it is worth checking the *albérlet* (to rent) advertisements in newspapers such as *Expressz* and *Hirdetés*.

CAMPING

Camping is only permitted at designated campsites. There are several of these situated on the outskirts of Budapest. The biggest and most picturesque of them all is **Római Camping**, which is located on the road leading from Óbuda to Szentendre. Campsites are open, in general, from May until the end of October. Some operations, such as the **EXPO**, are open only from 1 July to 31 August, while others are open throughout the year.

The restaurant of the Danubius Hotel Erzsébet *(see p185)*, in the city centre

DIRECTORY

INFORMATION

Hungarian National Tourist Office (UK)
Embassy of the Republic of Hungary, 46 Eaton Place, London SW1X 8AL.
Tel 020 7823 1032.
www.hungarywelcomes britain.com

Hungarian National Tourist Office (US)
150 East 58th Street, 33rd Floor, New York, NY 10155-3398.
Tel 212 355 0240.
www.gotohungary.com

Tourinform Call Centre
24-hour Tel 438 80 80.
From abroad +36 30 30 30 600.
From Hungary 06 80 630 800.

Tourinform Buda Castle
1016 Budapest, Szentháromság tér.
Map 1 B4 (9 A2).
Tel 488 04 75.

Tourinform Ferihegy 2 Airport
1185 Budapest, Terminal 2A/B.
Tel 438 80 80.

Tourinform Liszt Ferenc tér
1061 Budapest, Liszt Ferenc tér 11.
Map 7 A1.
Tel 322 40 98.

Tourinform Nyugati Pu
Left wing of main station.
Map 2 F2.
Tel 302 85 80.

AGENCIES

Express Utazási Iroda
1052 Budapest, Semmelweis utca 4.
Map 4 F1 (10 E4).
Tel 327 70 92.
www.express-travel.hu

Hungarian Youth Hostels Federation
1077 Budapest, Almássy tér 6.
Map 7 B2.
Tel 343 51 67.
www.miszsz.hu

IBUSZ Travel Agency
1053 Budapest, Ferenciek tere 10.
Map 4 F1 (10 E4).
Tel 485 27 65/6.
www.ibusz.hu

SELF-CATERING

Charles Apartment House
1016 Budapest, Hegyalja út 23.
Map 3 B2 (9 B5).
Tel 212 91 69.
www.charleshotel.hu

HOSTELS

Citadella
1118 Budapest, Citadella sétány. **Map** 4 D3.
Tel 466 57 94.
www.citadella.hu

Marco Polo Hostel
1072 Budapest, Nyár utca 6.
Map 7 A3.
Tel 413 25 55. **www**
marcopolohostel.com

Red Bus Hostel
V. Semmelweis utca 14.
Map 4 F1. **Tel** 321 71 00.
www.redbusbudapest.hu

Boat Hostel Fortuna
1137 Szent István Park, Alsó rakpart. **Map** 2 D1.
Tel 288 81 00.
www.fortunahajo.hu

Back Pack Guesthouse
XI, Takás Menyhért utca 33.
Map 3 B5. **Tel** 209 84 06.

SEASONAL HOSTELS

Mellow Mood Travel Agency
1056 Budapest, Molnár utca 3. **Map** 4 D2 (10 E5).
Tel 411 23 90.
www.youthhostels.hu

PRIVATE ROOMS AND APARTMENTS

TO-MA Tour
1051 Budapest, Oktober 6 utca 22.
Map 2 E4. **Tel** 353 08 19.
www.tomatour.hu

IBUSZ Travel
1053 Budapest, Ferenciek tere 10. **Map** 4 F1 (10 E4).
Tel 485 27 70.
www.ibusz.hu

CAMPING

Csillebérc Autós
1121 Budapest, Konkoly Thege út 21.
Tel 395 65 27.

Haller Camping
1096 Budapest, Haller utca 27. **Tel** 215 47 75.

Római Camping
1031 Budapest, Szentendrei út 189.
Tel 368 62 60.

Choosing a Hotel

Hotels have been selected across a wide price range for good value, facilities and location. They are listed by area of the city, in the same order as the rest of the guide. Within each area, they are listed alphabetically within each price category, from the least to the most expensive. Where breakfast is an optional extra, this is indicated.

PRICE CATEGORIES
For a standard double room with bathroom per night, including breakfast, service charges:

(HUF) under 15,000 HUF
(HUF)(HUF) 15,000–25,000 HUF
(HUF)(HUF)(HUF) 25,000–35,000 HUF
(HUF)(HUF)(HUF)(HUF) 35,000–50,000 HUF
(HUF)(HUF)(HUF)(HUF)(HUF) over 50,000 HUF

CASTLE DISTRICT

Burg

P ⑪ ✪   (HUF)(HUF)(HUF)

Szentháromság tér 7–8, 1014 **Tel** *212 02 69* **Fax** *212 39 70* **Rooms** *26*   **Map** *1 B4*

Located almost directly opposite the Mátyás Church in the heart of the Castle District, location is everything at the Burg.The rooms are comfortable, if a little spartan, and the bathrooms (all ensuite) are quite small. There is no extra charge for a room overlooking the church – ask for one when booking. **www.burghotelbudapest.com**

Carlton Hotel Budapest

🖥 P ⑪ ✪ ▼ 🛢   (HUF)(HUF)(HUF)

Apor Péter utca 3, 1011 **Tel** *224 09 99* **Fax** *224 09 90* **Rooms** *95*   **Map** *1 C5*

Despite its rather bleak exterior, this is a very comfortable hotel, situated beneath the Royal Palace just off Fő utca, close to Clark Ádám tér and handy for the Chain Bridge and Pest. It has good-sized, if slightly basic, single, double and triple rooms, all with large, bright bathrooms. A hearty buffet breakfast is available. **www.carltonhotel.hu**

Kulturinnov

P ⑪   (HUF)(HUF)(HUF)(HUF)

Szentháromság tér 6, 1014 **Tel** *355 01 22* **Fax** *375 18 86* **Rooms** *16*   **Map** *1 B4*

At the heart of Budapest's Castle District, the Kulturinnov is a reasonably priced, simple hotel where location is paramount. Guests are not overwhelmed by luxury here, but the rooms are all large, have ensuite facilities and offer peace and quiet. For serious sightseers it's a great choice, and the hotel building itself is a Neo-Gothic treat.

Hilton

🖥 P ⑪ ✪ ▼ 🛢   (HUF)(HUF)(HUF)(HUF)(HUF)

Hess Andrástér 1–3, 1014 **Tel** *889 66 00* **Fax** *889 66 44* **Rooms** *322*   **Map** *1 B4*

The Hilton *(see p81)*, one of the most luxurious hotels in Budapest, is located in a remarkable old-new building in a great location. It offers three restaurants, serving Hungarian and international cuisine. With magnificent views over the Danube and the Pest cityscape, the high prices here are more than justified. **www.budapest.hilton.com**

GELLÉRT HILL AND TABÁN

Citadella

🖥 P   (HUF)

Citadella sétány, 1118 **Tel** *466 57 94.* **Fax** *386 05 05* **Rooms** *13*   **Map** *4 D3*

This hostel-style hotel occupies the casements of the Citadel *(see p92)*. It offers relatively inexpensive, neat and clean double and multiple-occupancy rooms, and there's no curfew. Getting back here late at night can be a trek, however. A popular wine bar, restaurant and nightclub are nearby in the Citadella complex. **www.citadella.hu**

Best Western Orion

P ⑪ ✪ ▼ 🛢   (HUF)(HUF)

Döbrentei utca 13, 1013 **Tel** *356 85 83* **Fax** *375 54 18* **Rooms** *30*   **Map** *4 D1*

Hidden in a secluded spot, this pleasant hotel offers clean, plainly decorated rooms with bathrooms, controlled air conditioning and colour TVs. A small restaurant serves a good range of inexpensive Hungarian and international cuisine. It recently became a Best Western hotel, and service has improved. **www.bestwestern.hu/orion**

Astra

P ✪ 🛢   (HUF)(HUF)(HUF)

Vám utca 6, 1011 **Tel** *214 19 06* **Fax** *214 19 07* **Rooms** *9*   **Map** *1 C4*

A good-value hotel, set in a 300-year-old listed building. Recently renovated, it is small and cozy. The larger rooms – all set around a courtyard – need to be booked well in advance in high summer. A very good buffet breakfast is included in the price. There's a cellar bar and games room, too. **www.hotelastra.hu**

Congress Parkhotel Flamenco

🖥 P ⑪ ▼ 🛢   (HUF)(HUF)(HUF)

Tas vezérutca 3–7, 1113 **Tel** *889 56 00* **Fax** *889 56 51* **Rooms** *355*   **Map** *3 C5*

This good-value hotel is close to Buda's main sights, though the 1960s is extremely ugly. The interior depicts Spanish themes, and the Solero restaurant and La Bodega wine bar offer Spanish specialities. Rooms are large, well furnished and comfortable. Popular with businessmen. **www.danubiusgroup.com/flamenco**

Key to Symbols *see back cover flap*

Buda Gold
🚗 🅿 🍴 ♨ 🛗   🌐🌐🌐

Hegyalja út 14, 1016 **Tel** *209 47 75* **Fax** *209 54 31* **Rooms** *30*   **Map** *3 A2*

This wonderful, grand house in the Buda hills offers panoramic views – many including a view of the garden – and luxurious bathrooms. There's a very smart restaurant on site, and the buffet breakfast is hearty. Families should go for the good-value apartments, romantics for the tower rooms. **www.goldhotel.hu**

Gellért
🚗 🅿 🍴 ♨ 🛗 🛗   🌐🌐🌐🌐

Szent Gellért tér1, 1111 **Tel** *889 55 00* **Fax** *889 55 05* **Rooms** *234*   **Map** *4 D2*

This legendary spa hotel *(see pp90–91)* has both indoor and outdoor pools. Treatments such as massage are available. Other facilities include a restaurant, a bar, a nightclub and banqueting halls. The guests' rooms, it should be said, have probably seen grander days. **www.danubiusgroup.com/gellert**

NORTH OF THE CASTLE

Mercure Budapest Buda
🚗 🅿 🍴 ♨ 🛗 🛗   🌐🌐

Krisztina körút 41–3, 1013 **Tel** *488 81 00* **Fax** *488 81 78* **Rooms** *399*   **Map** *1 A4*

This 1950s hotel is close to the Vérmező park and has a large car park. Some of the rooms have beautiful views overlooking the Castle District, and there's no extra charge for these. The facilities include a swimming pool, a vegetarian restaurant, a bar and a beer bar. Dogs and children are welcome. **www.mercure-buda.hu**

Papillon
🚗 🅿 🍴 ♨   🌐🌐

Rózsahegy utca 3/B, 1024 **Tel** *212 47 50* **Fax** *212 40 03* **Rooms** *20*   **Map** *1 B2*

Small, garishly decorated in pinks and purples but charming all the same, this is an unpretentious place where the family who own and run it make all guests feel very welcome. Rooms are small but acceptable, pets are allowed, and there's a garden with a paddling pool for children. Breakfast is included in the price. @ **papillon2@axerlero.hu**

Victoria
🚗 🅿 🖥   🌐🌐🌐

Bem rakpart 11, 1011 **Tel** *457 80 80* **Fax** *457 80 88* **Rooms** *27*   **Map** *1 C4 (9 B2)*

On the western bank of Danube, within easy reach of Buda's main tourist sights, this hotel provides big, comfortable air-conditioned rooms, many with views of the Chain Bridge, the Elizabeth Bridge and Pest. There is no restaurant, so breakfast is served in the bar. Facilities include a sauna and an in-house doctor. **www.victoria.hu**

art 'otel
🚗 🅿 🍴 ♨ 🛗 🛗   🌐🌐🌐🌐

Bem rkp. 16–19, 1011 **Tel** *487 94 87* **Fax** *487 94 88* **Rooms** *164*   **Map** *1 C4 (9 B2)*

Everything – from the artwork decorating the rooms and halls, to the design of the carpets and chinaware – is the work of American designer Donald Sultan. Rooms are large, with high ceilings, and are individually styled in the best taste. There's a trendy restaurant on site and a bar. A buffet breakfast is included. **www.artotel.de**

AROUND PARLIAMENT

City Hotel Ring
🚗 🅿   🌐

Szent István körút 22, 1137 **Tel** *340 54 50* **Fax** *340 48 84* **Rooms** *39*   **Map** *7 A1 (10 F1)*

The City Hotel is within easy reach of Parliament *(see pp108–9)*. All rooms are clean and subtly decorated in neutral shades. There are few facilities and services, and this is reflected in the reasonable prices. There is a cheerful breakfast room but no restaurant. There are, however, many places to eat nearby. **www.taverna.hu/ring**

Medosz
🚗 🅿 🍴 🛗   🌐

Jókai tér 9, 1061 **Tel** *374 30 01* **Fax** *332 43 16* **Rooms** *67*   **Map** *7 A1*

This former trade union hostel has been successfully converted into a basic hotel. Designed for communist comrades as opposed to courting couples, most of the modest rooms have beds arranged end-to-end. Such hardships are compensated for by its excellent location close to Liszt Ferenc tér and Oktogon tér. **wwwmedoszhotel.hu**

Andrássy Hotel
🚗 🅿 🍴 ♨ 🛗   🌐🌐🌐🌐

Andrássy út 111, 1063 **Tel** *462 21 00* **Fax** *462 21 95* **Rooms** *70*   **Map** *2 F4 (10 E2)*

Elegance and charm meet in this hotel on Andrássy Avenue, one of the most prestigious streets in Budapest. Luxury shops, trendy cafés and historical monuments are minutes away, while the hotel itself provides beautiful Mediterranean-style rooms. The hotel's Zebrano restaurant is one of the city's best. **www.andrassyhotel.com**

K + K Opera
🚗 🅿 🍴 ♨ 🛗 🛗   🌐🌐🌐🌐

Révay utca 24, 1065 **Tel** *269 02 22* **Fax** *269 02 30* **Rooms** *205*   **Map** *2 F4 (10 E2)*

This hotel belongs to the K + K group and is situated close to the State Opera House *(see pp118–19)*. Behind a splendid façade it offers guests comfortable accommodation in modern, clean and incredibly spacious rooms. There is also a café, a pub, a bar and secure car parking. Buffet breakfast included. @ **kk.hotel.opera@kkhotel.hu**

Hilton Budapest WestEnd

Váci út 1–3. (inside WestEnd City Center), 1069 **Tel** *288 55 00* **Fax** *288 55 88* **Rooms** *230* **Map** *2 F2*

This is the second Hilton to open in the city. It is sited next to the hubbub of the WestEnd shopping centre, yet the contrast between the two places could not be greater. The hotel is an oasis of calm – especially in the charming rooftop garden – and offers the usual Hilton mix of modernity, efficiency and service. **www.hilton.com**

Radisson SAS Béke

Terézkörút 43, 1067 **Tel** *889 39 00* **Fax** *889 39 15* **Rooms** *247* **Map** *2 F3*

This old, magnificent hotel *(see p115)*, close to Nyugati pu metro station, has been restored and is now equipped with the latest facilities. The restaurants serve European and Hungarian delicacies, while the first-floor Zsolnay Café serves tea and coffee from Zsolnay porcelain *(see p56)*. **www.danubiusgroup.com/beke**

Four Seasons Gresham Palace

Roosevelt tér 5–6, 1051 **Tel** *268 60 00* **Fax** *268 50 00* **Rooms** *179* **Map** *2 D5 (9 C3)*

After 50 years of neglect the Gresham Palace *(see p114)* has been magnificently restored, and now houses one of the best hotels in central Europe. The lobby is a tourist attraction in itself, the restaurants among the city's finest, and the staff impeccable. If you can afford it, look nowhere else. **www.fourseasons.com**

Sofitel Atrium Budapest

Roosevelt tér 2, 1051 **Tel** *266 12 34* **Fax** *266 91 01* **Rooms** *350* **Map** *2 D5 (9 C3)*

Located close to the Danube, most of the Atrium's rooms have terrific views of the Castle District and Pest. There are stylish restaurants, serving international and Hungarian cuisine, terrace cafés and a cocktail bar. Souvenir boutiques and the Las Vegas Casino *(see p217)* are on the ground floor. **www.budapest.hyatt.com**

CENTRAL PEST

Anna

Gyulai Pál utca 14, 1085 **Tel** *327 20 00* **Fax** *327 20 01* **Rooms** *31* **Map** *7 A3*

A small, charming hotel in the centre of the city. Standard rooms are on the small side, but are stuffed full of amenities, while the two apartments come with classic wooden furniture, including enormous beds, original wooden floors and an antique table and chairs. A good buffet breakfast is included. Parking in the courtyard costs 10 euros per day.

City Hotel Pilvax

Pilvax köz 1–3, 1052 **Tel** *266 76 60* **Fax** *317 63 96* **Rooms** *32* **Map** *4 F1*

While far from being luxurious, this is a comfortable hotel. Only a lack of baths (rooms have showers only) lets it down. That apart, it is very well located for shops, service is excellent and breakfast very good. The on-site restaurant, the historic Pilvax, is famed for its inventive Hungarian cuisine. **www.taverna.hu/pilvax**

City Panzió Mátyás

Március 15 tér 8, 1056 **Tel** *338 47 11* **Fax** *317 90 86* **Rooms** *85* **Map** *4 E1*

This small, neat pension offers basic rooms, all with showers (but no baths), at affordable prices. There is no bar or restaurant, but a very good buffet breakfast is available. The hotel is well located, and many of Budapest's attractions are within walking distance or are easily reached on public transport. **www.taverna.hu/matyas**

Club Hotel Ambra

Kisdiófa utca 13, 1077 **Tel** *321 15 38* **Fax** *321 15 40* **Rooms** *21* **Map** *7 A2*

The exterior is starkly modern, but the interior is a real joy, made all the more homely by the friendly staff. Rooms are actually apartments, all individually air conditioned, with satellite TV and comfy sofas. There's a small fitness centre with a sauna, and buffet breakfast is included in the price. **www.hotelambra.hu**

Domina Inn Fiesta

Király utca 20, 1061 **Tel** *328 30 00* **Fax** *266 60 24* **Rooms** *112* **Map** *2 F5*

It would be easy to walk past this hotel. The exterior is not out of the ordinary, with shops occupying most of the ground-floor frontage. Inside, however, the hotel comes into its own, with finely furnished 3-star rooms at a reasonable price. The hotel restaurant is good, and offers a range of vegetarian dishes. **www.dominafiesta.com**

Ibis Budapest Emke

Akácfa utca 1–3, 1072 **Tel** *478 30 50* **Fax** *478 30 55* **Rooms** *84* **Map** *7 B3*

Situated in the city centre, in a quiet side street close to Blaha Lujza tér. Recently added to the Ibis chain of low-price, good-quality hotels, the Emke offers pleasant accommodation, including non-smoking rooms, and rooms that have been adapted for the needs of disabled visitors. Service is very friendly and breakfast is good. **www.ibis-emke.hu**

Ibis Centrum

Ráday utca 6, 1092 **Tel** *456 41 00* **Fax** *456 41 16* **Rooms** *126* **Map** *7 A5*

This hotel is located close to the Hungarian National Museum *(see pp130–3)*, Kálvin tér and several restaurants. The less-than-luxurious but nevertheless comfortable rooms and friendly service ensure a restful stay, and, as with all Ibis hotels, the buffet breakfast is excellent. Four rooms have been adapted for disabled use. **www.ibis-centrum.hu**

King's Hotel Kosher
Nagy Diófa utca 25–27, 1072 **Tel** *352 76 75* **Fax** *352 76 17* **Rooms** *100*   **Map** *7 A2 (10 F3)*

Right in the heart of the Jewish Quarter *(see p134)*, this beautifully restored 19th-century building has been a hotel since 1995. The rooms are modern and plain, but many have small balconies overlooking the quiet residential street outside. The hotel's restaurant offers a tasty range of strictly Kosher meals. **kingshotel@alexero.hu**

Leo Panzio
Kossuth Lajos utca 2/A, 1053 **Tel** *266 90 41* **Fax** *66 90 42* **Rooms** *14*   **Map** *4 F1*

In the very heart of Budapest, this is a superb little pension that offers good accommodation at a more than reasonable price. Rooms have private bathrooms (with shower and toilet), air conditioning and TVs. Some have great views of the lively streets below. A good buffet breakfast is included in the price. **www.leopanzio.hu**

Marco Polo Hostel
Nyár utca 6, 1072 **Tel** *413 25 55* **Fax** *413 60 58* **Rooms** *47*   **Map** *7 A3*

Excellent value backpacker hostel, right in the heart of the city and close to public transport, nightlife and sights. Dormitory rooms are partitioned into two-bed cubicles for a little extra privacy. There are also double, triple and quad rooms with en-suite facilities, a lively bar and an Internet café. Breakfast is included. **www.marcopolohostel.com**

Mercure Budapest Metropol
Rákóczi út 58, 1074 **Tel** *462 81 00* **Fax** *462 81 81* **Rooms** *130*   **Map** *7 A3*

Located in the city centre, close to all amenities and transport links, the Mercure Budapest is a newly renovated hotel housed in a 19th-century building. It offers every modern convenience, including sound-proofing – much needed in this location – and Internet access in all rooms. It is popular with business travellers. **www.mercure-metropol.hu**

Astoria
Kossuth Lajos utca 19–21, 1053 **Tel** *889 60 00* **Fax** *889 60 91* **Rooms** *131*   **Map** *4 F1 (10 E4)*

This old hotel, designed in the Secession style *(see pp54–5)* but with a Neo-Baroque breakfast room, has been refurbished in its original style. Non-guests should visit the café just to admire the new interior. Guests can enjoy luxurious rooms that are now in tune with the rest of the building. **www.danubiusgroup.com/astoria**

Cotton House
Jókai utca 26, 1066 **Tel** *354 08 86* **Tel** *354 13 41* **Rooms** *18*   **Map** *2 F3*

Upstairs at the Cotton Club bar is the Cotton House, offering some of the best decorated rooms in Hungary. Luxurious and classy, this is a great choice for couples or music fans – all the rooms are named and decorated in honour of a star of the stage or screen. This hotel offers incredible value for money. **www.cottonhouse.hu**

Danubius Hotel Erzsébet
Károlyi Mihály utca 11–15, 1053 **Tel** *889 37 00* **Tel** *889 37 63* **Rooms** *123*   **Map** *10 E5*

Despite the rather awful façade, this hotel almost in the very heart of Budapest is tremendous value. There's been a hotel on this site since 1873, though the current building went up in 1976. Renovated entirely in 2002, it offers comfortable rooms, all with large bathrooms, pay TV and sound-proofed windows. **www.danubiushotels.com**

Mercure Nemzeti
József körút 4, 1088 **Tel** *477 20 00* **Fax** *477 20 01* **Rooms** *76*   **Map** *7 B3*

Built at the end of 19th century, this remarkable, almost Art Deco-style hotel features an impressive grand staircase. Other main attractions are a brightly coloured façade and a Secession-style restaurant, which offers good food. Rooms are comfortable; those facing the courtyard are particularly pleasant. **www.mercure-nemzeti.hu**

Marriott
Apáczai Csere János utca 4, 1052 **Tel** *266 70 00* **Fax** *266 50 00* **Rooms** *362*   **Map** *4 E1*

The Marriott's excellent facilities include banqueting rooms, three restaurants, a business centre, and a fitness centre. The rooms are of a high standard and the staff provide an exemplary level of service. It was here, in 1991, that the decision was taken to dissolve the Warsaw Pact and Comecon *(see p35)*. **www.marriott.com/budhu**

Mercure Budapest Korona
Kecskeméti utca 14, 1053 **Tel** *486 88 00* **Fax** *318 38 67* **Rooms** *424*   **Map** *4 F2*

Big, modern and sophisticated, the Mercure Korona is situated in a small street off Kálvin tér, close to cafés and restaurants. The hotel has a wide range of amenities, including its own swimming pool, gymnasium, sauna and solarium. Room rates are reasonable, but breakfast costs an extra 15 euros. **www.mercure-korona.hu**

Taverna
Váci utca 20, 1052 **Tel** *485 31 00* **Fax** *485 31 11* **Rooms** *227*   **Map** *4 E1 (10 D4)*

This is the most centrally located hotel in Budapest, situated right on Vaci utca, or Váci Street *(see p127)*. The sound-proofed, elegant rooms are oases of calm amid the noise and bustle of this busy commercial district. Suites come with jacuzzis and saunas. The Zsolnay Café on the ground floor is famous for its pastries. **www.taverna.hu**

Corinthia Grand Hotel Royal
Erzsébet körút 43–49, 1073 **Tel** *479 40 00* **Fax** *479 43 33* **Rooms** *414*   **Map** *7 A2*

Behind its distinguished façade, what was the Grand Hotel Royal has been transformed into the modern and elegant Corinthia Grand Hotel Royal. The lobby is a joy in itself, setting a luxurious scene even before guests reach their rooms, which are equally stunning. All are classically furnished in mahogany. **www.corinthiahotels.com**

InterContinental

Apáczai Csere János utca 12–14, 1052 **Tel** *327 63 33* **Fax** *327 63 57* **Rooms** *398*   *Map 2 D5 (9 C3).*

This luxury hotel, situated close to Pest's riverside promenade, offers a magnificent view across the Danube to Buda's Castle District. Rooms are enormous with wonderful bathrooms. The facilities include a cocktail bar and a buffet restaurant. The beautifully decorated Viennese Café is on the first floor. **www.budapest.intercontinental.com**

Kempinski Corvinus

Erzsébettér 7–8, 1051 **Tel** *429 37 77* **Fax** *429 47 77* **Rooms** *365*   *Map 2 E5 (10 D5)*

This exclusive hotel – all glass and class – often welcomes heads of state and other notable personalities among its guests. The large and expensively furnished rooms are enormously relaxing, and perfectly mix luxury with modernity. The hotel has excellent fitness facilities, two good restaurants, bars and a pub. **www.kempinski-budapest.com**

Le Meridien Budapest

Erzsébet tér 9–10, 1050 **Tel** *429 55 00* **Fax** *429 55 55* **Rooms** *218*   *Map 2 E5 (10 D5)*

Housed in the centrally located and tastefully renovated Adria Palace, Le Meridien Budapest is an elegantly furnished hotel, where attention to detail is evident. Standard-size rooms are among the largest in Budapest. The fitness centre is one of the city's best, complete with an enchanting plunge-pool and jacuzzi. **www.budapest.lemeridien.com**

Marriott Millennium Court

Pesti Barnabás utca 4, 1052 **Tel** *235 18 00* **Fax** *235 19 00* **Rooms** *108*   *Map 4 E1*

A luxury, centrally located executive apartment block, with individual apartments available for the night or for longer. All apartments are serviced and impeccably tasteful. The price is not cheap but, for a family, taking space in one of these apartments can actually work out to be highly economical. **www.execapartments.com**

AROUND VÁROSLIGET

Golden Park

Baross tér 10, 1087 **Tel** *477 47 77* **Fax** *477 47 70* **Rooms** *172*   *Map 7 C2 (10 F5)*

The Golden Park Hotel is located in the heart of the business centre, and has good public transport links to the city's major sites. Newly reconstructed and refurbished, it serves a rich buffet-style breakfast and offers comfortable accommodation for individuals and group travellers alike. **www.goldenparkhotel.com**

Ibis Budapest Váci út

Dózsa György út 65, 1134 **Tel** *329 02 00* **Fax** *340 83 16* **Rooms** *322*   *Map 5 A1*

Almost equidistant from Margaret Island and City Park, the Ibis Vaci út is a hotel that appeals to families looking for a good base away from the crowds. Rooms are far from large, but well furnished and equipped, and bathrooms are surprisingly spacious. As with all Ibis hotels, the buffet breakfast is very good. **www.ibis-volga.hu**

Radio Inn

Benczúr utca 19, 1068 **Tel** *342 83 47* **Fax** *342 83 84* **Rooms** *34*   *Map 5 C4*

This pension-style hotel is the official guesthouse of Hungarian National Radio and entertains many visiting personalities. Accommodation is in spacious suites with well-equipped kitchens. Facilities are quite basic, but the Inn is ideal for families as it is situated in the peaceful embassy quarter and there is a garden. **www.radioinn.hu**

Unio

Dob utca 73, 1077 **Tel** *479 04 00* **Fax** *479 04 01* **Rooms** *52*   *Map 7 B1*

The rooms in this reasonably priced hotel are not spectacular, but they are nicely furnished with tasteful wooden beds, wardrobes and desks, and bright blue carpets (that might be a little garish for some). Bathrooms have a bath and a toilet. There is a good restaurant, and breakfast is included in the room rate. **www.uniohotel.hu**

Benczúr

Benczúr utca 35, 1068 **Tel** *479 56 50* **Fax** *342 15 58* **Rooms** *93*   *Map 5 C4*

Situated in a quiet street close to Városliget *(see p142)*, this hotel offers small but comfortable rooms. In addition, there is a good restaurant, as well as a terrace and a garden. Guests are able to make use of the services of an in-house dentist. Prices are sometimes considerably reduced out of the high season. **www.hotelbenczur.hu**

Best Western Grand Hotel Hungaria

Rákóczi út 90, 1074 **Tel** *889 44 00* **Fax** *889 44 11* **Rooms** *499*   *Map 7 C2*

Reputedly the largest hotel in the country, the Hungaria could feel dark and forbidding, but it doesn't because recent renovations have added life and colour to the warren-like corridors that lead visitors to their rooms. Rooms are comfortable, though not big, and the location is super. **www.danubiusgroup.com/grandhotel-hungaria**

Liget

Dózsa György út 106, 1068 **Tel** *269 53 00* **Fax** *269 53 29* **Rooms** *139*   *Map 5 C3*

Situated on the edge of the Hősök tere or Heroes' Square *(see pp142–3)*, close to the Museum of Fine Arts *(see pp146–9)*, the bright, modern Liget offers pleasant rooms, a sauna, a solarium, wireless Internet and a rent-a-bike scheme. The buffet breakfast (included in the price) is excellent. **www.liget.hu**

Key to Price Guide *see p182* **Key to Symbols** *see back cover flap*

Residence Izabella

Izabella utca 61, 1064 **Tel** *475 59 00* **Fax** *475 59 02* **Rooms** *38* **Map** *5 A5*

An apartment hotel offering spacious, one-, two- and three-bedroom apartments just off Budapest's most exclusive street, Andrássy út. There's a 24-hour reception, security, parking, and a health club with sauna. Apartments have DVD and sound systems, and fitted kitchens. Rates exclude parking and breakfast. **www.residenceizabella.com**

FURTHER AFIELD

Agro

Normafa út 54, 1121 **Tel** *458 39 00* **Fax** *458 39 01* **Rooms** *145*

This out-of-town hotel, situated on Sváb Hill *(see p161)*, retains echoes of Budapest's communist past. However, relaxing surroundings and good food are matched by excellent sports and leisure facilities. There are also splendid views, and walking in the Buda Hills *(see p161)* is an enjoyable pastime. **www.hotelagropanorama.hu**

Charles Apartment Hotel

Hegyalja út 23, 1016 **Tel** *212 91 69* **Fax** *202 29 84* **Rooms** *66* **Map** *3 B2*

The studio apartments are a bit larger than hotel rooms and have a tiny kitchen. Standard rooms are unrenovated, business-class rooms were recently given a makeover. Rooms on the quiet side of the building do not suffer from traffic noise in the morning. The hotel's restaurant is very good, and breakfast is a real treat. **www.charleshotel.hu**

Nordic

Gyopár utca 6, 1028 **Tel** *274 62 92* **Fax** *274 62 94* **Rooms** *12*

Simple but clean and bright rooms await guests at this miniature castle in the Buda Hills *(see p161)*. The tower at the front is striking. A good breakfast is available, though at a small extra cost, and there is a sauna and plunge pool for guests' use (also for a small fee). To get here, take Bus 56 from Moszkva tér. **www.hotelnordic.hu**

Panda

Pasaréti út 133, 1026 **Tel** *394 19 32* **Fax** *394 10 02* **Rooms** *28*

This small hotel in the somewhat troubling shape of a step pyramid is situated in Pasarét, a quiet and exclusive residential district of Buda. Rooms are a little like boxes, but the hotel in general offers a family atmosphere and a substantial, tasty breakfast. Bus 5 provides quick transport to the centre. **www.budapesthotelpanda.hu**

Platánus

Könyves Kálmán körút 44, 1087 **Tel** *333 65 05* **Fax** *210 43 86* **Rooms** *128*

A comfortable, inexpensive hotel situated on the edge of the People's Park and close to the Népliget metro station. From the outside it looks like a suburban block of flats, but inside it has clean, functional rooms, and offers good food. Other facilities available include a sauna, a solarium and an in-house doctor. **www.hunguesthotels.hu**

Vadvirág Panzió

Nagybányai út 18., 1025 **Tel** *275 02 00* **Fax** *394 42 92* **Rooms** *16*

A homely, family owned and operated pension, located in a quiet, green district of the Buda Hills *(see p161)*. There are comfortable rooms with balconies, and a restaurant, terrace and sauna. To get there, take Bus 11 from Batthany tér to the end of the line. **@** **vadviragpanzio@t-online.hu**

Villa Korda

Szikla utca 9, 1025 **Tel** *325 91 23* **Fax** *325 91 27* **Rooms** *21*

The popular Hungarian singer, György Kordahis, built this exclusive pension-style hotel in a smart residential district on the slopes of Mátyás Hill. It offers a high standard of service and exclusive company. There is no lift, and it is best reached by car due to its location and the steep road that leads to it. A genuine bargain. **www.villakorda.com**

Boat Hotel Fortuna

Szent István Park, Alsó rakpart, 1137 **Tel** *288 81 00* **Fax** *270 03 51* **Rooms** *60* **Map** *2 D1*

For something out of the ordinary, try this boat-hotel-cum-youth-hostel on the Danube, moored next to Margaret Bridge on the Pest side of the river. Some of the rooms are surprisingly large, though some are smaller than a cabin boy's quarters. There's a bar and restaurant, and a super lounge with classy leather sofas. **www.fortunathajo.hu**

Bobbio

Béla Király út 47, 1121 **Tel** *274 40 00* **Fax** *395 83 77* **Rooms** *22*

A bargain. One of the best kept secrets in Budapest. Find it by taking Bus 28 from Moszkva tér to the end of the line. Set in a small house, the rooms all have individual charms – from sloping ceilings to garden views from small balconies – and modern facilities such as wireless Internet access. The buffet breakfast is superb. **www.bobbio.hu**

Budapest

Szilágyi Erzsébet fasor 47, 1026 **Tel** *889 42 00* **Fax** *889 42 03* **Rooms** *289*

This establishment was built in the late 1960s and was the pride of the local hotel industry for many years. Its unique cylindrical shape makes it a landmark still. Its location in the Buda Hills *(see p161)*, and the magnificent view from the roof terrace remains unrivalled. There are two restaurants and a wine cellar. **www.danubiusgroup.com/budapest**

Classic

Zólyomi út 6, 1118 **Tel** *319 72 22* **Fax** *319 34 50* **Rooms** *32*   **Map** *3 A4*

A lovely, almost alpine villa in the Buda foothills, with basic but homely accommodation at a good price. Rooms are quite big, a little austere but very clean and well looked after. There's a restaurant and a sauna, as well as conference and meeting rooms. Classic is reached by Bus 139 from Deli station (Metro Line 3). **www.classichotel.hu**

Gerand Hotel Ventura

Fehérvári út 179, 1119 **Tel** *208 12 32* **Fax** *208 12 41* **Rooms** *149*

The façade is intended to be Neo-Classical but is in fact Neo-Socialist, but that shouldn't put anyone off this presentable and well-run hotel. Rooms (some are non-smoking) are a reasonable size and furnished in a modern style. There's a fitness centre, and a restaurant with a small terrace. Dogs are welcome. **www.gerandhotels.hu**

Gizella

Arató utca 42/B, 1121 **Tel** *249 02 01* **Fax** *249 22 81* **Rooms** *8*

A small pension high up in the Buda hills that may be difficult to get to without a car, but is well worth the effort. Rooms are tasteful and comfortable, all with ensuite bathrooms, and there is a superb garden, complete with a small pool. Take Bus 8 from Március 15 tér to Farkasréti tér, then follow the signs. **www.gizellapanzio.hu**

Gloria

Bláthy Ottó utca 22, 1089 **Tel** *210 41 20* **Fax** *210 41 29* **Rooms** *28*

On the edge of Nepliget, the Gloria is a good hotel at a great price. Looking like a little cottage in the forest, it is not luxurious (the rooms are a bit stuffy), but there is enough here to keep most guests happy. Staff are very friendly and speak all major languages. Breakfast is included in the price. **www.hotelgloria.com**

Griff

Bartók Béla út 152, 1113 **Tel** *204 00 44* **Fax** *204 00 62* **Rooms** *108*

Hardly welcoming from the outside, nevertheless this three-star hotel offers more than adequate facilities, including colour television in small but bright rooms, and child-minding. There's an excellent fitness centre, including a sauna, jacuzzi, solarium and squash courts. The restaurant features live Hungarian music. **www.hunguesthotels.hu**

Helios Hotel & Pension

Lidérc utca 5/A, 1121 **Tel** *246 46 58* **Fax** *246 46 58* **Rooms** *11*

Situated in the Buda Hills, but not too far from the centre by Bus 8, Helios Panzio offers peace and quiet. Rooms and apartments are comfortable and clean, and most have balconies that overlook the city. There's also a pleasant breakfast terrace and garden. Breakfast is included in the room rate. **www.heliospanzio.hu**

Ibis Budapest Aero

Ferde utca 1–3, 1091 **Tel** *347 97 00* **Fax** *280 64 03* **Rooms** *139*

By virtue of its situation close to Ferihegy airport, this hotel is particularly convenient for those making only a short visit to Budapest. The rooms are cosy and tastefully decorated, and there are suites for families and rooms for non-smokers. All rooms have balconies, and some are adapted for the use of disabled guests. **www.ibis-aero.hu**

Mediterran

Budaörsi út 20/A, 1118 **Tel** *372 70 20* **Fax** *372 70 21* **Rooms** *40*   **Map** *3 A2*

This bright hotel is a good choice for people who don't mind being a bus ride away from the city centre. Rooms are well sized and have modern facilities including wireless Internet, and bathrooms with both a bath and a shower. Bus 112 from Ferenciek tér reaches Mediterran in about 10 minutes. Children welcome. **www.hotelmediterran.hu**

Mohácsi Panzió

Bimbó út 25/A, 1022 **Tel** *326 77 41* **Fax** *326 7784* **Rooms** *9*

Small, pleasant and inexpensive, this pension is located just off Margit körút, in the Rózsadomb area of the Buda Hills *(see p161)*. Rooms are clean and have either a shower or a bath, and television. Those on the upper floor have marvellous views of Budapest. Underground parking costs 5 euros. **www.hotelmohacsipanzio.hu**

Molnár Panzió

Fodor utca 143, 1124 **Tel** *395 18 73* **Fax** *395 18 74* **Rooms** *23*

A mid-range pension in a residential district on the slopes of the Buda Hills *(see p161)*. Its green surroundings add to the homely atmosphere and offer guests complete peace. Family rooms are available. The amenities include a bar, fitness facilities and secure parking. There's also a restaurant with a bright, sunny terrace. **www.hotel-molnar.hu**

NH Budapest

Vigszínház utca 3, 1137 **Tel** *814 00 00* **Fax** *814 01 00* **Rooms** *160*

Smart and stylish hotel north of Nyugati station. Rooms are not large, but are well furnished, with many extras – including high-speed Internet access – and terrific bathrooms. A delicious breakfast is included in the price, and on-site dining is good. The bar is popular late in the evening. Fitness facilities include a sauna. **www.nh-hotels.com**

Normafa

Eötvösút 52–54, 1121 **Tel** *395 65 05* **Fax** *395 65 04* **Rooms** *62*

Guests have the option of indulging in complete relaxation at the Normafa, or exploring the beautiful scenery on foot. All rooms have terraces, and there is a large swimming pool, a sauna, tennis courts, a restaurant, a café and a beer bar. Rooms are not the biggest in the world, but represent terrific value for money. **www.normafahotel.com**

Key to Price Guide *see p182* **Key to Symbols** *see back cover flap*

Rege

🏠 P 🍴 ♿ 📺 🛄   💷💷

Pálos utca 2, 1021 **Tel** *391 23 00* **Fax** *391 15 00* **Rooms** *164*

An ugly glass and concrete high-rise building in the Buda Hills *(see p161)*, this hotel surprises by offering peace and quiet, beautiful views, and recreational facilities including a fitness centre with sauna. It is often patronized by actors. Rooms may be a little old fashioned, but they are more than adequate. **hunguesthotels.hu**

Veritas

🏠 P 🍴 ♿ 📺 🛄   💷💷

Mogyoródi út 8, 1143 **Tel** *273 22 33* **Fax** *222 47 92* **Rooms** *54*

Yellow, orange and blue from the outside, the Veritas is no less garish inside. Rooms are well sized with large, comfortable beds and TV, though bathrooms are smallish – most have shower and toilet only. Breakfast is included in the room rate, and airport transfers are available at extra cost. **www.hotelveritas.hu**

Budai

🏠 P 🍴 ♿ 📺 🛄   💷💷💷

Rácz Aladár út 45–47, 1121 **Tel** *249 02 08* **Fax** *249 21 86* **Rooms** *23*

Small but really rather charming pension, well hidden from the city's bustle in the Buda Hills *(see p161)*. Some of the rooms have a great view, and some have balconies. (Not all do, so it is a good idea to ask when booking.) The best are loft rooms, with wooden beams and sloping ceilings. Tram 59 (from Moszkva tér) stops right outside.

Danubius Grand Hotel Margitsziget

🏠 P 🍴 ♿ 📺 🛄   💷💷💷

Margitsziget, 1138 **Tel** *889 47 00* **Fax** *889 49 39* **Rooms** *164*

This hotel on Margaret Island *(see pp172–3)* is linked by a tunnel to the Danubius Thermal Hotel, whose spa facilities guests at the Grand can use. Other attractions include shaded terrace cafés and restaurants, a swimming pool and tranquil walks. Bike hire is also available. **www.danubiusgroup.com/grandhotel**

Novotel Budapest Congress

🏠 P 🍴 📺 🛄   💷💷💷

Alkotásutca 63–67, 1123 **Tel** *372 54 00* **Fax** *466 56 36* **Rooms** *319*   **Map** *3 A2*

Situated in the immediate vicinity of the Congress and World Trade Centre *(see p160)*, the hotel offers modern rooms, swimming pool, sauna, bowling alley and cocktail bar. There is also a large car park. The reception rooms and banqueting halls can accommodate approximately 2,500 people. **www.novotel-bud-congress.hu**

Rubin Hotel & Business Center

🏠 P 🍴 ♿ 📺 🛄   💷💷💷

Dayka Gábor utca 3, 1118 **Tel** *319 32 31* **Fax** *319 26 56* **Rooms** *85*

There are various relaxation and sporting facilities at this modern hotel, including sauna, swimming pool, tennis courts and bowling alley. In a quiet location close to the M1 and M7 motorways, the accommodation includes some suites with kitchenettes and some larger maisonettes for families. **www.hotelrubin.com**

Sissi

🏠 P 🍴 ♿ 🛄   💷💷💷

Angyal utca 33, 1094 **Tel** *215 00 82* **Fax** *216 60 63* **Rooms** *44*

Sissi was the affectionate name by which Hungarians referred to Empress Elizabeth, wife of Emperor Franz Joseph. She certainly did not stay in this modern and rather odd-looking hotel, but she might have enjoyed the luxury of the rooms, most of which have small balconies. There is a nice garden and terrace, too. **www.hotelsissi.hu**

Thermal & Conference Hotel Helia

🏠 P 🍴 ♿ 📺 🛄   💷💷💷

Kárpátutca 62–64, 1133 **Tel** *889 58 00* **Fax** *889 58 01* **Rooms** *262*

One of the most modern spa hotels in Budapest. Light and airy, and located on the bank of the Danube with views of the boats on the river and Margaret Island *(see pp172–3)*. The Thermal Helia offers a full range of health and beauty facilities including massage, thermal waters and qualified medical advice. **www.danubiusgroup.com/helia**

Thermal Hotel Margitsziget

🏠 P 🍴 ♿ 📺 🛄   💷💷💷

Margitsziget, 1138 **Tel** *889 47 00* **Fax** *889 49 88* **Rooms** *267*

The hotel hosts one of Europe's leading wellness centres, and sits on top of a natural spa that brings water to the surface at 70°C. It is then cooled to a range of temperatures and used for healing all sorts of ailments. The rooms are recently renovated, and offer comfort and luxury. Good restaurants. **www.danubiushotels.com/thermalhotel.**

Corinthia Aquincum

🏠 P 🍴 ♿ 📺 🛄   💷💷💷💷

Árpádfejedelem utca 94, 1036 **Tel** *436 41 00* **Fax** *436 41 56* **Rooms** *310*

This hotel offers everything guests need to relax or to improve their health. Facilities include a swimming pool, hot- and warm-water spas, a jacuzzi and sauna, massage and a gymnasium. There is a resident doctor, and some staff are dedicated to the needs of disabled guests. Some rooms have views of the Danube. **www.corinthiahotels.com**

Hunguest Aparthotel Europa

🏠 P ♿ 🛄   💷💷💷💷💷

Hárshegyi út 5–7, 1021 **Tel** *391 51 79* **Fax** *391 23 99* **Rooms** *91*

Modern, exclusive apartment-hotel in the Buda Hills *(see p161)*. Accommodation ranges from large apartments to studios. All rooms have a fully equipped kitchen, and upper floors have great views. Guests can use the facilities of the neighbouring Rege hotel *(see p189)* for an additional fee. Breakfast is included. **www.hunguesthotels.hu**

Sydney Apartment Hotel

🏠 P ♿ 📺 🛄   💷💷💷💷💷

Hegedűs Gyula utca 52–54, 1133 **Tel** *236 88 00* **Tel** *236 88 99* **Rooms** *97*   **Map** *2 F1*

Total luxury. Modern, serviced apartments are set around an exclusive, leafy courtyard. There is an indoor swimming pool, jacuzzi, steam room, gym, parking and 24-hour security. The apartments and studios are huge, far bigger than any hotel room in the city. Prices are deservedly high. Long-term rentals are available.

RESTAURANTS, CAFES AND BARS

ollowing a visit to Budapest, the Nobel Prize-winning Latin American writer Miguel Ángel Asturias said that "the exquisite taste of Hungarian cuisine is a language understood by all". The numerous restaurants, cafés and bars in Budapest give the visitor ample opportunity to sample the delights of this distinctive cuisine. The most typical examples of

Mascot for the Pipi Grill

traditional Hungarian cooking can be seen on pages 192–3, while information on what to drink is given on pages 194–5. A detailed guide to around 110 of the city's best restaurants, highlighting Hungarian specialities and covering a selection of price categories, is provided on pages 196–205. Cafés, wine bars, beer houses, pubs and clubs can be found on pages 206–9.

WHERE TO LOOK

There are a great many eating establishments in Budapest and the surrounding suburbs. Good traditional Hungarian dishes can be found within all price ranges in restaurants and inns, but in recent years Budapest has seen the arrival of cuisine from all over the world. Among the ethnic eating options now available are Italian, Greek, Chinese and Thai restaurants. American-style fast food chains are also appearing and are rapidly becoming popular.

The city's main tourist areas are well off for places to eat, but may not offer the best fare or prices. It is often worth looking off the main roads or away from popular areas to find establishments frequented by local Budapest residents. The restaurants, cafés and bars on Váci utca (Váci Street, *see p127*) are notorious for over-charging, especially at night.

Entrance to Ruszwurm Cukrászda
(see p207), in the Castle District

TYPES OF RESTAURANTS, CAFES AND BARS

Budapest offers a variety of places to eat and a range of prices to suit most budgets. The differences between the types of establishments can be subtle, but they break down roughly into the following types. *Étterem* simply means restaurant – any type of cuisine may be served. A *csárda* comes in various forms. Most are folky restaurants typically offering interesting local specialities. A fisherman's *csárda*, known as a *halászcsárda*, will offer mainly fish dishes and soups. There are two types of inn, a *vendéglő*, which has an informal ambience, and a *kisvendéglő*, (literally a "small inn"), which is similar to a cosy pub. Cafés range from a *kávéház* (coffee house) to a *cukrászda* (patisserie), and types of bars include a *borozó*, a *söröző* and an *eszpresszó (see pp206–9)*.

Lantern outside the Gerbeaud Cukrászda

WHAT TO ORDER

Ordering a Hungarian meal may not be as simple as it may first seem. There are many different varieties of Hungarian soups, some of which are a meal in themselves. *Bogrács*, which is often served in a kettle, and bean soups are the heartiest soups and would normally be followed by a light, hot pudding or pancakes. Hungarian fish soup is a particular speciality

and owes its red colour to paprika. This should be followed by delicate home-made noodles served with crackling, cheese and cream. There are also many light soups, or small portions of the more substantial soups, which can be eaten as a starter, thus leaving room for the main course.

The archetypal Hungarian main dish is goulash and there are several versions of the basic thick meat stew. Another Hungarian speciality is *pörkölt* (a paprika stew very similar to goulash). This stew is made with lean meat such as veal, poultry or fish, with sour cream added at the end of cooking. Almost all meals are eaten with bread; the white wheat variety is particularly delicious.

Food served in bars or bought from street kiosks is a different matter. More akin to fast food, it is often eaten standing up or on the move. Spicy sausages, liberally seasoned with paprika and garlic are served grilled or boiled. Grilled chicken and various smoked meats are also widely available. Another alternative is the delicious *lángos* (pronounced "langosh"), which is sold at markets. This flat, savoury, yeast cake is served with cream or cheese.

More detailed information on this subject is contained in *What to Eat* in Budapest on pages 192–3.

VEGETARIAN FOOD

Vegetarian cuisine *per se* is not found in abundance in Budapest. There are very few vegetarian restaurants, of which one, Govinda, is recommended in this guide *(see p198)*. Ethnic restaurants may offer a wider vegetarian choice.

Nevertheless, meat-free dishes can be found on most Hungarian menus. *Főzelék*, a vegetable dish that normally accompanies steak, sausage or a hamburger, can be ordered on its own or with egg. *Lecsó* is another popular vegetable side dish that makes a substantial meal by itself. Other specialities include *túrós csusza*, a pasta dish served with cottage cheese and sour cream. There are also many sweet and savoury varieties of *palacsinta* (pancake).

RESERVING A TABLE

In Hungary it is customary to join other guests at a table, especially during the busy lunch period. To secure a private table, it is advisable to book in advance. This applies equally to Budapest's exclusive restaurants and cheaper establishments.

MENUS AND PRICES

All Hungarian restaurants display a menu by the entrance, and, as a rule, this is translated into English or German. The name of the dish is followed by a brief description. The day's "specials" – a set meal consisting of a soup, a main course and a dessert –

A charming outdoor café on Margaret Island

are listed at the head of the menu. Set menus are often very good value and provide an ideal opportunity to sample several Hungarian specialities.

The prices should also be displayed. If they are not, it is wise to go elsewhere or at least see the prices, including any surcharges, before ordering the meal. The introduction of printed and itemized bills has made it more difficult for hidden "extras" to be added to the final bill.

In most Hungarian restaurants the waiters tend to round up the bill, particularly when serving foreign customers. This practice led to a minor scandal in 1997 when several embassies, including the American and British delegations, compiled a blacklist of dishonest restaurants, after receiving numerous complaints, and published it on the Internet. The government closed the offending establishments and the situation has

now improved. Visitors should still be cautious, however. By selecting a restaurant from those listed in this guide *(see pp196–205)*, this problem should be easily avoided.

TIPPING

In some restaurants a service charge is included in the final bill, in others it is customary to tip. If a service charge is added, this should be stated on either the menu or the bill; this could be up to 15 per cent. However, if there is any doubt, it is courteous to leave a tip. In general, an acceptable tip is between 10–15 per cent of the cost of the meal.

CHILDREN

Children are welcomed in all restaurants without exception. If children's portions do not appear on the menu, the chef will prepare suitable dishes to order. These are usually charged at half price. The only exception is dessert, but this can often be shared. However, the desserts in Hungarian restaurants are so delicious that most children will happily eat a whole portion.

OUTDOOR EATING

Hungarian summers are long and dry, and eating *al fresco* has been popular throughout the country, and especially in the capital, since the early 1930s. Those who are looking for a quick lunch or to stop for coffee and watch the world go by during their city wanderings, should head for one of two recently redeveloped and fashionable locations on the Pest side of the Danube: Liszt Ferenc tér *(see p206)*, which runs off Andrássy út, not far from Oktogon metro station; or Ráday utca, which starts at Kálvin tér. Both areas are full of cosy restaurants, bars and cafés, and attract a youthful clientele. Every kind of restaurant can be found in these locations, too – from those serving traditional Hungarian food to Italian, Chinese and even Argentinian establishments.

The coffee shop at the Four Seasons Gresham Palace Hotel *(see p114)*

The Flavours of Budapest

The fusion of Magyar, Turkish, Balkan and even French influences has made Hungarian cuisine one of the most interesting and flavourful in central Europe. Hungary is a country where cooking know-how has always been a key aspect of the national culture. The improvised stews of nomadic Asiatic settlers survive as a delicacy to this day. Noted for its game, *foie gras* and rich meaty preparations, such as goulash and the legendary Debrecziner sausages, it is also a good place to enjoy freshwater fish and an array of delicious cakes and pastries.

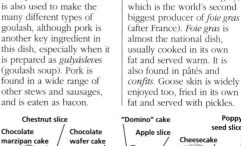

Hungarian peppers

Sausages and cured meats on sale in the Central Market

MEAT

Beef is Hungary's favourite meat and, as a result, is produced in large quantities, usually to a very high standard. Cuts of beef are a regular feature on Hungarian tables and menus, especially in Budapest, and veal is becoming increasingly

popular too. Steak is widely dished up, often with a rich sauce as in *Budapest módra* (Budapest medallions). Beef is also used to make the many different types of goulash, although pork is another key ingredient in this dish, especially when it is prepared as *gulyásleves* (goulash soup). Pork is found in a wide range of other stews and sausages, and is eaten as bacon.

POULTRY & GAME

Geese are an important farmyard animal in Hungary, which is the world's second biggest producer of *foie gras* (after France). *Foie gras* is almost the national dish, usually cooked in its own fat and served warm. It is also found in pâtés and *confits*. Goose skin is widely enjoyed too, fried in its own fat and served with pickles.

Chestnut slice
Chocolate marzipan cake
Chocolate wafer cake
"Domino" cake
Apple slice
Poppy seed slice
Cheesecake

Selection of typical Hungarian cakes and pastries

LOCAL DISHES AND SPECIALITIES

Despite strong foreign influences, the classic dishes of Hungary dominate menus in the restaurants and cafés of Budapest. Many show their roots in one of the country's three historical regions. Goulash and its many variants, for example, is a dish of the Great Plain, the traditional method of cooking it in a kettle reflecting the nomadic past of the Plain's inhabitants. *Foie gras* may have been introduced into the country by the Austrian Habsburgs, but has become so popular

White asparagus that it is key to the cuisine of eastern Hungary, where most geese are now bred. The centre of the country, and the area around Budapest, has always had the sweetest tooth and nearly all the nation's favourite cakes and desserts originate from here.

Lángos *Crisp and golden, these deep-fried potato cakes make a popular, filling snack, served with soured cream.*

Market stall, laden with root vegetables and strings of dried peppers

Duck is another regular on Hungarian menus, frequently roasted with chestnuts or berries and served with red cabbage. Partridge may also be on offer, roasted with bacon and herbs. Rabbit, hare and venison are common as well, usually dished-up in spicy, goulash-style sauces.

FISH

Trout is probably the most widely eaten fish, although carp, perch, roach, zander and even eels can be found on most menus. A popular soup is *balászlé*, made with trout and carp and seasoned with a generous dash of paprika. Another favourite is *csuka teifölös tormával* (pike in horseradish sauce). Many Budapest restaurants offer a variety of imported fish, but these are usually expensive.

VEGETABLES

Potatoes, parsnips and cabbage are usually the main vegetables. But from May to July, fine white asparagus appears on market stalls, with many restaurants

Roasting chestnuts, a common sight on Budapest's winter streets

serving *spárgaleves*, a rich creamy soup made from asparagus and veal stock.

Paprika peppers are a culinary staple. They are either cooked as part of a dish – *töltött paprika* (peppers stuffed with meat and rice) are served up everywhere – or dried and ground up to be used as a spice. There are hundreds of different types of ground paprika, which vary in flavour and strength, but they all fit into seven broad categories: "special" (sweet and very mild); "mild" (faintly spicy); "delicatesse" (slightly hot); "sweet" (mild but fairly aromatic); "semi-sweet" (medium hot); "rose" (hot); and "hot" (fiery).

BEST LOCAL SNACKS

Sausages Street vendors everywhere offer the lightly smoked Debrecziner sausage, made from beef, pork, paprika and garlic. It is generally eaten with bread and mustard.

Chestnuts In winter, Budapest is crammed with stalls selling freshly roasted chestnuts.

Pancakes, fritters and doughnuts Snack bars all over the country serve tasty, fried, doughy snacks all day long. Try *alma pongyolában* (apple fritters).

Gingerbread Shops devoted to selling gingerbread are everywhere. At Christmas it is often highly decorated and given as a present.

Budapest Módra *Slices of fine sirloin steak are lightly cooked and served in a creamy, peppered sauce.*

Gulyásleves *A type of goulash, this pork, beef and vegetable soup is flavoured with garlic, caraway and paprika.*

Dobos torta *Fine slices of sponge cake are layered with chocolate cream and topped with chocolate icing.*

to Drink in Budapest

American-style
drinks cabinet

Hungary is famous for its excellent wines and, although it is not a big country, it has as many as 22 wine regions. These regions produce all the characteristic wine styles, from *pezsgő* (sparkling wine) and light whites that come from Mátra, near Lake Balaton, to dry reds from Villány or Eger, as well as Tokaji, a distinctive sweet dessert wine. Many wines from different vineyards are matured in a maze of underground of cellars in Budafok. They are all widely available in Budapest's many restaurants, wine bars and wine shops. As well as being a prominent wine producer, Hungary also makes beer, *pálinka* (a drink distilled from different orchard fruits), several types of brandy and a bitter herb liqueur called Unicum.

Light Hungarian beers

PÁLINKA

Kecskemét is the largest region that produces the alcoholic drink *pálinka*, which is distilled from fruit grown in the orchards situated on the Great Hungarian Plain, some 100 km (60 miles) southeast of Budapest. *Pálinka* is a spirit native to Hungary and comes in a variety of flavours including *barack* (apricot) and *cseresznye* (cherry). The best of them, however, is *szilva* (plum) which comes from the Szatmár district and is much favoured by the Hungarians.

Pálinka is not the only spirit indigenous to Hungary. Other examples include Törköly, a spirit distilled from rape, which possesses a very delicate flavour, and Vilmos, a brandy made from Williams pears.

Barack
pálinka

SPARKLING WINES

Sparkling wine, called *pezsgő* (the Hungarian word for "sparkling"), enjoys a good reputation in Hungary. The classic method of producing these wines was introduced to Hungary from France by József Törley, in 1881. It was Törley *(see p161)* who built

Pezsgő by Törley and Hungaria

the first production plant in Budafok, which continues to produce excellent sparkling wines over 100 years on. Today, Hungary has several other vineyards producing *pezsgő*, mainly concentrated around Budapest, in the Pannonia and Balatonboglár regions. As well as Törley, Hungaria is another good label to look out for.

HUNGARIAN BEERS

In recent years Hungarians have been turning increasingly to beer as their chosen drink as it goes exceptionally well with many traditional, paprika-flavoured Hungarian dishes, goulash among them. There are three remaining authentic Hungarian breweries. These are Arany Ászok, Kőbányai (which was established in the Kőbánya district of Budapest some 150 years ago) and the excellent Dreher. Unfortunately, many other formerly Hungarian breweries have now been taken over by large foreign corporations. However, many of these brands are also well known and all are widely available in Budapest.

HUNGARIAN WINES

The choice of good wine available in Hungary has increased dramatically over the past few years. This is thanks to the ever-improving wines being matured in private cellars. The styles currently

One of Budafok's cellars, where wines are aged in barrels

Egri Bikavér, "Bulls' Blood", a full-bodied red wine

A dry white wine from the Badacsony vineyards

favoured by the producers include dry white Chardonnay and Reisling, medium-dry Zödszilváni, Hárslevelű and Szürkebarát, medium-sweet Tramini and the aromatic Muskotály, which is produced in Badacsony, Balatonboglár, Csopak and Somló.

Among red wines, the dry Kékfrankos, Burgundi, Oportó, Cabernet and Pinot Noir are popular, as is the medium-dry Merlot, which is produced in Siklós, Sopron, Szekszárd, Tihány and Villány.

Another vine-growing district is Eger, which is famous for its aromatic, robust red Egri Leányka and the dry red Egri Bikavér, or "Bulls' Blood", which is produced from a combination of three grape varieties. Other Hungarian wines take their names from their place of origin or the variety of grape from which they are produced.

TOKAJI

The dessert wine Tokaji has a very different style. Its bouquet and flavour come from a mould that grows only in the fork of the Bodrog and Tisza rivers and the volcanic soil in which the vines grow.

Tokaji ranges from sweet to dry and is full-bodied and rich. Particularly worth sampling is Aszú, which is made with the addition of over-ripe grapes harvested after the first frost. The proportion of these grapes added to the must (grape juice) determines the wine's body and sweetness. The more of these grapes used, the sweeter and richer the Aszú.

Although cheap varieties of Tokaji do exist, they do not share the quality of the genuine article.

UNICUM

For over 150 years, a blend of 40 Hungarian herbs has been used to create Unicum. The herbs, which are gathered in three separate areas, are combined to produce this bitter liqueur. Unicum can be drunk either as an apéritif before a meal or afterwards as a digestif with coffee.

The recipe has been held by the Zwack family, and remained a secret, since the reign of King Franz I (*see p19*). Originally, Unicum was prescribed as a remedy for the king by the court physician, who was himself a member of the Zwack family.

Unicum herb liqueur

Sweet Tokaji Szamorodni

Dry Tokaji Szamorodni

Tokaji Aszú, a renowned golden dessert wine

Pear-flavoured Vilmos liqueur

Sisi, an apricot liqueur

sing a Restaurant

The restaurants in this section have been selected for their good value and exceptional food. Within each area, entries are listed alphabetically within each price category, from the least to the most expensive. For details of Budapest's best cafés and bars, beer halls, pubs and clubs, refer to pp206–09.

PRICE CATEGORIES
For a three-course meal for one with half a bottle of wine, including all unavoidable charges and service:

(HUF) under 3,000 HUF
(HUF)(HUF) 3,000–4,000 HUF
(HUF)(HUF)(HUF) 4,000–5,000 HUF
(HUF)(HUF)(HUF)(HUF) 5,000–6,000 HUF
(HUF)(HUF)(HUF)(HUF)(HUF) over 6,000 HUF

CASTLE DISTRICT

Pierrot Café Restaurant

Fortuna utca 14, 1014 **Tel** 375 69 71   **Map** 1 B4

This popular place opened as a private café during socialist times when it was one of a kind. Though it now faces stiff competition, it still attracts a loyal crowd. The café has been redesigned but retains the original, elegant interior and a cosy café atmosphere. Live piano music in the evening, and all day at weekends. **www.pierrot.hu**

Pest Buda Vendéglő

Fortuna utca. 3, 1014 **Tel** 212 58 80   **Map** 1 B4

Small, elegant restaurant with arcaded walls in a listed building. Part of an ancient system of underground caves (see p85) provides space for a popular and extensive Hungarian and international wine cellar. The food menu itself is not all that extensive, but is interesting nevertheless, and everything is excellently prepared.

Alabárdos Étterem

Országház utca 2, 1014 **Tel** 356 08 51   **Map** 1 B4

A truly exclusive place in an outstanding Gothic building. Hungarian specialities of pre-paprika times are made to please today's taste buds. Everything from the service to the atmosphere reeks of class, though the prices are as expensive as anywhere in the city. Guitar music adds to the candle-lit medieval atmosphere. **www.alabardos.hu**

Rivalda Café & Restaurant

Színház utca. 5–9, 1014 **Tel** 489 02 36   **Map** 1 C5

Next to the Castle Theatre, with tasteful theatre-inspired décor. Contemporary international cuisine with a frequently changing menu reflects the seasons, and most dishes are based on local, fresh ingredients. Many dishes are inventive, and all are superbly presented. There's pleasant jazz piano music in the evenings. **www.rivalda.net**

GELLÉRT & TABÁN

Tabáni Kakas Vendéglő

Attila út 27, 1013 **Tel** 375 71 65   **Map** 3 C1

Small restaurant with a family atmosphere. Poultry dishes are a speciality. Goose and duck can be found in soups and main courses, including the excellent goose breast with bread dumplings and vegetable sauce. And there's no shortage of foie gras, or after-dinner port. Super, cheap prices. **tabanikakas.freeweb.hu**

Hemingway

Kosztolányi Dezső tér 2, (on Feneketlen Lake), 1113 **Tel** 381 05 22   **Map** 3 C5

Papa Hemingway sure knew how to live large. He would have appreciated the spread-out, island-resort feel of this restaurant, set on a small lake. The terrace is one of Budapest's more impressive al fresco dining venues. The menu's flexible, and offers plenty of choice. Weekend lunchtime "playhouse" for children. **www.hemmingwayetterem.hu**

Márványmenyasszony Étterem

Márvány utca 6, 1012 **Tel** 487 30 90   **Map** 3 A1

An old-style Hungarian restaurant with a fine gypsy band every night. Although hidden away, tourists tend to find it because the tales of fine food, great prices and roll-about atmosphere are legendary. Its many different rooms make it a great choice for groups, families or those wanting peace and quiet. **www.marvanymenyasszony.hu**

Rolling Rock

Bartók Béla út 76, 1113 **Tel** 385 33 48   **Map** 3 C5

The rather unadventurous but reliable Rolling Rock restaurant is located in the heart of Buda, and serves up Tex Mex food for Tex Mex kinds of people. There are salads, too, some pasta and loads of very sweet desserts, and this is a popular choice for the new Budapest rich who are making the surrounding area one of the city's most expensive.

Key to Symbols see back cover flap

Szeged Étterem.

Bartók Béla út 1, 114 **Tel** *209 16 68*

Next to the Gellért Hotel *(see pp90–91)*, this is a traditional Hungarian restaura
specialities including several river fish dishes. The *Szegedi halászlé* (Szeged fish s
gypsy band belts out local popular favourites every evening. **www.szegedvend**

Citadella Étterem

Citadella sétány, 1118 **Tel** *386 48 02*

The casements of the Citadel up above southern Buda have been turned into a
which can suffer from disappearing wait staff. Once that problem is dealt with,
Hungarian food, though prices are steep. A gypsy band plays every night. **www.**

Marcello

🚶 Ⅴ   ⓦⓦⓦⓦ

Bartók Béla út 40, 1111 **Tel** *466 6231*   **Map** *4 E4*

A super little treat where all sorts of tourists, locals, expatriates and businessmen meet and become equals. Housed in a cellar accessed by a low staircase, Marcello is famed for its pasta and its great salad bar – there is a wide range of choice for vegetarians. Make a reservation if you want to get a table in the evening.

Búsuló Juhász Étterem

🚶 🎵 Ⅴ   ⓦⓦⓦⓦⓦ

Kelenhegyi út 58, 1118 **Tel** *209 16 49*   **Map** *3 C3*

Traditional Hungarian restaurant on the western slopes of Gellért Hill, offering spectacular views and pleasant gypsy music. A wide choice of Hungarian specialities have been made lighter in the spirit of international gastronomy, but the often astronomically priced bill can leave a nasty aftertaste.

NORTH OF THE CASTLE

À la carte Kisétterem

♿ Ⅴ   ⓦⓦ

Iskola utca 29, 1011 **Tel** *202 05 80*   **Map** *1 C3*

A small and really rather charming restaurant conveniently situated near Batthyány tér (on the red metro line). There is an unusually wide choice of fish dishes on the respectably long menu, and everything is given a homely, home-cooked touch by two caring chefs. Reservation is recommended for both lunch and dinner.

Csalogány Étterem és Kávézó

♿ Ⅴ   ⓦⓦ

Csalogány utca 26, 1015 **Tel** *487 08 73*   **Map** *1 A3*

Popular and really quite trendy restaurant/café with a modern, bright and breezy Mediterranean interior. Excellent poultry, fish and meat dishes are all grilled on lava stones for a real burst of flavour. For such a meat-orientated place, there's also a surprisingly good selection of vegetarian dishes and salads. A small selection of good wines.

Georgian Restaurant

♿   ⓦⓦⓦ

Frankel Leó utca 30–34, 1015 **Tel** *326 04 06*   **Map** *1 B1*

A somewhat less than original name for a nevertheless super restaurant close to the Margaret Bridge. The food is impeccably authentic, featuring enormous shashlik kebabs cooked by Georgian chefs on a huge open grill. The decor is less Georgian, and far more contemporary. The homemade Georgian bread is great.

Arany Kaviár

🚶 🎵 Ⅴ   ⓦⓦⓦⓦ

Ostrom utca 19, 1015 **Tel** *201 67 37*   **Map** *1 A3*

Superb Russian seafood restaurant where, provided you do not over-indulge in caviar, you need not spend a fortune. Most dishes are based around fish and seafood, but there are Russian specialities on the menu, too, such as *pelmenyi* (Russian ravioli). Also, a surprisingly good vegetarian selection. **www.aranykaviar.hu**

Le Jardin de Paris

🚶 ♿ 🎵 Ⅴ   ⓦⓦⓦⓦ

Fő utca 20, 1011 **Tel** *201 0047*   **Map** *1 C5*

This French restaurant is impressive in every aspect. The building is a national treasure, and protected as such, and the main dining room is a sparsely decorated, tasteful treat. The service is efficient and friendly without being pretentious, and live jazz softens the mood most evenings. The food is international-French, and there's a garden.

Fekete Hollo

🚶   ⓦⓦⓦⓦⓦ

Országház utca 10, 1014 **Tel** *356 2367*   **Map** *1 B4*

In a terrific location up on Castle Hill, this little gem is a traditional Hungarian restaurant where the kitsch medieval decor does little to detract from the excellent food. All Hungarian favourites are on the menu, though there is little for vegetarians. Service can be slow, but that's because the place is always full of happy diners.

Kasca

🚶 ♿ 🎵 Ⅴ   ⓦⓦⓦⓦ

Fő utca 75, 1027 **Tel** *201 99 92*   **Map** *1 C2*

Kasca serves some of the finest food in the country. The service is as ostentatious as the food is splendid, with dishes presented under silver serving domes, whisked away with great ceremony. Though duck dominates the menu, there is far more on offer, including inventive vegetarian options. Outstanding, but dreadfully expensive.

D PARLIAMENT

...város Lugas Étterem

Bajcsy-Zsilinszky út 15/A, 1065 **Tel** *302 53 93*

Map 2 E4

Well-made, hearty dishes are served in a simple, appealing atmosphere. It's a favourite with locals, informal and relaxed. The food is great value, especially the daily specials that are chalked up on a blackboard. Great soups. In the summer a terrace is set up on the pavement, although constant traffic noise may disturb any conversation.

Bombay Palace

Andrássy út. 44, 1061 **Tel** *332 83 63*

Map 7 A1

Since 1994 this place, which is part of an international chain, has been serving reasonably authentic Indian cuisine to expatriates and visitors. Occasionally, a curious local drops by. The food is unusually mild, but it is certainly tasty, and the ingredients are fresh and good. **www.bombay-palace.com**

Govinda

Vigyázó Ferenc utca 4, 1051 **Tel** *269 16 25*

Map 2 D4

Popular at lunchtimes. this fast food-style restaurant serves vegetarian meals and salads. Here, no meat doesn't mean no flavour. In fact, some of the dishes are hotter than many people will ever have tasted – choose carefully. There's a shop attached, selling Eastern-style gifts and Krishna literature, and a meditation room.

Művész Vendéglő

Vígszínház utca 5, 1136 **Tel** *339 80 08*

Map 2 E2

Located behind the Vígszínház (Variety Theatre), this is an intimate, homely restaurant. The walls display photos of theatre personalities and, with its antique furniture, it looks like a grandmother's dining room. The cooking is also home-style and simple, but effortlessly tasty. A late breakfast is served.

Shakespeare Étterem és Kávéház

Sas utca 4, 1051 **Tel** *266 87 58*

Map 2 E4

Gorgeously decorated café and restaurant – the Shakespeare theme is almost too strong – with a warm welcome. The food is inventive, and there's plenty for vegetarians. The crowd is casual, friendly and young. The smart leather chairs and round tables fill up quickly in the evening, so it is advisable to make a reservation. **www.shakespeare.hu**

Via Luna

Nagysándor József utca 1, 1054 **Tel** *312 80 58*

Map 2 E4

A truly Italian place, owned and operated by Italians, with an extensive menu of trattoria favourites. Excellent pasta is made on the premises, which is a rarity in Budapest, and so word has got out and the restaurant is always crowded. It is best to reserve a table. Both Hungarian and Italian wines are available.

Café Kör

Sas utca 17, 1051 **Tel** *311 00 53*

Map 2 E4

Popular bistro-style place, serving good salad plates and Hungarian/European-inspired dishes. None will win prizes, but all offer great value. Vegetarian food is made to order. A good selection of Hungarian wines offered by the glass betray the fact that this was once a wine bar. Reserving is recommended.

Cotton Club

Jókai utca 26, 1066 **Tel** *354 08 86*

Map 2 F3

Part of a three-part project on the same premises – with Cotton Club bar *(see p209)* and Cotton House hotel *(see p185)* – the restaurant is classy and clean, and serves unusual dishes in a unique atmosphere. It's a great place for a long evening: eat, then head downstairs for the live music. **www.cottonclub.hu**

Dzsungel

Jókai utca 30, 1065 **Tel** *302 40 03*

Map 2 F3

Children love Dzsungel (it means jungle), decorated as it is with parrots and monkeys and elephants, all making a vocal contribution at regular intervals. Most of the really rather original food is a little too fancy for some children, but there are more simple dishes on offer if you ask. A 10% service charge is imposed. **www.crazycafe.hu**

Marquis de Salade

Hajós utca 43, 1065 **Tel** *302 40 86*

Map 2 F4

This wonderfully named restaurant boasts an extensive menu featuring recipes from around the world, including interesting lamb dishes from Azerbaijan and Georgia. Basic Hungarian fare, such as *goulash*, is also on offer. Vegetarians have plenty to choose from, too. The reasonable prices are rare in this part of town.

Abszint

Andrássy út 34., 1061 **Tel** *332 49 93*

Map 2 F4

Abszint does serve a green absinthe, but without the wormwood. Still, it is the food that people flock here for: a French-inspired bistro menu that changes regularly, always features a good selection of game dishes, and never costs a great deal of money. A popular breakfast and lunchtime spot. **www.abszint.hu**

Key to Price Guide *see p196* **Key to Symbols** *see back cover flap*

Articsóka

Zichy Jenő utca 17, 1066 **Tel** *302 77 57* **Map** *2 F4*

Wonderfully bright and breezy Articsóka, decorated with hanging plants, pastel-shaded paintwork and superb contemporary art, is as un-Hungarian as a restaurant can be. The Mediterranean cuisine on offer – with a good vegetarian selection – is prepared and presented with equal flair.

Belcanto

Dalszínház utca 8, 1061 **Tel** *269 27 86* **Map** *2 F4*

A legendary Hungarian restaurant, as famous for its good-time atmosphere as for its excellent food. In the evenings, diners enjoy favourite international and Hungarian dishes while waiters sing well-known operatic arias. Customers and visiting professional singers join in, and an orchestra plays dance music. **www.belcanto.hu**

Focáccia

Roosevelt tér 2, 1051 **Tel** *266 12 34 ext. 657* **Map** *2 D5 (9 C3)*

This Italian establishment at the Sofitel Atrium Budapest has just about everything that is required in a fine restaurant: great food, superb service and lovely views over the Danube. Diners are mostly regulars – locals and businessmen – who know their Italian food. Exemplary wine list. **www.sofitel.hu**

Sir Lancelot lovagi étterem

Podmaniczky utca 14, 1065 **Tel** *302 44 56* **Map** *2 F3*

Excellent Renaissance-inspired dishes, brought to the table by waiters in period costume. Only knives and spoons are provided with the food, which is served in such substantial portions that diners rarely manage to finish. Renaissance music is played in the evenings. Reserving is advisable, especially at weekends. **www.sirlancelot.hu**

Trattoria Pomo D'oro

Arany János utca. 9, 1051 **Tel** *302 64 73* **Map** *2 D4*

Far too big to be a genuine Italian restaurant, this place is recommended nonetheless for its superb atmosphere, created by different dining levels and excellent staff, who ensure that everyone has a good time. There's little besides the usual tourist fare on the menu, but the fresh mussel dishes are exceptional. **www.pomodorobudapest.co**

Wabi Sabi

Visegrádi utca 2, 1136 **Tel** *412 0427* **Map** *2 E2*

With its low, Japanese-inspired seating, relaxed, mood-setting music and entirely vegan menu, Wabi Sabi is a favourite of the trendy crowd. Lovers of vegetarian food, or those who would like to discover that eschewing meat does not mean foregoing taste, cannot do better than visit this place. **www.wabisabi.hu**

Arigato

Ó utca 3, 1066 **Tel** *353 35 49* **Map** *2 F4*

A good Japanese restaurant, where simple flavours are allowed to come to the fore and no expense has been spared to bring diners the best ingredients. As a result the food is good, but prices are very high. That doesn't stop people flocking here, though. Reservations are essential in the evenings.

Iguana

Zoltán utca 16, 1054 **Tel** *331 43 52* **Map** *2 D4*

Iguana is a perennial expatriate favourite. The food is standard Tex Mex fare, such as *chorizo*, *jalepeno* soup, *quesadillas* and *burritos*. On the menu a helpful green "Y" points the way to the many vegetarian choices, while a red chilli marks out the hot dishes. It is wise to reserve a table in the evening. **www.iguana.hu**

Mare Croaticum

Nagymező utca 49 (entrance on Weiner Leo utca), 1065 **Tel** *311 7345* **Map** *10 E1*

Croatia is famous for its fish, and this place does its homeland proud by offering only the freshest produce, along with tangy Croatian white wines. There is a wide selection of good, non-fish dishes too, but it's the the sea treats that keep this restaurant very busy. Reservations needed. **www.hbcetterem.hu**

Gresham Kávéház

Roosevelt Tér 5-6, 1051 **Tel** *268 60 00* **Map** *2 D5*

The more informal of the two restaurants at the Gresham Palace Four Seasons hotel *(see p114)* is the perfect place for a light lunch or early evening dinner. The stand-out choice on the menu is the exquisite "Three Foie Gras", the dessert menu is a real treat, and there is a wicked selection of freshly made cakes. **www.fourseasons.com**

La Fontaine

Mérleg utca 10, 1051 **Tel** *317 37 15* **Map** *2 E5*

An authentic French restaurant with a French owner and chef, offering freshly made, high-quality French cuisine with an inventive, contemporary and daily-changing menu. Good salads and fish dishes, excellent Hungarian wines and a wide selection of French wines are on offer. Prices are high, but everything here is the very best. **www.lafontaine.hu**

Páva

Roosevelt Tér 5-6, 1051 **Tel** *268 60 00* **Map** *2 D5*

Doubts about the wisdom of dining at a hotel should be dispelled by the splendour of this restaurant. Pava is an establishment where fine food, fine wine and outstanding service combine with luxurious surroundings in a sophisticated, understated way. Not cheap, by any means, but still superb value for money. **www.fourseasons.com**

CENTRAL PEST

Al-Amir
Király utca 17, 1075 **Tel** *352 14 22*   **Map** *2 F5*

Cheap and cheerful Middle-Eastern food cooked and served by experts. It's a long-time favourite of Budapest's expatriates from all backgrounds – members of almost every nationality congregate here to enjoy the city's best hummus, *shwoarma* and pitta bread. Simple, unfussy, and the perfect place for a quick lunch between sights.

Alföldi Étterem
Kecskeméti utca 4, 1053 **Tel** *317 44 04*   **Map** *4 F2*

Popular, cheap and simple restaurant serving tasty Hungarian food in enormous portions. *Pogácsa* (savoury, heavy scones) are always fresh and on the table. It's tremendously crowded at lunchtime. The menu has been extended to include a choice of salads, though it must be said that this is not a great place for vegetarians.

BohémTanya
Paulay Ede utca 6, 1061 **Tel** *267 35 04*   **Map** *2 F5*

Reasonably priced, hearty Hungarian food in plain surroundings. (Bohém Tanya means Bohemian Farm.) Customers are allocated places in wooden cubicles big enough for eight, but when the place is busy they are often required to share the cubicle with other diners. **http://web.axelero.hu/bohemtanya**

Fatál
Váci utca 67, 1056 **Tel** *266 26 07*   **Map** *4 F2*

Often crowded, cellar restaurant serving enormous portions of standard Hungarian fare as made at home, with a huge quantity of beef and pork. It's a no-frills, all-comers-welcome type of place, where the cheap prices compensate for the often unreliable service. Little English is spoken.

Hanna Ortodoxkóser Étterem
Dob utca 35, 1074 **Tel** *342 10 72*   **Map** *7 A2*

A simple, Orthodox, kosher eating place in the courtyard of the Orthodox Synagogue on Kazinczy utca. Traditional Jewish dishes and kosher wines are served. Note that it is open from 8am–3:30pm, except on Friday and the Sabbath, when it opens in the evenings too. For Sabbath meals, customers pay the day before or after.

Két Szerecsen
Nagymez utca 14, 1065 **Tel** *343 19 84*   **Map** *2 F4*

A bright, friendly place with a pleasant atmosphere on Pest's "Broadway". It offers a good range of tasty salads, and Hungarian and French main courses. Most wines are available by the glass, keeping prices down, and food this good usually costs a lot more in Budapest. Booking is recommended, especially in the evening. **www.ketszerecsen.com**

Bangkok House
Só utca 3, 1056 **Tel** *266 05 84*   **Map** *4 F2*

The food served here may not be convincingly Thai, but it is certainly a good imitation, and about as authentic as you will find in this part of the world. The decor is great – all statuettes and funky South East Asian artwork – and the staff are extremely helpful. Prices aren't too bad, though portions can be a little small.

Baraka
Magyar utca 12–14, 1053 **Tel** *483 13 55*   **Map** *4 F1*

Here customers can enjoy fine French-inspired food, much of it genuinely inventive, in the centre of Budapest and at reasonable prices. As a result, Baraka is popular and it is necessary to reserve a table for dinner. A great wine list can encourage over-spending, but those who keep off the imported wines can eat here relatively cheaply.

Carmel Étterem.
Kazinczy utca 31, 1074 **Tel** *322 18 34*   **Map** *10 F3*

Legendary, non-kosher, Hungarian-Jewish cellar restaurant, always crowded with locals and tourists enjoying its famed *sólet (cholent)* with smoked goose. The food may not be entirely kosher but there are some super kosher wines available. Reservations recommended, especially at the weekend. **www.carmel.hu**

Club Verne
Váci utca 60, 1056 **Tel** *318 62 74*   **Map** *4 F2*

Rapidly becoming something of a Budapest legend, Club Verne is both a restaurant and a night-time venue for the city's hip crowd. Its dead-central location also makes it popular with visitors. The menu is based around American seafood favourites, though there is plenty for vegetarians too. The submarine decor may too much for some.

Columbus Pub
Vigadó tér, Port No. 4, 1051 **Tel** *266 75 14*   **Map** *4 D1*

All aboard for superb food and good times on probably the most kitsch theme boat in Europe. Nobody complains, however, as the prices are great, the views superb and the jazz mellow. Once on board, most people don't want to get off, and stay here long into the night. Reservations are essential for the restaurant.

Key to Price Guide *see p196* **Key to Symbols** *see back cover flap*

Dionysos Taverna

Belgrád rakpart 16, 1056 **Tel** *318 12 22*

Map *4 F3*

Designed not entirely without success to recreate the atmosphere of a traditional Greek village, Dionysos is a good place for groups. The *meze* (of which there are at least 30), are great, and the main dishes authentic. The management deserves full marks for serving Italian not Greek olive oil, too. Reservations essential in the evenings.

Dupla

Kertész utca 48, 1073 **Tel** *321 91 19*

Map *7 A2*

This split-level restaurant has something of a pleasantly cluttered Bohemian feel, where the ensemble becomes more than the individual pieces. Enormous portions of less than original but tasty Hungarian food are on offer at terrific prices, and there's good live music most nights of the week, though not at weekends.

Eklektika

Semmelweis utca 21, 1053 **Tel** *266 30 54*

Map *4 F1*

Though the decor may be a little kitsch for some, and the management are clearly trying too hard to be trendy, the ambience and food here make a visit worthwhile. Food is simple, Mediterranean-inspired, with plenty for vegetarians, and prices are reasonable. It's popular with a hip crowd that stays drinking cocktails long into the night.

Fészek Klub

Kertész utca 36, 1073 **Tel** *322 60 43*

Map *7 A2*

People come here for two things: the sublime courtyard in summer, and the reasonable prices. The food is nothing special, but at these prices nobody complains. The staff are polite, professional and accommodating, and the menu even says that if you don't find your favourite dish, the house will make it for you. **www.feszeketterem.hu**

Kaltenberg Bajor Királyi Söröz

Kinizsi utca 30–36, 1092 **Tel** *215 97 92*

Map *7 A5*

Attractively furnished beer cellar close to the Museum of Applied Arts. Huge portions of simple Hungarian and Bavarian specialities (plenty of sausage and cabbage) are served by friendly staff and eaten by a friendly patronage. Beer is brewed in the restaurant's own, on-site brewery and several good wines are available. **www.kaltenberg.hu**

Kispipa Étterem

Akácfa utca 38, 1073 **Tel** *342 25 87*

Map *7 A2*

An establishment that hasn't changed in essence in 25 years that serves a wide choice of international and Hungarian dishes. Rezső Seres, composer of "Gloomy Sunday", no longer sits at the piano, but many of his songs are still played. Both the food and the service are as good now as they were in his day. **www.kisipa.hu**

Kulacs

Osvát utca 11, 1073 **Tel** *322 3611*

Map *7 B2*

This restaurant serves a very good selection of tasty Hungarian specialities, including some delicious and devilishly hot *goulash* soup. A gypsy band serenades the diners, many of whom don't appear to like being serenaded. Though entertaining for a while, the attention can become wearing. To encourage the band to ignore your table, tip them well.

Centrál Kávéház és Étterem

Károlyi Mihály utca 9, 1053 **Tel** *266 21 10*

Map *4 F1*

A recently revived, relaxed café-cum-restaurant with an authentic Central European, pre-War feel. Open for breakfast and late-night dinner. Good Hungarian and international cuisine with excellent cakes – betraying the fact that this place is as popular for coffee and cakes as it is for lunch and dinner. **www.central kavehaz.hu**

Cyrano

Kristóf tér 7, 1052 **Tel** *266 47 47*

Map *10 D4*

The central location of this chic eaterie keeps prices higher than they should be, but the food is never less than outstanding, and the ambience is hard to beat in this city. The fusion menu is inventive to the point of being extraordinary, but that's how most of the patrons like things to be. It is advisable to reserve a table for the evening.

Il Terzo Cerchio

Nagydiófa utca 3, 1072 **Tel** *352 86 69*

Map *7 A3*

The Third Circle of the title is the third circle of Dante's Hell, but here it alludes not to the acid rain with which gluttons were punished in the original, but to the gluttonous portions of fantastic Italian food that are served in this restaurant. Prices are good if you avoid the Italian wines. **www.ilterzocerchio.hu**

Kárpátia Étterem és Söröz

Ferenciek tere 7–8, 1053 **Tel** *317 35 96*

Map *4 F1*

First opened in 1877, this is Hungarian cuisine, hospitality and imperial elegance at its best, set in an understated, beautifully ornamented interior. The beer hall on the premises serves the same dishes, but at cheaper prices and in a less formal atmosphere. Gypsy music is played in the evenings. Reservation recommended. **www.karpatia.hu**

Matyas Pince

Március 15. tér 7, 1056 **Tel** *318 1693*

Map *10 D5*

This place is unquestionably touristy, and tour groups make getting a table a challenge, but it's great. The food is super – huge portions of Hungarian classics are served up by friendly waiters – and there's usually a gypsy band on hand to create a rollicking atmosphere. **www.taverna.hu/matyas**.

Pertu Station

Váci utca 41A, 1056 **Tel** *317 79 77*   **Map** *10 E5*

This basement diner is decorated exactly like one of the stations on Budapest's Millennium Metro. Indeed, bricks were brought from the metro to adorn the walls. The food is adequate – standard Hungarian fare at reasonable prices – and on Váci utca that's usually about all you can expect. **www.perturestaurant.com**

Soul Café & Restaurant

Ráday utca 11–13, 1092 **Tel** *217 69 86*   **Map** *7 A5*

An intimate restaurant with a pleasant and easy atmosphere on the once-gloomy but now thriving Ráday utca, which has filled with cafés, restaurants and shops. Well-prepared and tasty international cuisine vies for space on the menu with standard Hungarian dishes. It's all good, and there's plenty for vegetarians. **www.soulcafe.hu**

Vista Café and Restaurant

Paulay Ede utca 7, 1061 **Tel** *268 08 88*   **Map** *2 F5*

The vista referred to is the superb view from the enormous windows that overlook one of Budapest's busiest streets. A lively atmosphere is guaranteed here, and there is an extensive, delightfully designed menu of contemporary international cuisine. Also a large area for non-smokers. Live jazz some evenings. **www.vistacafe.hu**

Aranybárány

Harmincad utca 4, 1051 **Tel** *317 27 03*   **Map** *2 E5*

A legendary, traditional Transylvanian restaurant, where fine stews are served up in enormous portions. There is plenty of lamb on the menu (the title of the restaurant translates as "The Golden Lamb"), though lamb is certainly not a Hungarian speciality. Famous the world over, prices are high. **www.aranybaranyetterem.hu**

Bistro Jardin

Erzsébet tér 7–8, 1051 **Tel** *429 37 77*   **Map** *2 F2*

The flagship restaurant of the Kempinski Corvinus hotel. The hotel management has every right to be proud. From the jazz brunch on Sundays, which has become an expatriate institution, to the many theme weeks during which the menu is given over to a country or region, the food is never less than sensational. **www.kempinski-budapest.com**

Comme Chez Soi

Aranykéz utca 2, 1052 **Tel** *318 39 43*   **Map** *4 E1*

Not to be confused with the three-Michelin-starred Brussels establishment of the same name, nevertheless this Budapest restaurant does offer Belgian food, including the usual number of dishes cooked in beer, and mussels galore. Though some of the prices are high, there are less expensive choices on the menu.

Jazz Garden

Veres Pálné utca 44/A, 1053 **Tel** *266 73 64*   **Map** *4 F2*

A cellar, but it looks and feels like a garden, so the name is not entirely misleading. It's very popular among jazz fans, not only for the daily changing music, but also for its fine international cuisine featuring vegetarian options. Booking is recommended for the evening. Jazz usually kicks off around 9:30pm. **www.jazzgarden.hu**

Károlyi Étterem és Kávéház

Károlyi Mihály utca 16, 1053 **Tel** *328 02 40*   **Map** *4 F2*

An elegant restaurant in the lovely courtyard of the Károlyi Palace. Worth trying is the *borjúpaprikás lángosban* (veal paprika stew in potato pancake). The attractive gardens are uncommon in the city centre and therefore often booked for weddings. At weekends, it is worth phoning to check it is open. **www.karolyietterem.hu**

Lou Lou

Vigyázó Ferenc utca 4, 1051 **Tel** *312 45 05*   **Map** *2 D4*

A charming, intimate French restaurant where everything is perfect, from the tightly packed tables which are so good for eavesdropping, to the service and outstanding food. The sublime lighting should be *de rigueur* in all restaurants, but Lou Lou is one of a kind. Make a reservation or you will not get a table. **www.lou-lou.hu**

Vörös és Fehér Borbár

Andrássy út 41,1061 **Tel** *413 15 45*   **Map** *10 F1*

Excellent international and Mediterranean cuisine, with an extremely wide range of wines that can be sampled by the glass – the restaurant was established by the Budapest Wine Society. Booking is recommended, as is arriving with spare room on a credit card. All-round excellence does not come cheap. **www.voresfeher.com**

Empire

Kossuth Lajos utca 19–21, 1053 **Tel** *889 6022*   **Map** *10 E4*

The recently renovated Astoria hotel is the home of the Empire, which has fortunately retained its imperial charms, being all marble columns and fine-liveried, classically designed chairs. Male staff in immaculate attire serve traditional dishes to business people and travellers. Breakfast is served until 10am. **www.danubiusgroup.comm/astoria**

Fausto's

Dohány utca 5, 1072 **Tel** *269 68 06*   **Map** *10 F4*

Probably the best Italian restaurant in Budapest, indeed the country. It is popular with power-diners who like to impress clients, while well-to-do couples also enjoy its understated atmosphere. Try the duck *carpaccio*, followed by the black ravioli with cottage cheese. There isn't a pizza in sight. **www.fausto.hu**

Key to Price Guide *see p196* **Key to Symbols** *see back cover flap*

Múzeum Kávéház és Étterem

Múzeum körút 12, 1088 **Tel** *338 42 21*

Map 10 F5

Next to the National Museum, this is a distinguished restaurant and café, established in 1855. It serves Hungarian specialities, though visitors should always be aware of what they are ordering, and how much it costs. Ostensibly friendly waiters often try to tempt the undecided with expensive items on the menu. **www.muzeumkavehz.hu**

Százéves Étterem.

Pesti Barnabás utca 2, 1052 **Tel** *266 52 40*

Map 4 E1

This is apparently the oldest restaurant in Budapest. First opened in 1831, it is housed in a beautiful Baroque building furnished with antique pieces. It offers Hungarian and international cuisine, and gypsy music is played in the background. Desserts are outstanding. Expensive, but justifiably so.

AROUND VÁROSLIGET

Baross Étterem

Baross tér 11/A, 1087 **Tel** *343 62 38*

Map 8 D2

A beautifully restored restaurant in Budapest's late-19th-century eastern railway station, Keleti pu. The food is excellent, and the whole dining experience has echoes of the *Orient Express*, which did once stop here. It's good value for money, and there's live piano music in the evenings.

HanKukGuan

Ilka utca 22, 1143 **Tel** *460 08 38*

Map 6 F4

The food of Korea has never been as celebrated as that of its Chinese or Japanese neighbours, but a few more restaurants like HanKukGuan might change that. The menu is short, but everything on it is authentic, and some ingredients are clearly imported at great cost. It is astonishing then that prices are so reasonable.

Bagolyvár Étterem.

Állatkerti út 2, 1141 **Tel** *468 31 10*

Map 5 C3

In the heart of Városliget (City Park), this enchanting restaurant whose name means "Owl's Castle" offers home-style cooking of a high standard – the chef and waiting staff are all female. There is gypsy music in the evenings. And, for those who have been inspired by their visit, cookery courses are available. **www.bagolyvar.com/angol**

Haxen Kiraly

Király utca 100, 1068 **Tel** *351 6793*

Map 7 B1

This place serves up the classic Germanic experience of leather-trouser-wearing gentlemen playing accordion music as pretty waitresses serve up *bratwurst*, *sauerkraut* and huge mugs of beer – all to Budapest's friendliest patrons. It's raucous and not for the faint-hearted, but for an all-round good time it's hard to beat.

Jorgosz

Csengery utca 24, 1074 **Tel** *341 0772*

Map 7 B1

A terrific choice for all those people who are fed up with Hungarian cuisine, and for vegetarians who are looking for a bit more choice than is usually on offer in Budapest. Jorgosz provides an array of outstanding *meze*, main courses with meat or fish or cheese or beans, and probably the best salads in town.

Picasso Point

Hajós utca 31, 1065 **Tel** *312 1727*

Map 2 F4

Just a short hop from the Opera House *(see pp118–9)*, Picasso Point is a café-cum-restaurant serving good bistro food, good coffee and superb cakes. Though food is served all day, Picasso Point is more popular in the evenings as a bar and café. There's even a nightclub in the cellar.

Zebrano

Andrássy út 111, 1063 **Tel** *462 21 00*

Map 5 C4

If you are the kind of person who feels that food should be presented beautifully, by beautiful people and in beautiful surroundings, then Zebrano, one of Budapest's trendiest restaurants, is just for you. The food is inventive, and if enjoyed in the lovely garden on a warm summer evening, just perfect. You'll find it in the Andrássy hotel.

1894 BorVendéglő

Állatkerti út 2, 1146 **Tel** *468 40 44*

Map 5 C3

There is a stunning choice of over a hundred Hungarian wines in this cellar restaurant at the Gundel Palace in Varosliget (City Park). Dishes are prepared by the kitchen that serves Gundel Étterem, but are less expensive. As with Gundel, the emphasis is on quality and Hungarian specialities. **www.gundel.hu**

Premier

Andrássy út 101, 1062 **Tel** *342 17 68*

Map 5 B4

International cuisine and Hungarian specialities in an elegant restaurant in the villa of the Hungarian Journalists' Union. Daily specials at lunchtime. There are three dining rooms, one of which has a long table for formal occasions. The terrace, with its wrought-iron borders, is especially appealing in good weather. **www.premier-restaurant.hu**

Gundel Étterem

Állatkerti út 2, 1146 **Tel** *468 40 40*

Map *5 C3*

Probably Hungary's most famous restaurant. Not cheap, but no longer the most expensive. It features innovative Hungarian and international cuisine, including goose liver prepared in many different ways – warm, confit or paté. Gypsy music livens up the atmosphere and Sunday brunch is excellent value. Lovely gardens. **www.gundel.hu**

Robinson

Városligeti-tó, 1146 **Tel** *422 02 22*

Map *5 C3*

Robinson is justly renowned for one of the most unforgettable outdoor dining areas in Budapest, on a platform in the midst of Városliget (City Park). Indoors, the setting is equally exquisite, and, wherever you sit, the food is tremendous – modern Hungarian prepared by one of the country's best teams of chefs.

FURTHER AFIELD

BioPont

Krúdy Gyula utca 8, 1088 **Tel** *266 46 01*

Map *7 B4*

Here everything is natural and organic. There isn't a piece of meat, a dairy product or a fish in sight, and those who like what they eat can buy most of the ingredients in the shop attached. A bright café atmosphere attracts a student crowd, who flock here at lunchtimes. The whole restaurant is non-smoking.

Fenyőgyöngye Vendéglő

Szépvölgyi út 155, 1025 **Tel** *325 97 83*

Small, incredibly popular restaurant up in the Buda Hills, offering traditional Hungarian fare made in a lighter, healthier way. The garden area is perfect for families, and popular with Buda's middle classes on Sunday afternoons. Reserving a table is a good idea. Bus 65 runs to the door from Szépvölgyi út HEV station. **www. fenyogyongye.hu**

Jókai Étterem

Hollós út 5, 1121 **Tel** *395 36 58*

Relaxed restaurant in a lovely 19th-century villa in the hills near the Svábhegy cog-wheel station. Attentive service and well-prepared classic Hungarian dishes at incredibly good prices. The terrace is pleasant in the summer. For those who don't fancy the journey on the cog-wheel railway, Bus 21 from Moszkva tér runs close by.

Kerék Vendéglő

Bécsi út 103, 1034 **Tel** *250 42 61*

An authentic Old Buda restaurant from the 1960s, offering Hungarian cuisine to the music of an accordion player. It's not the most exclusive place in the city, nor will it win any design contests, but the garden is lovely and the food is great – both hearty and cheap. Tram 17 from Margaret Bridge gets you there. Booking is advised at weekends.

Náncsi Néni Vendéglője

Ördögárok út 80, 1029 **Tel** *398 71 27*

Customers are offered a wide choice of interesting, home-style interpretations of traditional Hungarian dishes. Giant *túrógombóc* (curd cheese dumplings) is a favourite dessert – with those who have remembered to save room. Booking is essential, especially for the popular garden area in summer. **www.nancsineni.hu**

Szép Ilona Vendéglő

Budakeszi út 1–3, 1021 **Tel** *275 13 92*

A long established, pleasant restaurant offering Hungarian and German specialities, including some tremendous sausages, and all at knockdown prices. It's a good place to compare the relative merits of German and Hungarian cuisines. The well-sized garden is lovely, and popular in summer. Bus 22 from Moszkva tér runs close by.

Vasas Családi Vendéglő

Pasaréti út 11–13, 1026 **Tel** *212 87 77*

Popular family restaurant with a relaxed and friendly atmosphere, a bright and breezy interior, and a lovely terrace. Cooking is home-style. There is a good menu for children and an excellent-value, three-course set lunch. Booking is recommended, especially for lunch. Bus 5 from Moszkva tér gets you there.

Bajai Halászcsárda

Hollós út 2, 1121 **Tel** *275 52 45*

Located next to the Svábhegy cog-wheel stop. Traditional Hungarian dishes specializing in fresh river fish. A real treat is the Bajai fish soup with a huge portion of carp fillets served on the side. There is also *goulash*, and for dessert the fried doughnuts are worth trying. If you don't fancy the cog-rail, Bus 21 from Moskva tér runs close by.

Külvárosi Kávéház

István út 26, 1041 **Tel** *379 15 68*

A gem in the district of Újpest. International cuisine with excellent Hungarian dishes, including a three-course *betyárleves* (bone marrow on toast, golden soup with noodles and vegetables, beef cooked in soup). The absurdly cheap prices make this one of Budapest's most popular restaurants so reserve a table. Take metro M3 to Újpest-Központ.

Key to Price Guide *see p196* **Key to Symbols** *see back cover flap*

Nefrit Chinese Restaurant
Apor Vilmos tér 4k, 1124 **Tel** *213 90 39*

Cantonese and Sechaun specialities in a pleasant restaurant in an old villa. Tasty *dim sum* are on offer, and prices are remarkably reasonable. Finding Chinese food in Budapest is easy; finding good Chinese food is tricky, so make your way here. You can do so on Bus 105 from Erszebet tér.

Öreghalász Étterem
Árpád út 20–22, 1042 **Tel** *231 08 00*

There's a homely atmosphere in this restaurant, where fresh river fish is the speciality. The decor is nautical but not over-the-top, and it enhances enjoyment of the super food. It is worth trying any fish soup from the wide range on offer, though non-fish dishes are also available. Booking recommended. **www.oreg-halasz.hu**

Arcade Bistro
Kiss János Altáb utca 38, 1126 **Tel** *225 19 69*

Map *3 A1*

Few restaurants in Budapest can match the outstanding patio that attracts the Budapest jet set to Arcade during the summer. The food here is excellent, too, contemporary and inventive, and beautifully presented. Prices are a little high but represent real value for money. **www.arcadebistro.hu**

Kisbuda Gyöngye Étterem
Kenyeres utca 34, 1043 **Tel** *368 64 02*

This restaurant has a natural, old-time drawing room atmosphere, where guests relax and enjoy excellent dishes from international and Hungarian cuisines to the soft music of a piano. A lunch here, where nothing should be hurried, usually turns into a long afternoon as the wine continues to flow. **www.remiz.hu**

Ristorante Krizia
Mozsár utca 12, 1066 **Tel** *331 87 11*

Krizia is a celebration of Mediterranean food and atmosphere. Elegance is balanced by hints of rusticity, from the terracotta pots to the overcrowded shelves of wine. The food is mainly Italian, and the pasta is made on the premises. There is a super wine list. Take the Millennium Metro to Oktagon to get here. **www.ristorantekrizia.hu**

Voros Postakocsi
Ráday utca 15, 1092 **Tel** *217 67 56*

It's worth eating here simply to gaze out of the enormous windows at the super-trendy people passing by on up-and-coming Ráday utca. The main dining room is large, but charmingly decorated. The food is good – mainly Hungarian but with an international and contemporary twist. The name means Red Post Wagon.

Chez Daniel
Sziv utca 32, 1063 **Tel** *302 40 39*

Choose from the daily specials chalked up on the blackboard, then kick back and enjoy great food in one of Budapest's most relaxed restaurants. The food is mainly French, unfussy and accessible. The wine list is very good, and evenings here tend to be long. The small terrace-cum-courtyard is lovely. You'll need a reservation.

Jardinette
Németvölgyi út 136, 1112 **Tel** *248 16 52*

During the summer there are a number of tables in the garden, where chestnut trees provide shade from the sun, and the whole ambience is warm and Mediterranean. Sitting inside in winter, however, can feel a little like sitting in a greenhouse. Food is contemporary European – not fancy, but good. **www.jardinette.hu**

Kéhli Vendéglő
Mókus utca 22, 1036 **Tel** *250 42 41*

Excellent, long-forgotten tastes of Pest and Buda are served here in large portions. Established more than a century ago in Old Buda, this was the favourite eating place of Gyula Krúdy, the great Hungarian gourmet writer. Standards have not dropped a notch since he dined here. Reservations recommended. **www.kehli.hu**

King Arthur's
Bécsi út 38-44 (Új Udvar Shopping Centre), 1036. **Tel** *437 82 43*

This theme restaurant on the second floor of a giant shopping mall may not be everyone's idea of fine dining, but if you want great food and a good time at a reasonable price, you can do a lot worse in Budapest. Serving girls dress in period costume and deliver enormous portions of meat on the bone. **www.kingarthur.hu**

Fuji Japan
Csatárka utca 54, 1025 **Tel** *325 71 11*

In a pagoda-style interior, Japanese food enthusiasts can watch the chef at work while enjoying dishes such as a beautifully presented selection of *sashimi*. There is more than raw fish on the menu, however. This is a real Japanese restaurant, with the high prices to prove it. **www.fujirestaurant.hu**

Vadrózsa Étterem
Pentelei Molnár utca 15, 1025 **Tel** *326 58 17*

Exclusive restaurant set in a beautiful Neo-Baroque villa and run by one family for 30 years. Soft piano music plays in the evenings. The gardens are lovely in summer. A taxi is required to get here, but the house will tell you when, at the end of the meal, it's time for carriages. The food? Outstanding, adventurous and expensive. **www.vadorzsa.hu**

Cafés and Wine Bars

To sample the true atmosphere of Hungary, it is essential to visit the smaller eating and drinking establishments that are scattered across the city and into the suburbs. Behind even the most ordinary of buildings, there could be hiding a timeless pocket of old Hungarian culture. Elsewhere, bright neon and loud music reflect the contemporary cultural interests of Budapest's youth. And between these extremes, visitors can still find a taste of 19th-century opulence in the old coffee houses and patisseries that once sat comfortably at the heart of the city's life.

CAFES & COFFEE HOUSES

Hungary has one of the oldest coffee-drinking traditions in Europe. Introduced by the Turks in the mid-16th century during their occupation *(see pp26–7)*, the coffee culture blossomed towards the end of the Habsburg era *(see pp32–3)*, when there were almost 600 *kávéházes* (cafés) in the city.

The 19th-century café scene was a hotbed of intellectual activity dominated by literary and artistic circles. **New York Kávéház** *(see p129)*, which opened in 1894, was for many years the centre of this creative scene; its walls adorned with frescoes painted by the leading artists of the day. At the former Café Pilvax the seeds of the national uprising of 1848-49 *(see pp30–31)* were sown.

Today's café scene is much changed. Almost every luxurious *cukrászda* (cake shop) and *kávéház* has closed down, giving way to a new variety of coffee bar. *Eszpresszó* bars first appeared in the 1930s but were most popular in the 1960s. Much cheaper than their predecessors, they catered for teenagers with a taste for Western culture. These have subsequently been replaced by more modern cafés, such as **Pierrot Café** up in the Castle District; or **Pesti Est Café** and **Mozart Café**, two of the many cafés and bars that line trendy Liszt Ferenc tér in the city centre.

Fortunately, a couple of the old gems remain. **Gerbeaud Cukrázsda** still serves the best coffee and cakes in the land, as it has done for well over a hundred years, while the **Gellért Eszpresszó** is a sublime recreation of a Habsburg-era coffee house, situated on the ground floor of the Gellért Hotel *(see pp183)*. Both of these places offer the genuine Budapest coffee-house experience, complete with immaculately liveried waitresses in pinafore dresses, and an old lady who insists on taking your coat. They are sublime reminders of a bygone age.

There are many styles of coffee in Budapest. A *kávé* is an espresso with milk and sugar, and a *dupla* is a double espresso. French-style milky coffee is called a *tejeskávé*, while cappuccinos are often served with whipped cream or in the Viennese-style – that is, without either chocolate or cinnamon. For decaffeinated coffee, ask for *koffeinmentes*.

WINE BARS

Wine and wine bars occupy a different position in the social hierarchy in Hungary than they do in, say, Britain or the United States. Whereas in these countries wine drinking is regarded as a somewhat middle-class pursuit, in Hungary it has traditionally been considered a workers' pastime. Furthermore, despite the fact that young men are now starting to adopt beer as their drink of choice, the old ways of drinking wine are still to be found underground, in the *borozók of* Budapest.

A *borozó* is, generally speaking, an unglamorous, cheap wine cellar, where wine is served straight from the barrel and sold by the decilitre. Few places have tables and chairs. In the city centre, however, there is the more stylish **Rondella Borozó**, where wine is drawn from barrels and served in curious jugs with a tap at the bottom.

The Castle District is home to a range of *borozók*. **The Hattyú**, meaning "Swan", at No. 1 Hattyú utca, and the **Várfok Borozó**, at No. 9 Várfok utca are of the simple kind. At the other end of the spectrum, there are places like the **Hilton Hotel** *(see p182)*, which houses a stylish wine bar in an authentic medieval cellar. Such establishments tend to serve expensive wines in bottles, rather than straight from the barrel.

The popular, full-bodied range of dessert wines called Tokaji *(see p195)* also has a number of wine bars dedicated to it. Arguably, the best is found in **Tokaji Borozó**, in central Pest, where most customers drink standing up.

COCKTAIL BARS

Budapest is currently alive with trendy cocktail bars that buzz from the early evening onwards with a young crowd, enjoying after-work drinks in the Italian fashion *(aperitivo)*.

There are cocktail bars all over the city, but the trendiest establishments, such as arthouse-style **Vian**, tend to be found on "the tér" (Liszt Ferenc tér). Indeed, Liszt Ferenc tér is quite simply the social heart and soul of Budapest during the spring and summer months. There are at least 16 bars, cafés and discos on the ter, and all have seating *al fresco*. Nevertheless, the area is so popular that it can often be difficult to get a seat. Favourite places nearby include **Incognito** and **Karma**.

On the other side of the Danube, a hip crowd meets every evening at **Oscar's American Bar**, famous for its selection of more than 200 cocktails. The lucky few for whom money is no object head for the **Four Seasons Bar**, in the Gresham Palace hotel. Visitors to the city may like to follow suite, not least to enjoy the hotel's splendid interiors.

FOOD AND CUSTOMS

Wine bars, where people can pop in for a glass of wine or a spritzer *(see p195)* at any time of day, do not generally serve food. Occasionally, however, light snacks are available. Typically, these consist of a slice of bread and dripping garnished with raw onion and sprinkled with paprika; or *pogácsa*, a yeast pan-bread, served with crackling, cheese, caraway seeds or paprika. Wine bars with tables sometimes serve frankfurters or knuckle.

Visitors should take note of the following warning. In Hungary, unlike most other Europeans countries, it is not done to clink beer glasses together with fellow drinkers. This apparently innocent gesture was adopted by the Austrians as they executed Hungarian generals after the uprising of 1848–9, and can still cause great offence.

DIRECTORY

CAFÉS

Anna Café
Váci utca 7. **Map** 4 E1.
Tel 266 90 80. **Open**
8:30am–midnight daily.

Auguszt Cukrászda
Kossuth Lajos utca 14–16.
Map 4 F1. *Tel 316 89 31.*
Open 10am–6pm Tue–Fri,
10am–2pm Sat.

Café Firenze
Szalay utca 5a. **Map** 2 E3.
Tel 331 83 99.
Open 9am–8pm daily.

Gerbeaud Cukrászda
Vörösmarty tér 7.
Map 2 E5. *Tel 429 90 00.*
Open 9am–9pm daily.

Grinzingi Borozó
Veres Pálné utca 10.
Map 4 F2 (10 E5).
Tel 317 46 24. **Open**
9am–1am Mon–Sat,
3pm–11pm Sun.

Havana Café
Török pal utca 6.
Map 7 A5. *Tel 061 215
42 88.* **Open**
11.30am–1am daily.

Károlyi "R" Café
Károlyi Mihály utca 19.
Map 4 F2 (10 E5).
Tel 266 02 44. **Open**
9am– midnight Sat & Sun.

Leroy Café
Liszt Ferenc tér 2.
Map 7 A1. **Open**
10am–midnight daily.

Lukács Café
Andrássy út 70. **Map** 5 A5.
Tel 302 87 47.
Open 9am–8pm Mon–Fri,
10am–8pm Sat & Sun.

Menza
Liszt Ferenc tér 2. **Map** 7
A1. *Tel 413 14 83.* **Open**
11am–midnight daily.

Mozart Café
Erzsébet körút 36. **Map** 7
B2. *Tel 352 06 64.* **Open**
9am–11pm Mon–Fri,
9am–10pm Sat & Sun.

Mvész Cukrászda
Andrássy út 29.
Map 2 F4 (10 E2).
Tel 352 13 37. **Open**
9am–midnight daily.

New York Kávéház
Erzsébet körút 9–11.
Map 7 B2. *Tel 322 38 49.*
Open 9am–midnight daily.

1000 Tea
Vaci utca 65. **Map** 4 F2.
Tel 337 82 17.
Open noon–9pm
Mon–Sat, 3pm–8pm Sun.

Pesti Est Cafe
Liszt Ferenc tér 5. **Map** 7A.
Tel 344 43 81. **Open**
11am–midnight daily.

Pierrot
Fortuna utca 14.
Map B4. *Tel 375 69 71.*
Open 11am–11pm daily.

Ruszwurm Cukrászda
Szentháromság utca 7.
Map B4 (9 A2).
Tel 375 52 84.
Open 10am–7pm daily.

WINE BARS

Alkoholos Filc Kávézó
Várfok utca 15/B. **Map** 1
A3. **Open** 9am– 10pm
Mon–Sat. **Closed** Sun.

Bástya Borozó
Székely utca 2–4. **Map** C4
(10 E2). *Tel 212 38 19.*
Open 10am–10pm daily.

Badacsonyi Borozó
Károlyi István utca 24.
Map 4 F2. *Tel 269 32 07.*
Open 9am–midnight
Mon–Fri (from noon Sat).

Fehér Galamb
Szentháromság utca 9–11.
Map 1 B4 (9 A2).
Tel 212 56 04. **Open**
noon–midnight daily.

Hattyu
Hattyú utca 14.
Map 1 A3.
Tel 202 77 77.
Open 24 hours daily.

Karma
Liszt Ferenc tér 11.
Map 7 A1.
Tel 413 67 64.
Open 11am–1am daily.

Kékfrankos Borozó
Keleti Károly utca 4.
Map 1 A2.
Tel 212 53 86.
Open 10am–9pm daily.

Móri Borozó
Fiáth János utca 16.
Map 1 A3.
Tel 214 92 16.
Open 2–11pm Mon–Fri,
4–9pm Sat & Sun.

Pince Csárda
Török utca 1. **Map** 1 B1.
Tel 212 45 08. **Open**
11am–10pm Mon–Fri.

Rondella Borozó
Régiposta utca 4.
Map 4 E1.
Tel 483 08 30.
Open 5pm–2am daily.

Söröz a Szent Jupáthoz
Retek utca 16.
Map 1 A3.
Tel 212 29 23.
Open noon–6am daily.

Vincellér Borszaküzlet
Erd utca 10.
Map 1 B3.
Tel 201 15 61. **Open**
10am–6pm Tue–Fri,
8pm–midnight Sat & Sun.

Vidocq Borozó
Lajos utca 98.
Tel 388 83 14.
Open noon–11pm
Mon–Fri, noon–midnight
Sat & Sun.

Villányi-Siklósi Borozó
Gerlóczy utca 13.
Map 4 F1 (10 E4).
Tel 267 02 41. **Open**
6am–11pm Mon–Fri.

Tokaji Borozó
Falk Miksa utca 32.
Map 2 D2. *Tel 269 31 43.*
Open noon–10pm
Mon–Fri, 4–11pm Sat.

COCKTAIL BARS

Crew Bar
Szondi utca 11. **Map** 2 F3.
Tel 269 49 04.
Open 11am–2am daily.

Four Seasons Bar
Four Seasons Gresham
Palace Hotel. Roosevelt tér
5–6. **Map** 2 D5.
Tel 268 60 00 **Open**
11am–1am daily

Incognito
Liszt Ferenc tér 3.
Map 7 A1. *Tel 342 14 71.*
Open 10am–midnight
daily.

Karma
Liszt Ferenc tér 11.
Map 7 A1. *Tel 413 67 64*
Open 11.30am–midnight
daily.

Oscar's American Bar
Ostrom utca 14.
Map 1 A3.
Tel 212 80 17.
Open 5pm–2am daily.

Vian
Liszt Ferenc tér 9.
Map 7 A1. *Tel 268 11 54.*
Open 9am–midnight daily.

Beer Halls, Pubs and Clubs

There are drinking establishments in Budapest to suit practically every taste, from traditional Hungarian beer halls to high-tech nightclubs, and many stay open late. The most recent developments on the scene – themed Irish, English or sports bars – cater to crowds of English ruffians who visit the city on "stag" weekends. It is still possible, however, simply to stroll around the city and drop into the places frequented by locals. You will find Budapest a very friendly and informal place to drink; if you sit at an empty table, others will probably join you. Note that in traditional pubs a waiter will automatically bring more beer as soon as you appear to be close to finishing your glass, unless you indicate otherwise.

TRADITIONAL BEER HALLS

In recent years, beer has started to take over from wine as Hungary's favourite drink. Driven by this fashion, in Budapest many wine bars have been turned into *sörözs* (beer halls), and several new establishments modelled on the German *bierstube* and the English pub have opened. As a result, beer-drinking has become an aspirational pastime, and prices in the *sörözs* and pubs are much higher than in the *borozós* (traditional wine bars, *see p206*). This price difference is particularly noticeable in the popular tourist areas.

The cost of drinking beer is, however, reflected in the relative sophistication of the pastime; it is possible to buy almost all the major brands in the city, as well as Hungarian *világos* (light) and *barna* (dark) beers (*see p194*).

Beer is measured by the *korsó*, the equivalent of a pint, and the *pohár*, a smaller glass. A variety of good and moderately priced snacks and hot dishes, including smoked knuckle, is available in *sörözs*, as, indeed, is wine. By contrast, the *borozós* rarely offer food, and never beer.

The best of the old-style beer halls is probably historic **Budavari**, located in the Castle District. A more mainstream drinking experience can be had in the **Jam Pub** in the Mammut Shopping Centre, which even has live music most nights of the week, at 9pm.

IRISH PUBS & THEME BARS

Like many Eastern European cities, Budapest has been invaded by theme bars and pubs, notably Irish pubs. Some are friendlier than others, some are more Irish than others, but all have Guinness at the usual, extortionate prices. **Becketts** was the first Irish pub in Budapest and it remains popular with tourists, locals and expatriates. There's great pub food on offer, and good music at weekends. Equally celebrated is **Fregatt**, a hybrid Irish-English-Hungarian pub decked out in bizarre naval style. **Janis' Pub** is named after Janis Joplin and is a gem – with a bright blue exterior and live music at weekends. The small but enjoyable **Zappa Café** pays homage to another great legend of rock, Frank Zappa.

Budapest also has many easy-going venues where the music is less important than the atmosphere. For example, the **Cotton Club**, where sultry female singers croon to a trendy, upmarket crowd; and the **Old Man's Music Pub**, where a range of performers from Irish fiddlers to Hungarian punk bands entertain happy, drunk crowds from 9–11pm daily.

For Hungarian "oompah" music, complete with floor show, head for the peerless **Kalamajka Dance House**. It is touristy and expensive, but great. **Alcatraz**, where clients sit behind bars in their own private cells and staff wear prison warden's costumes, takes the theme pub concept perhaps too far; but it is still around after years on the scene, is more popular than ever, and has good live music most nights.

BOHEMIAN HANGOUTS

Though not in the same league as Prague, Budapest has nevertheless long been a haven for individualists looking for something a little different. Many are attracted by its glut of unusual places to eat and drink, such as the **Red Lion Tea House**, an Eastern-style retreat from modern life, where the serving of tea is an art form. Another favourite hangout is **Piaf**, a superbly decadent dive reminiscent of a speakeasy.

NIGHTCLUBS & DISCOS

Nightlife in Budapest is on its way to competing with that of other European capitals and new clubs open daily. Among the most recent arrivals are **Dokk Jazz Bistro**, a huge, high-tech club set in a converted dry dock; **Tütü Tango**, offering a mix of live bands, hip DJs and drinking and dining; and **Complex** in Szentendre (*see p165*), which is Hungary's first "superclub" and features top-name DJs.

The biggest and probably the most popular club in the city is **Bahnhof**, which is found, predictably enough, behind Nyugati train station and is frequented by a terrific mix of locals, expatriates and tourists, attracted by the relatively cheap drinks and mainstream dance music. It's open on Thursday, Friday and Saturday. Also popular is the disco boat **A38**, moored just past Petfi bridge on the Buda side of the river.

Older clubs are often centered around student venues. **Petőfi Csarnok**, a cavernous youth entertainment centre built in 1984 during the Communist era, is a stage and disco complex that hosts local and international rock bands. **E-Klub** is open on Fridays and Saturdays and is always crowded with Technical

University students. **Közgáz Pince Klub** is a really vibrant student club held in the huge hall of the University of Corvinus (*see p138*).

The chic set meet at **Made Inn**, which has two dance floors, a room for live music, and an attractive patio and garden which are full to bursting in summer.

GAY VENUES

Budapest's trendy gay crowd usually heads for **Angyal Bár**, which always has great disco music from all eras and a friendly atmosphere. Friday nights are male-only, but at other times there is a mixed crowd. Also good is **Upside Down**, which attracts all sorts

to its celebrated karaoke nights on Mondays and Wednesdays. Weekends are for hardcore techno fans and almost exclusively male. **Coxx**, a massive men-only complex with bar, disco, restaurant, internet café and gallery is famous for its theme nights – anything from fancy dress to no dress at all.

DIRECTORY

BEER HALLS

Alagút Sörház
Alagút utca 4.
Map 1 B5 (9 A3).
Tel 212 37 64.
Open 24 hours daily.

Aranyászok Sörház
József nádor tér 12.
Map 2 E5 (10 D4).
Tel 267 24 63.
Open 11am–11pm daily.

Astoria Café Mirror
Kossoth Lajos utca 19.
Map 4 F1.
Tel 317 34 11.
Open 7am–11pm daily.

Bajor Sörsátor
Kós Károly sétány.
Map 6 D3.
Tel 363 19 04.
Open 10am–11pm daily.

Bécsi Söröz
Papnövelde utca 8.
Map 4 F2 (10 E5).
Tel 267 02 25. **Open** 10am–10pm Mon–Fri, 10am–4pm Sat & Sun.

Budavári
Fortuna Spaten, Hess András tér 4. **Map** 1 B5.
Tel 375 61 75.
Open 11am–midnight daily.

Gösser Söröz
Régiposta utca 4.
Map 4 E1 (10 D4).
Tel 318 26 08. **Open** 10am–midnight daily.

Jam Pub
Lövház utca 1–3,
Mammut II. **Map** 1 A3.
Open 8am–4am Mon–Fri, 8am–6pm Sat–Sun.

Kaltenberg Royal Bavarian Brasserie
Kinizsi utca 30–36. **Map** 7 A5. **Tel** 215 9792. **Open** noon–midnight daily.

Tóth Kocsma
Falk Miksa utca 17.
Map 2 D2.
Tel 302 40 20.
Open 11am–11pm daily.

IRISH PUBS & THEME BARS

Alcatraz
Nyár utca 1. **Map** 7 A3.
Tel 478 60 10. **Open** 4pm–2am Sun–Thu, 4pm–2am Fri & Sat.
www.alcatraz.hu

Becketts Irish Pub
Bajcsy Zsilinszky út 72.
Map 2 E3 (10 E1).
Tel 311 10 33. **Open** noon–1am Mon–Fri, noon–3am Sat & Sun.

Cotton Club
Jókai utca 26.
Map 2 F3.
Tel 354 08 86.
Open noon–1am daily.
www.cottonclub.hu

Fregatt
Molnár utca 26.
Map 4 E2 (10 D5).
Tel 318 99 97.
Open 11am–11pm daily.

Janis' Pub
Királyi Pál utca 8.
Map 4 F2.
Tel 266 26 19.
Open 4pm–3am Mon–Sat, 6pm–midnight Sun.

John Bull Pub
Apáczai Csere János utca 17. **Map** 2 D5.
Tel 338 21 68.
Open noon–11pm Mon–Sat, 5–11pm Sun.

Kalamajka Dance House
Molnár utca 17.
Budapest V. **Map** 4 E2.
Tel 266 78 66.
Open 11am–1am daily.

Old Man's Music Pub
Akácfa utca 13.
Map 7 A2.
Tel 322 76 45.
Open 3pm–4am daily.

Zappa Café
Miksáth Kálmán tér 2
Map 7 A4.
Tel 972 47 11.
Open 10am–2am daily.

BOHEMIAN HANGOUTS

Piaf
Nagymező utca 25.
Map 2 F3.
Tel 312 38 23. **Open** 10pm–5am Sun–Thu, 10pm–7am Fri–Sat.

Red Lion Tea House
Jókai tér 8. **Map** 10 F1.
Tel 269 05 79.
Open 11am–11pm daily.

NIGHTCLUBS & DISCOS

A38
Pázmány Pétér setány, Petfi híd.
Tel 464 39 40.
Open 4pm–4am
www.a38.hu

Bahnhof
Váci út 1. **Map** 2 F2.
Tel 302 47 51.
Open 9pm–4am Thu–Sat.
www.bahnhofmusic.hu

Complex
Rószá utca 8,
Szentendre.
Tel 936 77 19.
Open 10pm–6pm daily

Dokk Jazz Bistro
Hajogyari Sziget 12.
Tel 535 27 47.
Open 9pm–5am daily.

E–Klub
Népliget út 2.
Tel 263 16 14.
Open 9pm–5am daily.

Közgáz Pince Klub
Fvám tér 8. **Map** 4 F3.
Tel 215 43 59. **Open** 10pm–5am Tue–Sat.
Closed Sun & Mon.

Made Inn
Andrássy út 112.
Map 7 A1.
Tel 311 34 37.
Open 5pm–2am daily.

Petőfi Csarnok
Zichy Mihály utca 14.
Map 6 E4. **Tel** 363 37 30.
Open Times vary with events.

Tütü Tango
Hajós utca 2. **Map** 2 F4.
Tel 321 27 15. **Open** 11am–1am Mon–Sat, noon–midnight Sun.

GAY VENUES

Angyal Bár
Szövetség utca 33.
Map 7 B1.
Tel 351 64 90.
Open 10pm–5am daily.

Coxx
Dohany utca 38.
Map 7 A3.
Tel 344 48 84.
Open 11am–4am daily.
www.coxx.hu

Upside Down
Podmaniczky Tér 1.
Map 2 F3.
Tel 070 367 96 19 (mob.).
Open 10pm–5am daily.

SHOPS AND MARKETS

Shopping in Budapest has changed dramatically since the more spartan days of Communism. A huge variety of consumer goods, both foreign and home produced, are now available here. Major shopping streets include the pedestrianized and fashionable Váci utca (Váci Street, *see p127)* good for folk art and Zsolnay porcelain, and the less fashionable, but much cheaper

String of paprika peppers

Nagykörút, where locals come to do their shopping. For a more traditional shopping experience, don't miss a visit to some of Budapest's many markets. These range from stunning 19th-century food halls such as the Great Market Hall (Nagy Vásárcsarnok), to flea markets such as the huge and lively Ecseri Flea Market, for everything from bric-a-brac to furniture and antiques.

OPENING HOURS

Most shops in Budapest open from 9am to 5:30 or 6pm Monday to Friday, and from 9am to 1pm on Saturday. Department stores open at 10am, while green-grocers, bakeries and super-markets are open from 7am until 8pm. Many shops stay open until 8 or 9pm on Thursday. Indoor markets and department stores open on Sunday, and most cafés sell milk and bread on Sunday morning. One result of the increase in private enterprise since 1989 is a large number of small shops which open 24 hours a day and sell groceries, cigarettes and alcohol.

Duna Plaza Shopping Centre on Váci út

HOW TO PAY

Credit cards and Euro-cheques can be used to pay for goods and services in many of the more touristy parts

of Budapest. Outside these areas it is best to carry plenty of cash in Hungarian forints.

VAT EXEMPTION

The price of all goods in Hungary includes a value-added tax of 25% (ÁFA). With the exception of works of art and antiques, it is possible to claim back the value-added tax on anything costing more than 50,000 forints when you leave the country. First, present your goods at customs within 90 days of purchase to receive your customs certification and a refund claim form. You will need your sales receipt and currency exchange or credit card receipt, plus the customs certification, to apply for your refund within 183 days of your return home.

DEPARTMENT STORES AND MALLS

There are a number of department stores in the city, many housed in spectacular old buildings. The

Traditional folk crafts, on sale around Váci utca

Secession-style **Luxus** on Vörösmarty tér offers three floors of smart men's and women's clothing, as well as accessories and perfumes. More of a mall than a department store, the **Duna Plaza** on Váci út is smart but overpriced. It is equipped with an ice-skating rink, a video arcade and a bowling alley. Another store worth a look is **Skála Metro** on Nyugati tér opposite the railway station in Pest.

Over the past decade more than 10 major shopping malls have opened in Budapest, and have proved popular with both locals and visitors . The most exciting new mall is **Westend City Center**. Central Europe's largest, the centre has over 350 stores, including Armani, Benetton and Marks & Spencer, in addition to a 14-screen cinema and a food court.

The new and stylish **Mammut** on Moszkva tér is frequented by the better off inhabitants of Buda, and is easily accessible for those who do not have the good fortune to live nearby.

Delicate lace, an example of traditional Hungarian folk art

MARKETS

Markets of all sorts are an essential part of life in Budapest, and offer a delightfully traditional shopping experience to visitors. Perhaps the most spectacular are the five cavernous market halls which dot the city. All were built in the late 19th

Sausages on sale at the Central Market Hall

century and several are still used as markets. The three-level Great Market Hall (Nagy Vásárcsarnok) known officially as the **Central Market Hall** (Központi Vásárcsarnok) on Fővám tér is the largest of all. More than 180 stalls display a huge variety of vegetables, fruit, meat and cheese, under a gleaming roof of brightly-coloured Zsolnay tiles. The market opens from 7am–6pm Mon–Fri and 7am–1pm Sat.

In addition to the covered market halls, there are open-air food markets in every Budapest neighbourhood. In many you will see country women in traditional costumes selling fruit and vegetables, as well as local cheeses, honey and sausages. Some of the best markets are at Lehel tér (district XIII), Bosnyák tér (XIV) and Fehérvári út (IX). Delicious hot sausages with mustard and fresh bread, or *lángos*, a flat bread served with cream or grated cheese, are traditional and widely available market snacks.

Beginning at 156 Nagykőrösi út in district XIX, is the **Ecseri Flea Market**. Outside, a maze of wooden tables is covered in

Communist artifacts, second-hand clothes and all sorts of bric-a-brac, while from tiny cubicles inside the market, serious antique dealers sell porcelain, icons, silverware, jewellery and much more. It is necessary to obtain permission from the Museum of Applied Arts *(see pp136–7)* before you can take antiques out of the country. The flea market is open on Saturdays and Sundays.

Another market well worth a visit is the extremely busy **Józsefvárosi Market**, situated close to Józsefváros pu on Kőbányai út and open 7am–6pm daily. Many of the traders here are Chinese, often with Roma assistants, using the Trans-Siberian railway to transport a huge variety of new goods from China, southeast Asia, the former Soviet Union and eastern Europe, all sold at knock-down prices. Look out for all sorts of entertaining and obvious southeast Asian fashion fakes, as well as electronic goods, Chinese silks, Russian caviar and vodka, and Stalinist memorabilia.

Marks & Spencer, a branch of the British department store

What to Buy in Budapest

Despite price rises since the return to a free-market economy, many Hungarian goods are still great bargains. Embroidered peasant blouses and wooden carvings make unique souvenirs, as does the distinctive porcelain produced at the world-famous Zsolnay and Herend factories. Cheap, good quality CDs and records are widely available, and Hungarian wines, salamis and other foodstuffs can be bought in the city's many lively markets. Clothes and shoes made to your specifications represent one of the city's most luxurious bargains.

FOLK ART

Hungarian folk culture is still alive and well in many parts of rural Hungary. You can buy textiles, ceramics and woodwork from flea markets *(see p211)* and from street vendors around Moszkva tér and Parliament *(see pp108–9)*. Folk art shops such as **Folkart Centrum**, sell machine-made products, and, for genuine Transylvanian textiles there is the **Judit Kézmüves** hand-made shop. For the cheapest authentic folk costumes, head for the **Central Market Hall** (Nagy Vásárcsarnok).

ANTIQUES

Dominated by 18th- and 19th-century pieces in the Habsburg style, the Budapest antiques scene is concentrated in the Castle District, around Falk Miksa utca and on Váci utca *(Váci Street, see p127)*. **Moró Antik** is a tiny shop specializing in 18th-century weapons, while the huge **Nagyházi Gallery** sells everything from jewellery to furniture. The **Ecseri Flea Market** *(see p211)* is also a good place for antiques.

PORCELAIN

There are two major porcelain manufacturors in Hungary, **Herend** and **Zsolnay**. Herend enjoys a reputation as the producer of the country's finest porcelain, while Zsolnay's brightly glazed tiles can be seen on many of the city's notable buildings. Second-hand porcelain can be bought in antiques shops and markets. Both companies have shops selling new pieces.

CLOTHES AND SHOES

Made-to-measure clothes and shoes, and ready-made designer clothes offer some of the best deals to be had by visitors to Budapest. Many people have clothes made up in their choice of fabric by a local designer – who is likely to be happy to oblige for a fairly modest fee. At the smart end of the market, there is **Naray Tamás Boutique**, the showcase for one of the most famous designers in Hungary. **Budapesti Brilliáns Börze**, which opened in 2004, is already one of the country's most exclusive jewellers. Shoemakers in Budapest tend to make only men's shoes. **Vass** will make you a one-off pair of dress shoes in about a month. They will cost around 130,000 Hungarian forints.

FOOD AND WINE

Food and wine in Hungary are great value and make excellent souvenirs for you to take home after your stay. Sausage is a national passion and can be bought in shops and markets all over the city. Some of the most popular types include spicy sausages from Debrecen, smoked sausages from Gyulai and a whole range of world-famous salamis. Also worth bringing home are dried mushrooms, *paté de foie gras*, a string of paprika or some fresh sheep's cheese. All these can be bought in Budapest's markets and in major supermarkets like **Pick**. Hungary's national beverage is wine *(see pp194–5)* and there are various top-quality bottles to look out for. These include fine desert wines from the Tokaji region, Muscats from Kiskunhalas on the central plain, and Chardonnays from Mátraalja. Also popular are the herbal liqueur Unicum, and the strong, fiery *pálinka*, which is made from plums, cherries or apricots. Wines and spirits are available in supermarkets and in specialist shops such as the **House of Hungarian Wines**, Borház and the **House of Palinka**.

MUSIC

Hungary's rich folk and classical music traditions make low-priced CDs, tapes and vinyl a tempting purchase in Budapest. For Hungarian folk music, from traditional Roma (Gypsy) music to recordings of village folk music, the old-style **Rózsavölgyi Zeneműbolt** is a good choice. In nearby Dob utca, **Concerto Records** offers a selection of new and second-hand vinyl and CDs, specializing in classical and opera, with some jazz, folk and funk. The state label, **Hungaroton**, has a shop in Rottenbiller utca that sells a wide range of classical music as well as some pop.

BOOKS

For illustrated books and English-language guide-books, try the **Litea Bookstore and Café**, where you can brouse through the books while enjoying coffee and cakes at tables set among the shelves. The large **Studium Libri** stocks many books in English. A wide range of English-language newspapers, magazines and novels are available at **Bestsellers**. **Írók Boltja** sells art books and some English-language books, while **Pendragon** stocks a varied assortment of fiction in English. One of the best places for maps and English-language guide books is **Párizsi Udvar**. **Librotrade-Kodex** stocks books in English, French and German. For antique books, etchings and maps a good place to try is **Központi Antikvárium**.

DIRECTORY

DEPARTMENT STORES

Duna Plaza
Váci út 178.
Tel 465 16 66.

Luxus
Vörösmarty tér 3.
Map 2 E5 (10 D3).
Tel 235 03 95.

Mammut I–II Mall
Lövőhaz utca 3.
Map 1 A2.
Open *10am–9pm*
Mon–Sat, 10am–6pm Sun.
Tel 345 80 20.
www.mammut.hu

Westend City Center
Váci út 1–3.
Map 2 F2.
Tel 238 77 77.

MARKETS

Central Market Hall (Központi Vásárcsarnok)
Vámház Körút 1–3
(Fővam tér).
Map 4 F3.
Open *6am–5pm Mon,*
6am–6pm Tue–Fri,
6am–2pm Sat.
Tel 217 60 67.

Ecseri Flea Market
Nagykőrösi út 156.
Open *Sat & Sun.*
Tel 282 95 63.

Fehérvári út Market
Fehérvári út 20.
Map 4 D5.

Fény utca Market
Near Moszkva tér.
Map 1 A3.

Józsefvárosi Market
Kőbányai út.
Map 8 F4.

Lehel tér Market
Lehel tér.
Map 2 F1.

FOLK ART

Folkart Centrum
Váci utca 58.
Map 4 E1 (10 D3).
Tel 318 58 40.

Judit Kézműves
Szentháromság utca 5.
Map 1 B4.
Tel 212 76 40.

ANTIQUES

Moró Antik
Falk Miksa utca 13.
Map 2 D2.
Tel 311 08 14.

Nagyházi Gallery
Balaton utca 8.
Map 2 D2.
Tel 475 60 00.

PORCELAIN

Herend Shops
József Nádor tér 11.
Map 2 E5 (10 D3).
Tel 317 26 22.
Szentháromság utca 5.
Tel 225 10 50.
Kigyó utca 5.
Map 4 E1 (10 D4).
Tel 318 34 39.

Zsolnay Shops
Kígyó utca 4.
Map 4 E1 (10 D4).
Tel 318 37 12.
Váci utca 19–21.
Map 2F1 (5 A2).
Tel 266 63 05.

CLOTHES AND ACCESSORIES

Budapesti Brilliáns Börze
Kristóf tér 8.
Map 10 D4.
Tel 266 65 20.

Naray Tamás Boutique
Károlyi Mihály utca 12.
Map 10 E5.
Tel 266 24 73.

Vass Cipőlt
Haris köz 2.
Map 4 E1.
Tel 318 23 75.
www.vasshoe.hu

FOOD AND DRINK

Borház
Jókai tér 7.
Map 2 F3 (10 F1).
Tel 353 48 49.

La Boutique des Vins
József Attila utca 12.
Map 2 E5 (10 D3).
Tel 317 59 19.

House of Hungarian Wines
Szentháromság tér 6.
Map 9 A2.
Open *noon–8pm.*
Tel 212 10 32.
www.winehouse.hu

House of Palinka
Rakoczi utca 17.
Map 7 A3. **Open**
9am–7pm Mon–Sat.
Free tasting: Fri.
www.magyarpalinkaha
za.hu

Pick
Kossuth Lajos tér 9.
Map 2 D3 (9 C1).
Tel 331 77 83.

MUSIC

Concerto Records
Dob utca 33.
Map 2 F5 (10 F3).
Tel 268 96 31.

Hungaroton Records
Rottenbiller utca 47.
Map 7 C1.
Tel 322 88 39.

Liszt Ferenc Zeneműboltja
Andrássy út 45.
Map 2 F5 (10 E2).
Tel 352 7314.
www.lizstbolt.hu

Rózsavölgyi Zeneműbolt
Szervita tér 5.
Map 4 E1 (10 D4).
Tel 318 35 00.

BOOKS

Bestsellers
Október 6 utca 11.
Map 2 E4 (10 D2).
Tel 312 12 95.
www.bestsellers.hu

Írók Boltja
Andrássy út 45.
Map 2 F4 (10 E2).
Tel 322 16 45.

Központi Antikvárium
Múzeum Körút 13–15.
Map 4 F1 (10 E4).
Tel 317 35 14.

Librotrade-Kodex
Honvéd utca 5.
Map 7 C3.
Tel 428 10 10.

Litea Bookstore and Café
Hess András tér 4.
Map 1 B4 (9 A2).
Open *10am–6pm.*
Tel 375 69 87.

Párizsi Udvar
Petőfi Sándor utca 2.
Map 4 E1 (10 E4).
Tel 235 03 79.
www.parisiudvar.hu

Pendragon
Pozsonyi út 21–23.
Map 2 F1.
Open *10am–6pm*
Mon–Fri, 10am–1pm Sat.
Closed *Sun.*
Tel 340 44 26.

Pendragon at CU
Nador utca 9. **Map** 2 D4.
Tel 327 30 96.
Open *10am–6pm*
Mon–Fri.
Closed *Sat & Sun.*

Studium Libri
Váci utca 22 (main
pedestrian precinct).
Map 4 E1 (10 D4).
Tel 318 56 80.
www.libri.hu

ENTERTAINMENT IN BUDAPEST

Budapest has been known as a city of entertainment since the late 19th century, when people would travel here from Vienna in search of a good time. Its buzzing nightclubs were frequented for their electric atmosphere and the beautiful girls that danced the spirited *csárdás* and the cancan. Nowhere else did fiddlers play such heartrending music or were the gambling casinos wit-

Street performer

ness to such staggering losses as in Budapest. Between the wars the city was as famous for its glittering society balls as for its libertine delights. The half-century of Communist rule dampened the revelry, but since 1990 the music scene has flourished and theatres, cabarets, festivals, cinemas and discotheques are all buzzing. Above all, renowned nightclubs have risen convincingly from their ashes.

ENTERTAINMENT HIGHLIGHTS

Budapest has two opera houses, an orchestral concert hall at the **Franz Liszt Academy of Music** (*see p208*), several other concert halls including the new **National Concert Hall** at the Palace of Arts (*see p156*), an operetta theatre, numerous cabarets and more than 50 theatres, including the fringe. Among them is the **Merlin Theatre** (*see p217*), which performs only in English.

The greatest concentration of theatres is in district V, in Nagymez utca, which has been nicknamed "Budapest's Broadway". Along this 100-m (328-ft) stretch there are two theatres, the **Operetta Theatre** (*see p216*), the satirical cabaret **Mikroszkóp Színpad** (*see p217*), reputed to be the best in Hungary, and the **Moulin Rouge** (*see p217*) revue theatre. Film-lovers are

spoilt for choice, as Budapest boasts many **cinemas**.

Városliget (*see pp142–3*) offers a permanent circus, funfair and zoo, with bars and beer tents in the summer.

The youth entertainment centre, **Petőfi Csarnok** (*see p217*), hosts rock concerts and the largest disco in town. **A38 Hájo**, a music club in a converted ship, and **Millenáris**, a relatively new concert venue with a varied programme, are both popular. The **Budapest Arena** holds 12,000 spectators, and stages a range of cultural events. Casinos and striptease clubs are the latest addition to the city's nightlife.

FREE ENTERTAINMENT

It is not difficult to find excellent, free entertainment in Budapest. During the summer, there always seem to be street entertainers and musicians wandering around the **Castle District**, often in elaborate period costume, playing instruments or acting out scenes from Hungarian history. During the **Budapesti Búcsú** (*see page 59*), all entertainments, from singing and dancing to theatre, are staged by the city council for free. In July, the **Danube Water Carnival** offers most of its thrills without charge, and the **Budapest Parade** (*see p59*) at the end of August is another great free day out.

The Hungarian government has decreed that the country's **museums** should be free. In practice, most charge for access to semi-permanent

exhibitions, but visitors who protest gently may find their entrance fees are waived.

Last but not least, guided tours of Budapest's leading sight, **Parliament**, are now free for citizens of the EU.

BUYING TICKETS

Tickets for all plays and concerts can be purchased in advance, either at a booking office or by telephoning the venue direct. Addresses and telephone

Lavishly staged opera at the State Opera House (*see p216*)

numbers are listed in the directory on pages 216–17. The most difficult to obtain are tickets to the **Franz Liszt Academy of Music** concerts, as these tend to be sold many days in advance. Similarly, seats at opera and operetta performances sell out quickly. The best way of securing a seat, particularly for summer performances, is via **Rózsavölgyi Jegyirodá** or **Ticket Express**, which are

Actors in satirical cabaret at Mikroszkóp Színpad (*see p217*)

located right in the centre of town, close to Vörösmarty tér. In Budapest, like anywhere else, you can risk it and try buying returned tickets at the last minute. A cheap alternative, but not for the weary, is to buy a standing-room pass.

LATE NIGHT TRANSPORT

Budapest's metro (see p238) runs until just after 11pm. Buses marked with black numbers and the letter 'E' provide the night transport on busy routes. There are also night trams running on some routes, though their frequency varies from between one and three an hour. Night buses should be boarded through the front door, and tickets shown to the driver. The stop-request button is situated above the exit door.

The HÉV train (see p239) that connects Budapest with its suburbs stops running at about 11:30pm.

DISABLED ACCESS

Much work has been done since Hungary joined the European Union to make the country's venues accessible to as wide a range of people as possible. However, a lot of Budapest's older venues are far from wheelchair-friendly. Places which are equipped for

Poster pillar

disabled visitors include the **Mátyás Church** (see pp82–3), the **State Opera House** (see pp118–19) and the **Franz Liszt Academy** (see p1129). The pedestrianized **Liszt Ferenc tér**, with its preponderance of outdoor cafés and terraces is also perfect for disabled travellers. The bars and pubs of Central Pest, many of which are located in basements, are not. Note that many venues (including the State Opera House) offer small reductions for disabled visitors.

The Hungarian Disabled Association
San Marco utca 76. *Tel* 250 90 13.
www.meosz.hu

LISTINGS MAGAZINES

The best Budapest listings publication is the free weekly *Pesti Est*, which, though published almost entirely in Hungarian, is comprehensible to most people. It is available in bars, restaurants, hotels and shops. Visitors should also try the *Budapest Times*, an English-language free weekly newspaper that carries very good event, English-language cinema screening, theatre, opera and classical music listings. Other cultural bulletins include *Exit* and *Programme*, which are published in English and German,

The dramatic entrance to the Moulin Rouge theatre (see p217)

and *Budapest Panorama* (published in English, German, Russian, Italian and French). The latest bars and restaurants are found in *Budapest in Your Pocket,* a bi-monthly English-language listings and events guide.

LATE-NIGHT SCAMS

Budapest is generally a very safe city, but it is not without its dangers, especially late at night. Tourists are seen as easy prey by fraudsters, and it is important to stay alert at all times. Attractive peroxide-blondes promenading Váci utca and introducing themselves to single men may appear friendly and genuine at first sight, but, alas, they are not. It they insist you join them for a drink in a bar of their choice, you should refrain from doing so. They are not prostitutes, but "consumption girls", employed by bars to bring in foreign men to buy them drinks – which, as will become apparent only after the bill arrives, cost thousands of Hungarian forints.

Although a number of bars that carry out this practice have been closed by the authorities, it still goes on. Always check how much you are paying for a drink and be wary of instant female friends.

Late nights are also the delight of unscrupulous taxi drivers, eager to make a killing from tipsy tourists. Never get into a taxi that does not clearly state it belongs to a reputable taxi company, or which does not display its tariffs on the side of the driver's door. Always ask for a rough estimate of the cost before getting in.

The elegant interior of the Franz Liszt Music Academy (see p216)

Music

Thanks to great composers such as Liszt, Bartók and Kodály (see p144), and the wealth of its folk tradition, Hungary is famous for its music. Hungarians have always been a nation of music lovers; in addition to performances by national artists, Budapest is frequently visited by revered musicians from around the world.

OPERA AND OPERETTA

The standard of opera in Budapest is high. Performances are at either the **State Opera House** (see pp118–9) or the **Erkel Theatre** (see p151). At both there is a mainly classical repertoire, sung in Italian. The secondary focus is on Hungarian works. The **Operetta Theatre** (see p115) stages Hungarian operettas.

CLASSICAL MUSIC

The **Franz Liszt Academy of Music** (see p129) is the leading venue for classical music. The city's largest venue is the new **National Concert Hall** (see p156). Concerts are sometimes held in the domed hall of **Parliament** (see pp108–9), which has excellent acoustics, and at the **Congress Centre** (see p160). Budapest also has a strong tradition of music festivals, (see pp58–61).

SACRED MUSIC

Concerts of organ music are held between March and December in the magnificent setting of the **Mátyás Church** (see pp82–3). Among the composers whose works are featured, Bach is the most popular. **St Stephen's Basilica** (see pp116–7) serves sporadically as the venue for concerts of choral music. Between March and October the Musica Sacra Agency organizes concerts in the **Great Synagogue** (see p134).

FOLK & GYPSY MUSIC

Performances of folk and gypsy music are held at the **Duna Palota** and **Hungarian Heritage House**. Watch out for shows by the Hungarian State Song and Dance Ensemble and a Gypsy band that is part of the ensemble but also stages independent concerts.

During July and August the city is visited by folk troupes from all over the country.

From October to May, the city's dance houses rock to the sounds of fiddles and flutes. One of the most renowned is **Fonó Budai Zeneház**, which stages peasant and gypsy bands from Transylvania. The popular **Marcibányi téri** cultural centre stages folk and gypsy music events, and house music, as well as playing host to various other arts events and shows.

JAZZ

Jazz was very late in reaching Hungary. The best known and revered Hungarian jazz band is the Benkó Dixieland Band, which during Spring Festivals (see p58) plays in various theatres and large halls. The best place for jazzlovers to congregate is **Columbus Jazz Club**, where Hungary's best players perform from 8:30pm every evening. The club boasts views of the Danube and it is a good idea to reserve a table. The **Cotton Club** (see p198) is also very popular.

DIRECTORY

TICKETS

Rosavolgyi
Jegyiroda Szervita tér 5.
Map 4 E1.
Tel 318 35 00.

Ticket Express
Andrássy út 18.
Map 10 E2. **Tel** 312 00 00.
Deák Ferenc út 19.
Map 4 E1. **Tel** 266 70 70.

OPERA AND OPERETTA

Erkel Theatre
Köztársaság tér 30.
Map 7 C3. **Tel** 333 05 40.

Operetta Theatre
Nagymez utca 17.
Map 2 F3.
Tel 472 20 30.

State Opera House
Andrássy út 22.
Map 2 F4. **Tel** 331 25 50.

CLASSICAL MUSIC

Congress Centre
Jagelló út 1–3.
Tel 372 57 00.

Franz Liszt Academy of Music
Liszt Ferenc tér 8.
Map 7 A1. Tel 462 46 79.

National Concert Hall
Palace of Arts
Komor Marcell utca 1.
Tel 555 30 00.

Parliament
Kossuth Lajos tér. **Map** 2 D3 (9 C1). **Tel** 441 49 04.

SACRED MUSIC

Great Synagogue
Dohány utca 2–8. **Map** 7 A3. **Tel** 342 89 49.

Mátyás Church
Szentháromság tér 2.
Map 1 B4 (9 A2).
Tel 355 56 57.

St Stephen's Basilica
Szent István tér.
Map 2 E4 (10 D2).
Tel 403 53 70.

FOLK AND GYPSY MUSIC

Hungarian Heritage House
Corvin tér 8. **Map** 1 C4 (9 A2). **Tel** 201 50 17.

Duna Palota
Zrínyi utca 5. **Map** 2 E5 (10 D2). **Tel** 317 13 77.

Fonó Budai Zeneház
Sztregova utca 3. **Map** 2 E5 (10 D3). **Tel** 206 53 00.

Marcibányi téri
Müvelödesi Központ
Marczibányi tér 5/A.
Tel 212 28 20.

JAZZ

Columbus Jazz Club
Vigadó tér, Dock 4.
Map 4 D1. **Tel** 205 30 41.

Cotton Club
Jókai utca 26. **Map** 2 F3.
Tel 354 08 86.

Theatre, Cinema and Casinos

Budapest has many theatres, which are worth visiting not only for their impressive repertoires, but also because they are invariably located in beautiful, historic buildings. Cinemas show the latest films, although few retain the original soundtrack. For late-night dancing, the city has a wealth of popular clubs to choose from.

THEATRE

The first theatre to stage plays in Hungary was the National Dance Theatre, now the **Castle Theatre** *(see p73)*. Other established theatres include the **Madách Theatre**, **Nemzeti Theatre**, **Pesti Theatre** and **Lézerszínház**. The **Merlin Theatre** performs in English. **Trafó** is an exciting showcase for all the contemporary arts.

Budapest has over 30 drama and cabaret theatres including **Mikroszkóp Színpad**, which hosts satirical cabaret shows *(see p214)*, and the **Moulin Rouge**. The most prestigious is the **József Katona Theatre**, which became famous following performances in Paris and London. The **Vígszínház**, meaning "comedy theatre", specializes in musicals (as does the Madách Theatre*)*. In summer rock-operas are staged on Margaret Island. These shows are remarkable for their quality and magnificent setting.

CINEMA

Many of Budapest's cinemas were built during the 1920s and 1930s and, despite renovations, have been superceded by modern multiplexes such as those in the shopping malls **Duna Plaza**, **Westend City Center**, and **Corvin Filmpalota**.

Most foreign films in Hungary are now both dubbed and subtitled into Hungarian, leaving cinema-goers free to choose which version they prefer. Those who do not understand Hungarian should choose the *angyol nelvű* (English soundtrack) version of the film. For films in English with no subtitles at all, look out for the words, *angol nyelvű, felirat nélkül*.

Apart from foreign films, the cinemas also show native Hungarian films. The range covers both the latest releases and vintage films from a time of Hungarian cinematic glory, notably when Miklós Jancsó and István Szabó received international awards for directing. The renovated, Moorish style **Uránia Filmszínház** film palace dates from this time.

All cinema tickets can be bought a few hours in advance. Some cinemas will sell tickets for showings the next day.

CASINOS

Budapest has several casinos. Most occupy historical buildings next to smart hotels.

Casino Vakert, for example, occupies one of the city's finest Secession-era buildings, built to a design by Miklós Ybl *(see p119)*. It originally functioned as the engine room of the water supply system of the Royal Palace. For the past 40 years it has operated as an elegant restaurant and, since 1992, as both a casino and a restaurant.

At any of the casinos listed below, players can try their hand at roulette, Black Jack, poker and the wheel of fortune. All are open 24 hours a day and, with the exception of the Las Vegas Casino, require evening dress. Passports are also universally required.

DIRECTORY

THEATRE

Castle Theatre
Színház 1-3. Map 9 A3.
Tel 356 40 85.

József Katona Theatre
Petöfi Sándor utca 6.
Map 4 E1 (10 D4).
Tel 318 37 25.

Lézerszínház
Népliget, Planetárium.
Tel 263 08 71.

Madách Theatre
Erzsébet körút 29–33.
Map 7 A2. **Tel** 478 20 41.

Merlin Theatre
Gerlóczy utca 4.
Map 4 F1 (10 E4).
Tel 317 93 38.

Mikroszkóp Színpad
Nagymező utca 22–24.
Map 2 F3 (10 E1).
Tel 332 53 22.

Moulin Rouge
Nagymező utca 17.
Map 2 F3. (10 E1.)
Tel 332 90 90.

Nemzeti Theatre
Bajor Gizi Park 1.
Map 7 B1. **Tel** 476 68 68.

Pesti Theatre
Váci utca 9.
Map 4 E1 (10 D4).
Tel 266 52 45.

Trafó
Lilom utca 41.
Map 7 B5.
Tel 215 16 00.

Vígszínház
Pannónia utca 1.
Map 2 E1. **Tel** 340 46 50.

CINEMA

Corvin Filmpalota
Corvin köz 1.
Tel 459 50 50.

Hollywood Multi-plex Duna Plaza
Váci út 178.
Tel 467 42 67.

Palace West End
Váci út 1–3.
Map 2 F2. **Tel** 238 72 22.

Uránia Nemzeti Filmszínház
Rákózi út 21
Map 7 A3.
Tel 486 34 00.

CASINOS

Çasino Tropicana
Vigadó utca 2.
Map 4 D1.
Tel 327 72 50.

Casino Vakert
Ybl Miklós tér 9.
Map 9 C4.
Tel 202 42 44.

Grand Casino Budapest
Deak Ferenc tér 13.
Map 2 E5.
Tel 483 01 70.

Las Vegas Casino
Roosevelt tér 2
(Sofitel Atrium Hotel).
Map 2 D5.
Tel 266 20 81.

Sports

Hungarians are fine athletes, as is testified by their consistently outstanding performances at competitive events, such as the Olympic Games. Budapest's world-class sports facilities serve as venues for many of these international events, including European and World championships. Sporting opportunities for visitors to the city are both varied and accessible.

SPECTATOR SPORTS

Most competitive sporting events are held either in the magnificent **Ferenc Puskás Stadium** (see p155), which seats 80,000 spectators, or in the modern, indoor **Budapest Aréna**.

Soccer remains the most popular spectator sport, although Hungarian fans can only look wistfully back to the time when their national side was highly successful. In the 1950s, for instance, Hungary beat England 6:3 at Wembley. League matches in Budapest attract big crowds. The atmosphere is particularly electric when local favourites Ferencváros, FTC, take to the pitch.

Two of the three great events regularly held in Budapest are the Welcom Marathon Hungary and the Budapest Marathon. These are run on the last Sundays of April and September, respectively. The third big sporting event of the year is the Hungarian Grand Prix (see p59), which takes place during August at the Mogyoród racing circuit.

Hungarians achieve impressive results in boxing, canoeing, swimming, water polo and fencing, which are all widely supported.

HORSE RACING AND RIDING

As a nation of former nomads, the Hungarians have retained a great love of horses. In Budapest this passion finds its expression in horse racing, which is enormously popular. A few hours spent at a racetrack can be a cheap and fun way of soaking up the local atmosphere. Near Keleti pu (see p234) is the Trotters' Racecourse, the **Ügetőpálya**.

Those wishing to be rather more energetic and ride instead of watch horses, should contact the **National Riding School**, the **Petneházy School**, the **Kincsem Horsepark** or the **Budapest Riding Club**.

SPORTING ACTIVITIES

Practising sport for fitness and pleasure is both cheap and popular in Budapest.

Strolling through the city's parks, particularly on Margaret Island, you will encounter scores of eager joggers, both young and not so young. The indoor and outdoor swimming pools are also full of regular visitors, who come here for an hour

or so of healthy exercise. Particularly popular is the **Hajós Olympic Pool** on Margaret Island, which is named after Hungary's first Olympic gold winner for swimming, who was also the pool's architect. Busy open-air swimming options include **Komjádi Pool** (see p52) and the neighbouring **Lukács Baths** (see p101), both of which can be enjoyed even in winter as the hot spring water creates a steamy atmosphere over the water's surface. For the hottest spa water in the city, head to the **Széchenyi Baths** (see p151), which is the largest bathing complex in Europe. However, the most atmospheric and beautiful baths are undoubtedly the 16th-century Turkish **Rudas Baths** (see p93).

Cycling is also gaining in popularity, particularly since the introduction of cycling lanes to the city's roads (see p229). If you want to play tennis, there are numerous courts available, but these tend to be monopolized by local Hungarians. Your best bet for a game is to befriend a local tennis player, or find a hotel that has its own court.

Despite the moderate climate, it is also possible to undertake winter sports in Budapest. From December until March the **Városliget Lake** (see pp142–3) is turned into a skating ring and many people take to the ice. **Sváb Hill** (see p161) is generally snow-covered from December to March and has several ski runs and ski lifts.

DIRECTORY

STADIA

Budapest Aréna
Stefánia út 2.
Map 10 F4.
Tel 222 26 00.

Ferenc Puskás Stadium
Kerepesi út.
Map 8 F1.
Tel 471 43 21.

HORSE RACING AND RIDING

Budapest Riding Club
Kerepesi út 7.
Tel 0629 313 52 10.

Kincsem Horsepark
2711 Tápiószentmárton.
Tel 0629 423 056.

National Riding School
Kerepesi út 7. **Tel** 210 26 61.

Petneházy School
Feketefej utca 2–4.
Tel 397 12 08.

Ügetőpálya
Kerepest út 9–11.

SWIMMING POOLS

Császár Komjádi Uszoda
Frankel Leó út 55.
Map 1 B1. **Tel** 212 27 50.

Lukács Baths
Frankel Leó utca 25–29.
Map 1 C1. **Tel** 326 16 95.

Hajós Olympic Pool
Margitsziget. **Tel** 450 42 20.

Rudas Baths
Döbrentei tér 9. **Map** 4 D2.
Tel 356 13 22.

Széchenyi Baths
Allatkerti körút 11.
Map 6 D3. **Tel** 363 32 10.

Children's Budapest

Visiting Budapest can be made great fun for children. There are several choices of energetic outdoor pursuits, including a funfair, a terrific zoo and, of course, a range of glorious of swimming venues. If the weather is poor, the city's historic buildings, museums and art galleries will entertain and inform. In addition, a handful of puppet theatres cater specifically for younger audiences.

SIGHTSEEING FOR KIDS

Busy Pest is a difficult area in which to entertain small people, but the **Postal Museum**, set in an opulent 19th-century mansion, is well worth a morning's visit.

In Buda's **Royal Palace** (see pp70–1) and **Castle District** (see pp68–85), the city's long history can be understood instinctively just by wandering round the ancient and lovely buildings. The **Hungarian National Gallery** (see pp74–7) feeds young imaginations, as does the fabulous *turul*, the statue of a mythical giant bird that stands in the Palace Court-yard. The magnificently carved **Mátyás Fountain** (see pp72–3) is also worth a look.

In the Old Town, the **Labyrinth** (see p85) on Lords' Street is a bizarre underground exhibition that fascinates kids, and there are displays of armour and weapons in the **Museum of Military History** (see p85). A final "must" is a ride on the **Budavári Sikló** funicular railway (see p239).

SWIMMING

The most suitable complex for young families is **Palatinus Strand** (see p53) on Margaret Island, where there are pools of varying temperatures, water slides, artificial waves, and all sorts of fun and games. Numerous kiosks sell snacks, ice cream and fruit.

During the winter season, the **Gellért Hotel and Baths Complex** (see pp90–1) is a better alternative. Here, the large swimming pool has artificial waves, and the paddling pool's warm water is wonderful for toddlers.

Széchnyi Baths (see p151) also welcome children.

CIRCUS, FUNFAIR & ZOO

People of all ages love the Budapest **Zoo** (see pp150–51), which is one of the best in Europe. Attractions include a large sea-water aquarium, a terrarium with splendid snakes, and an impressive aviary.

A visit to the **Great Capital Circus** is an easy way to keep youngsters occupied. Shows, which often star international artists, take place daily.

At **Vidám Park Funfair** (see p151) in Városliget, there are merry-go-rounds, a railway, shooting galleries and games machines.

INDOOR ATTRACTIONS

Bu'pest Bábszínház and **Kolibri Színház** are two of several puppet theatres that stage international favourites, such as *The Jungle Book*, *Cinderella* and *Snow White*, as well as Hungarian classics.

In People's Park, the **Planetárium** is known for its special entertainment shows – remarkable compositions of laser effects, pictorial projections and music, staged under an impressively large dome.

SCENIC RAILWAYS

Children love the trip up into the **Buda Hills** (see p161). The first stage is a ride on the cog-wheel railway that runs up Széchényi Hill. At the top, there is a playground and the start of the Children's Railway, which follows the ridge of the hills to the Hvös Valley. The way back down is on the Libeg chair-lift that runs from the top of János Hill to Zugliget (linked by bus 158 to Moszkva tér). Young railway enthusiasts also enjoy the **Railway History Park** (see p156).

DIRECTORY

SIGHTSEEING

Budavári Sikló
Clark Ádám tér,
Szent György tér.
Map 1 C5 (9 B3).

Hungarian National Gallery
Szent György tér 2.
Map 3 C5. **Tel** 439 73 25.

Labyrinth
Úri utca 9.
Map 1 A4 (9 A2).
Tel 489 32 81.

Postal Museum
Andrássy út 3.
Map 2 F4 (10 E2).
Tel 342 69 97.

Mátyás Fountain
Royal Palace.
Map 1 C5 (9 B3).

Museum of Military History
Tóth Árpád Sétány 40.
Map 1 A4. **Tel** 356 95 22.

Railway History Park
Tatia út 95. **Tel.** 450 14 97.

Royal Palace
Map 1 5C (9 4B).

SWIMMING

Gellért Hotel and Baths Complex
Kelenhegyi út 4–6. **Map** 3 C3. **Tel** 466 61 66.

Palatinus Strand
Margitsziget.
Tel 340 45 05.

Széchnyi Baths
Állatkerti körút 11.
Map 6 D3.
Tel 363 32 10.

RECREATION

Great Capital Circus
Állatkerti körút 7.
Map 5 C3.
Tel 344 60 08 00.

Vidám Park Funfair
Állatkerti körut 14–16.
Map 5 C3.
Tel 363 83 10.

Zoo
Állatkerti körút 6–12.
Tel 363 37 10.
Map 5 C3.

INDOOR ATTRACTIONS

Bu'pest Bábszínház
Andrássy út 69.
Map 5 A5 (10 E2).
Tel 321 52 00.

Kolibri Színház
Jókai tér 10.
Map 2 F3 (10 F1).
Tel 311 08 70.

Planetárium
Népliget.
Tel 263 18 11.

SURVIVAL
GUIDE

PRACTICAL INFORMATION

Budapest was always famous for its hospitality and the Hungarians, particularly in recent years, have been emphasizing tourism as an important part of the national economy. The biggest problem in its development is the formidable barrier posed by the Hungarian language, which hinders access to information. The Hungarians are therefore trying hard to learn foreign languages.

Tourist information sign

In all tourist offices, bigger hotels and most restaurants either English or German is spoken. Information brochures and tourist pamphlets are now published in several languages. It is difficult to get lost in Budapest as the road sign system is easy to follow. The historic monuments in the city centre are best visited on foot, while the more distant sights can be easily reached by public transport *(see pp236–41)*.

TOURIST INFORMATION

Prior to your arrival in Budapest it is worthwhile getting in touch with your nearest **Hungarian National Tourist Office**, who can supply useful information and put you in touch with reputable tour operators.

Many agencies specialize in organizing individual trips and tours to Hungary including **Travellers Cities Ltd, Kirker Holidays** and **Page & Moy**. They can all provide you with detailed information on meals and accommodation and help you to make reservations.

Official tourist information centres (Tourinform) in Budapest can be found at a number of locations, including **Liszt Ferenc tér**, **Nyugati Pu**, **Sütő utca** and **Ferihegy 1 and 2** airports.

General tourist information in a variety of languages is provided by these centres. They also sell the Budapest Card *(see p224)* – which enables unlimited travel around the city – as well as souvenirs, guide books and maps. Brown tourist signs can be found at all the important points of the city to help visitors find their way around.

ADVICE FOR VISITORS

Budapest has a favourable climate year round, but the best time to visit is between March and the end of June, and from the middle of August until October. July is generally very hot.

Various festivals and cultural programmes take place throughout the year. The end of the year is a fun time, when visitors can experience the Christmas Fair and the New Year's Eve street party.

On arriving in Budapest it is a good idea to get hold of the foreign language information booklets. The *Budapest Panorama*, the *Budapest Programme Visitor's Guide*, the *Budapest Guide* and the *Dining Guide* each contain a calendar of cultural and tourist events for the month. They are free and are easily available from tourist centres and hotel reception desks. They all contain maps of Budapest, and free city maps are also published by the Tourism Office of Budapest.

It is also worth investing in the Budapest Card *(see p224)*, which, as well as entitling cardholders to unlimited use of public transport and free admission to museums, gives reductions on the price of tickets for various cultural events.

OPENING HOURS

Museums and galleries are open all year round. Opening times for specific venues are given under their individual entries.

One of several tourist information offices in Budapest

Horses on a tourist carriage

As a general rule, the winter season from November until March sees museums offering shorter opening hours. In the summer, from April until October, they tend to stay open a couple of hours longer, typically from 10am until 6pm. Museums remain closed on Monday, except for the National Jewish Museum (see p134), which is closed on Saturday instead. Most museums, both state and private tend to charge an entrance fee, though it is worth checking to see if there are any applicable discounts.

Shopping centres in Budapest are open each day of the week, grocery stores are open from 7am to 7pm and other shops from 10am until 6pm during the week. On Saturdays shops close at 1pm, while on Sundays some department stores and market halls are open, often until 2pm. Detailed information on the opening hours of particular shops and markets can be found on pages 202–5 of this guide. Hungarians tend to take lunch early, between noon and 1pm.

ENTRY TICKETS

Tickets to museums and historical monuments can be purchased on the spot.

Average prices vary from 700 to 1,500 forints per person, but some can be as much as 2,000 forints. Nevertheless, students and school children are always entitled to reductions. Opera, concert and other tickets can be bought at ticket agencies (see pp214–15). Theatre and opera tickets are also sold at individual box offices, either for shows on the same day or in advance. Ticket prices can vary from 1,500 to 10,000 forints, depending on the show.

ETIQUETTE

Casual clothes are often worn to the theatre, particularly during summer. By comparison classical music concerts and operas are much smarter affairs and even tourists will feel more comfortable wearing evening dress. Traditionally, Hungarians attach great importance to being properly dressed when going to an opera or concert hall.

DIRECTORY

Additional Information

Tourists in Szentháromság tér

PASSPORT AND CUSTOMS REGULATIONS

Citizens of the US, Canada, and Australia need only a valid passport to visit Hungary for up to 90 days. EU visitors may stay as long as they please. Visitors from other countries require a visa which can be obtained from any Hungarian embassy. All visitors should check their requirements prior to travelling. Only visitors on long-term visas can apply for and obtain a residency permit.

The loss or theft of a passport should be reported to the appropriate consulate or embassy as soon as possible. Carry your passport or a copy of it to identify yourself. For safety reasons, keep a copy in your hotel. As well as personal belongings, visitors can bring the following items into the country tax-free (fees up to 175 Euros): 200 cigarettes, 2 litres wine, 1 litre liqueur, 500 g coffee or 100 g tea.

Signs showing facilitites and major tourist attractions in Budapest

TAX-FREE GOODS

Non-EU residents can apply for the refund of VAT (ÁFA in Hungarian) charged on goods purchased in Hungary. To reclaim it, visitors need to present the ÁFA invoice at the border. This only applies to sums in excess of 50,000 Hungarian forints (175 Euros), and does not apply to works of art. The exported goods must be new and not previously used in Hungary. They must also have been bought within the last 90 days.

BUDAPEST CARD

This splendid new facility, introduced in 1997, is designed for tourists visiting the city for two or three days.

The Budapest Card entitles a visitor, together with one child under 14, to use all city transport – metro, bus, tram, trolley bus, funicular and HÉV – free of charge, as well as providing free entry to 60 museums, the zoo and the funfair. It also entitles the holder to a 50 per cent discount on guided tours of the city, a 10 to 20 per cent discount on tickets to selected spas and cultural events,

and a 10 to 20 per cent discount in recommended restaurants.

The card costs about 5,000 Hungarian forints for 48 hours and 6,000 forints for 72 hours. Cards can be purchased at tourist offices, hotel reception desks, museums and at the ticket offices of the majority of the larger metro stations.

Enclosed with the card is an information pamphlet, in four languages, listing its benefits.

Budapest Card

PRESS, RADIO AND TV

In Budapest all the world's top newspapers and magazines are easily accessible at hotels. A number of the larger news stands maintain a constant stock of international newspapers and magazines. The largest number of these can be found at the underpasses near Nyugati and Keleti stations. As well as these, there are also various shops around town which specialize in English-language newspapers, books and maps (see pp212–3).

Bear in mind that the foreign daily newspapers on sale tend to be yesterday's editions, but even so they often sell out by lunchtime. For English-speaking tourists there are also quite a few magazines, including *Budapest in your Pocket, The Budapest Sun* and *NLG*. These provide the most comprehensive information on local and, in some cases, world events as well as full entertainment guides.

The city's larger hotels are geared up for the needs of the international traveller and, in addition to the state and independent Hungarian television channels, most offer tens of satellite TV channels in English and other European languages.

English language magazines, published in Budapest

DISABLED TRAVELLERS

Budapest is becoming more accessible for disabled visitors, although it is best to call ahead to the sights or obtain specialist information prior to your visit to ensure it is as hassle free as possible. Many buses are now equipped for boarding and some metro stations have special lifts. For advice and help, contact the **Hungarian Disabled Association**. Many museums and monuments present difficulties for the disabled, although increasingly they are being renovated to be wheelchair-friendly.

BUDAPEST TIME

Budapest uses Central European time, in keeping with the rest of mainland Europe, which means it is two hours ahead of Greenwich Mean Time (GMT) in the summer and one hour ahead in the winter.

Examples of the winter time differences between Budapest and other major cities are as follows: London: -1 hour; New York: -6 hours; Dallas: -7 hours; Los Angeles: -9 hours; Perth: +7 hours; Sydney: +9 hours; Auckland: +11 hours; Tokyo: +8 hours.

PUBLIC TOILETS

There are not many public toilets in Budapest, and most require a small fee for their use. It is worth carrying some small change if you anticipate having to use them.

The cubicle type is found in some squares and parks and these are usually free. In cafés and restaurants there are toilet attendants and the price for using the facility is usually clearly displayed.

There are no public toilets in metro stations, except for Batthyány tér.

Sign for the ladies' toilet

URAK

Sign for the gentlemen's toilet

Apart from the generally understood picture symbols, the toilets are signed in Hungarian: *Hölgyek* (ladies) and *Urak* (gentlemen), or *Nők* (women) and *Férfiak* (men).

ELECTRICAL AND GAS APPLIANCES

Hungarian electricity supply is 220 V and the plugs needed are the standard continental type. Adapters can be purchased in most countries. Since sockets are generally earthed, the most commonly used plugs are the flat type.

Hungarian gas cookers are equipped with a bimetal safety device, which means that after lighting the knob should be held down until the burner warms up. This is an effective means of preventing the escape of any unlit gas.

Hungarian plug with two pins

DIRECTORY

FOREIGN EMBASSIES AND CONSULATES IN BUDAPEST

Australia
Királyhágó tér 8–9.
Tel 457 9777.
Fax 201 97 92.
www.ausembbp.hu

Canada
Budakeszi út 32.
Tel 392 33 60.
Fax 392 33 90.

New Zealand
Teréz körút 38.
Map 2 F3.
Tel 428 2208.
Fax 428 2208.

South Africa
Gárdonyi Géza utca 17.
Tel 392 09 99.
Tel 200 72 77.
@ dha@axelero.hu
www.sa-embassy.hu

United Kingdom
Harmincad utca 6.
Map 2 E5.
Tel 266 28 88.
Fax 266 09 07.
@ info@britemb.hu
www.britishembassy.
gov.hu

United States
Szabadság tér 12.
Map 2 E4. *Tel 475 44 00.*
Fax 374 00 34.
@ usconsular.budapest
@state.gov
www.usembassy.hu

HUNGARIAN EMBASSIES

United Kingdom
35 Eaton Place,
London SW1X 8BY.
Tel 020 7235 5218.
www.huemblon. org.uk

United States
3910 Shoemakers Street
NW, Washington DC,
20008.
Tel 202 362 6730.
www.huemblwas.org

INTERNATIONAL NEWSPAPERS

A Világsajtó Háza
V. Városház utca 3–5.

Map 10 E4. *Tel 317 13
11.* **Open** 7am–7pm
Mon–Fri, 7am–2pm Sat,
8am–12 noon Sun.

Bestsellers
V. Október 6 utca 11.
Map 10 D2. *Tel 312 12 95.*
Open 9am–6.30pm
Mon–Fri, 10am–5pm Sat,
10am–4pm Sun.

DISABLED TRAVELLERS

Hungarian Disabled Association
San Marco utca 76.
Tel 250 9013.
Fax 454 1144.
www.meosz.hu.

Security and Health

Police Symbol

Budapest is not just a beautiful city, it is also one with efficient and well-maintained services which help to ensure the safety and well-being of its residents. The public telephones generally work, the bus and tram stops display timetables and public transport is both clean and reliable. Nevertheless, as with all other central European countries, there are a growing number of negative social phenomena. Local people are increasingly complaining about rising crime rates, the plague of pickpockets and incidences of car theft. Visitors to Budapest will also be sadly aware of the growing numbers of homeless people living on the streets.

Police car

ADVICE TO VISITORS

Documents and money should be carried in a secure inside pocket or in a money belt. Traveller's cheques are widely accepted, so there is no need to carry much cash on you.

Money should be exchanged at a bank, your hotel or an exchange bureau, never on the black market. Do not leave valuables in your car.

There are four multistorey car parks in the city centre: at Nos. 4–6 Aranykéz utca, No. 20 Nyár utca, and on Erzsébet tér and Szervita tér. A lot of the larger hotels have an underground garage. Cars parked improperly may be clamped or towed away to a car park outside the centre. To find out where a car has been taken, call the **Removed Cars Information** line. Fines of up to 7,000 HUF can also be imposed for parking offences.

Police badge

Pickpockets operate during rush hours, targeting people in crowded metro stations, buses and shopping centres. They also operate at all the main tourist sights, and on nearby public transport. When working as a group, they may surround unsuspecting tourists and jostle or distract them. For this reason it is a good idea to have a photocopy of your passport and your travel insurance. If a passport is lost call the police in Szalay utca

11–13 (373 10 00), where English is spoken. Once the appropriate police certificate is obtained, report the loss to your embassy (*see p225*).

SECURITY

Hungarian police are frequently seen patrolling the streets on motorbikes, on foot or in cars. In addition, every district has its own police station. The Hungarian word for police is *rendőrség*. In the event of anything going missing, because of loss or theft, a report should be made immediately to the police. In the event of a lost passport, see the section under the heading *Advice to Visitors*.

All visitors should check their visa requirements prior to travelling. Australian tourists will need a visa, but Europeans and Americans can stay for three to six months without one. However, after one month make sure to check the registration requirements at a local police station. In reality, this applies mainly to tourists staying in private accommodation or with friends, since all hotels, hostels and pensions automatically register foreign guests. For more information, see the Hungarian Ministry of Foreign Affairs' website (www.mfa.gov.hu).

Tourists coming to Budapest by car are obliged to have the green insurance card, while those hiring a car need only present their driving licences. Hitchhiking, although not against the law, is not a recommended way of travelling in Hungary.

Women should not walk unaccompanied late at night in poorly lit areas and should avoid deserted streets.

Rákóczi tér and Mátyás tér, in district VIII, have been infamous for their brothels since the 19th century and have a long-standing tradition as hangouts for prostitutes. Prostitution has been officially outlawed in Hungary since 1950. In recent years, however, it has been tolerated more.

Road policeman on a motorbike

MEDICAL MATTERS

When travelling to Hungary it is highly recommended that visitors take out travel insurance.

Foreign nationals are only entitled to free medical help in emergencies, such as accidents or a sudden illness requiring immediate medical intervention. Any other medical care, including hospitalization, must be paid for. The cost depends on the type of insurance policy held and the relevant agreement between Hungary and the visitor's home country. Most insurance companies expect policy holders to pay for their treatment as they receive it and then apply for a refund on their return home. All the relevant bills and police reports must be submitted with any insurance claim. Remember that, where applicable, a report must be made to the police within seven days of any incident.

Budapest's pharmacies *(Gyógyszertár or Patika)* are well stocked and, in case of a minor ailment, the chemist will be able to recommend a suitable treatment. Some drugs require a prescription, while others can be sold over

Pharmacy sign

the counter. If your nearest pharmacy is closed, there should be a list displayed, either on the door or in the window, of all the local chemists and it will indicate which ones are on 24-hour emergency duty.

No special vaccinations are required for Hungary and the general standard of hygiene in the country is reasonably good. That said, allergy sufferers and people with breathing difficulties should take account of the summer smog conditions, which are particularly acute in the crowded streets of Pest. Those susceptible should consider staying in the Castle District, from which cars are banned, or retreating to the wooded Buda Hills *(see p161)*

Pharmacy shop front

or the greenery of Margaret Island *(see pp170–71)*.

The water in Budapest is of good quality. It is generally considered safe to drink water straight from the tap. There are also numerous thermal baths *(see pp50–53)* which are an excellent way to relax.

Ambulance

DIRECTORY

EMERGENCY SERVICES

Ambulance
Tel 104 (also 311 16 66).

Fire
Tel 105.

Police
Tel 107.

Metropolitan Police
Tel 443 50 00.

Electricity Emergency Service
Tel 40 383 838 (ask for number of local service) or 238 38 38.

Gas Emergency Service
Tel 477 11 11 (24 hours)

Water Emergency Service
Tel 40 247 247.

HELPLINES

Aids Helpline
Tel 251 00 51 (8am–4pm Mon–Thu); 469 22 83 (9am–noon Tue & Fri, 5–8pm Mon, Wed, Thu); 338 24 19 (8am–1pm Fri).

Alcoholics Anonymous
Tel 251 00 51.

BKV Lost Property
Tel 267 52 99 ext. 3.
Tel 461 65 00 ext. 12778 or 12779.

Fönix SOS Medical Service
1025 Budapest,
Kapy utca 49.
Tel 200 01 00.
www.fonixsos.hu

Foreigners' Registry Office
Izabella utca 61.
Map 2 F3. *Tel 436 91 00.*
Open 8am–noon
Mon–Wed & Fri,
8am–6pm Thu.

International Vehicle Insurance
Tel 061 209 07 30.

Removed Cars Information
Tel 383 07 00.

SOS Non-Stop Dental Service
Kiraly Utca 14. **Map** 2 F5.
Tel 267 96 02 (24 hours).

Telefon-doktor
Tel 317 21 11.

Vehicle Assistance & Breakdown Emergency Service
Tel 188.
Mak-Magyar Autóklub
Tel 345 16 87 (English spoken).

PHARMACIES

Déli Gyógyszertár
Alkotás u.1/b. *Tel 355 46 91.*

Teréz Patika
Teréz krt. 41. **Map** 10 F1.
Tel 311 44 39

Local Currency and Banking

Bureau de change sign

The Hungarian currency system is rapidly approaching the European standard. Budapest now boasts many modern banks, both Hungarian and foreign, which are located in smart and spacious buildings. The service is efficient and courteous. There are many automatic cash dispensers and bureaux de change in the town centre and around the railway stations. An increasing number of shops and restaurants now accept credit cards, but it is still more common in Budapest to pay for goods and services in cash. Most banks will now also advance money on a credit card.

Cash dispenser

CURRENCY REGULATIONS

Foreigners are allowed to bring 350,000 Hungarian forints into Hungary, which at the beginning of 2000 was equal to about US $1,400 (890 pounds sterling). The same amount of money can be taken out of the country. There are no restrictions concerning the denominations of the Hungarian currency brought in or taken out.

Tourists who bring in foreign currencies totalling in excess of 100,000 Hungarian forints should declare them on arrival and ask the customs official for a receipt. This can then be presented when leaving the country, as the same limit applies to foreign currencies brought in and taken out of the country, without the need for an additional licence.

Foreign currencies can be easily exchanged into forints in banks, bureaux de change and hotels, but there is a limit of 20,000 Hungarian forints per day. To exchange any unspent forints back into a convertible currency, visitors have to present the proof of purchase. So keep all the exchange receipts until the end of the visit. Otherwise, tourists will find themselves at home with forints that devalue quite rapidly, at a rate of 10–15 per cent relative to the major foreign currencies.

BANKS AND BUREAUX DE CHANGE

For the best rate of exchange, take foreign currency to a bank or bureau de change, which are generally run by Hungarian banks. Before changing money, check the rate of exchange, as they do tend to vary quite widely. The rates quoted by some exchange offices can be misleading as they could apply only to sums in excess of 200,000 forints, which is stated in a very small print.

The least favourable rates are in hotels and at the airport, while the best are offered by the bureaux de change near the railway stations and in the city centre, in Petőfi Sándor utca. A reasonable, average rate can usually be found at Hungarian banks.

The branches of **Budapest Bank** are open Monday till Friday, from 10:30am until 2pm. Merchant banks, such as **K & H Bank**, are open Monday till Thursday, between 8am and 3pm, and on Friday between 8am and 1pm. Most banks are closed on Saturdays and Sundays, but the bureaux de change and automatic cash dispensers remain open.

Exchanging money is only permitted in licensed, designated places. Transactions on the street are illegal, and those who enter into such transactions are likely to receive counterfeit money.

Most hotels, stores and restaurants accept credit cards. The most widely accepted are VISA, American Express, MasterCard and Diners Club. The logos of accepted credit cards are usually on display.

DIRECTORY

BANKS

Budapest Bank
Báthori utca 1.
Tel 477 77 77.

CIB Bank
Váci utca 19–21.
Tel 485 98 00.

K & H Bank
Vigadó tér 1.
Tel 328 90 00.

Magyar Külkereskedelmi Bank Rt
Váci utca 38.
Tel 268 84 72.

OTP Bank
Deák F. utca 7–9.
Tel 486 60 00.

Erste Bank
Jósef Nádor tér 5.
Tel 266 85 52.

Entrance to a branch of the Budapest Bank, in Váci utca

Hungarian currency

The Hungarian currency unit is the forint (HUF or Ft). Banknotes are issued in denominations of 200, 500, 1,000, 2,000, 5,000, 10,000 and 20,000 forints. Both an old and a new style of some notes are currently legal tender, but an older version of the 5,000 than the one shown here is no longer accepted.

200 HUF

500 HUF

1,000 HUF

2,000 HUF

5,000 HUF

10,000 HUF

20,000 HUF

Coins

Currently in circulation are coins of 1, 2, 5, 10, 20, 50 and 100 forints. As with the banknotes, new coins are gradually being phased in – the new 100 forint coin, with a brass disc inside a nickel ring, is now the only legal version.

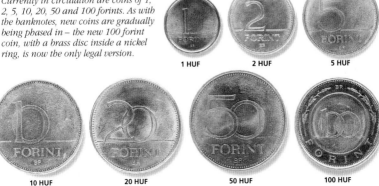

1 HUF

2 HUF

5 HUF

10 HUF

20 HUF

50 HUF

100 HUF

Communications

Telephone symbol

The Hungarian telephone operating system has undergone enormous changes in the last few years. Nowadays, you can easily access the telephone number you require. There are many telephone boxes throughout the city, although card-operated telephones are much more widespread than coin-operated ones. Most telephone boxes no longer contain a telephone directory. However, by dialling 198, the telephone information system provides a directory enquiry service.

Telephone box

USING THE TELEPHONE

Telephone cards are the best option, and can be obtained in units of 800, 1,800 or 5,000 forints. They are widely available from tobacconist shops, post offices, street vendors and some newspaper kiosks. Alternatively, coin phone boxes accept 10, 20 50 and 100 forint coins. The minimum rate for a local call is 20 forints, and 100 for an international call. To make an international call dial 00, wait for the dialing signal and then dial the country code, followed by the rest of the number.

Budapest telephone numbers consist of seven digits (when combined with the dialing code there are eight digits). There is really no advantage in using the services of a hotel operator, as this only adds to the length of the call and makes the call very much more expensive.

Cheaper off-peak rates apply throughout the night and on public holidays.

USING A CARD TELEPHONE

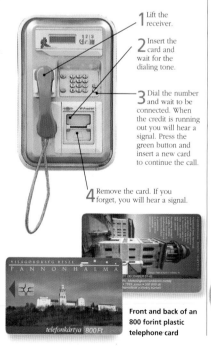

1 Lift the receiver.

2 Insert the card and wait for the dialing tone.

3 Dial the number and wait to be connected. When the credit is running out you will hear a signal. Press the green button and insert a new card to continue the call.

4 Remove the card. If you forget, you will hear a signal.

Front and back of an 800 forint plastic telephone card

USING A COIN TELEPHONE

1 Lift the receiver.

2 Insert coins and wait for the dialling tone.

3 Dial the number and wait to be connected. When the credit is running out you will hear a signal and should then insert more coins.

4 When you have finished speaking, replace the receiver. Wait for any unused coins to be returned.

10 HUF   **20 HUF**   **50 HUF**

Budapest's Districts

Budapest is divided into 23 districts. Streets of the same name may appear in several different districts, so it is important when addressing a letter to quote the four-digit postal code.

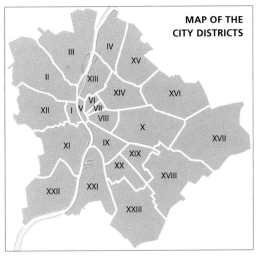

MAP OF THE CITY DISTRICTS

INTERNET CAFES

Email is a popular way to communicate from abroad. Budapest has several internet cafés offering coffee and snacks while you check your emails or search the internet.

Internet Galéria & Café
VI Szondi utca 79. **Map** 5 A5. **Tel** 269 00 73. **Open** 8am–midnight daily.

Kávészünet Internet Café
XIII Tátra utca 12/b. **Map** 2 E3. **Tel** 236 08 53. **Open** 8am–10pm Mon–Fri, 10am–8pm Sat–Sun.

Siesta Netcafé
VI Izabella utca 85. **Map** 7 B1 **Tel** 312 32 59. **Open** 10am–2am Mon–Fri, noon–2am Sat, noon–midnight Sun.

POSTAL SERVICES

When going to a post office in Budapest, you must be prepared to spend some time there. Postage stamps cost between 60 to 130 Hungarian forints for sending a postcard. Apart from ordinary stamps, all post offices sell various special issues that are very pretty. Ask the cashier if you can see the different designs.

On weekdays, most post offices are open from 8am until 6pm, and they usually close at 2pm on Saturday and are closed all day Sunday. If

Post office logo

you know the values of the stamps you require, it is easier to buy them from a *trafik* (a tobacconist shop or a newspaper kiosk), as often there are long queues at post offices.

Post offices cannot be avoided, however. Airmail (*légiposta*) or registered letters have to be posted at a post office and poste restante mail has to be collected there. Telegrams can also be sent by telephone from post offices. Public fax machines can be found at most post offices.

Budapest postal codes are four-digit numbers. The first digit refers to Budapest, the second and third digits refer to the district number and the fourth digit defines the postal area within the district.

Post boxes are emptied daily at the times indicated on the front of the box.

POST OFFICE ADDRESSES

Bajcsy-Zsilinszky út 16. **Map** 10 E1. **Open** 8am–8pm Mon–Fri, 8am–2pm Sat.

Baross tér 11. **Map** 8 D2. **Open** 7am–9pm Mon–Fri, 8am–2pm Sat.

Krisztina körút. **Map** 3 C1. **Open** 8am–8pm Mon–Fri, 8am–2pm Sat.

Teréz körút 51. **Map** 10 F1. **Open** 7am–9pm Mon–Sat, 10am–5pm Sun.

Városház utca 18. **Map** 10 E4. 8am–8pm Mon–Fri, 8am–2pm Sat.

Red post box for national and international mail

USEFUL TELEPHONE NUMBERS AND DIALLING CODES

- Sending telegrams: 192
- International operator calls: 190
- Inland operator calls: 191
- Inland information: 198
- International information: 199
- SDC for international calls: 00
- SDC from Budapest to other Hungarian towns: 06
- SDC from Budapest to Australia: 00 61
- SDC from Budapest to France: 00 33
- SDC from Budapest to New Zealand: 00 64
- SDC from Budapest to South Africa: 00 27
- SDC from Budapest to the UK: 00 44
- SDC from Budapest to the US: 00 1
- For Budapest from UK and most of Europe: 00 361
- For Budapest from US and Australia: 00 11 361

GETTING TO BUDAPEST

Hungarians like to boast that Budapest is the heart of central Europe – a claim with some justification, as the city acts as a major crossroads linking north to south and west to east. It has excellent rail links with the whole of Europe and its two largest railway stations, Keleti and Nyugati (*see p235*) are conveniently situated in the centre of town. The country's motorway network has undergone improvements in recent years, making up for decades of neglect.

A plane owned by the Hungarian airline, Malév

Budapest can now be reached by motorway from all directions but the north. Travelling down by car from Slovakia and Poland, via Vác, is not recommended. The poorly maintained, narrow road makes for a very tedious journey, particularly at peak travelling times. For convenience, it is better to make use of the air links Budapest has with major cities throughout Europe. The journey from London to Budapest, for example, takes just two and a half hours.

ARRIVING BY AIR

Airlines from around 60 towns and cities, in 30 different countries, now fly to Budapest. The city's Ferihegy airport is used by many major international airlines, including **Air France, British Airways, Northwest, Lufthansa**, the Hungarian national carrier **Malév**, and the major low-cost airlines. Between them, British Airways, Malév and the low-cost airlines operate eight flights daily between Budapest and London's international airports.

It is possible to fly to Budapest from other airports in the UK, including Manchester, only by taking a connecting flight from another European city, such as Brussels or Frankfurt. Consequently, flight times and costs are greater.

Northwest airline's flights

from the United States involve a transfer or touchdown in Frankfurt or Zurich, but there is a daily direct code-share flight from New York's JFK airport with Northwest reservations on a Malév-owned plane. The flight takes around ten hours.

A direct flight service now operates between Beijing and Budapest.

TICKETS AND CONCESSIONS

When planning to travel to Budapest by air, bear in mind that substantial savings can be made by purchasing APEX tickets, although they do carry certain conditions. The tickets require fixed dates for departure and return, and the stay must include at least one

Malév stewardess

Saturday and last no longer than one month. APEX tickets usually need to be bought in advance but it is worth checking purchasing arrangements with individual airlines. For those aged 2–24, British Airways offer youth fares to Budapest which, although nominally higher than the lowest APEX fare, carry none of the normal restrictions. Low-cost airlines offer good deals year-round. The low autumn-winter season is a good time to look for special offers from the major carriers. Look out also for low-price weekend flight-plus-hotel deals between September and March.

FERIHEGY AIRPORT

Budapest's international airport terminals, Ferihegy 1 and Ferihegy 2, are 16 km (10 miles) from the city centre. Ferihegy 2, built in 1985, was extended to accommodate more flights in 1997–8 and, in 1999 took on all Budapest's passenger services. Ferihegy 1, an older terminal, has been modernised and now mainly handles low-cost airlines. Terminal 2a deals with the arrivals and departures of the Hungarian carrier, Malév; Terminal 2b handles those of all foreign airlines.

Both terminals offer good amenities to passengers.

Check-in desk at Budapest's modern Ferihegy 2

A Malév aircraft parked outside Ferihegy 2

Catering facilities include bars, cafés and restaurants, and there are numerous boutiques and shops. Both airports have tourist offices and currency exchange facilities. All the major car rental firms have desks in the arrivals halls of Ferihegy 1, Ferihegy 2a and Ferihegy 2b. The main names to look out for are Avis, Budget and Europcar *(see p236)*.

For departing travellers, there are several duty-free shops selling all kinds of goods – not only Hungarian products.

Airport taxi company logo

Malév airlines' logo

GETTING TO THE CENTRE

For around 2,300 Hungarian forints (3,900 forints return) the **Airport Minibus Shuttle** takes passengers from either terminal to any address in the city centre. Tickets are sold in the Arrivals Hall. Minibuses have wheelchair access and can pick up returning passengers. (Call 24 hours before departure.) BKV+ runs to Kőbánya-Kispest metro station, followed by the blue M3 metro line.

Taxis from the airport are very costly. As elsewhere in the city, to avoid over-charging ask the driver to use the meter and to quote the approximate fare in advance.

Pest Barnabás utca 4.
Map 4 E1.
Tel 411 05 03 or 483 88 00.

British Airways
Rákóczi út 1–3.
Map 10 F4.
Tel 411 55 55.

Lufthansa
Váci utca 19–21.
Map 4 E1.
Tel 411 99 00.

Malév Airlines
Váci út 26.
Map 2 F1.
Tel 235 38 88.

Northwest (KLM)
East West Business Centre,
Rákóczi út 1–3.
Map 10 F4.
Tel 373 7737.

AIRPORT MINIBUS

Airport Minibus Shuttle
Tel 296 85 55.
(Phone booking 6am–10pm daily.)

BUDAPEST'S AIR LINKS WITH EUROPE

Budapest has air links with major cities in every European country. From each of the locations marked on the map you can travel to Budapest in under three hours.

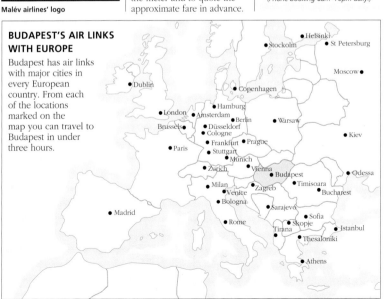

Ticket offices at a main railway station in Budapest

RAIL TRAVEL

Budapest has direct rail links with 25 other capital cities. Every day, more than 50 international trains, many of them express services, arrive and depart from the city's four railway stations. Some trains terminate here, while others enable passengers to join connecting services. Hungarian trains are widely considered to be a very efficient means of getting around, and their reputation is well deserved. Most importantly, they invariably depart and arrive at the right time.

Trains from Budapest to Vienna, the main communication hub for western Europe, depart approximately every three hours. The fastest trains run at top speeds of 140–160 km/h (85–100 mph). The travelling time is an efficient 2 hours 50 minutes. The "Transbalkan" train, which also has car carriages, runs from Keleti pu to Thessaloníki in Greece every day.

Detailed information on all domestic and international rail travel running to and from Budapest can be obtained from either Keleti pu or the MÁV (Hungarian Railways) ticket sales office, which is centrally located at No. 35 Andrássy út.

It is worth knowing that there are several concessionary fares available. Foreign visitors to Hungary can buy a season ticket that is valid for between seven and ten days

and offers unlimited travel throughout the country. There are also a number of Europe-wide passes that allow you to travel cheaply on trains throughout Europe and Hungary.

Local trains can be either "slow" *(személy)* or "speedy" *(sebes)*, but both invariably make frequent stops. A much better option if time is tight is for you to take the fast *(gyors)* train. There are also modern Intercity trains, which take passengers to Pécs, Miskolc, Debrecen, Szeged, Békéscsaba and all the larger cities in Hungary in around 1–3 hours. Seat reservations, costing a small extra charge, are required on these clean and comfortable trains.

Railwayman

RAILWAY STATIONS

There are three main railway stations in Budapest – Keleti pu (East), Nyugati pu (West) and Déli pu (South). A fourth station, Józsefváros pu, handles mainly domestic

traffic, although it does cater for a handful of longer routes. Most international trains run from Keleti pu. The express train to Croatia ("Maestral") and trains to the Lake Balaton resorts leave from Déli pu, almost hourly in high season.

The easiest way to get to Keleti pu is by the M2 metro. The same line connects Keleti pu with Déli pu. For Nyugati pu take the M3 metro line, or trams 4 or 6. A special minibus runs between the various railway stations.

Rail information
Tel 461 55 00 (English).
Tel 461 59 00 (national).
www.elvira.hu
Central Ticket Office
Andrássy út 35. *Tel 322 80 82.*

COACH TRAVEL

Budapest has one international coach station, called Népliget (Üllői út 131), which can easily be accessed by the M3 metro line. There are three national coach stations: Népliget (to Western Hungary), Stadionok (to Eastern Hungary), and Árpád Bridge (to Northern Hungary and the Danube Bend). Népstadion station can be reached by the M2 metro line, while Árpád Bridge is served by the M3 line. The international routes are served by luxury coaches, which have all the usual facilities. The domestic and main international traffic is served by Volánbusz coaches, which operate routes to most of the major towns throughout Hungary.

Coach information
Tel 382 08 88.

The imposing exterior of the Nyugati Railway Station

Luxury air-conditioned tourist coach

TRAVELLING BY BOAT

From April until October hydrofoils cruise the Danube from Vienna to Budapest, via Bratislava. It is also possible to take a hydrofoil or pleasure boat along to the Danube bend, to towns such as Esztergom and Visegrád *(see p164)*. See the timetable at the departure point at Vigadó tér for details.

Cruise companies
Mahart Passnave *Tel 484 40 13.*
Legenda Ltd *Tel 317 22 03.*

TRAVELLING BY CAR

Note that parking in Budapest is extremely difficult.

Motorways are marked "M" and international highways "E". The speed limit is 130 km/h (80 mph). Seven main roads lead out of Budapest and one, the A8, starts in Székésfehérvár. The M1 stretches from Budapest to the Hegyeshalom border crossing, where it joins the Austrian motorway network. Tolls are payable on all motorways. The M3 links

Budapest to Polgár and is being extended to join up with the Slovak road network. From Budapest the M5 leads to Kecskemét *(see p166)*, while the M7 links to the Balaton resorts.

Minor roads have three or four digits, with the first digit indicating the number of the connecting main road.

Traffic regulations include: driving with the headlights on, wearing seatbelts in the back and keeping to the speed limit of 50 km/h (30 mph) in built-up areas.

Drivers must purchase a motorway sticker for the M1, M3 and M7 motorways. On the M5, a toll is levied.

Vehicle assistance
Tel 188 (for breakdowns).
Tel 0640 40 50 60 (for information).

A road sign directing traffic to Margaret Bridge and the M3

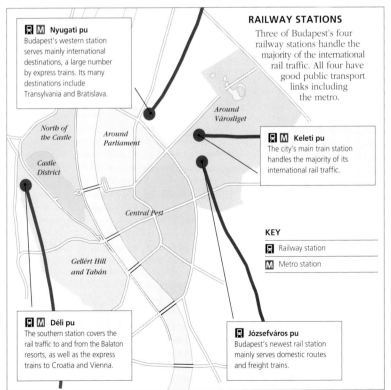

RAILWAY STATIONS

Three of Budapest's four railway stations handle the majority of the international rail traffic. All four have good public transport links including the metro.

🚊 Ⓜ Nyugati pu
Budapest's western station serves mainly international destinations, a large number by express trains. Its many destinations include Transylvania and Bratislava.

Around Városliget

North of the Castle

Around Parliament

Castle District

🚊 Ⓜ Keleti pu
The city's main train station handles the majority of its international rail traffic.

Central Pest

KEY

🚊 Railway station

Ⓜ Metro station

Gellért Hill and Tabán

🚊 Ⓜ Déli pu
The southern station covers the rail traffic to and from the Balaton resorts, as well as the express trains to Croatia and Vienna.

🚊 Józsefváros pu
Budapest's newest rail station mainly serves domestic routes and freight trains.

GETTING AROUND BUDAPEST

Budapest is a sprawling city with many suburban districts. However, most of its main tourist attractions are centrally located and can be easily reached by the city's public transport system, or on foot. The many choices of transport by rail, road and even water provide the visitor to Budapest with ample opportunity to travel through and around the city to reach their chosen

One of Budapest's environmentally friendly city buses

destinations. The infrastructure of Budapest is chiefly determined by the *körúts* (ring roads), which radiate out from the city centre and into the city's suburbs. The metro system mainly operates in Pest, although the red M2 line crosses the Danube at Batthyány tér and runs just north of the Castle District. The overland HÉV train provides a service from the city centre to the suburbs.

DRIVING IN BUDAPEST

The large number of one-way streets in Budapest make it a very difficult city for visitors to navigate by car. The many changes of direction often result in unfamiliar drivers becoming lost. Any confusion brought about by the complex system of roads is further aggravated by the heavy rush-hour traffic. There are also few places to park in the city, so it is much better to sightsee on foot or by public transport.

In Hungary it is strictly forbidden to drive following

One-way traffic in direction indicated

Stop sign at road junction

End of pedestrian and cycle zone

any alcohol consumption. If any trace of alcohol is found in the bloodstream, the fine for drink-driving can be as high as 50,000 Hungarian forints (approximately US $220) and is only payable in forints.

All car occupants, both in the front and the back seats, are required by law to wear seat belts. Motorcycle drivers and passengers must wear helmets at all times.

In built-up areas the speed limit is 50 km/h (30 mph), and most of the road signs follow the European pattern. In towns the use of the horn is legally restricted to cases of imminent danger. Despite this, Hungarian drivers hoot loudly and often at both pedestrians and other drivers.

New regulations permit the use of mobile telephones by drivers only when the car is fitted with a hands-free system. Otherwise, it is advisable to pull over and stop if you wish to make or receive a call.

HIRING A CAR

Cars can be hired from the airport on arrival in Budapest *(see p233)*, or from one of several car hire offices, such as **Avalon Rent Kft**, **Avis**, **Budget Hungary** or **World Wide Rent A Car**. Be prepared to leave a credit card deposit ranging between 100,000 forints and 800,000 forints and to pay US $80–240 per day for unlimited mileage.

BUDAPEST ON FOOT

Budapest is a city in which every pedestrian will find something of interest. Visitors who enjoy rambling along leafy trails should take the railway or bus 21 from Moszkva tér to the Buda Hills *(see p161)*. Those who prefer to stroll through picturesque streets and alleyways should go to Buda's Castle District, which is closed to traffic. Váci utca (Váci Street, *see p127*) is fully pedestrianized and has seats where weary walkers can rest and watch the bustle. The promenade along the Danube is one of the most pleasant walks in Budapest.

Pedestrian zone

V. Kerület, Lipótváros
Báthori utca
2 ———— 2

New street name plate

OKTÓBER 6. UTCA

Old street name plate

Pedestrian crossing

Walk signal at a pedestrian crossing

PARKING

Budapest's car parks, indicated by a blue "P", reduce the problem of on-street parking (and also relieve traffic congestion). There are more covered car parks in the centre, for example at Nyár utca, Aranykéz utca, Osvát utca and Szervita tér. There are attended and unattended car parks situated in other busy parts of the city as well. Several hotels also have car parks, and may offer spare parking spaces to non-guests. Parking charges vary from 120 to 400 Hungarian forints per hour. Parking cards for use in meters can be bought from outlets in the city.

Parking at the main tourist attractions, for example, near Hősök tere (Heroes' Square, *see pp142–3*) or the Citadel (*see pp92–3*), is free for the duration of the visit. These car parks cannot be used by people not visiting the particular sight.

When parking in a metered parking bay, the length of stay must be specified in advance. Parking without a valid ticket or overstaying the allocated time can lead to either a parking fine or wheel-clamping.

CLAMPING AND TOWING

Stopping and parking prohibited

Parking of cars allowed in this zone for a maximum of two hours

Wheel-clamping is growing in Budapest; all illegally parked vehicles are subject to clamping. As well as paying a fine, it costs around 7,000 forints (US $34) to release a car from a clamp, and around 9,300 forints (US $45) if a car has been towed away – usually to a car park outside the city. Parking meters often display the telephone number to contact in the event of wheel-clamping. It is also worth asking a car park attendant for advice. If the car has been towed away, details on its whereabouts and retrieval can be obtained by telephoning 383 07 00.

A wheel-clamped car

CYCLING

Cycling around Budapest is difficult and fairly angerous. Cyclists have to be careful of the tram rails and the uneven, cobblestoned surface of some roads.

Budapest's main roads are closed to cyclists and designated cycle lanes continue to be in short supply. Until recently, Szentendrei út was the only road with a cycle lane. However, the provision of other new cycle routes in Budapest has made cycling an increasingly popular pastime.

The best way to see some of Budapest on a bicycle is by taking a cycling trip around Margaret Island (*see pp172–3*). There are several bike-hire shops on the island, which can provide everything needed for a day's cycling. The range of bicycles includes children's bikes, thus enabling family groups to explore the paths and avenues of this quiet, picturesque island. Many kiosks selling food and drinks can be found on the island, so cyclists can spend the whole day there.

USING A PARKING METER

2 The display panel shows the maximum and minimum parking charges. If you are using a parking card it indicates the value remaining on the card.

1 Insert coins to the value of your ticket, or insert a parking card.

3 When the display shows the correct amount of time you require, press the green button to request a ticket.

4 When using a parking card, each time the blue button is pressed, the machine deducts a fee equal to 15 minutes of parking time.

5 Turn the red button to abhort the process at any time.

6 Ticket appears here.

Getting Around by Metro

Budapest has three metro lines *(see inside back cover)*, which intersect only at Deák tér station. Here passengers can change trains (stamping their tickets once again), by following the clearly marked passageways. The oldest line, the yellow M1 line, runs just beneath the surface of the city. Built in 1894, it is known as the Millennium Line after the celebrations that took place two years later *(see p142)*. Recently it has been modernized and extended. Two more lines – the red M2 and blue M3 lines – have been added since 1970, serving the rest of the city.

Sign over the entrance to the M1 metro line at Oktogon tér station

Signs for the M2 and M3 lines

display maps of the local area, and maps of each line are placed over the doors inside the trains. A recorded voice message announces when the door is closing and gives the name of the next station.

Smoking and eating are not permitted on the trains, and music can only be listened to through headphones. Dogs are allowed to travel on the metro, but only when muzzled. They are required to have a franked ticket for the normal fare on all forms of public transport.

The metro service runs from 4:30am until just after 11pm.

THE METRO SYSTEM

A journey on the Millennium Line (M1) is an event in itself, with beautifully preserved late-19th century stations and wooden carriages *(see p10)*.

Two words to remember when using the metro system are *bejárat*, meaning entrance and *kijárat*, meaning exit, both of which are always clearly marked.

To plan a journey, consult the map at the back of this guide. Most metro stations

A typical station on the original M1 metro line

USING A TICKET

Tickets are bought in advance and need to be franked in a machine before a journey is made. On the metro, the machines are located outside the platforms. Tickets are checked frequently, and there is a fine of 2,000 forints to be paid on the spot for travelling without a valid ticket.

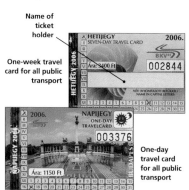

Name of ticket holder

One-week travel card for all public transport

One-day travel card for all public transport

TRAVEL CARDS AND SEASON TICKETS

Travel cards are available for 1, 3 or 7 days; and season tickets (for which a photo is needed), for 14 or 30 days, or one calendar month. Prices change constantly. A Budapest Card *(see p224)*, entitles the holder to free city transport and entry to many sights for 5,000 or 6,000 forints for 2 or 3 days, respectively.

SINGLE TICKETS

These can be purchased separately, or more economically in booklets, for journeys with or without transfers on public transport. There are cheaper tickets for metro journeys of 3 stops (no transfers), 5 stops (with transfers) and unrestricted travel. When changing metro lines a new single ticket must be validated.

Single ticket for all public transport

Travelling on the HÉV

The suburban railway logo

The overland HÉV railway provides an essential means of transport that connects Budapest with its suburban districts. It carries residents to and from work and tourists to attractions located 20–30 km (10–20 miles) away from the city centre. The standard tickets *(see p238)* used on other forms of transport can be used to travel to the central destinations on the HÉV line, but additional fares are payable to more distant destinations. Tickets can either be bought at stations before travelling or from the conductor while on the train.

A standard HÉV train carriage

SUBURBAN RAIL LINES

The HÉV line most commonly used by tourists runs north from Batthyány tér *(see p100)* towards Szentendre *(see p165)*, taking in such sights as Aquincum *(see pp162–3)* along the way. Many of the trains on this line terminate at Békásmegyer rather than running on to Szentendre. Check the destination on the front of the train before boarding. Another line runs from Örs vezér tere (at the eastern terminus of the M2 metro line)

to Gödöllő, passing the *Hungororing* Grand Prix race track *(see p59)* near Mogyoród en route. Gödöllő, a small Baroque town, was once the summer residence of the Habsburgs *(see pp28–9)*.

The third HÉV line begins at Közvágóhíd and terminates at Ráckeve *(see p167)*. Tourists who make this long journey can enjoy a visit to the palace of Prince Eugene of Savoy.

The HÉV service between Boráros tér and Csepel Island is the longest at approximately 50 km (30 miles).

OTHER TOWN TRANSPORT

The Budavári Sikló is an old funicular railway, which takes passengers from the head of the Chain Bridge in Buda to the top of Castle Hill.

Several modes of transport operate in the Buda Hills *(see p161)*. A cog-wheel railway connects Szilágyi Erszébet fasor with Széchenyi Hill, with its picturesque walking trails, while the Children's Railway runs from there to the Hűvös Valley. A chair lift, or *libegő*, descends from the top of János Hill down onto Zugligeti út.

Getting Around by Taxi

Taxi sign

It has always been easy to find a taxi in Budapest, and now, with over 15,000 registered cabs, the competition for passengers is fierce. Nevertheless, not all taxi drivers read the meter correctly and they have been known to exploit foreign visitors, especially those unfamiliar with Budapest who are travelling to the city centre from airports or railway stations. To reduce this risk, choose a taxi whose tariffs and meters are clearly displayed.

USEFUL TAXI NUMBERS:

Budataxi 233 33 33.
City Taxi 211 11 11.
Főtaxi 222 22 22.
Budapest Taxi 433 33 33.
Rádiótaxi 777 77 77.
Taxi 2000 200 00 00.
Tele5 355 55 55.
6x6 Taxi 466 66 66.

A typical taxi meter

FARES

Taxi ranks can be found throughout Budapest and are seldom empty. Taxis can also be hailed on the street but it is often better to book one from your hotel. Before getting in to the taxi, ask

what the fare will be. Ensure that the meter is set at the beginning of the journey and get a receipt for the fare. Fares increase from year to

year but can be negotiated with unlicenced taxis. This price should always be agreed in advance. The total charge is made up of three parts; a basic charge, a per-kilometer charge, and a waiting charge.

A licenced taxi in Budapest

Getting Around by Tram

There are over 30 tram lines in Budapest, which extend to practically every part of the city. These yellow trams are an efficient and speedy means of getting around Budapest, as they avoid traffic and run very frequently. Services start early in the morning, at around 4:30am, and run regularly throughout the day until 11pm or midnight, depending on the route. Night trams operate only on certain routes, at an average of four trams per hour. Timetables are displayed at each stop. It is worth knowing that *utolsó indul* means "last tram".

THE TRAM SYSTEM

Tickets for trams can be bought at metro stations, tobacconist shops *(trafiks)* and some newspaper kiosks. Passes valid for a week or more require a photograph and can only be bought at metro stations. When ticket

Yellow Budapest tram

offices are closed, tickets can be bought from vending machines. Tickets should be franked in a machine found inside the tram. Each ticket is valid for a single journey without changes, and can be used on any form of public transport. It can be cheaper and more convenient to buy books of 20 tickets.

When a tram line is closed for maintenance, replacement buses are provided. These display the tram number preceded by the letter "V".

TRAVELLING WITH LUGGAGE

Every passenger on the tram, just as on the bus or trolley bus, is entitled to carry two pieces of luggage. These should not exceed 40 by 50 by 80 cm (16 by 20 by 30 inches) or 20 by 20 by 200 cm (8 by 8 by 80 inches) in

TRAM STOP

Every tram stop displays the appropriate tram numbers and the timetable.

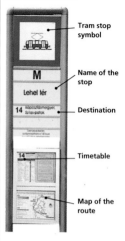

- Tram stop symbol
- Name of the stop
- Destination
- Timetable
- Map of the route

size. You can also carry one pair of ice skates and one pair of skis, providing they are clean, as well as a child's buggy. If you need to transport a bicycle or a larger item of luggage, up to 100 by 100 by 200 cm (40 by 40 by 80 inches) in size, then the rack railway or the designated carriages of the HÉV trains should be used. Any items left on public transport can be traced at the Lost Property Office, at No. 18 Akácfa utca *(see p227)*.

USEFUL TRAM ROUTES

Budapest trams are possibly the most convenient form of public transport for tourists. Particularly valuable sightseeing routes are trams 18, 19 and 61 on the Buda side of town and trams 2, 4 and 6 on the Pest side.

KEY

O	Interchange tram stop
▬	Line 2
▬	Line 4
▬	Line 6
▬	Line 18
▬	Line 19
▬	Line 61

0 kilometres   1

0 miles   1

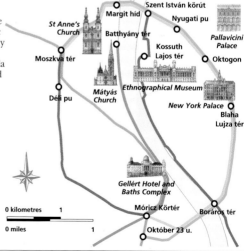

Szent István körút
Margit híd
Nyugati pu
St Anne's Church
Batthyány tér
Pallavicini Palace
Moszkva tér
Kossuth Lajos tér
Oktogon
Déli pu
Mátyás Church
Ethnographical Museum
New York Palace
Blaha Lujza tér
Gellért Hotel and Baths Complex
Móricz Körtér
Boráros tér
Október 23 u.

Getting Around by Bus

Budapest has about 200 different bus routes, which altogether cover most of the city. The blue Ikarus and new Volvo buses generally run from 4:30am until 11pm, with departures on most routes every 10–20 minutes. Times and a list of destinations are on display at most stops. Ordinary buses are indicated by black numbers and stop at every stop. Buses with red numbers follow express routes and omit a number of

THE BUS SYSTEM

Budapest's bus transport is extremely efficient and makes exploring the city easy, even for first-time visitors. Tickets can be purchased at metro stations and from tobacconist shops *(trafiks)*. They must be punched upon entering the bus.

The driver always announces the next stop, often informing the passengers about any interchanges. To ensure that the bus stops, passengers should press the button located by the door before their required stop, otherwise the bus may carry on. When arriving at or leaving a bus stop, most drivers will welcome or bid farewell to passengers. Remember that Budapest's bus drivers tend to drive fast and that the streets, particularly in Buda, can be steep. This combination makes it advisable

A clean and efficient Ikarus bus in Budapest

BUS STOP

The layout of bus stops is very similar to that of trams and trolley bus stops.

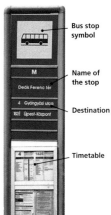

Bus stop symbol

Name of the stop

Destination

Timetable

to hang on tightly to the hand grips when standing on a bus.

It is advisable to avoid buses in the centre of town during rush hours, when traffic becomes congested. At these times it is best to take the metro or even to walk.

Getting Around by Trolley Bus

Trolley buses serve mainly the suburbs and as such are little used by tourists. They are a particularly uncomfortable form of transport, as they move slowly along narrow streets. In addition, their pantographs often get dislodged, causing short breaks in the journey.

Trolley bus stop symbol

THE TROLLEY BUS SYSTEM

The same rules apply to travelling on a trolley bus as to travelling on a bus. Again, remember to signal to the driver by pressing the button located above the door when approaching your stop. Otherwise, if there are no passengers waiting at the stop, the driver will not automatically come to a halt.

Trolley buses are numbered from 70 upwards and there are about 15 different routes in Budapest. Tickets must be punched upon entering the bus, and are the same type as for other forms of public transport. Failure to punch the ticket may result in an on-the-spot fine of 2,000 forints. A particularly pleasant route is trolley bus 70, which runs between Kossuth Lajos tér and Erzsébet Királyné útja.

TICKET VENDING MACHINE

Tickets are sold at tobacconist shops (trafiks), *metro stations and the vending machines at major transport junctions and HÉV railway stations. (These are often out of order.)*

Insert 1, 2, 5, 10, 20, 50 or 100 HUF coins

Press button to receive ticket

Check the amount paid

Collect the ticket and change

STREET FINDER

The map references for all the sights, hotels, bars, restaurants, shops and entertainment venues described in this book refer to the maps in this section. A complete index of street names marked on the maps appears on pages 254–6. The map below shows the area of Budapest covered by the *Street Finder* and is colour-coded by area. The *Street Finder* also includes bus and tram routes, major sights and places of interest together with other useful information listed in the key below. As an aid to navigation, all street names, both on the *Street Finder* and in the index, are in Hungarian. Slightly confusing are the terms *utca* (often abbreviated to *u*), which means street, and *út* meaning avenue, a term mainly applied to wide, busy roads. Other commonly used terms are *körút* (ring road), *tér* (square), *köz* (lane), *körtér* (circus) and *híd* (bridge).

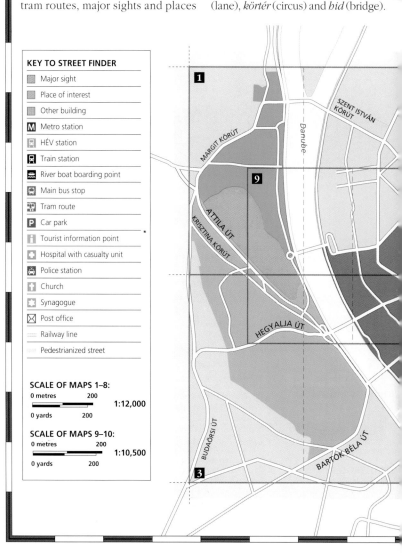

KEY TO STREET FINDER

	Major sight
	Place of interest
	Other building
M	Metro station
	HÉV station
	Train station
	River boat boarding point
	Main bus stop
	Tram route
P	Car park
	Tourist information point
	Hospital with casualty unit
	Police station
	Church
	Synagogue
	Post office
	Railway line
	Pedestrianized street

SCALE OF MAPS 1–8:

0 metres   200
0 yards   200
1:12,000

SCALE OF MAPS 9–10:

0 metres   200
0 yards   200
1:10,500

House in the leafy Tabán district *(see p94)*

Deák tér *(see p121)*, named after politician Ferenc Deák and home to the city's first ever public toilet

Flag-lined avenue in the Castle District *(see pp 78–9)*

Statue of King Ludwig I, part of the colossal Millennium Monument on Heroes' Square *(see p145)*, which was completed in 1929

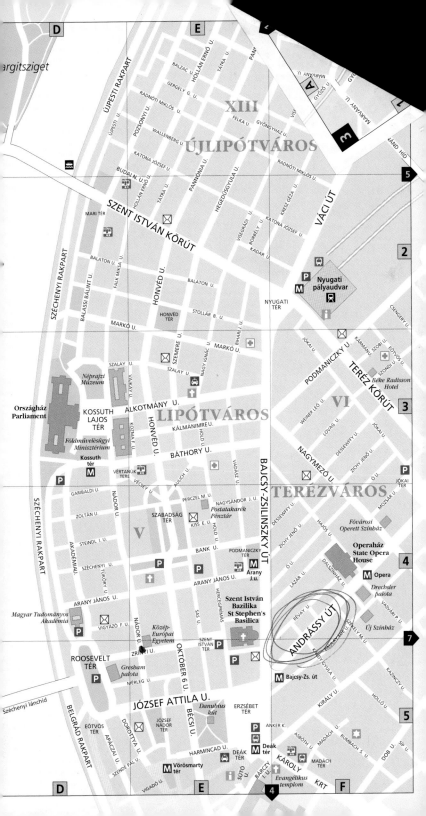

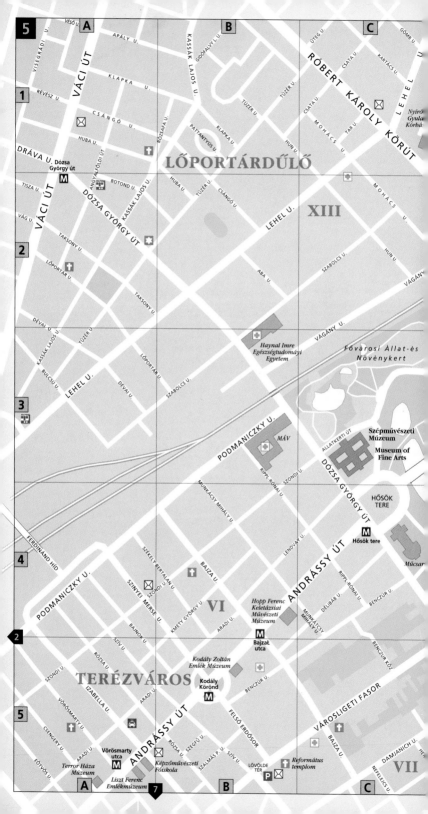

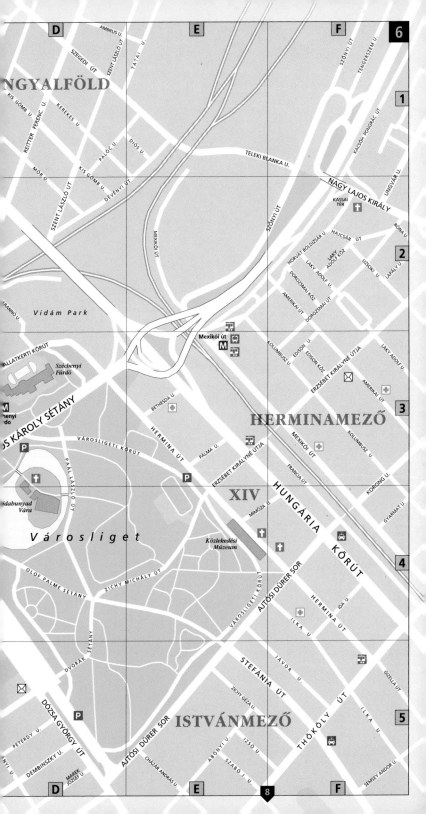

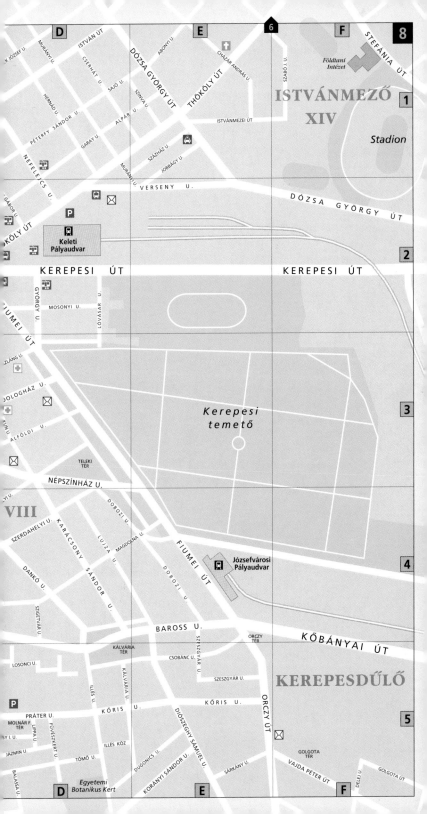

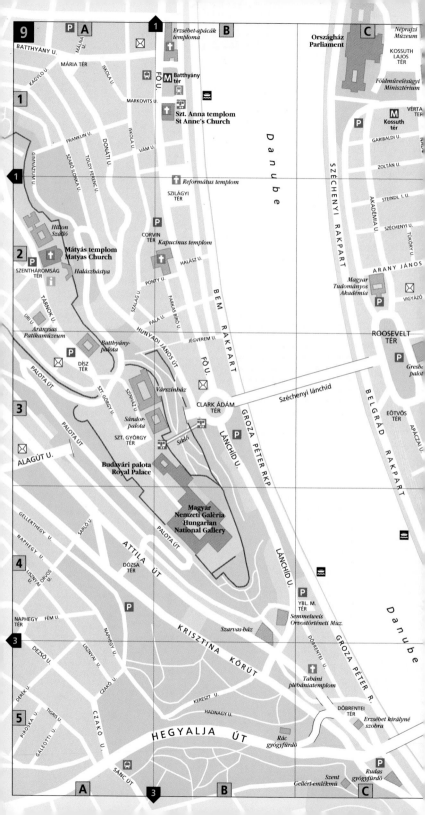

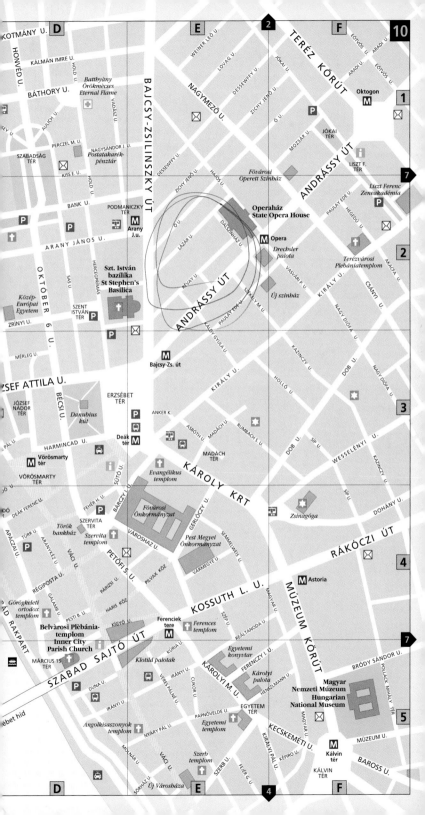

Street Finder Index

Index

Acknowledgments

Dorling Kindersley would like to thank the following people whose contributions and assistance have made this book possible:

Main Contributor
Tadeusz Olszanski was born in 1929 in Poland. During World War II, he fled with his parents to Hungary, where he attended a Polish school in Balatonboglar. He has since visited Hungary many times as a journalist and is the author of five books about the country. These include a volume of articles, Budapesztanskíe ABC. In addition, he has translated over 30 Hungarian novels and dramas into Polish. From 1986 to 1994, he lived in Hungary, working both as the manager of the Institute of Polish Culture and as a correspondent for Polish Radio and TV. In recognition of his activities in promoting Hungarian literature and culture, he was awarded the Pro-Hungarian Culture Award and the Tibor Derye Literary Prize.

Additional Contributors
Sławomir Fangrat, Mariusz Jarymowicz, Iza Mo cicka, Barbara Olszanska, Ágnes Ördög, Ewa Roguska, Craig Turp.

Editorial and Design
SENIOR MANAGING EDITOR Vivien Crump
DEPUTY ART DIRECTOR Gillian Allan
PRODUCTION Jo Blackmore, David Proffit
DTP DESIGNERS Lee Redmond, Ingrid Vienings
MAPS Maria Wojciechowska, Dariusz Osuch
(D Osuch i Spółka)
Elizabeth Atherton, Arwen Burnett, Lucinda Cooke, Fay Franklin, Anna Freiberger, Vicki Ingle, Maite Lantaron, Rebecca Milner, Amir Reuveni, Rachel Symons, Anna Streiffert, Andrew Szudek, Ros Walford, Sophie Warne.

Researchers
Julia Bennett, Javier Espinosa de los Monteros.

Indexer
Hilary Bird.

Additional Photography
Demetrio Carrasco, Ian O'Leary.

Special Assistance
The Publisher would like to thank the staff at shops, museums, hotels, restaurants and other organizations in Budapest for their invaluable help. Particular thanks go to: the Ambassador for the Republic of Hungary in Warsaw; the Ambassador for the Republic of Poland in Budapest; Gábor Bányai; Katalin Bara and the rest of the staff at the Hungarian airline, Malév; Beatrix Basics, Tibor Kovács, Izabella Bősze and Péter Gaál at the Hungarian National Museum; Éva Benkő and Judit Füredi Hamvasné at the Museum of Fine Arts; Zoltan Fejős and Endre Stefana Szemkeő at the Ethnographical Museum; Béla Juszel and Éva Orosz at the Hungarian National Bank; the staff of the Kiscelli Museum; Imre Kiss, Zsuzsa Mátyus and Tivadar Mihalkovics at the State Opera House; Konrad Adenauer Stifung; the staff of the Franz Liszt Museum; Zsuzsa Lovag at the Museum of Applied Arts; the Meteorological Office of the Republic of Hungary; the staff at the Hungarian Post Office; Katalin Neray at the Ludwig Museum; Anita Obrotfa at the Budapesti Turisztikai Hivatal; Csilla Pataky at Cartographia Ltd; Géza Szabó; Mária Vida at the Semmelweis Museum of Medical History; Annamária Vigh at the Budapest History Museum. Ágnes Ördög and Judit Mihalcsik at the Tourism Office of Budapest, 1056 Március 15 tér 7, for sourcing pictures and providing new information.

Photography Permissions
Dorling Kindersley would like to thank the following for their kind permission to photograph at their establishments: Ágnes Bakos, Margit Bakos and Bence Tihanyi at the Budapest History Museum; the staff of the Budapesti Turisztikai Hivatal; Eszter Gordon; István Gordon at the Kurir Archive; Astoria Hotel; Dénes Józsa at the Museum of Fine Arts; Ágnes Kolozs at the Museum of Applied Arts; the Ludwig Museum; the Hungarian National Museum; the Hungarian Academy of Sciences; Tibor Mester at the Hungarian National Gallery; Béla Mezey; the Imre Varga Gallery; András Rázsó at the Museum of Fine Arts; the Semmelweis Museum of Medical History; Judit Szalatnyay at the Kiscelli Museum; Ágnes Szél; Ferenc Tobias and Erzsébet Winter at the Ethnographical Museum; Richard Wagner at the Museum of Applied Arts; the Hungarian airline, Malév.

Dorling Kindersley would also like to thank all the shops, restaurants, cafés, hotels, churches and public services who aided us with our photography. These are too numerous to mention individually.

Particular thanks are due to Marta Zámbó at the Gundel Étterem, who provided the Hungarian cuisine photographed for this guidebook.

Picture Credits
t=top; tc=top centre; tr=top right; tl=top left; cla=centre left above; ca=centre above; cra=centre right above; cl=centre left; c=centre; cr=centre right; clb=centre left below; cb=centre below; crb=centre right below; bl=bottom left; bc=bottom centre; br=bottom right; b=bottom.

The publisher is grateful to the following individuals, companies and picture libraries for permission to reproduce their photographs:

ALAMY IMAGES: Tibor Bognar 175tl; Kevin Foy

10cla; 47tr; Chris Fredriksson 232bl; Peter Horree 126br; INSADCO Photography/Martin Bobrovski 193c; Jon Arnold Images/Doug Pearson 192cl; nagelestock.com 80cr; Sergio Pitamitz 41bc, 79c; Travelog Picture Library 11br; Westend61/Johannes Simon 174cla; ASTORIA HOTEL: 180b.

WWW.BRIDGEMAN.CO.UK: Bibliotheque Polonaise, Paris, Aleksander Lesser (1814-84) *Grand Duke of Lithuania* (engraving) 25br; Magyar Nemzeti Galeria, Budapest 77tr; BUDAPEST FESTIVAL CENTRE: 58ca; BUDAPEST HISTORY MUSEUM: 32c, 33c, 38cb, 38b, 72t; BUDAPEST SPA LLC: 51tc, 53tr, 143tc; BUDAPESTI TURISZTIKAI HIVATAL: 50cr, 50clb, 50br, 51b, 58t, 59b, 60b, 156b.

CORBIS: Jon Hicks 175cr, Barry Lewis 91tl, 193tl.

DANUBIUS HOTEL GROUP: 180b.

EUROPRESS FOTOUGYNOKSEG: 11tr, 25crb, 27crb, 51crb, 83cr, 95cl, 122bl, 140, 152, 156cl, 166tl, 166tr, 214bl; Darnay Katalin 93tr, Szabu Tibor 123crb.

ESZTER GORDON: 35ca.

ROBERT HARDING PICTURE LIBRARY: Gavin Hellier 174bl; HOUSE OF TERROR: 144tl; HUNGARIAN NATIONAL GALLERY: 16, 23b, 24cb, 26ca, 38ca, 54cla, 56cl, 74tl, 74tr, 75ca, 75cr, 75cra, 75b, 76t, 76c, 76b, 77t, 77c, 77b; HUNGARIAN NATIONAL MUSEUM: 8, 20t, 20ca, 20cr, 20cb, 20b, 21t, 21cra, 21c, 21crb, 22t, 22c, 22cl, 22br, 23t, 23c, 23cra, 23crb, 23b, 24cl, 24c, 25t, 25c, 26t, 26b, 27t, 27cra, 27crb, 27cla, 28t, 28ca, 28c, 28cb, 29t, 29c, 29cra, 29crb, 30cl, 31tr, 32t, 32cra, 32cl, 32crb, 33cr, 37cl, 40tl, 130tr, 130tl, 130ca, 130cb, 131t, 131ca, 131cb, 131bc, 133t, 133c, 133b; HUNGARIAN NATIONAL TOURIST OFFICE: 226t.

JEWISH MUSEUM: 39cr.

KURIR ARCHIVE: 34tr, 34br, 35br.

LUDWIG MUSEUM: 40b, 73b.

BÉLA MEZEY 34ca; MUSEUM OF APPLIED ARTS: Ágnes Kolozs 5br, 56tr, 57bl, 136tr, 136tl, 136c, 137tl, 137cra, 137cr, 137crb, 137b; MUSEUM OF FINE ARTS: 39tr, 146tl, 146tr, 146ca, 146cb, 146b, 147t, 147ca, 147cb, 147b, 148tl, 148tr, 148c, 148bl, 149t, 149c, 149b.

OFFICE OF THE PRESIDENT OF THE REPUBLIC: 19tr.

RED DOT, BUDAPEST: 50t, 85tr; Serenc Isza 51cra, 190cla, 190br, 190t, 191cb, 191bl,   bl, 216bl; REUTERS:STR 59cr.

SZÉCHENYI NATIONAL GALLERY: 39tl, 126tr, 110t; SZÉCHENYI NATIONAL LIBRARY: 24c, 25c, 26c, 27c, 72b; ÁGNES SZÉL: 34tl, 37br, 41c, 78bc, 84b, 160b.

TOURISM OFFICE OF BUDAPEST: 10tc, 10br, 45tr, 50br, 65tl, 78clb, 114tl, 151tr, 175br, 215tr.

FRONT ENDPAPER: EUROPRESS FOTOUGYNOKSEG: crb.

JACKET
Front - ALAMY IMAGES: Jon Arnold Images/Doug Pearson main; HUNGARIAN NATIONAL MUSEUM: bl. Back - ALAMY IMAGES: Peter Horree bl; DK IMAGES: Demetrio Carrasco cla; Dorota and Mariusz Jarymowiczowie tl, clb. Spine - ALAMY IMAGES: Jon Arnold Images/Doug Pearson t; DK IMAGES: b.

All other images © Dorling Kindersley. For further information see: www.dkimages.com

DORLING KINDERSLEY SPECIAL EDITIONS

DK Travel Guides can be purchased in bulk quantities at discounted prices for use in promotions or as premiums.
We are also able to offer special editions and personalized jackets, corporate imprints, and excerpts from all of our books, tailored specifically to meet your own needs.

To find out more, please contact:
(in the United States) **SpecialSales@dk.com**
(in the UK) **Sarah.Burgess@dk.com**
(in Canada) DK Special Sales at **general@tourmaline.ca**
(in Australia)
business.development@pearson.com.au

Phrase Book

Pronunciation

When reading the literal pronunciation given in the right-hand column of this phrase book, pronounce each syllable as if it formed part of an English word. Remember the points below, and your pronunciation will be even closer to correct Hungarian. The first syllable of each word should be stressed (and is shown in bold). When asking a question the pitch should be raised on the penultimate syllable. "R"s in Hungarian words are rolled.

a	as the long 'a' in father
ay	as in 'pay'
e	as in 'Ted'
ew	similar to the sound in 'hew'
g	always as in 'goat'
i	as in 'bit'
o	as in the 'ou' in 'ought'
u	as in 'tuck'
y	always as in 'yes' (except as in *ay* above)
yuh	as the 'yo' in 'canyon'
zh	like the 's' in leisure

In Emergency

Help!	**Segítség!**	sheg**ee**tshayg
Stop!	**Stop!**	shtop
Look out!	**Tessék vigyázni**	teshayk vid**y**ahzni
Call a doctor	**Hívjon orvost!**	heevyon **o**rvosht
Call an ambulance	**Hívjon mentőt!**	heevyon m**e**nturt
Call the police	**Hívja a rendőrséget**	heevya a r**e**ndur shayget
Call the fire department	**Hívja a tüzoltókat!**	heevya a t**e**wzoltowkot
Where is the nearest telephone?	**Hol van a legköze-lebbi telefon?**	hol von a l**e**gkurzelebbi t**e**lefon
Where is the nearest hospital?	**Hol van a legköze-lebbi kórház?**	hol von a l**e**gkurzelebbi k**oo**rhahz

Communications Essentials

Yes/No	**Igen/Nem**	igen/nem
Please (offering)	**Tessék**	teshayk
Please (asking)	**Kérem**	kayrem
Thank you	**Köszönöm**	kurss**u**rnurm
No, thank you	**Köszönöm nem**	kurss**u**rnurm nem
Excuse me, please	**Bocsánatot kérek**	bochanutot kayrek
Hello	**Jó napot**	yow n**o**pot
Goodbye	**Viszontlátásra**	vissontlatashruh
Good night	**Jó éjszakát/jó éjt**	yaw-**ay**ssukat/yaw-ayt
morning (4–9 am)	**reggel**	reggel
morning (9am–noon)	**délelőtt**	d**ay**lelurt
morning (midnight–4am)	**éjjel**	ay-yel
afternoon	**délután**	d**ay**lootan
evening	**este**	**e**shteh
yesterday	**tegnap**	t**e**gnup
today	**ma**	muh
tomorrow	**holnap**	h**o**lnup
here	**itt**	it
there	**ott**	ot
What?	**mi**	mi
When?	**mikor**	mikor
Why?	**miért**	m**i**ayrt
Where?	**hol**	hol

Useful Phrases

How are you?	**Hogy van?**	hod-**y**uh vun
Very well, thank you	**köszönöm nagyon jól**	kurss**u**rnurm n**o**jjon yowl
Pleased to meet you	**Örülök hogy megis-merhettem**	ur-r**e**wlurk hod-yuh megishmerhettem
See you soon	**Szia!**	seeyuh
Excellent!	**Nagyszerű!**	nud-**y**usserew
Is there ... here?	**Van itt ... ?**	vun itt
Where can I get ...?	**Hol kaphatok ...-t?**	hol k**u**phutok ...-t
How do you get to?	**Hogy lehet.../-ba eljutni?**	hod-yuh l**e**het ...-buh el-yootni
How far is ...?	**milyen messze van ...**	m**ee**yen m**e**sseh van ...
Do you speak English?	**Beszél angolul?**	bessayl **u**ngolool
I can't speak Hungarian	**Nem beszélek magyarul**	nem b**e**ssaylek mud-yarool
I don't understand	**Nem értem**	nem **ay**rtem
Can you help me?	**Kérhetem a segítségét?**	k**ay**rhetem uh sheg**ee**chaygayt
Please speak slowly	**Tessék lassabban beszélni**	teshayk l**u**shubbon bess**ay**lni
Sorry!	**Elnézést!**	eln**ay**zaysht

Useful Words

big	**nagy**	noj
small	**kicsi**	kichi
hot	**forró**	meleg
cold	**hideg**	h**i**deg
good	**jó**	yow
bad	**rossz**	ross
enough	**elég**	el**ay**g
well	**jól**	yowl
open	**nyitva**	n**y**itva
closed	**zárva**	z**a**rva
left	**bal**	bol
right	**jobb**	yob
straight on	**egyenesen**	e**j**eneshen
near	**közel**	k**u**rzel
far	**messze**	m**e**sseh
up	**fel**	fel
down	**le**	leh
early	**korán**	k**o**ran
late	**késő**	k**ay**shur
entrance	**bejárat**	b**e**h-yarut
exit	**kijárat**	k**i**-yarut
toilet	**WC**	vaytsay
free/unoccupied	**szabad**	s**o**bbod
free/no charge	**ingyen**	i**n**jen

Making a Telephone Call

Can I call abroad from here?	**Telefonálhatok innen külföldre?**	telefonalhutok inen kewlfurldreh
I would like to call collect	**Szeretnék egy R-beszélgetést lebonyolítani**	seretnayk ed-yuh er-bessaylgetaysht lebon-yoleetuni
local call	**helyi beszélgetés**	hayee bessaylgetaysht
I'll ring back later	**Visszahívom később**	vissuh-heevom kayshurb
Could I leave a message?	**Hagyhatnék egy üzenetet?**	hud-yuhutnayk ed-yuh ewzenetet
Hold on	**Várjon!**	vahr-yon
Could you speak up a little please?	**kicsit hangosab-ban, kérem!**	kichit hungosh-shob-bon kayrem

Shopping

How much is this?	**Ez mennyibe kerül?**	ez **menn**-yibeh kerewl
I would like ...	**Szeretnék egy ...-t**	seretnayk ed-yuh ...-t
Do you have ...?	**Kapható önöknél ...?**	k**u**phutaw **ur**nurknayl
I'm just looking	**Csak körülnézek**	chuk kur-rewlnayzek
Do you take credit cards?	**Elfogadják a hitelkártyákat?**	elfogud-yak uh hitelkart-yakut
What time do you open?	**Hány kor nyitnak?**	Hahn kor n**y**itnak?
What time do you close?	**Hány kor zárnak?**	Hahn kor z**a**rnak?
this one	**ez**	ez
that one	**az**	oz
expensive	**drága**	dr**a**hga
cheap	**olcsó**	o**l**chow
size	**méret**	m**a**yret
white	**fehér**	feheer
black	**fekete**	feketeh
red	**piros**	p**i**rosh
yellow	**sárga**	sh**a**rga
green	**zöld**	zurld
blue	**kék**	cake
brown	**barna**	b**o**rna

Types of Shop

antique dealer	**antikvárius**	ontikvahrioosh
baker's	**pékség**	paykshayg
bank	**bank**	bonk
bookshop	**könyvesbolt**	kurn-yuveshbolt
cake shop	**cukrászda**	tsookrassduh
chemist	**patika**	p**u**tikuh
department store	**áruház**	aroo-haz
florist	**virágüzlet**	virag-ewzlet
greengrocer	**zöldséges**	zurld-shaygesh
market	**piac**	p**i**-uts
newsagent	**újságos**	oo-yushagosh
post office	**postahivatal**	posht**a**-hivatal
shoe shop	**cipőbolt**	tsipurbolt
souvenir shop	**ajándékbolt**	uy-yandaykbolt
supermarket	**ábécé/ABC**	abaytsay
travel agent	**utazási iroda**	ootuzashi iroduh

Staying in a Hotel

Have you any vacancies?	Van kiadó szobájuk?	vun ki-udaw soba-yook
double room with double bed	francia-ágyas szoba	frontsia-ahjosh sobuh
twin room	kétágyas szoba	kaytad-yush sobuh
single room	egyágyas szoba	ed-yad-yush sobuh
room with a bath/shower	fürdőszobás/ zuhanyzós szoba	fewrdur-sobahsh/ zoohonzahsh soba
porter	portás	portahsh
key	kulcs	koolch
I have a reservation	Foglaltam egy szobát	foglultum ed-yuh sobat

Sightseeing

bus	autóbusz	owtawbooss
tram	villamos	villumosh
trolley bus	troli(busz)	troli(booss)
train	vonat	vonut
underground	metró	metraw
bus stop	buszmegálló	boossmegallaw
tram stop	villamosmegálló	villomosh-megahllaw
art gallery	képcsarnok	kayp-chornok
palace	palota	polola
cathedral	székesegyház	saykesh-ejhajz
church	templom	templom
garden	kert	kert
library	könyvtár	kurnvtar
museum	múzeum	moozayoom
tourist information	turista információ	toorishta informatzeeo
closed for public holiday	ünnepnap zárva	ewn-nepnap zarva

Eating Out

A table for ... please	Egy asztalt szeretnék... személyre	ed-yuh usstult seretnayk ... semayreh
I want to reserve a table	Szeretnék egy asztalt foglalni	seretnayk ed-yuh usstult foglolni
The bill please	Kérem a számlát	kayrem uh samlat
I am a vegetarian	Vegetáriánnus vagyok	vegetari-ahnoosh vojok
I'd like ...	Szeret nék egy ...-t	seret nayk ed-yuh ...-t
waiter/waitress	pincér/pincérnő	pintsayr/pintsaymur
menu	étlap	aytlup
wine list	itallap	itullup
chef's special	konyhafőnök ajánlata	konha-furnurt oyahu-lotta
tip	borravaló	borovolo
glass	pohár	pohar
bottle	üveg	ewveg
knife	kés	kaysh
fork	villa	villuh
spoon	kanál	kunal
breakfast	reggeli	reg-geli
lunch	ebéd	ebayd
dinner	vacsora	vochora
main courses	főételek	fur-aytelek
starters	előételek	elur-aytelek
vegetables	zöldség	zurld-shayg
desserts	édességek	aydesh-shaydek
rare	angolosan	ongoloshan
well done	átsütve	ahtshewtveh

Menu Decoder

alma	olma	apple
ásványvíz	ahshvahnvcez	mineral water
bab	bob	beans
banán	bonahn	banana
barack	borotsk	apricot
bárány	bahrahn	lamb
bors	borsh	pepper
csirke	cheerkeh	chicken
csokoládé	chokolahday	chocolate
cukor	tsookor	sugar
ecet	etset	vinegar
fagylalt	fodyuhloot	ice cream
fehérbor	feheerbor	white wine
fokhagyma	fokhodyuhma	garlic
főtt	furt	boiled
gomba	gomba	mushrooms
gulyás	gooyahsh	goulash
gyümölcs	dyewmurlch	fruit
gyümölcslé	dyewmurlch-lay	fruit juice
hagyma	hojma	onions
hal	hol	fish
hús	hoosh	meat
kávé	kavay	coffee

kenyér	ken-yeer	bread
krumpli	kroompli	potatoes
kolbász	kolbahss	sausage
leves	levesh	soup
máj	my	liver
marha	marha	beef
mustár	mooshtahr	mustard
narancs	noronch	orange
olaj	oloy	oil
paradicsom	porodichom	tomatoes
párolt	pahrolt	steamed
pite	pitch	pie
sertéshús	shertaysh-hoosh	pork
rántott	rahntsott	fried in batter
rizs	rizh	rice
rostélyos szelet	bifstek	steak
roston	roshton-	grilled
sajt	shoyt	cheese
saláta	sholahta	salad
só	shaw	salt
sonka	shonka	ham
sör	shur	beer
sült	shewlt	fried/roasted
sült burgonya	shewlt boorgonya	chips
sütemény	shewtemayn-yuh	cake, pastry
szendvics	sendvich	sandwich
szósz	sowss	sauce
tea	tay-uh	tea
tej	tay	milk
tejszín	taysseen	cream
tengeri hal	tengeri hol	seafood
tojás	toyahsh	egg
töltött	turlturt	stuffed
vörösbor	vur-rurshbor	red wine
zsemle	zhemlch	roll
zsemlegombóc	zhemlch-gombowts	dumplings

Numbers

0	nulla	noolluh
1	egy	ed-yuh
2	kettő, két	kettur, kayt
3	három	harom
4	négy	nayd-yuh
5	öt	urt
6	hat	hut
7	hét	hayt
8	nyolc	n-yolts
9	kilenc	kilents
10	tíz	teez
11	tizenegy	tizened-yuh
12	tizenkettő	tizenkettur
13	tizenhárom	tizenharom
14	tizennégy	tizen-nayd-yuh
15	tizenöt	tizenurt
16	tizenhat	tizenhut
17	tizenhét	tizenhayt
18	tizennyolc	tizenn-yolts
19	tizenkilenc	tizenkilents
20	húsz	hooss
21	huszonegy	hoossoned-yuh
22	huszonkettő	hoossonkettur
30	harminc	hurmints
31	harmincegy	hurmintsed-yuh
32	harminckettő	hurmintskettur
40	negyven	ned-yuven
50	ötven	urtven
60	hatvan	hutvun
70	hetven	hetven
80	nyolcvan	n-yoltsvun
90	kilencven	kilentsven
100	száz	saz
110	száztíz	sazteez
200	kétszáz	kayt-saz
300	háromszáz	haromssaz
1000	ezer	ezer
10,000	tízezer	teezczer
1,000,000	millió	milliaw

Time

one minute	egy perc	ed-yuh perts
hour	óra	awruh
half an hour	félóra	faylawruh
Sunday	vasárnap	vusharnup
Monday	hétfő	haytfur
Tuesday	kedd	kedd
Wednesday	szerda	serduh
Thursday	csütörtök	chewturturk
Friday	péntek	payntek
Saturday	szombat	sombut

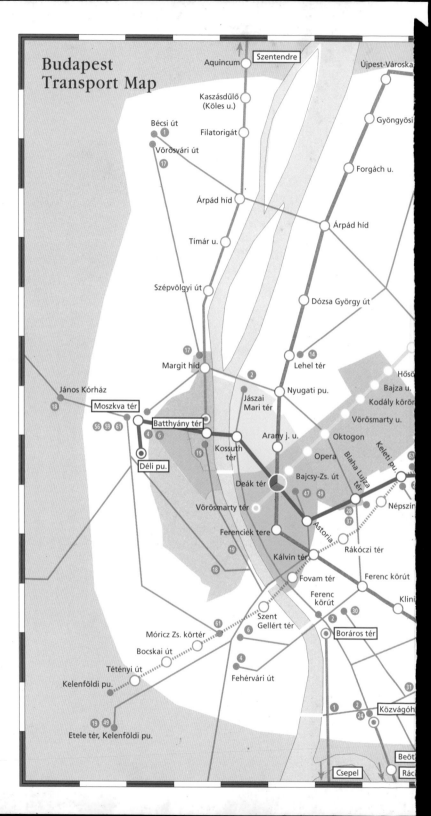